ALTERNATE WORLDS

THE ILLUSTRATED HISTORY
OF SCIENCE FICTION

BY JAMES GUNN

PRENTICE-HALL, INC.,

Englewood Cliffs, N.J.

Alternate Worlds, The Illustrated History of Science Fiction, by James Gunn

Copyright © 1975 by James Gunn

Copyright under International and Pan American Copyright Conventions

All rights reserved. No part of this book may be reproduced in
any form or by any means, except for the inclusion of brief quotations
in a review, without permission in writing from the publisher.

DESIGNED BY PHILIP GRUSHKIN

Printed in the United States of America

Prentice-Hall International, Inc., London
Prentice-Hall of Australia, Pty. Ltd., Sydney
Prentice-Hall of Canada, Ltd., Toronto
Prentice-Hall of India Private Ltd., New Delhi
Prentice-Hall of Japan, Inc., Tokyo

LIBRARY OF CONGRESS CATALOGING IN PUBLICATION DATA

Gunn, James E.
 Alternate worlds.

 1. Science fiction—History and criticism. I. Title.
PN3448.S45G8   809.3'876   75-8561
ISBN 0-13-023267-X

OVERSIZED

CONTENTS

PREFACE

Alternate Worlds is an illustrated history of science fiction. But it is more than just illustrations and history; it has a particular method, and that method is to explain science fiction in terms of the influences that created it and then affected its subsequent development. *Alternate Worlds* (abbreviated *AW* and pronounced *awe*) tries to describe what science fiction is and how it differs from other kinds of fiction (fantasies and utopias and "mainstream" stories), how it got to be what it is, and how it achieves its effects.

It discusses and excerpts the basic works in the field and the authors who created them; but note that the word "basic" is not synonymous with "best," though they may sometimes coincide. *AW* does not ferret out little-known examples of science fiction which other historians of the field have missed, nor does it trace strictly literary influences. Other books have done this, most notably and delightfully Brian Aldiss' *Billion Year Spree*.

Science fiction has always been a popular literary form, closely related to the public mind and the state of public awareness. *AW* is concerned with those books and stories that influenced the genre and helped develop science fiction into what it is, the books and stories that everyone who is interested in science fiction—or who thinks he might be interested in science fiction—ought to know. The books that few people ever read, and that few influential science fiction authors have ever read, obviously had no effect on the shaping of science fiction. *AW* is a book about a genre, and genres are defined by their types, not by isolated masterpieces. Great books, by definition, are unique; and if they launch genres, or cap them, the qualities we value in them are those which transcend their circumstances.

Books about fiction are of two kinds, it seems to me. One kind puts aside the wonder with which readers discover narrative, with which even the critic originally was enraptured, and discards such delights as childish while it discovers adult pleasure through more subtle distinctions. The other kind tries to incorporate within an adult vision the ingenuous eyes of discovery; it tries to explain why some fiction palls and other fiction enthralls.

Leslie Fiedler has remarked that for too long literary critics have tried to tell people why they should like what they don't like. What they should do, he continues, is to discover why people like what they like.

There's no doubt where I stand.

Those of us who are fascinated by why people like what they like tend to write about ourselves and our infatuation with story. In a sense, then, this book recapitulates my own experience, my discovery of science fiction; my excitement and insights and growing sophistication; this is my way of saying, as Isaac Asimov says more directly in his introduction, "Science fiction, I love you."

A book with the scope of this one is never the work of one person. Dozens of others helped in major or minor ways, and I want to give credit to them here for their contributions. To any I have forgotten or overlooked, my apologies.

I begin with all the historians and critics and scholars and anthologists who have shaped my critical theories and understandings (whether I agreed or disagreed with them), and who helped make this a kind of consensus history of science fiction: Isaac Asimov, H. O. Bailey, James Blish, Anthony Boucher, Reginald Bretnor, John W. Campbell, Thomas Clareson, I. F. Clarke, Edmund Crispin, Basil Davenport, August Derleth, H. Bruce Franklin, Robert Heinlein, Mark R. Hillegas, Damon Knight, Sam Moskowitz, Theodore Sturgeon, Darko Suvin, Jack Williamson, and Donald A. Wollheim.

For permission to quote from their work, or to quote or to reproduce pictures from their magazines, I thank Isaac Asimov, Paul H. Bonner, Jr., for Condé Nast Publications, Sol Cohen for *Amazing Stories* and *Fantastic Adventures,* Edmund Crispin, Judy-Lynn Benjamin del Rey for the UPD Publishing Company, Ed Ferman for the *Magazine of Fantasy and Science Fiction,* the Ford Archives and the Henry Ford Museum, M. H. Gernsback, H. L. Gold, Sam Moskowitz, the Viking Press for permission to use four illustrations by Chesley Bonestell from *The Conquest of Space* and *The Exploration of Space* by Bonestell and Willy Ley, Harry Warner, Jr., the Estate of H. G. Wells, and Donald A. Wollheim; and the following artists for permission to reproduce their work: the Bokanalia Memorial Foundation for the late Hannes Bok, Chesley Bonestell, Ed Emshwiller, Frank Kelly Freas, Mel Hunter, Richard M. Powers, Betty J. Schneeman for the late Charles Schneeman, John Schoenherr, William F. Timmins, and Henry R. Van Dongen. To those artists and magazines I was unable to contact for permission because addresses were inadequate or unknown, my apologies and, I hope, their understanding in return.

Obtaining photographs was an incredible task made possible only by the help of many friends: Forrest J. Ackerman of the incredible collections, Herb Arnold, Ruth Berman, Harvey Bilker, Ben Bova, Bill and Margie Bowers, Charlie Brown, John Brunner, Hulbert Burroughs for Edgar Rice Burroughs, Inc., Mrs. John W. Campbell, Ed Cartwright, Mildred Clingerman, Tom Collins, Rita and Vern Coriell, Avram Davidson, Morris Dollens, John Ellis, Harlan Ellison, Meade Friarson III, Robert Gardner, M. H. Gernsback, Sam Glavas, Randall Hawkins, Robert and Virginia Heinlein, Jim Loehr, Will F. Jenkins, Jay Kay Klein out of his lifelong avocation of taking convention pictures, Roy Lavendar, Raylyn Moore, Paramount Television, Christopher Priest, Catherine Reggie (C. L. Moore), Gerry de la Ree, Harvey J. Satty, Leon Stover, Art Tofte, A. E. Van Vogt, Mort Weisinger, Phyllis White, Robert Wilson, Richard Wilson, Donald Wollheim, and all the individual authors and editors pictured in this book who contributed photographs of themselves.

My special thanks for innumerable favors and unlimited assistance to Alexandra Mason and the staff of the Kenneth Spencer Research Library at the University of Kansas.

And finally there was the general help of my graduate assistants, Barry Baddock and John J. Kessell; my two photographers, Doug Delano and Gary Glendening; my sons, Christopher and Kevin; Jay Haldeman; Alan Huff; Joe Kaiser; Ken Keller; and William P. Younger, head of the Public Services Section of the Library of Congress. And my wife, Jane, who helped read proof and compile the index, and who corrected my excesses.

JAMES GUNN
Lawrence, Kansas

SCIENCE FICTION, I LOVE YOU

BY ISAAC ASIMOV

I suppose it is rather unusual to ask someone to write an introduction to a book in which that someone is frequently mentioned in a very favorable fashion. It is even more unusual for that someone to accept such a task.

But because James Gunn knows that I am inhibited by no silly notions of false modesty (or any other kind), he asked me. And I, of course, accepted eagerly.

I'm not even going to try to disinfect the situation by assuming a blush. Quite the contrary. I accept Jim's assessment of my place in science fiction with my usual frank and engaging grin, and I only wish he had seen fit to mention my story *The Last Question* * which, in my professional opinion, is the best science fiction short story ever published.

But there was a time, forty years ago, when I was not one of the great seminal influences of contemporary science fiction. I was only a kid, reading science fiction and experiencing in it an extreme of joy beyond description.

I envy that kid, for I have never known such joy since and I never expect to. I have known other joys—the sales of stories, the discovery of sexual love, the earning of advanced degrees, the sight of my newborn children—but none has been as unalloyed, as all-pervasive, as *through and through*, as reaching out for a new issue of a science fiction magazine, grasping it, holding it, opening it, reading it, reading it, reading it. . . .

It was such a different joy because there was no other reading like it, no other worlds like those it described, no other dangers like those it lived with. It was such a private joy because there was no one else you knew who read it, so that all its universe was yours alone. It was such an intense joy because it was tied to the calendar; because longing built and built within you until it reached a kind of ecstatic pain by the time that emerald moment came when the new issue arrived.

I have a montage of memories of stories that shone before me in my boyhood with a great luminous flame that out-glamored the sun.

---

* I confess: I had never read "The Last Question" until Isaac mentioned it. The story appeared originally in *Science Fiction Quarterly*, November 1956, and was reprinted in Isaac's 1959 Doubleday collection, *Nine Tomorrows*. But, challenged by Isaac's superlative, I searched it out, read it, enjoyed it, and can report that it is not (sorry, Isaac) the best science fiction short story ever published—that judgment is easy enough; to decide what is the best is infinitely more difficult—but it is an ideal example of what science fiction is all about: a big, brilliant, mind-expanding concept that could only be told as science fiction, a story which concerns the end and the beginning of the universe, whose last two lines might well serve as an epigraph for this history of science fiction:

And AC said, "LET THERE BE LIGHT!"
And there was light—

The first science fiction story I ever read (secretly, for I had not yet obtained my father's permission to read such literature) was "Barton's Island" by Harl Vincent, which appeared in the August 1929 issue of *Amazing Stories*.

Magazine science fiction had begun only a few years earlier with the first issue of *Amazing* in April 1926. A couple of months before my introduction to science fiction, two new magazines had come out: *Science Wonder Stories* and *Air Wonder Stories*. A couple of months afterward, *Astounding Stories of Super Science* appeared. We were off!

I remember "Drums of Tapajos" by Captain S. P. Meek, serialized in the 1930 *Amazing*, which introduced me to the lost civilizations of the Amazon and made *Matto Grosso* a phrase of infinite mystery to me. I remember the same author's "Submicroscopic" and its sequel, "Awlo of Ulm," both published in 1931. I remember the cover that went with "Awlo of Ulm," on which two antagonists dueled with colored rays, each ray possessing a different set of arcane and deadly properties—which made for a scene of suspense infinitely superior to the dull clanging of sword and shield.

There was Charles R. Tanner's "Tumithak of the Corridors," in the January 1932 *Amazing*, which created a vision of an underground world that never left me, and that appeared again, transmuted, in my own "The Caves of Steel."

There was Clifford Simak's "World of the Red Sun" in the December 1931 *Wonder Stories*. I told and retold this story to fellow students in the junior high school I attended—without ever dreaming that the time would come when Cliff and I would be old friends sharing the dais at the 1971 World Convention, where he was guest of honor.

Jack Williamson was another favorite. In one of his stories (I've forgotten the name, blast it *) he wrote of a moon-girl, quite inhuman in appearance, with whom I fell deeply in love. There was his "Legion of Space," a futuristic version of the three musketeers, with old Giles Habibula as a kind of super-Falstaff, and with its suspense so incredibly cliff-hanging that to this day I don't know how I survived the gap between the first and second installments, the second and third, the third and fourth. . . . (There were *six* installments, and I never had the willpower to wait for completion so I could read a serial straight through.)

How about Nat Schachner, with his "Isotope Men" in a 1936 *Astounding* and his "Past, Present and Future" in a 1937 one? I read the latter while hiding behind the cigar counter in my father's candy store and traitorously praying that no customer would come in to interrupt me.

And there were Murray Leinster's "Sidewise in Time" and "Proxima Centauri" in *Astounding* issues of 1934 and 1935 respectively. There was Howard Wandrei's "Colossus" in the *Astounding* of 1934. There was Leslie Stone's "Human Pets of Mars" in *Amazing* in 1936 and Walter Rose's "By Jove" in *Amazing* in 1937.

Even a story I didn't particularly like could leave a sharp memory. I still recall a perfect June day in Brooklyn's Prospect Park, reading Harry Walton's "Quicksilver, Unlimited" in an *Astounding* of 1937.

I remember holding the December 1936 *Astounding* in my hand, and holding it and holding it because my family was involved in a social engagement and I couldn't read. The cover, all in shades of purple, burnt itself hypnotically and permanently into my mind, even though it only illustrated Warner Van Lorne's "World of Purple Light," a real stinker of a story.

But the peak came with the September 1937 issue of *Astounding*, the issue in which appeared the first installment of "Galactic Patrol" by E. E. Smith. If I had to pick the moment in my life when my reading experience hit its peak, when every word was fire, and when the print itself, the images it provoked, the smell of the pulp paper, the feel and weight of the magazine, all combined into a vivid and agonizing transport because I wanted to be *part* of the story and couldn't, that was the moment.

Alas for the passage of time and the vanishing of youth. At that very instant, in my delirium of happiness, the shades were closing in about me, and I didn't even know. I was already trying to write science fiction of my own, and in

---

* "The Moon Girl," *Wonder Stories*, February 1932.

the course of the next year—1938—I was to begin submitting, and selling. (You will find that story in some detail in my book *The Early Asimov*, Doubleday, 1972).

Writing and selling science fiction had joys of its own, but it evicted me from Arcadia. I was now constructing science fiction stories on my own, and the intimate knowledge of their anatomy and physiology destroyed the fragile wonder.

By the time John W. Campbell's "Who Goes There?" appeared in the August 1938 *Astounding*—probably the greatest science fiction story written up to its time—I was reading with a cold and thoughtful pleasure, a world removed from the uncritical transports of the year before.

Mind you, I can't go back. The stories that ravished my soul and opened it to a music of the spheres that few can hear, still exist. I can go to M.I.T.'s library of science fiction and read every one of those old wonderful tales. The trouble is that whatever it was that received them has long since vanished. What I was I no longer am, and the bitter loss is mine.

I tried rereading "Galactic Patrol" some years ago. It read like the memory of dead love, like the reminiscence of summer in midwinter. It was the rustling scurry of fallen and brittle leaves.

But you know. . . . In those wonderful days of four decades ago, I had no notion that there was a history to science fiction. Science fiction began as I watched. When I read stories by Jules Verne and H. G. Wells, I recognized them (with impatience) to be science fiction, in the same way I recognized the pyramids to be skyscrapers.

Even now, when I know the long and respectable history of science fiction, I can't accept it with my heart. I cannot shake the worship felt by a 9-year-old I once knew long ago. To me, deep in my soul, science fiction began in April 1926, and its father was Hugo Gernsback.

But don't *you* fall for that, because James Gunn doesn't. His field is English literature (mine isn't) and he is not to be shaken by childish emotionalism. More than half the book passes before he reaches April, 1926, and in that more-than-half he lays the foundation, explains the ancestry, and traces the development of science fiction.

What was wonderful to me out of innocence should be more wonderful to you out of sophistication.

And yet—those memories . . .

CHAPTER 1
THE SHAPE OF
THE PRESENT

THE WORLD finally has caught up with science fiction.

That statement is true and false, and the ways in which it is both true and false illuminate what science fiction is, how it got to be what it is, and what it may become—as well as how the world got to be what it is.

Science fiction and the world. They have created each other, and that process of mutual creation is what this book is about. Obviously the world's influence on science fiction has been much more massive, but the influence of science fiction on the world has been much more purposeful. Perhaps it balances out.

In any case we live, indisputably, in a science fiction world. All around us we see evidences of a new order: life is not what it was for our fathers and certainly not what it was for their fathers. Life moves faster, and we move with it. We are on the back of galloping technology, and we cannot dismount without breaking our necks. We—at least most of us—are watching pictures in our living rooms that move and speak. We are traveling in roaring vehicles that reach speeds of more than one hundred miles an hour across transcontinental systems of broad, paved roads—or in machines that fly through the air at speeds surpassing sound. We are living in houses where climate is automatically controlled and working in buildings that scrape the sky. We—at least a few of us—have at our fingertips the power to destroy another nation, or the world. We—or at least a handful of us—have walked on the moon.

What kind of world is it where men travel faster than the speed of sound, where they control the immense power of the atom, where they travel to the moon? What else but a science fiction world?

Interviewers once asked science fiction writers, "Where do you get those crazy ideas?" Now the first question asked is "What are you going to write about now that we've put men on the moon?" This question is not much more knowledgeable than the first one, but it illustrates the way in which the world has caught up with science fiction. As Donald Wollheim and Isaac Asimov and probably many others have pointed out, this world we live in today is what they were writing about back in the thirties and forties. (As late as 1957, I wrote a series of stories about the first steps in the conquest of space, followed by a 1958 book called *Station in Space*. Even then space flight still was considered science fiction.)

As early as 1863 Jules Verne was writing about the wonders to come from the laboratories of science and engineering, beginning with *Five Weeks in a Balloon*. Germany's Kurd Lasswitz wrote *On Two Planets* in 1897, in this country Hugo Gernsback wrote *Ralph 124C 41+* in 1911, and even earlier, in 1849, Edgar Allan Poe wrote *Mellonta Tauta*—books and stories which were catalogs of future marvels, grand tours of wonderful, fantastic, exciting worlds to come. Yet

November, 1926 (Paul)

for more than a century—and most especially since 1926—the world at large, and a few distinguished scientists as well, had scoffed at the idea of heavier-than-air craft, atomic weapons and atomic power, and spaceflight. Any literary work that included these possibilities was dismissed as "mere science fiction."

Space travel, plastics, fluorescent lighting, jukeboxes, liquid fertilizer, loud-speakers, flying saucers, sleep learning, solar energy, radar, rustproof steel, micro-film, television, radio networks, skywriting, hydroponics, tape recorders, aquacades, vending machines, night baseball, cloth made of glass, synthetic fabrics—is this a description of our present world? It is taken directly from Gernsback's 1911 *Ralph 124C 41+*.

Science fiction is based upon a belief that the world is changing, that the way we live is changing, and that humanity will adjust to it, or will adjust change to humanity, or will perish. That is the theme of a best-selling nonfiction book of recent days, Alvin Toffler's *Future Shock*, which describes

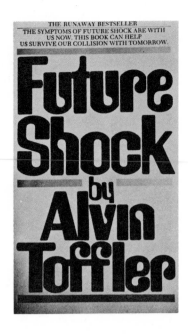

the roaring current of change, a current so powerful today that it overturns institutions, shifts our values, and shrivels our roots. Change is the process by which the future invades our lives, and it is important to look at it closely, not merely from the grand perspectives of history, but also from the vantage point of the living, breathing individuals who experience it.

The vantage point Toffler adopts is the vantage point of science fiction, and the mutual advantage both Toffler and science fiction have over such profes-sional futurism organizations as the Rand Corporation and the Hudson Institute—which deal largely with theories and hardware and when they touch upon people consider them mechanistically—is their concern for the effects of change upon the individual.

Toffler, at least, recognizes that he is poaching on the unknown territory ex-plored and staked out by science fiction, and he pays tribute to its legitimate heirs. He refers to the immunizing ability of science fiction against what "well may be the most important disease of tomorrow," future shock, which he defines as "the dizzying disorientation brought on by the premature arrival of the future."

Toffler quotes Robert Jungk, whom he regards as "one of Europe's leading futurist-philosophers," on the subject of education:

Nowadays almost exclusive stress is laid on learning what has happened and has been done. Tomorrow . . . at least one third of all lectures and exercises ought to be con-cerned with scientific, technical, artistic, and philosophical work in progress, anticipated crises and possible future answers to these challenges.

October, 1953 (Freas)

And Toffler adds:

We do not have a literature *of* the future for use in these courses, but we do have literature *about* the future, consisting not only of the great utopias but also of contempo-rary science fiction. . . . Science fiction has immense value as a mind-stretching force for the creation of the habit of anticipation. Our children should be studying Arthur C. Clarke, William Tenn, Robert Heinlein, Ray Bradbury, and Robert Sheckley, not because these writers can tell them about rocket ships and time machines but, more important, because they can lead young minds through an imaginative exploration of the jungle of political, social, psychological, and ethical issues that will confront these children as adults. Science fiction should be required reading for Future I.

All of this does not imply that this science fiction world in which we live is the world that science fiction writers wanted, only that it is the world they envisioned. Most of them looked toward the future with impatience, it is true,

Although magazine covers were not always truly illustrative of the contents, they give a quick tour of the world science fiction writers were creating. The pages that follow illustrate the ways in which science fiction concepts have become today's reality, in space, in the laboratories and in the ways life was changing on earth.

(Cover artists are identified in parentheses.)

January, 1950 (Malcolm Smith)

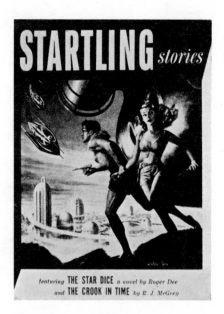

November, 1952 (Popp)

September, 1952 (Coggins)

Apollo 14, liftoff

September, 1953 (Coggins)

October, 1963 (Dember)

May, 1955, movie still,
Conquest of Space

October, 1955 (Walt
Disney Productions)

May, 1957 (Coggins)

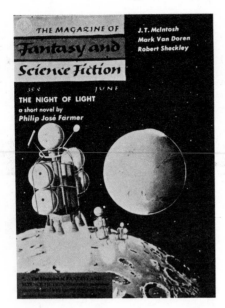

June, 1957 (Pederson)

January, 1958 (Hunter)

March, 1958 (Dember)

October, 1958 (Dember)

February, 1931 (Morey)

August, 1952 (Gibbons)

November, 1953 (Hunter)

December, 1952 (Welker)

November, 1957 (Pederson)

16

November, 1928 (Paul)

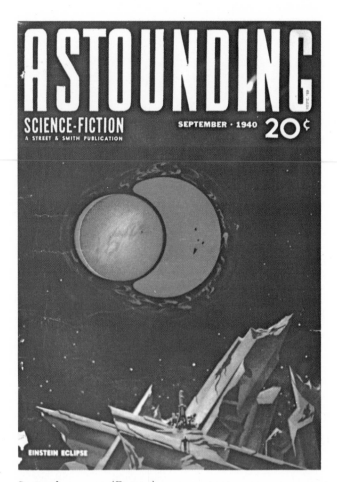

September, 1940 (Rogers)

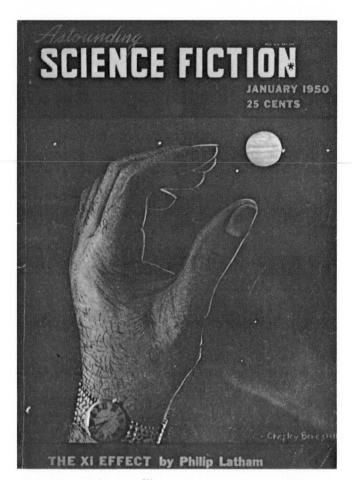

January, 1950 (Bonestell)

November, 1952 (Schneeman)

December, 1950 (Bonestell)

October, 1952 (Bonestell)

February, 1954 (Bonestell)

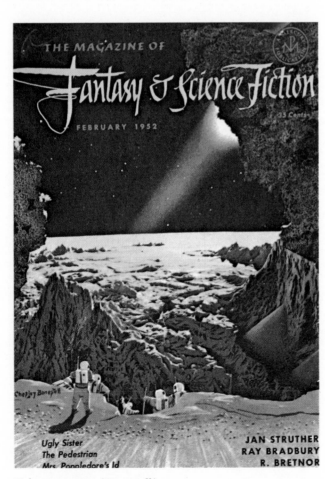

February, 1952 (Bonestell)

March, 1953 (Bonestell)

December, 1954 (Bonestell)

November, 1954 (Bonestell)

May, 1953 (Coggins)

April, 1956 (Bonestell)

THE MAGAZINE OF

Fantasy and Science Fiction

35 ¢   FEBRUARY

A TIME TO SURVIVE
a short novel by
JAMES BLISH

DAMON KNIGHT

FREDERIK POHL

C. S. LEWIS

EVERY STORY
in this issue NEW

February, 1956 (Bonestell)

August, 1926 (Paul)

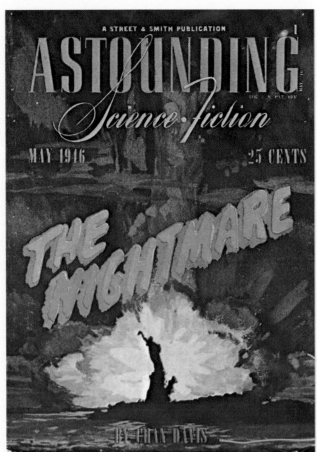

May, 1946 (Timmins)

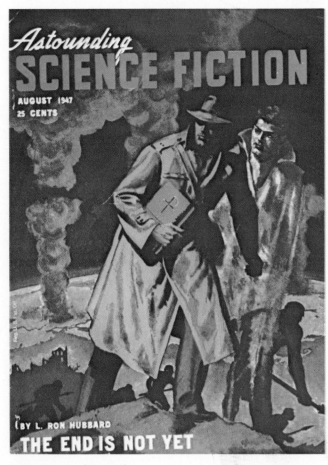

August, 1947 (Rogers)

February, 1947 (Sniffen)

July, 1949 (Rogers)

August, 1928 (Paul)

April, 1930 (Morey)

August, 1956 (Finlay)

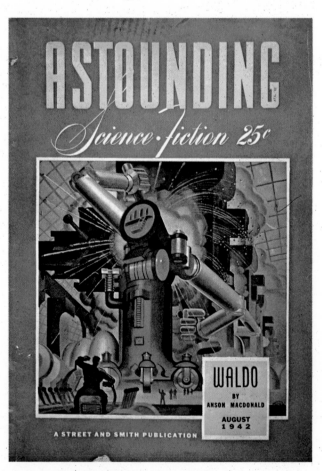

August, 1942 (Rogers)

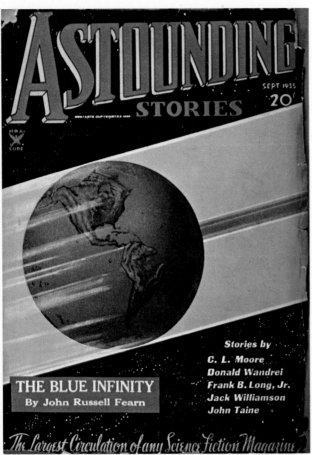

September, 1935 (Brown)

December, 1950 (Timmins)

September, 1952 (Miller)

August, 1948 (Canedo)

November, 1955 (Van Dongen)

October, 1954 (Van Dongen)

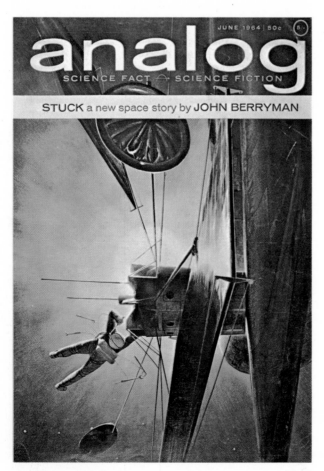

June, 1964 (Schoenherr)

April, 1966 (Freas)

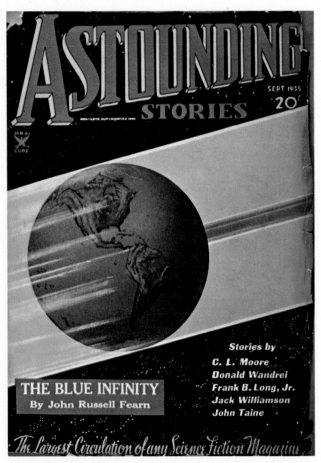

September, 1935 (Brown)

December, 1950 (Timmins)

September, 1952 (Miller)

August, 1948 (Canedo)

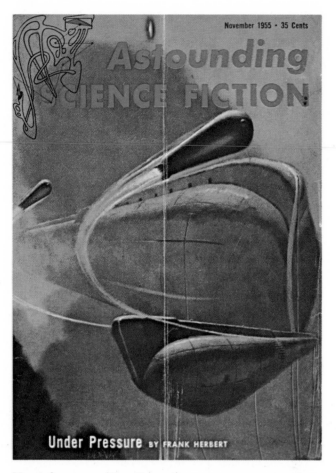

November, 1955 (Van Dongen)

October, 1954 (Van Dongen)

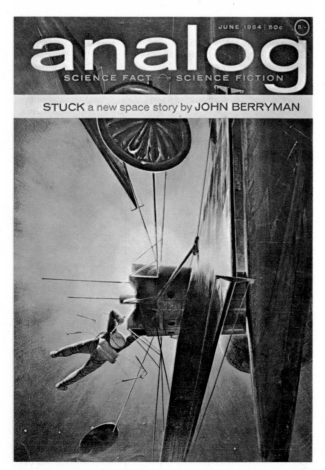

June, 1964 (Schoenherr)

April, 1966 (Freas)

June • 50 cents

analog
SCIENCE FACT ⌒ SCIENCE FICTION

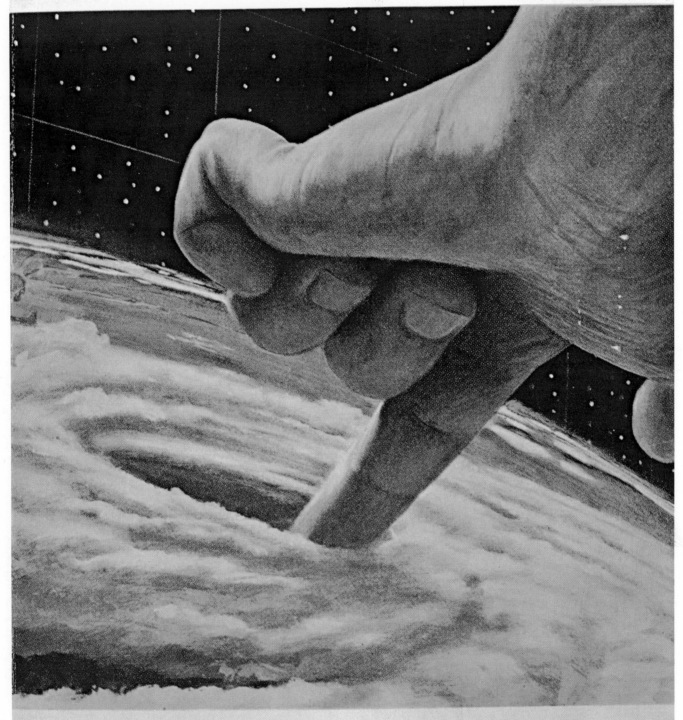

THE WEATHER MAN
A novelette by Theodore Thomas

June, 1962 (Schoenherr)

January, 1940 (Schneeman)

May, 1951 (Unknown)

October, 1957 (Van Dongen)

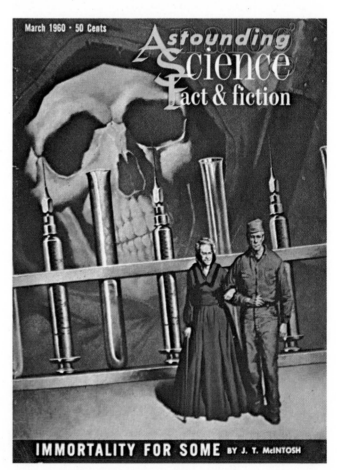

March, 1960 (Van Dongen)

and their readers, unlike the great masses of humanity who are fearful of change and subject to future shock, were unwilling to wait for the future to arrive in its own time. They sought to hurry it along by reading about it; but almost as many cautionary tales were published as stories glorifying the future, and even the most magnificent technological paradises usually had a wormy apple or two, for dramatic reasons if no other. Ecological problems, overpopulation, the horrors of mechanized warfare, the misuse of atomic power, the brainwashings of psychological war and of society—all these and more were decried by science fiction long before the rest of the world recognized them as problems.

This ability to foresee tomorrow's crises, to dramatize their human implications and consequences, and to act out alternatives is one of science fiction's major values. Its more celebrated ability to predict fades to insignificance beside its ability to dramatize.

If all this is true—and how it is true and how it came to be true will be documented in the chapters to come—science fiction should be the literature of a science fiction world. That particular happy epoch has not yet arrived, but the great day may be coming. More people are reading and viewing more science fiction than ever. More books are being published, more science fiction motion pictures are being made, more television series are being planned—and pervading the practitioners in the field is a general sense of being in the middle of what is going on.

Harlan Ellison

Harlan Ellison, the perennial angry young man of science fiction, wrote in *Dangerous Visions*, "It is 'steam-engine time' for the writers of speculative fiction. The millennium is at hand. We are what is happening."

Even discounting Ellison's hyperbole, such a sweeping statement demands documentation. What has been going on in science fiction the past few years?

Articles heralding the upsurge in science fiction have appeared in *The New York Times*, the *New Yorker*, the *National Observer*, the *Christian Science Monitor*, the *Wall Street Journal*, *Show Magazine*, *TV Guide*, the *Wilson Library Bulletin*, *American Libraries*, *Library Journal*, *Publisher's Weekly*, *Time*, numerous small specialized magazines like *Colloquy* and *Trend*, numerous grade-school and high-school classroom publications which have devoted entire issues to science fiction, and, probably, your local newspaper. Perhaps more important, the newspaper and magazine articles have dropped their "look at the nuts we just discovered in our attic" approach, which lumped science fiction writers with flying saucer fanatics, in favor of a surprised awe at the "prophets recently identified in our midst" and even an occasional note of respect for the literary qualities of the work.

Big-budget science fiction motion pictures are not uncommon. In the late forties and fifties there were *When Worlds Collide, The War of the Worlds, Destination Moon, The Day the Earth Stood Still,* and *On the Beach;* and in the sixties we had *From the Earth to the Moon, Fantastic Voyage, Fahrenheit 451, The Planet of the Apes,* the *Illustrated Man,* and *Dr. Strangelove.* But the fabulous box-office success of 1968 and 1969 was the biggest-budget production of them all, *2001: A Space Odyssey,* a motion picture even more popular with young audiences than *The Graduate.* Other films have come along since: the sequels to *Planet of the Apes, THX 1138, The Andromeda Strain, The Hellstrom Chronicle, Silent Running, A Clockwork Orange,* and there are more ahead, possibly including *Dune, Childhood's End,* and *Stranger in a Strange Land.*

Television coverage of the Apollo 11 moon flight featured commentary by science fiction writers. Not many years before, the networks—like the rest of the media—had ridiculed the science fiction premise that man someday would travel in space, but when the moon flights became reality the science fiction writers became prophets whose predictions had come true in their own time. When Apollo 12 took off, ABC-TV obtained prophecies about the year 2000 from a dozen science fiction writers and telecast these prophecies as serious commentary during the moon landing. And the Apollo 15 moon exploration was distinguished by the informal naming of two craters (Rhysling and Earthlight) for works by Robert Heinlein and Arthur C. Clarke, and by Mission Control's quoting from Heinlein's "The Green Hills of Earth."

The world has caught up with science fiction in other ways.

Two science fiction books, *The Andromeda Strain* and *Time and Again,* were selections of the Book-of-the-Month Club, and science fiction books are being reviewed reasonably seriously in the major popular media.

Two of the latest "in" books with students in high schools and colleges—succeeding *Lord of the Flies* and *The Fellowship of the Ring*, both more closely related to science fiction, incidentally, than to mainstream fiction—are Robert Heinlein's *Stranger in a Strange Land* and Frank Herbert's *Dune*.

More science fiction books were published in 1970 than in any five years during the fifties, the previous boom period for science fiction, and more science fiction books were published in 1969 than had been published in England through man's entire history up to 1950. By 1971, according to figures in *Publishers Weekly*, 9 percent of all fiction being published was science fiction.

Science fiction is being taught at colleges and universities as a branch of literature that has suddenly and unexpectedly achieved literary significance. More than 150 college courses have been reported, and the number is rising swiftly—and high-school courses, particularly in senior English, may be multiplying even more rapidly. Universities are building science fiction collections and vying for science fiction manuscripts, including Harvard and Syracuse University on the East Coast, Eastern New Mexico University in the West, California State College at Fullerton and Stanford on the West Coast, Mississippi State University in the South, and the University of Kansas in the Midwest. In 1950, when I wanted to write a thesis about science fiction, one senior faculty member informed me that science fiction was at best "subliterary." (I persisted, and some 20,000 words of the thesis were serialized in a science fiction magazine before it collapsed.) Now Stanford University has an annual Summer Institute for Science Fiction and Fantasy, with science fiction authors as visiting lecturers; summer workshops in the writing of science fiction have spread from Clarion State College in Pennsylvania to the University of Washington and Michigan State University. Other institutions are incorporating such courses into their regular curricula.

Other collegiate courses—such as political science and sociology—are being taught using science fiction stories as models. Early in the fifties M.I.T. was teaching an industrial design class using a science fiction format to liberate students from earthbound preconceptions; and other disciplines are now recognizing the unique ability of science fiction to separate concept from the matrix of prejudice and social convention which surround it. Articles about science fiction concepts are finding their way into such scholarly journals as *The Journal of Marriage and the Family*, which carried in its February 1969 issue the address delivered by the society's president at its annual meeting, "Marriage and the Family in Modern Science Fiction."

A Science Fiction Research Association, primarily composed of college professors who are teaching courses and doing research in science fiction, has been formed after a decade of regular meetings at the Modern Language Association. Scholarly journals are being published: *Extrapolation and Science Fiction Studies* in the United States, *Foundation* in Great Britain. Scholarly books about science fiction are beginning to stream from the university presses of the nation, such as Bruce Franklin's *Future Perfect*, Mark Hillegas' *The Future as Nightmare*, I. F. Clarke's *Voices Prophesying War*, Thomas Clareson's *SF: The Other Side of Realism*, and Robert Philmus' *Into the Unknown*, joining such earlier works as J. O. Bailey's *Pilgrims Through Space and Time* and Marjorie Nicholson's *Voyages to the Moon*. And the commercial presses are now beginning to produce books about the field. Kingsley Amis was the first, with a sympathetic study called *New Maps of Hell*; then after a gap of some years, came such books as Benjamin Appel's *The Fantastic Mirror*, Richard Ofshe's *The Sociology of the Possible*, Donald Wollheim's *The Universe Makers*, Dick Allen's *Science Fiction: The Future*, Sam Lundwall's *Science Fiction: What It's All About* and Brian Aldiss' *Billion Year Spree*. And this is only the beginning.

Science fiction has received little critical attention in this country (it is more highly regarded in England and in other foreign countries), and critics and reviewers generally have dismissed science fiction without a reading, if they thought of it at all. Mainstream writers have been more receptive. Now, after a meandering journey through secluded meadows, science fiction may be rejoining the mainstream. Or, as science fiction writer and critic Alexei Panshin puts

May, 1953 (Baer)

it, "In spite of the general attempt to drag science fiction into the mainstream, I think the mainstream will come to it." As proof of Panshin's position we might cite Huxley's classic *Brave New World,* Orwell's *1984,* Shute's *On the Beach,* Wolfe's *Limbo,* Wouk's *Lomokome Papers,* Rand's *Anthem,* Hersey's *White Lotus* and *Child Buyer,* Boulle's *Planet of the Apes,* Burgess' *A Clockwork Orange,* Vercors' *You Shall Know Them,* several of William Burroughs' books, Barth's *Giles Goat-boy,* Pynchon's *Gravity's Rainbow,* and Vonnegut's *Cat's Cradle, Player Piano,* and others. Among the ten books *Time* magazine listed as the Most Notable Books of the 1960s were *Cat's Cradle* and Burroughs' *Naked Lunch,* and two of the novels nominated for Nebula Awards of the Science Fiction Writers of America in 1969 were Vonnegut's *Slaughterhouse-Five* and Nabokov's *Ada.*

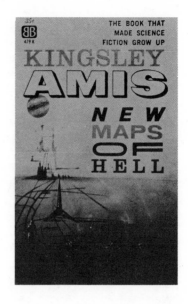

Articles about science fiction writers have been appearing in such magazines as the *New Yorker* and *The New York Times Magazine,* and articles by science fiction writers are appearing in such publications as *The New York Times, Harper's Magazine,* and *TV Guide.*

What is all the excitement about?

"Fiction is simply dreams written out," wrote the late John W. Campbell, long-time editor of the leading science fiction magazine, *Analog.* "Science fiction consists of the hopes and dreams and fears (for some dreams are nightmares) of a technically based society."

"It may be suggested that science fiction is composed of 'supernatural' writing for materialists," wrote the late Groff Conklin in the first big postwar anthology, *The Best of Science Fiction.* "You may read every science fiction story that is true science fiction, and never once have to compromise with your id. The stories all have rational explanations, provided you are willing to grant the word 'rational' a certain elasticity."

"Science fiction is fantasy wearing a tight girdle," said Sam Merwin, Jr., an editor of the late forties and fifties.

"Social science fiction is that branch of literature which is concerned with the impact of scientific advance upon human beings," wrote Isaac Asimov, a science fiction writer who has become even better known as a prolific author of science fact.

Kingsley Amis

Since we are well-launched into a sea of definitions—a sea from which we will extract ourselves only with great difficulty and almost certainly without what we came to seek—we may as well continue with a process which is basic to any book: describing what the book is about.

"A [good] science fiction story," said Theodore Sturgeon, one of the best of science fiction writers himself, "is a story built around human beings, with a human problem and a human solution, which would not have happened at all without its scientific content."

Sam Moskowitz, science fiction's self-appointed historian, has written, "Science fiction is a branch of fantasy identifiable by the fact that it eases the 'willing suspension of disbelief' on the part of its readers by utilizing an atmosphere of scientific credibility for its imaginative speculations in physical science, space, time, social science, and philosophy."

And Kingsley Amis, mainstream author and critic, wrote in a similar vein: "Science fiction is that class of prose narrative treating a situation that could not arise in the world we know, but which is hypothesized on the basis of some innovation in science or technology, or pseudo-science or pseudo-technology. It is distinguished from pure fantasy by its need to achieve verisimilitude and win the 'willing suspension of disbelief' through scientific plausibility."

Professor Bruce Franklin wrote in *Future Perfect:*

One may think of realistic fiction, historical fiction, science fiction, and fantasy as theoretically distinct strategies for describing what is real . . . realistic fiction tries to imitate actualities, historical fiction past probabilities, science fiction possibilities, fantasy impossibilities.

Robert Heinlein called science fiction "speculative fictions in which the author takes as his first postulate the real world as we know it, including all established facts and natural laws."

31

My own definition has, if nothing else, brevity: "In science fiction a fantastic event or development is considered rationally."

One problem with trying to define such an amorphous field as science fiction is that every definition tends to include stories which any panel of critics would agree were not science fiction or to exclude stories that the same panel would insist were science fiction; historically, science fiction has been defined as "what I mean when I point at it, or write it, or publish it."

But a common element in all these definitions is an underlying conviction that science fiction is a mutated form of fantasy that could not exist until science became a meaningful ingredient of civilization. This happened only a little more than two centuries ago, with the beginning of the Industrial Revolution. Until about the middle of the eighteenth century science was, even to scientists, a plaything, a philosophical pursuit or pastime. We can point to works in that non-scientific past that resemble science fiction: Plato's *Atlantis;* Lucian's *True History;* parts of Homer and Vergil; works by Heliodorus, Apuleius, Aristophanes, and Thucydides; Cyrano de Bergerac's *Voyages to the Moon and the Sun;* Voltaire's *Micromegas;* Sir Thomas More's *Utopia;* Francis Bacon's *New Atlantis;* Johannes Kepler's *Somnium;* Jonathan Swift's *Gulliver's Travels;* Bishop John Wilkins' *A Discourse Concerning a New World and Another Planet* and *Mercury: or the Secret and Swift Messenger;* and Baron Ludvig Holberg's *A Journey to the World Under-Ground.* But these were tales of wonder or far-traveling, or satires, or utopias, or even barely disguised works of scientific exposition or speculation; they did not contain the one indispensable ingredient of science fiction: a belief in a world being changed by man's intellect, a conviction that what was being written could really happen.

Then the Industrial Revolution happened. Not suddenly but gradually over the last half of the eighteenth century everyone who felt its effects—mainly in western Europe and the United States—was forced to the conclusion that change was now going to be man's fate, and that if he wished to be the master of change rather than its victim he would have to start thinking about the consequences of his actions and decisions.

In the entire seventeenth century only 1 book was published in England that I. F. Clarke calls futuristic fiction; in the eighteenth century, 6 (5 of them in the second half); in the first half of the nineteenth century, 12; in its second half, 172; and in the first half of the twentieth century, 510.

For a time most science fiction tended to portray man as victim rather than as mover; the optimistic view of science as a means to improve man's lot, right wrongs, and create a better world seemed to be largely restricted to the juveniles, such as the dime novels and the Tom Swift series.

Before the Industrial Revolution, men worked in the trades handed down in their families.

From alchemy to steam engine, man was driven by a desire to master his environment.

Two men have been called "the father of science fiction": Jules Verne and H. G. Wells. Verne began writing in the middle of the nineteenth century and became one of the most prolific and widely read authors in the world. He called his books "voyages extraordinaires," and they were largely romantic adventure stories. Wells enjoyed even greater prestige when his "scientific romances," which often were biting philosophical and social commentary, began to be printed in magazines and books in 1895.

One of the best-loved editors in the field, the late Anthony Boucher, once wrote, "Like the detective story, science fiction was first written and published by people who (like M. Jourdain speaking prose) had no specific notion that they were producing science fiction."

During the nineteenth century and the early twentieth century many writers turned to what we now call science fiction as casually as they published realistic fiction or historical fiction or detective stories: Poe, Hawthorne, Twain, Kipling, Bierce, London, Haggard, Stockton, Conan Doyle, Edward Bellamy, John Buchan. . . .

Verne died in 1905; Wells lived until 1946. Both continued writing up to the year of their death, but the most influential work of both was done early in their careers. Their immediate successors were more Vernian romantics than Wellsian social realists. The pulp adventure magazines, created in 1896 but achieving their greatest triumphs in the early twentieth century, featured in the pages of such magazines as *Argosy, Black Cat, Cavalier,* and *All Story* long serialized novels of romantic science fiction adventure as well as shorter works, by authors with a preference for three names or initials: George Allen England, Charles B. Stilson, Austin Hall, Homer Eon Flint, Garrett P. Serviss, A. Merritt and Edgar Rice Burroughs.

The nature of science fiction began to change in 1926, when a Luxembourg immigrant named Hugo Gernsback created *Amazing Stories,* the first science fiction magazine. Gernsback, who was an experimenter with radio and electronics, had founded the first radio magazine, *Modern Electrics,* in 1908. He sold it in 1912 (combined with others, it became *Popular Science*), and started *Electrical Experimenter,* which became *Science and Invention* in 1920. Gernsback, who wanted to popularize science and technology through fiction, himself wrote about engineering marvels in novels such as *Ralph 124C 41+.* Such stories as he encouraged were to give science fiction a piquant but misleading reputation for prophecy; the basic value of science fiction, as it later developed, lay not in its ability to predict a device, as Jules Verne inaccurately is said to have predicted the submarine or the periscope, but in its exploration and dramatization of a possible changing world.

But with *Amazing Stories* Gernsback created an entire new generation of

Jules Verne

H. G. Wells

science fiction writers—and condemned them to a ghetto wherein they could live in genteel poverty, much admired by their neighbors and largely ignored by the residents in more gracious neighborhoods.

Hugo Gernsback

Other magazines followed, some of them started by Gernsback himself, others by imitators: *Wonder Stories, Astounding Stories* (which became *Astounding Science Fiction* and then *Analog*), *Startling Stories, Planet Stories,* and, in the great boom-and-bust period about three years after the end of World War II, some sixty to seventy others of which only a handful survive, *Analog, Galaxy,* and *The Magazine of Fantasy and Science Fiction* being the most important.

Isaac Asimov has divided modern science fiction into three periods: "adventure-dominant" between 1926 and 1938, when stories were written by general writers with little knowledge of science, stories which emphasized space opera, monsters, and "dangerous discoveries"; "science-dominant," beginning around 1938, when the new editor of *Astounding,* John W. Campbell, made his influence effective, and continuing until 1950; and "sociology-dominant," created by the new magazines which appeared around 1950, particularly *Galaxy,* which emphasized the social response to scientific advances. Asimov thinks a fourth stage of science fiction may have come into being in the middle of the sixties to compete with the dominance of sociology: its concern with sex, violence, and experimental style might give it the name of "style-dominant."

The magazines that nurtured this new kind of literature have not thrived on it: the best of them do modestly well—*Analog* sells about 120,000 copies a month, *Galaxy* and *The Magazine of Fantasy and Science Fiction* about half that many—and the rest get by with shortcuts and economies and hope. The Big Three pay rates of two to five cents a word.

The major breakthrough for science fiction writers has come in the paperback field, and more recently in the hardcover market. Paperback publishers once published an occasional title, the most persistent among them as many as one a month; now many issue two or three a month, and almost every publishing house has a science fiction line. At every local paperback bookstore the shopper will see them grouped together on rack after rack. The old-line hardcover publishers, who once dealt only with the Heinleins and the Bradburys, are publishing science fiction as a regular practice. And anthologies of original stories, now being published in hardcover or paperback or both, are paying advances against royalties of as much as five cents a word, not only providing competition for the magazines but often allowing the writers to explore concepts farther out than the magazines feel they can touch.

Science fiction in paperbacks

For writers science fiction always has had two major appeals: its relevance and its freedom. It has been relevant because of its concern for contemporary issues: atomic weapons and their control, space travel, the machine and its impact upon man and upon society, aliens, pollution, social inventions such as advertising and television, robots, computers, overpopulation, and those eternal problems of communication, prejudice, intolerance, and injustice. The writer who wishes to deal with many of these problems will find himself writing science fiction or something resembling it.

English critic Edmund Crispin called science fiction, in the *Times Literary Supplement,* "origin of species" fiction. "Its basic valuation of man is as just one of a horde of different animals sharing the same planet. Given this, it is not difficult to see that in science fiction individuals are apt to count for very little in their own right. The multitudinousness of the human species forbids us—if we are going to adopt such a standpoint—to take really seriously Madame Bovary or Strether or Leopold Bloom."

If it could not deal in literary depth with character and such eternal themes as love, war, and death except as they had social significance, at least science fiction made it possible to dramatize the situations that nobody else was discussing or seemed able to discuss in print: no subject was too serious or too delicate for science fiction.

But it was a ghetto, and the ghetto dwellers were talking largely to themselves. Now science fiction has broken out of its ghetto, and for the writers, at least, the feeling is exhilarating.

What happened?

One big factor may have been the moon shots and all the scientific prepara-

Apollo 11's view of Earth   A scene from *Destination Moon* (1950)

tion that led up to them, beginning with the launching of Sputnik by the Russians, which shocked officials and the general public into the conviction that science and technology were important, space was important, going to the moon was important—and possible. The step-by-step progress into space demonstrated that the subject matter of science fiction was not dream but reality; that science fiction was, if anything, more real than most mainstream fiction, which deals not with the future or even the present, but with the past. In magazines and newspapers of the past decade, we have repeatedly come across such awed expressions as "the scene is straight out of science fiction" or "this may sound like science fiction, but. . . ."

In a recent issue *Time* magazine said, "Writing grand-design scenarios of the future is a more popular art now than science fiction, even if less reliable."

In fact, the actual televised scenes of the Apollo 11 astronauts on the moon looked like nothing so much as a science fiction movie out of the early fifties—*Destination Moon,* perhaps, with lunar landscapes by Chesley Bonestell. The picture might be a little indistinct, a bit blurred, but we could attribute that to a scratched print; all that was lacking for that late, late movie was a girl astronaut or the comic relief, a bumbling crew member from Brooklyn or Texas.

As Harlan Ellison has said, "We live in a fantasy world."

A similar sense of déjà vu occurred after the dropping of the atom bomb in 1945, though that was a triumph of death rather than accomplishment; it happened and was over, and the development of atomic energy afterward was a slow, unglamorous process with little public appeal. Moreover, atomic energy did not have television. Television and the space program seemed to be created for each other: television provided instant reality for the space program, and, to be honest, the space program has been staged, at least in part, for the benefit of the television viewer.

One might also speculate about the influence of science fiction on the space program—about the preparation of a nation to accept space flight as a dramatic reality, about all those NASA engineers who had grown up reading and dreaming about space—but we will deal with the influence of science fiction on society later in the book.

Another factor in science fiction's release from the ghetto is the rapidly increasing number of high-school and college students, of scientifically and technically trained men and women, and of professional people of all kinds. Science fiction always has appealed to the better-educated, to those with inquiring minds who enjoy speculation and can endure, if not even enjoy, uncertainty. Increasing levels of education, more young people completing high school and going on into college, more college graduates—all have multiplied the market for science fiction.

Once the high-school science fiction reader tended to be alienated from his society—he rejected it because he was too bright or it rejected him because he lacked the ability to get along—and he turned to science fiction as food for his restless mind, and to science fiction fandom as a society which accepted him on his own terms. Now increasing numbers of high-school students—a sizable minority if not yet a majority—feel alienated from the larger society and turn to science fiction as a literature of alternatives, a place to seek new answers to old problems or new ways of thinking about or looking at the world.

Until the recession of 1970–71 the affluent society had put money into the pockets of young people, and they spent it on records, on personal care and clothing and vehicles, on youth-oriented motion pictures, and on science fiction books. The recession hit youth jobs harder than any other: it reached the publishing industry in 1971, with some retrenching in science fiction. Although science fiction sales did not seem as much affected as the rest of the publishing business, the depressing effects continued into 1973, but the boom resumed in 1974.

One other factor which may have influenced science fiction readership among the young is the increasing availability of good juvenile science fiction to get youthful readers started and looking for the right things: books and series of books by such able writers as Heinlein, del Rey, Silverberg, Asimov, Williamson and Pohl, Dickson, André Norton, and others.

The appearance of science fiction in other media may also have been influential: some reasonably good science fiction television series have advertised the possibilities of the genre to a broader audience—*Outer Limits, Twilight Zone, Star Trek*, perhaps even the ill-fated series based on my book, *The Immortal*. The impact of one major creation cannot be overlooked: in spite of the fact that it was criticized for various reasons by a number of science fiction writers, *2001: A Space Odyssey* excited a great many filmgoers and turned them to books to seek more such excitement in ideas and speculation.

Some science fiction readers and writers say they were turned on by science fiction in the comic magazines.

The increasing sophistication of the times may have helped prepare the way for science fiction. The rapid pace of technological and even social change has become apparent to almost everyone. "Where will it all end?" everyone asks.

Apollo 14, liftoff

Apollo 14, space-walk

Apollo 14, exploring the moon

Scene from Stanley Kubrick's and Arthur C. Clarke's *2001: A Space Odyssey*

Science fiction, at least, poses the right questions. If its answers are not always solutions, science fiction may do more to get people thinking about the problems than any other kind of literature or medium, even television, and there is no question that for many it eases the transitions that change makes inevitable. Science fiction readers are not susceptible to future shock; they were part of the space generation long before anyone else. They don't fear change; they welcome it. They are impatient for the future to arrive.

In science fiction there is, as well, a kind of "nowness" that many young people are seeking, perhaps the kind of relevance they are asking for, and sometimes a kind of fictional experience that can be mind-expanding in its best sense. It can be a kind of psychedelic literature in the hands of skillful experimental stylists.

Then, too, the quality of writing in science fiction has improved considerably in recent years, or so we science fiction writers would like to believe.

The world has caught up with science fiction, but science fiction is not there. It has rocketed on farther into the unknown, charting new territories of the imagination, expanding once more the frontiers of the possible.

What it is, how it got to be that way, and where it may be going from here is what this book is about. We will begin at the beginning.

CHAPTER 2
IN THE BEGINNING

SCIENCE FICTION could not exist before the creation of a new world by invention and technology, a world in which change is apparent, a world in which people believe in progress. Neither could it exist without form, without a medium in which to relate its dreams and describe its visions.

The novel and the short story are of comparatively recent origin. Some literary historians find their sources in fourteenth century Italy (Boccaccio wrote his *Tales* in 1339, his *Decameron* in 1347), in fifteenth century France and England (Malory's *Le Morte d'Arthur* appeared in 1470), or in seventeenth century Spain (some critics insist that Cervantes' *Don Quixote*, first printed in 1605, was the first novel). Daniel Defoe published *Robinson Crusoe* in 1719 and *Moll Flanders* in 1722; but traditional scholarship points to Samuel Richardson's *Pamela* (1740) as the first English novel.

We can imagine—after all, imagination is the differentiating characteristic of the science fiction reader as well as the writer—science fiction existing in other forms. We can even find some examples: science fiction poems, such as Stephen Vincent Benet's "Nightmare No. 3" (there are two recent anthologies of science fiction poetry, *Holding Your Eight Hands*, edited by Edward Lucie-Smith, and *Inside Outer Space*, edited by Robert Vas Dias); and science fiction plays, such as Karel Čapek's classic *R.U.R.* if not Aristophanes' *The Birds*. But if these were the only forms of science fiction, most of what we value today would be unrealized.

LEFT: Italy's fourteenth century storyteller, Giovanni Boccaccio

RIGHT: A page from *Le Morte d'Arthur* by Sir Thomas Malory, England's fifteenth- century romancer

Before there were novels and short stories, however, men had the same human instincts and desires: to entertain and to be entertained, to instruct, to explain, to illuminate, to invent, to imagine things that are not. Conditions may change, but people remain the same. If it seems that people have changed, it is because the ways in which they express their instincts and desires have changed; it has become possible to think differently; the changing times force men and women to alter their ways of life; cultural shifts create a climate in which certain new modes of thought or expression, once unthinkable or unspeakable, now are encouraged, even applauded, by one's peers.

So the things that men do—the inventions they make, the economies they create, even the ideas they conceive and disseminate—change the conditions that control what men can do. Contemporary social conditions determined the ways in which those instincts and desires that ultimately created science fiction expressed themselves.

Those instincts and desires could not create what we know as science fiction before the Industrial Revolution brought the general realization that science and technology were producing irreversible change, were altering the way people lived, even within their lifetimes. This is not to imply that the ancient world had no scientists. The Greeks produced great philosophers of science; the Romans, great engineers; and the Egyptians before them knew enough to build the pyramids with the aid of what Lewis Mumford calls the first machine, masses of people moving as one at the command of a single man, "the collective human machine, the platonic model of all later machines."

Among the Greeks, for instance, Heraclitus (c.535–c.475 B.C.) maintained that permanence in the world is an illusion, that the only reality is change; Democritus (c.460–c.370 B.C.) believed that the world is made up of tiny particles imperceptible to the senses but indivisible and indestructible—in other words, atoms. But neither philosopher sought to verify his theories through experiment —in fact, Democritus held that the true nature of things can be discovered only by thought, for sense impressions are confusing—and so far as we know, no writers speculated about the implications to mankind or an individual if these beliefs were true and verifiable and could be harnessed to improve man's lot. At least the view held by many philosophers, including Democritus, was that the true purpose of life was happiness through inner tranquility.

The Greeks expressed their instincts and desires in other ways: in philosophical speculation sometimes framed as dialogues, like Plato's; in natural history; in history itself; in criticism; in tragedies and comedies for the Greek amphitheaters; and in the epic literature epitomized in the two works attributed to Homer, which look back toward a more heroic past. Of more interest to the scholar looking for literary influences is *The Odyssey*, which describes the wanderings of Odysseus, long delayed from returning home after his participation in the Trojan War, around the strange and unknown lands bordering the Mediterranean. Aside from the Babylonian epic "Gilgamesh," which itself has science fiction aspects, *The Iliad* and *The Odyssey* are two of the oldest literary works that have come down to us, and there may be significance in the fact that one is about war and the other is about a fabulous journey that would be a model for hundreds of others, including Vergil's *Aeneid*. Its themes would be picked up and used again and again: the island of Circe, for instance, where an enchantress cast a spell over Odysseus' men and changed them into animals (swine) may, much later, become H. G. Wells's *Island of Dr. Moreau*, where a scientific experimenter uses vivisection to turn animals into men.

Another myth, of greater similarity to the eventual subjects of science fiction, described the first great scientist-engineer, Daedalus, who built the Minotaur's labyrinth for King Minos of Crete, as well as a man of bronze to repel the Argonauts. Finally, when he fell out of favor with King Minos, Daedalus made artificial wings of feathers and wax with which he and his son Icarus escaped, although Icarus flew too near the sun, the wax melted, and he fell to his death in the sea. The myth, then, introduced not only the rewards of technology but the dangers of technology unwisely used.

Plato (c.427–347 B.C.) exhibited some of the speculative and model-building characteristics of the science fiction writer in *The Republic*, the first of the utopias which figure prominently in the history of science fiction. In *The Re-*

Spain's sixteenth century satirist, Miguel de Cervantes

England's seventeenth century journalist, Daniel Defoe

England's eighteenth century novelist, Samuel Richardson

LEFT: a Grecian urn shows the traditional bard

RIGHT: Homer

BELOW: Virgil, and the Roman world through which his epic hero Aeneas wandered

public Plato describes an ideal state, a self-contained, independent city whose population is divided into three fixed classes, each member of which knows his place, minds his own business, takes orders from above, and never answers back: husbandmen and craftsmen, military protectors, and guardians. In setting up his ideal Plato dismisses, as increasingly removed from it, the military state, the dominance of merchant princes, democracy, and tyranny. His one scientific proposal, if we exclude his concern with the science of government, is eugenic breeding.

But of course we cannot exclude the science of government, and later utopian and anti-utopian writers through H. G. Wells and his successors would deal with the same ideas and face the same problem: how do you compel people to like what is good for them? (Does B. F. Skinner have an answer?) They would not, in their search for the ideal government, quite get around to asking themselves the science fiction question: what would happen if we had a science of government? Perhaps this is why their visions always are flawed.

Plato believed in the search for knowledge which he believed, when true, was eternal and unchangeable. Behind the appearances we see in the world around us, Plato thought, was the idea, the general form, which was permanent and the only true reality, and which could be arrived at only through reason. Since the general ideas, which things in the physical world only imitate imperfectly, can be arrived at only through induction, through the logical process of dialectic, Plato cast his ideas into the form of dialogues between Socrates and others. Among his later dialogues is the first mention of the legend of Atlantis. In the "Timaeus" and "Critias" Plato tells of a land of fabled strength and wealth, which existed in prehistory beyond the pillars of Hercules—an island larger than Libya and Asia together.

Plato

But at a later time there occurred portentous earthquakes and floods, and one grievous day and night befell them, when the whole body of your warriors was swallowed up by the earth, and the island of Atlantis in like manner was swallowed up by the sea and vanished; wherefore also the ocean at that spot has now become impassable and unsearchable, being blocked up by the shoal mud which the island created as it settled down.

The great lost civilization entered the science fiction repertoire, to be joined a little later by the lost race and the distant lands where strange peoples lead fabulous or incredible lives. In *Imperial Purple,* Edgar Saltus wrote that the Roman Emperor Tiberius retired to his gardens by the sea and sought his entertainment in imaginative accounts of other worlds.

There was a work by Hecataeus, with which he could visit Hyperborea, that land where happiness was a birthright, inalienable at that; yet a happiness so sweet that it must have been cloying; for the people who enjoyed it, and with it the appendage of limitless life, killed themselves from sheer ennui. Theopompus disclosed to him a stranger vista—a continent beyond the ocean—one where there were immense cities and where two rivers flowed—the River of Pleasure and the River of Pain. With Iambulus he discovered the Fortunate Isles, where there were men with elastic bones, bifurcated tongues; men who never married, who worshipped the sun, whose life was an uninterrupted delight, and who, when overtaken by age, lay on a perfumed grass that produced a voluptuous death. Evhemerus, a terrible atheist, whose *Sacred History* the early bishops wielded against polytheism until they discovered it was double-edged, took him to Panchaia, an island where incense grew; where property was held in common; where there was but one law—Justice, yet a justice different from our own. . . . Aristeas of Proconnesus led him among the Arimaspi, a curious people who passed their lives fighting for gold with griffons in the dark. With Isogonus he descended the valley of Ismaus, where wild men were, whose feet turned inwards. In Albania he found a race with pink eyes and white hair; in Sarmatia another that ate only on alternate days. Agatharcides took him to Libya, and there introduced him to the Psyllians, in whose bodies was a poison deadly to serpents. . . . Callias took him further yet, to the home of the hermaphrodites; Nymphodorus showed him a race of fascinators who used enchanted words. With Apollonides he encountered women who killed with their eyes those on whom they looked too long. Megasthenes guided him to the Astomians, whose garments were the down of feathers, and who lived on the scent of the rose.

Lucian of Samosata

Something that more nearly resembled science fiction was written about A.D. 165 by the Greek writer, rhetorician, philosopher, and satirist Lucian of Samosata. Lucian's birthplace now is a ruined city in Syria on the banks of the Euphrates, but then it was part of the Roman Empire. Lucian traveled widely, settling in Athens at the age of forty and ending his life in Egypt, where he was appointed to a post by the Emperor Commodus; but his imagination carried him even farther. Lucian wrote the first accounts of what would become typical of the later utopian and then science fiction theme of far traveling, the voyage to the moon. Lucian's *Icaromenippus* describes a flight to the moon, with one wing from a vulture and one from an eagle, by a philosopher bent on proving that the earth is round. In addition to perceiving the earth's shape, Menippus sees the immorality of its philosophers, for Lucian's purpose was satire.

Lucian's more ambitious work was *A True History*. In it he sets forth with a company of fifty Greek athletes to reach the limits of the ocean and see the men "who live on the other side," but on the second day his ship is caught in a strange island inhabited by tree women. When the ship leaves the island

. . . we were suddenly caught by a whirlwind, which turned our vessel several times around in a circle with tremendous speed and lifted it more than three thousand stadia into the air, not setting it down again on the sea, but kept it suspended above the water at that height, and carried us on, with swelled sails, above the clouds.

After an aerial voyage of seven days and seven nights, we sighted land in the air. It was an island, luminous, spherical and shining with strong light.

We put into it, and having cast anchor, landed. On examining the country, we discovered that it was inhabited and cultivated.

In the daylight we could see nothing from where we were, but when night came, other islands became visible to us in the surrounding air, some close by, some larger and some smaller, with the appearance of fire.

There was also another land below us, with cities, rivers, seas, woods, and mountains on it. This, we concluded, was our own world. . . .

Voiage and Travaile of Sir John Mandeville

As in *Icaromenippus* Lucian's purpose was satire; the adventurers from Earth become involved in a war between Endymion, the king of the moon, and Phaeton, the king of the sun, about the colonization of the planet Jupiter; the war is fought between troops described as horse-vultures, cabbage-fowl, flea-archers, horse-pismires, radish-darters, stalky mushrooms, dog-acorns, and cloud-centaurs.

Both kinds of far traveling—to distant lands or unknown areas of the world, and to other planets, particularly the moon—became standard forms of fantasy in later centuries. In the Middle Ages, with legends like Siegfried and Parzival, Norse mythology, and the Arthurian cycle, the dominant motif was the journey and the quest. Just before the Age of Exploration came to full flower, the *Voiage and Travaile of Sir John Mandeville* (c. 1371), with its accounts of the pseudonymous author's travels through Jerusalem and the East, compiled from the authentic travels of others and fantastic lore, became popular in many languages. It seemed no more fantastic, perhaps, than the authentic travels of such adventurers as Marco Polo, whose experiences in the Far East were dictated after his return to Venice in 1295.

Ludovico Ariosto

So many fictional journeys to the moon have been published that at least one book has been written about them, Marjorie Hope Nicolson's *Voyages to the Moon* (1948). In spite of the tempting vision of another world hung every night before the eyes of authors and philosophers, however, nothing more was done with Lucian's theme for thirteen centuries. Then in 1532 the Italian poet Ariosto published his epic *Orlando Furioso;* in what has been called the greatest Renaissance poem, Orlando loses his wits and Astolpho, in search of them, goes to the moon in the same chariot that carried away Elijah and finds the moon to be a "rich champaign" filled with cities and towns. and the repository of all things lost on earth, including vows, prayers, forgotten poems, and Orlando's wits.

Then in 1608 a Dutch spectacle-maker named Hans Lippershey invented the telescope; in 1609 Galileo built his first telescope and began his observations of the heavens, reported the following year in his *Sidereus Nuncius;* and voyages to the moon began to incorporate the realities of scientific observation. The next such book was written, appropriately enough, by a German astronomer, Johannes Kepler. *Somnium* was published posthumously in 1634 and cast in the form of a dream, perhaps as a means of self-protection, since Kepler's method of getting to the moon was the witchcraft of the narrator's mother, Fiolxhilda; oddly enough, private circulation of the Latin manuscript may have led to the arrest of Kepler's mother for witchcraft. Once the narrator, Duracotus, and Fiolxhilda have reached the moon, the story becomes a means of describing conditions on the moon as Kepler believed them to be, which included air and water, and burning days and frozen nights equal to fourteen Earth-days each. Kepler's purpose was to deliver an exposition of the new Copernican-Galilean-Keplerian system of astronomy.

Early telescope

The first trip to the moon published in English was Bishop Francis Godwin's *The Man in the Moone* (1638), in which his hero, Domingo Gonsales, reaches the moon on a raft pulled through the air by swanlike birds called gansas. Following the example of Kepler and Godwin, another English bishop, John Wilkins, wrote a book called *A Discourse Concerning a New World* (first edition, 1638; third, 1640) arguing that the moon may be inhabited and men may learn how to reach it; the book expressed his belief that men someday will learn to fly and place colonies on the moon. Others followed: Cyrano de Bergerac's *Voy-*

Johannes Kepler

Scene from *The Man in the Moone*

From *A Discourse Concerning a New World*

Thomas More

Plan of More's *Utopia*

Thomas Campanella

Francis Bacon

ages to the Moon and the Sun (1657; in English, 1659 and 1687); Gabriel Daniel's *A Voyage to the World of Cartesius* (French, 1691; in English, 1694); David Russen's *Iter Lunare; or, A Voyage to the Moon* (1703); Ralph Morris's *John Daniel* (1751); Voltaire's *Micromegas* (1752), in which a giant from Sirius and a smaller companion from Saturn come to Earth; Aratus's *A Voyage to the Moon* (1793); and George Fowler's *A Flight to the Moon* (1813).

Many of these were vehicles for criticizing contemporary society or presenting an ideal society—that is, utopia. Intermixed with them in time were more typical examples, beginning with the work that gave the genre its name, Thomas More's *Utopia* (1516), and continuing through Campanella's *The City of the Sun* (1623), Francis Bacon's *The New Atlantis* (1627), and the first such work published in America, Louis Sebastien Mercier's *Memoirs of the Year Two Thousand Five Hundred* (1771).

Cyrano de Bergerac imagined
that man might be carried to
the moon on burning gasses.

Another way was to fasten
phials of dew to a harness
and be lifted upward by the
sun's attraction.

Laputa, the flying island of
Gulliver's Travels.

Today Cyrano de Bergerac is known almost entirely through his central role in the 1897 play by Edmond Rostand. But he existed in the flesh (1619–55) and apparently in detail as romantic as that portrayed on stage and screen. Like most of his predecessors, his purpose was to satirize his society, but in the process of getting to the moon he explored numerous scientific and mythological methods of travel. Rostand has Cyrano run through them all at one point in the play:

One way was to stand naked in the sunshine, in a harness thickly studded with glass phials, each filled with morning dew. The sun in drawing up the dew, you see, could not have helped drawing me up too!

I could have let the wind into a cedar coffer, then rarefied the imprisoned element by means of cunningly adjusted burning glasses, and soared up with it!

Or else, mechanic as well as artificer, I could have fashioned a giant grasshopper, with steel joints, which, impelled by successive explosions of saltpeter, would have hopped with me to the azure meadows where graze the starry flocks!

Since smoke by its nature ascends, I could have blown into an appropriate globe a sufficient quantity to ascend with me!

Since Phoebe, the moon-goddess, when she is at wane, is greedy, O beeves! of your marrow . . . with that marrow I may have besmeared myself!

Or else, I could have placed myself upon an iron plate, have taken a magnet of suitable size, and thrown it in the air! That way is a very good one! The magnet flies upward, the iron instantly after; the magnet no sooner overtaken than you fling it up again . . . The rest is clear! You can go upward indefinitely.

At the hour in which the moon attracts the deep, I lay down upon the sands, after a sea-bath . . . and, my head being drawn up first,—the reason of this, you see, that the hair will hold a quantity of water in its mop!—I rose in the air, straight, beautifully straight, like an angel. . . .

Actually Cyrano's narrator first is drawn into the air by his bottles of dew but lands in Canada; he crashes in a second machine driven by a spring; soldiers send him up again with rockets, but when these fail high in the air he is saved by the moon's attraction to the beef marrow he had rubbed on his bruises.

But perhaps Cyrano's most important contribution to science fiction was his influence on Jonathan Swift (1667–1745), just as Swift's gift to the genre may

Jonathan Swift

have been his influence on H. G. Wells, although Swift himself was a greater writer than either. All of *Gulliver's Travels* (1726) can be read as science fiction —and that is how it still is read by children—even though its intention was to satirize men and their institutions. The detail with which Swift described Gulliver's adventures and the strange people he was thrown among—the Lilliputians, the Brobdingnagians, the Laputans, the Houyhnhnms—creates in the reader a feeling of delight in the imagination and a concern for what happens to Gulliver that raises the narrative above the one-to-one relationship of satire.

Swift's science fiction theme—the distant wonders of the earth—was implemented by Gulliver's long sea voyages, which ended in three violent storms and a mutiny. Though a less-engrossing narrative, the most significant from a science fiction viewpoint is Gulliver's third travel adventure, in which he is picked up by the flying island of Laputa. The founding of England's Royal Society is said to have been inspired by Bacon's *New Atlantis;* through the scientists of Laputa, Swift was ridiculing the Royal Society. Laputa floats in the air through the repulsion of a giant natural magnet located in a cave:

> . . . the greatest Curiosity, upon which the Fate of the Island depends, is a Load-stone of a prodigious Size, in Shape resembling a Weaver's Shuttle. It is in Length six Yards, and in the thickest Part at least three Yards over. This Magnet is sustained by a very strong Axle of Adamant, passing through its Middle, upon which it plays, and is poized so exactly that the weakest Hand can turn it. It is hooped round with a hollow Cylinder of Adamant, four Foot deep, as many thick, and twelve Yards in Diameter, placed horizontally and supported by Eight Adamantine Feet, each Six Yards high. . . .
>
> By Means of this Load-stone, the Island is made to rise and fall, and move from one Place to another. For . . . the Stone is endued at one of its Sides with an attractive Power, and at the other with a repulsive. Upon placing the Magnet erect with its attracting End towards the Earth, the Island descends; but when the repelling Extremity points downwards, the Island mounts directly upwards. . . .

In 1740 the first English novel was published.

In 1763 one of the earliest, perhaps the first, stories of the future was published, the anonymous *Reign of King George VI, 1900–1925,* in which a patriot English king repels invasions by Russia and then France and finally an attack by Spain, and brings back England's greatness. The concept that men might write about events yet to happen was a startling leap of imagination, but life in twentieth-century England is viewed in the book as little different from life in the eighteenth century, and it falls short of achieving the feel and ends of science fiction because it falls so far short of recognizing the pervasive influence of change.

In 1764 the gothic romance entered literature with Horace Walpole's *The Castle of Otranto* and brought with it generations of frightened heroines, unseen horrors, and ghostly visitations in gloom-ridden medieval architecture, all of them enjoying an unexpected revival today. They were immensely popular in their own day, and *Otranto* was followed by William Beckford's *Vathek* (in English, 1784), Mrs. Ann Radcliffe's *The Mysteries of Udolpho* (1794), and M. G. "Monk" Lewis' *The Monk* (1796), among many others. Gradually semi-scientific explanations for all the midnight carryings-on became part of the genre, as in Charlotte Dacre's *Zofloya* (1806).

The union of science and the gothic romance brought forth a creation that has some right to be called the first science fiction novel: Mary Shelley's *Frankenstein* (1817). Mary Wollstonecraft Shelley, young mistress and soon-to-be wife of the English poet Percy Bysshe Shelley, set out to write a tale of terror. She was eighteen when she began. The Shelleys, Lord Byron, and a friend of Byron's, an Italian physician named Dr. Polidori, had been reading *Fantasmagoriana,* and Byron suggested that they each try to write a ghost story. At first Mary Shelley had no idea what to write about. Then one evening Byron and Shelley discussed Erasmus Darwin's studies about the nature of life; that night, lying sleepless, Mary Shelley had a vision of "the hideous phantasm of a man stretched out, and then, on the working of some powerful engine, show signs of life." Two years later the book was published. In a preface she said that she did not want the novel to be considered a story of the supernatural; if not the supernatural, then the events of the story had to rely upon the power of science to work miracles.

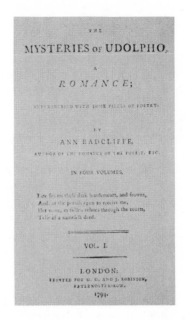

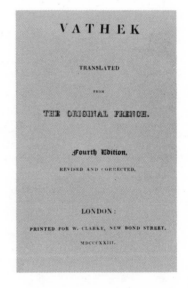

Mary Wollstonecraft Shelley

Thus the theme of man's creation of artificial life—and the inevitable retribution that comes to him for his presumption—entered science fiction. One of the book's side effects was to shape the concept of the "mad scientist" and his punishment for more than a century in spite of the fact that Frankenstein's monster is born with natural goodness and is soured only by the revulsion it meets from everyone, even its own creator. Conditioned by generations of simplistic motion-picture treatments, the general public has little occasion to reflect with Frankenstein, "For the first time . . . I felt what the duties of a creator toward his creature were, and that I ought to render him happy before I complained of his wickedness."

The myth of creation goes back far beyond *Frankenstein*, of course, and into the religious needs of man to explain the origins of his world and himself; and the attempt to encroach upon the exclusive prerogative of deity—whether through the alchemist's search to turn base metals into gold, or attempts to find the elixir of life that would prolong man's existence beyond its God-given span, or plans to create life itself—always has ended in punishment for its blasphemy. Daedalus built a man of bronze to repel the Argonauts, and Jewish folklore tells of the creation of the Golem, molded of clay and animated by a charm or shem (one of the names of God) by various medieval rabbis, the most famous of them Rabbi Löw of sixteenth century Prague. The Golem, too, turns against its creator. Only in recent times have robots and androids been treated without religious awe, and only with the development of Isaac Asimov's three laws of robotics (see Chapter 10) which built in a prohibition against harming man has the creation of artificial life not resulted in tragedy. And yet many recent considerations of computers, fictional and speculative, involve overtones of punishment for blasphemy; and HAL, the murderous computer in the Kubrick-Clarke motion picture *2001: A Space Odyssey*, harks back to Frankenstein and the Golem. (In a 1970 New York Nebula Award banquet discussion about research into artificial intelligence, the influence on that research of the fictional speculations of science fiction writers like Asimov and Clarke, and the need to estab-

The Frankenstein monster

From the wood engravers and the early presses to the modern rotary presses, the development of printing hastened the growth of a literate public—and the demand for popular writing.

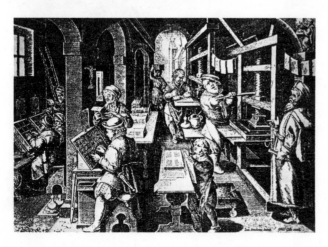

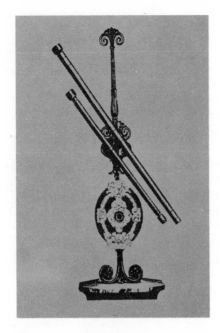

An early microscope

A nineteenth century harvest

lish teleological goals, Asimov responded, "What kinds of goals would a Golem have if a Golem could have goals?")

Frankenstein had other important attributes; it was, for instance, the first truly outstanding science fiction success, not only in print but on the stage and in motion pictures. Five years after the story first appeared, "Presumption: or the Fate of Frankenstein" was a hit on the London stage, and two other serious versions and three burlesque treatments were presented the same year. The story was an early motion picture favorite, first reaching the screen in 1910 through Thomas A. Edison's company; again as *Life Without Soul* in 1915; in an Italian version in 1920; and then in the definitive version, which made a star out of Boris Karloff, in 1931. It would be followed by one serious sequel, *The Bride of Frankenstein,* and then by a horde of imitations exploiting the theme for horror or humor, including recent spoofs by Andy Warhol and Mel Brooks.

What had happened in the world to make possible *Frankenstein*'s creation? While speculations about ideal systems and imaginary voyages for sport or satire were produced by writers from Homer on up through Plato, Lucian of Samosata, and the travel and utopian writers of the late Middle Ages and the Renaissance, during the centuries in which empires rose and fell, the modes of life and warfare remained virtually unchanged. Man seemed eternally at the mercy of the elements—subject to the natural processes of sun and storm, drought and disease, and the almost-as-inevitable and elemental tyranny of his fellow men.

Slowly then, but with increasing rapidity, like a flywheel gathering momentum, changes began to occur. The English longbow made the peasant a dangerous opponent and gave England its sturdy yeomen. The spinning wheel, invented in 1298, represented a new way of thinking about work. The printing press, invented in 1450 by Gutenberg (using movable type invented in eleventh-century China), had the potential to revolutionize the transmission—and hence the very nature—of knowledge. The Age of Exploration, with its sense of adventure and expanding horizons, began in the fifteenth century. In 1520 the invention of the rifle destroyed knighthood and the tradition of the warrior—and created the soldier.

In 1589 came the knitting machine; in 1590, the microscope; in 1608, the telescope. The process of invention was speeding up, feeding upon its own success, and beginning to change the way people lived.

At first it was only the scientists themselves who were influenced, as they read about the work of their contemporaries and were inspired to new work of their own. But the telescope destroyed the medieval universe and rocked the Catholic Church, and gradually Gutenberg's invention spread the written word—

James Watt

and only a little later the ability to read—among the growing middle class and eventually to the lower classes as well, who wished at least to read the word of God.

In 1628 came Harvey's discovery of the circulation of blood; in 1636, the invention of the micrometer; in 1661, the invention of the reflecting telescope. In 1660 English scientist Robert Boyle observed that "the invention of gunpowder hath quite altered the conditions of martial affairs over the world, both by sea and land."

The first Newcomen steam engine, the threshing machine, and the weaving machine all were invented in England before 1735; by 1750 the Industrial Revolution had begun. The blessings and curses of science and technology had come upon the land, and they were changing life for better or for worse, in spite of pain and protest. Angry weavers forced John Kay, inventor of the flying shuttle, to flee to France where he died in poverty. A London grain mill, powered by one of James Watt's steam engines, was destroyed by fire. Elias Howe's sewing machine was opposed by many midnineteenth-century Americans, who believed that it would put thousands out of work.

About this time, too, men were beginning to look ahead, to see if they could guess what the future might be like, how it could be changed for the better, or how it might get worse if conditions went on as they had been going. Extrapolation—a kind of crystal ball made up of observation, imagination, and logic—became the tool of seers as well as mathematicians. According to one editor, extrapolation is one of the two basic methods for constructing a science fiction story—spotting a trend and predicting its probable course into the future—a method summed up in the title of a story by Robert Heinlein, "If This Goes On . . ." The other method, speculating about the effect of some unique event, is summed up in the title of Isaac Asimov's "What If?"

There had been earlier prophets—but it was because they were prophets, with unique powers, who could predict what others could not foresee by means they could not describe, that their methods were beyond analysis and imitation, even discussion. But the ability to extrapolate—to observe a series of events, to connect them in sequence, to discern their trend, and to continue that trend into the future—came to be only when men realized that their lives were changing, and could be changed, through their own efforts; and that man's logic could determine the course of this change and possibly influence it.

The pace of scientific and technological discovery picked up. James Watt invented the condensing steam engine in 1765; two years later came Hargreaves' spinning jenny. Mesmer introduced his new "science" of mesmerism in Vienna about 1775. In 1776 Adam Smith published his *Wealth of Nations,* the application of the scientific method to political economy, and the Declaration of Independence, itself a scientific document, was signed.

The circular saw came in 1777; the steel pen in 1780; and the Age of Flight in 1783, with the first balloon ascensions in France by the Montgolfier brothers

Watt's steam engine

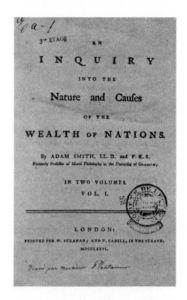

Montgolfier hot-air balloon

Robert Fulton

Fulton's steamboat, the *Claremont*

A Mediterranean galley

A pioneer steamship, the *Great Eastern*

Eighteenth century British canals

Inland waterway system of England and Wales

and Jacques Charles—and in the same year, fortuitously, the invention of the parachute.

The steamboat was invented in 1783; the iron plow in 1784; the power loom in 1785; and in 1789 came the French Revolution which, like the American Revolution, was at least in part a response of people to the new questioning attitudes of the scientific mind and its effort to seek a new scientific order based on natural law, in political systems as well as in other areas of life and commerce.

The wonders that men expected of the new age were put into verse in 1791, as were his later scientific observations, by an aspiring inventor, poet, and natural philosopher, Erasmus Darwin, who would father a famous scientific family:

> *Soon shall thy arm, UNCONQUER'D STEAM! afar*
> *Drag the slow barge, or drive the rapid car;*
> *Or on wide-waving wings expanded bear*
> *The flying-chariot through the field of air.*
> *Fair crews triumphant, leaning from above,*
> *Shall wave their fluttering kerchiefs as they move;*
> *Or warrior-bands alarm the gaping crowd,*
> *And armies shrink beneath the shadowy cloud.*

During the closing decades of the eighteenth century and the first decades of the nineteenth century the marriage of Watt's steam engine to various forms of transportation would begin the process of shortening distance and time in the world that would culminate in our present global village. Robert Fulton and

First passenger locomotive

The Suez Canal

John Stevens independently produced working steamboats by 1807, and by 1827 the first steamship had crossed the Atlantic; by 1833 the passage took twenty-five days, and five years later it was down to fifteen days.

Canals were built—beginning in England with the Bridgewater Canal in 1761 and continuing through the Erie Canal, completed in 1825, and the Suez, in 1869.

The first steam railways were opened in England (1825) and the United States (1830), and the transcontinental railroad was completed by 1869.

Public demonstrations of the results of the new laboratory sciences came with increasing frequency: Eli Whitney, who had invented the cotton gin in 1793, received in 1798 a government order for 10,000 guns and worked out machine tools to produce the necessary parts on an interchangeable basis, thus initiating America's major contribution to world industry, mass production.

In 1798 Robert Malthus published his "Essay on the Principle of Population," which for the first time suggested natural limits to the biblical injunction to "be fruitful, and multiply, and replenish the earth, and subdue it. . . ."

In 1799 Napoleon Bonaparte ended the French Revolution and launched an era of French conquest in which even the tactics of warfare seemed to have changed with the times. He also produced, through the application of scientific thought to the law, the Napoleonic Code.

In the quarter of a century between 1800 and 1825 the Latin American nations won their independence from Europe.

The nineteenth century loosed discovery after discovery upon the world. In electricity, Volta invented the electric battery in 1800; Ritter, the storage battery in 1812; Faraday, the electric motor in 1822; Sturgeon, the electromagnet in 1824; Pixii, the electric generator in 1832. Dalton announced his atomic theory in 1802.

Within little more than two decades came the invention of the breech-loading rifle, the bicycle, the stethoscope, the cultivator, the camera, the calculating machine, portland cement, the tractor, the reaper, the friction match, and the revolver.

In 1827 Goethe told Eckermann that he was confident of continual change, because "through my whole life down to the present hour one great discovery has followed on another." He felt, he said, like "one who walks towards the dawn and, when the sun rises, is astonished at its brilliancy."

In 1832 an American told De Tocqueville, who himself might be considered an early futurist, "There is a feeling among us about everything which prevents us aiming at permanence. There reigns in America a popular and universal be-

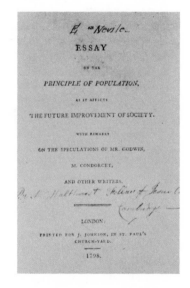

Michael Faraday

lief in the progress of the human spirit. We are always expecting an improvement to be found in everything."

The readiness of the American people to believe in the limitless miracles of science was demonstrated by articles which appeared in the New York *Sun* during the months of August and September 1835, as "Discoveries in the Moon Lately Made at the Cape of Good Hope, by Sir John Herschel." Herschel was a distinguished English astronomer and the son of an even more distinguished astronomer; the articles, which purported to be reprinted from the *Edinburgh Journal of Science,* described his years of work to perfect a telescope that could magnify astronomical objects 40,000 times and make visible objects on the moon as small as eighteen inches in diameter. First to be discovered among the lunar mountains were great claret-colored jewels, then bisonlike animals adjusted to the conditions of the moon by flaps over the eyes to protect them against extremes of light and darkness. Manlike creatures with batlike wings were discerned, then templelike structures. Finally, when the sun's rays struck the great lens, it acted as a burning-glass and the observatory was burned.

The articles stirred up great excitement and New York *Sun* circulation jumped, but finally the newspaper revealed that the articles had been written by a reporter for the newspaper, Richard Adams Locke. The series came to be known as "The Moon Hoax." Other hoaxes would follow.

The world—certainly the United States, probably England and France and the rest of Western civilization—was ready for science fiction, for the wildest flights of imagination which could be supported by the findings and speculations of science. By the 1840s Americans and most of the world, having passed through the trials and triumphs of the Industrial Revolution, had accepted the social doctrine that science had led mankind to a new and more desirable order of existence.

Men were looking forward to greater glories. In 1842, in his two-volume edition of *Poems,* Tennyson published "Locksley Hall." In it he described "nourishing a youth sublime/With the fairy tales of science, and the long result of time. . . ."

> *Men, my brothers, men the workers, ever reaping something new:*
> *That which they have done but earnest of the things that they shall do:*
>
> *For I dipt into the future, far as human eye could see,*
> *Saw the Vision of the world, and all the wonder that would be;*
>
> *Saw the heavens fill with commerce, argosies of magic sails,*
> *Pilots of the purple twilight, dropping down with costly bales;*
>
> *Heard the heavens fill with shouting, and there rained a ghastly dew*
> *From the nations' airy navies grappling in the central blue;*
>
> *Far along the world-wide whisper of the south-wind rushing warm,*
> *With the standards of the peoples plunging through the thunder-storm;*
>
> *Till the war-drum throbbed no longer, and the battle-flags were furl'd*
> *In the Parliament of man, the Federation of the World.*
>
> *There the common sense of most shall hold a fretful realm in awe,*
> *And the kindly earth shall slumber, lapt in universal law. . . .*
>
> *Through the shadow of the globe we sweep into the younger day:*
> *Better fifty years of Europe than a cycle of Cathay.*

Goethe

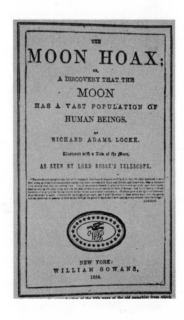

Alfred Lord Tennyson

CHAPTER 3
TOWARD VERNE:
1800-1885

THROUGHOUT most of man's history he has looked back toward a happier time, toward Paradise, toward a "golden age." Ahead lay only a hope of laying aside sufficient food to provide for a family until the next crop matured. The major changes in life were personal and natural: birth, marriage, death. From outside came war, disease, drought, flood, violence, theft, murder, execution.

The rise and fall of empires meant little to the peasant; he tilled his patch of land and seldom ventured beyond the nearest village. Everything beyond was unknown, and even for the educated, maps contained vast areas and even continents labeled "terra incognita." Men hoped to live in tranquil times so that they could enjoy at least the comfort and safety of their fathers. Almost no one could read; books, for most of the life of man, have been non-existent; science was a mental exercise; and technology was a toy.

In times like these only visionaries dream of a better way; they wrote the utopias. Then, slowly, the Industrial Revolution brought man-made change; the great wheel of invention began to accelerate. As C. P. Snow said in his "Two Cultures" lecture, "With singular unanimity, in any country where they have had the chance, the poor have walked off the land into the factories as fast as the factories would take them."

The Hereford Mappa Mundi

Technology shortened the distances between places; steam made man independent of wind and animal; weapons changed warfare from a courtly sport to a grim business for citizens; books, periodicals, and literacy spread rapidly. And the promise and threat of science brought literary responses such as *Frankenstein,* the "Moon Hoax," and "Locksley Hall."

A feeling of hope for the future was not universal. Blake wrote of "dark satanic mills," and Emerson said, "Things are in the saddle, and ride mankind." But many men, if not most, agreed with the Marquis de Concercet who, facing death at the hands of the French Revolution, still was able to proclaim his undying faith in "the future progress of mankind."

The world was ready for science fiction, and when the world is ready someone always steps forward to provide or invent whatever the times require. A later prophet, whose work was closely related to science fiction and whose ideas suggested a significant number of stories, put the concept of ripeness into more memorable words. "When it's steam-engine time people invent steam engines," Charles Fort said.

Occasionally, as we know, the world is not ready, and the pioneer before his time must endure ridicule or oblivion, like Billy Mitchell or Robert Goddard, apostles of air power and rocketry. Or like Leonardo da Vinci and his drawings of tanks and helicopters. Science fiction can cite similar examples.

This chapter in the evolving history of science fiction is devoted to the authors who worked in the middle half of the nineteenth century, who helped

Chappe telegraph tower

shape protoplasmic science fiction into the almost-human creation it would later become, authors who prepared the way for Jules Verne and H. G. Wells, authors of the mainstream because there was no other stream to be of, authors such as Nathaniel Hawthorne, Honoré de Balzac, Edgar Allan Poe, Fitz-James O'Brien, Herman Melville, Edward Everett Hale, Mary Griffith, Sir Edward Bulwer-Lytton, Samuel Butler, and others.

By the nineteenth century increasing emphasis on production for trade had created a middle class, and the middle class had adopted as its philosophy the ideal of rationalism—the establishment of rational goals (in business the goal was profits) and the conscious examination of the best methods for attaining those goals. So deeply ingrained is rationalism in our society that such a philosophy seems like mere common sense, but it was not so when larger, less-measurable goals were held up by emperors or priests or warriors, when ideal rather than practical states were considered to be the proper pursuit of man. In recent days, of course, rationalism has been challenged by sensationalism, which ranks feeling above thought, but that is another story to be covered in Chapter 13.

Robert Goddard and an early rocket

Rationalism, with its emphasis on the posing of theories and the checking of those theories by careful measurement of phenomena, became significant in Renaissance science. In the nineteenth century it spread from business to society in general, affecting law, family ties, religious beliefs, and the host of loyalties normally held by men. One immediate consequence of industrialization and rationalism was a vastly increased division of labor. In *The Republic* Plato had justified philosophically the principle of division of labor, but industrialization made it essential. New occupations appeared: the numbers and types of doctors, lawyers, and engineers multiplied. Full-time scientists, who made their livings at science, appeared for the first time in the nineteenth century, and inventors applied their ingenuity to the findings of science and their own observations of the natural world, and kept the world in a turmoil of change.

One of the eternal dreams (and bureaucratic necessities) of man has been rapid communication over great distances; governments had come up with couriers, swift vehicles and ships, and such signals as the semaphore, created in France in 1794. In 1835 Samuel Morse invented the telegraph and brought each man the potential for instant communication with the rest of the civilized world. The first submarine cable was laid in 1855; successive attempts to lay a transatlantic cable finally succeeded in 1866.

Samuel Morse and the first telegraph

Man's dreams of abundance were coming true. Marx and Engels recognized that fact in 1848:

> The bourgeoisie during its rule of scarce 100 years has created more massive and more colossal productive forces than have all preceding generations together. Subjection of nature's forces to man, machinery, application of chemistry to industry and agriculture, steam navigation, railways, electric telegraphs, clearing of whole continents for cultivation, canalization of rivers, whole populations conjured out of the ground— what earlier century had even a presentiment that such productive forces slumbered in the lap of social labour?

Other inventions followed: electrotyping and vulcanized rubber, 1839; nitroglycerin, 1846; the safety pin and the rifle bullet, 1849; the passenger elevator (which made possible the skyscraper), 1852; the firearm magazine, 1854; the Bessemer process for turning iron into steel, 1856; the railroad sleeping car, 1858; the internal combustion engine, 1859, as well as the spectroscope. In 1843 the term "hypnotism" began to be applied to mesmerism.

Critical changes were occurring in other fields: natural disasters such as the potato blight, which began in Ireland in 1845 and resulted in the death of one million people from starvation and disease over the next six years; political documents and upheavals such as the publication by Marx and Engels of the *Communist Manifesto* in 1848 and revolutions in France, Germany, Austria, Hungary, Bohemia, and Italy; and scientific events such as the publication in 1859 of Charles Darwin's *Origin of the Species*.

The Origin of the Species, possibly the most important event of the century, would have an impact not only on science and natural history but on philosophy, politics, sociology, and warfare, and thus directly and indirectly on science fic-

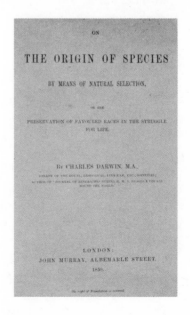

tion. Much of the work of H. G. Wells developed out of his immersion in Darwinism through his studies under Thomas Huxley.

The process of invention accelerated: the steam warship, 1860; dynamite and the machine gun, 1862; smokeless powder in 1863 and 1864, as well as the player piano and the typewriter; the refrigerator car, 1868, which made practicable the transportation of meat and other perishables to urban dwellers, and, thus, perhaps, made possible the city itself.

Meanwhile the Civil War tore apart the United States, Karl Marx organized the First International in London and three years later published *Das Kapital*, and the Franco-Prussian War of 1870 led to the first Paris Commune.

In this environment science fiction developed rapidly.

Nathaniel Hawthorne (1804–64), the gloomy, brooding recorder of Puritan guilt in such novels as *The Scarlet Letter* (1850) and *The House of the Seven Gables* (1851), was a persistent author of science fiction and fantasy as well; in fact, even his attempts at realism may have been thwarted by his inability to suppress the dark symbols that snake their way up from his narratives. Even at his most fantastic, however, Hawthorne kept to the spirit of the new science (and of nascent science fiction) by providing natural explanations for what happened in his stories. This fact was noted by Dorville Libby, a contemporary critic, in 1869: "Hawthorne's are not fairy stories. In dealing with either nature or art he never violates physical laws."

Hawthorne's "Young Goodman Brown" might be called science fiction; one possible explanation of the witch's sabbath and other supernatural events, Bruce Franklin has suggested, is that psychological processes have actually given different shape to external reality. More typical, and more typical of science fiction, are "The Artist of the Beautiful," "The Birthmark," "Rappaccini's Daughter," "Dr. Heidegger's Experiment," and *The Blithesdale Romance* (1852), a novel about hypnotism which was considered at least a potential science at that time.

Hawthorne's notebooks are even more revealing of his turn of mind. After graduating from Bowdoin College in 1825, he secluded himself for years in his home, turning out literary hackwork and the short stories that first attracted critical notice (collected in *Twice Told Tales*, 1837; second series, 1842), and jotting down in his notebook such story ideas as:

Questions as to unsettled points of History, and Mysteries of Nature, to be asked of a mesmerized person.

Imaginary diseases to be cured by impossible remedies—as a dose of the Grand Elixir, in the yolk of a Phoenix's egg. The diseases may be either moral or physical.

A physician for the cure of moral diseases.

A moral philosopher to buy a slave, or otherwise get possession of a human being, and to use him for the sake of experiment, by trying the operation of a certain vice on him.

These are the notes of a science fiction writer. I have put down similar ideas on note cards, and Alfred Bester (in the 1965 anthology edited by Robert P. Mills, *The Worlds of Science Fiction*) published the following selections from his *Commonplace Book:*

A circulating brain library in a Womrath's of the future, where you can rent a brain for any purpose.

Tell a story from the POV of a calculating machine.

The Lucky Man. Suppose good fortune is a question of ether or sunspots?

A story about weather smugglers.

There must be a place where you can go to remember all the things that never happened to you.

In his survey of American science fiction of the nineteenth century, *Future Perfect*, Bruce Franklin points out that "one typical genesis for Hawthorne's fiction is the genesis which typifies science fiction—a speculation generated immediately out of a brush with science."

Hawthorne's stories include one about a man who turns into stone through calcification, rejuvenation by means of the elixir of life (a theme that would echo through science fiction up to my own novel, *The Immortals*), the removal

Nathaniel Hawthorne

of physical defects through drugs and the misuse of science, the creation of a beautiful mechanical butterfly, and the accustoming of the body to poisons. The origin of the latter theme, used in "Rappacini's Daughter," is recorded in another notebook entry:

> Madame Calderon de la B [in "Life in Mexico"] speaks of persons who have been inoculated with the venom of rattlesnakes by pricking them in various places with the tooth. These persons are thus secured forever against the bite of any venomous reptile. They have the power of calling snakes, and feel great pleasure in playing with and handling them. Their own bite becomes poisonous to people not inoculated in the same manner. Thus a part of the serpent's nature appears to be transfused into them.

Later in his life, in the quaint custom of the nineteenth century, Hawthorne's writings would be subsidized by a series of public positions: measurer at the Boston customhouse, surveyor of the port at Salem, consul to Liverpool. His son, Julian, carried the Hawthorne science fiction tradition into the twentieth century.

Even earlier than Hawthorne's stories were those of the great French realistic novelist of manners, types, classes, and professions, Honoré de Balzac. He wrote at least two science fiction works; one was "Elixir of Life" (1830), about a wealthy dying scientist who discovered an elixir of life which he asked his wastrel son to rub on his body; the son revivified only an eye, and *his* son, in turn, brought back to life only his father's arm and head. A Balzac novel, *The Quest of the Absolute* (1834), described a futile scientific effort to transmute base elements into gold—a frequent theme in later magazine fiction.

Edgar Allan Poe (1809–49), a major figure in poetry, the short story, and literary criticism, helped shape detective fiction and science fiction in the first half of the nineteenth century; in fact, the annual awards presented by the Mystery Writers of America are called Edgars. The extent of Poe's influence on science fiction is difficult to overestimate: one line of development leads through his carefully wrought mood stories of horror and terror, "The Fall of the House of Usher," "The Tell-Tale Heart," and "The Pit and the Pendulum," up to the writings of H. P. Lovecraft and Ray Bradbury; another runs through his more factual and science fictional stories, "Ms. Found in a Bottle," "A Descent into the Maelstrom," "Hans Pfaall," and *The Narrative of Arthur Gordon Pym*, to Jules Verne and more scientifically oriented science fiction.

Poe's life was a strange mixture of personal tragedies, small successes, large disappointments, and genius relatively unrecognized until after his early death at the age of 40. He was born in Boston in 1809, son of a touring actor and actress who died, one of pneumonia, the other of consumption, when Poe was two (or perhaps, as some accounts have it, the father simply disappeared). Poe was adopted by a Richmond, Virginia, merchant, John Allan, and schooled in the English classic tradition, including five years spent in England. He attended the University of Virginia for one year, where he led, according to a brief autobiographical note, "a very dissipated life—the college at that period being shamefully dissolute."

One fortunate influence may have been the presence of Professor George Tucker, author of *A Voyage to the Moon*, which was published under the pseudonym of Joseph Atterly in 1827, while Poe was at the university. The book presented the concept that a traveler to the moon must cross an airless void in bitter cold; Tucker's mechanism is a countergravitational substance coated on the car, a device remarkably similar to the "Cavorite" H. G. Wells used in *The First Men in the Moon*.

Poe quarreled with Allan, first about Allan's refusal to pay Poe's university gambling debts and later concerning Allan's second wife; and although Allan had inherited a substantial amount late in life, he cut Poe off without further support or inheritance. Poe appears to have spent two years in the army and five months at West Point before he resigned, turned to literary pursuits which brought him little money, married a 14-year-old tubercular cousin, and struggled with personality problems, alcohol, and drugs through a series of poorly paying editorial positions and poorer-paying publications of his work until his death.

Poe's first volume of poetry, *Tamerlane and Other Poems*, was published in

Honoré de Balzac

Edgar Allan Poe

1827, when he was only 18; and his second, *Poems*, in 1831. His first published science fiction story, "Ms. Found in a Bottle," won first prize of one hundred dollars offered in 1833 by the *Baltimore Saturday Visitor*. It is related by a jaded traveler whose sailing ship is dismasted by an incredible hurricane; he is thrown aboard a mysterious ancient ship whose aged crew go about their enigmatic tasks without noticing him until the ship at last sinks in a giant whirlpool surrounded by Antarctic ice. Another of the half-dozen stories Poe submitted to the *Baltimore Saturday Visitor* contest was "A Descent into the Maelstrom," which described another giant whirlpool off the Norwegian coast and a fisherman whose smack was caught in it:

Illustration from "Hans Pfaall"

> Never shall I forget the sensations of awe, horror, and admiration with which I gazed about me. The boat appeared to be hanging, as if by magic, midway down, upon the interior surface of a funnel vast in circumference, prodigious in depth, and whose perfectly smooth sides might have been mistaken for ebony, but for the bewildering rapidity with which they spun around, and for the gleaming and ghastly radiance they shot forth, as the rays of the full moon, from that circular rift amid the clouds . . . streamed in a flood of golden glory along the black walls, and far away down into the inmost recesses of the abyss. . . .

A factual story about a trip to the moon, "Hans Pfaall," appeared in 1835 in *The Southern Literary Messenger*, a magazine for which he was then a correspondent and a few months later, editor. Pfaall gets to the moon by means of a balloon aided in its first ascent by a large explosion, and solves the problem of the increasing rarefaction of the air through a compressor (which Poe calls a condensor). Possibly to protect himself against ridicule, Poe surrounded the story of the trip with a facetious framework in which Pfaall is a Dutch bankrupt bedeviled by creditors, and the conclusion casts doubt on whether the trip was actually made. But this may have been due to Poe's custom of framing his stories in ways which explain how the stories happen to get into the hands of the reader and thus achieve the proper credibility. On the other hand, Poe may have felt that in spite of the research and calculations that went into "Hans Pfaall," whirlpools and hypnotism were possible but a trip to the moon was not.

Poe apparently intended to write a sequel about life on the moon. "Hans Pfaall" ends:

> I have much to say of the climate of the planet; of its wonderful alternations of heat and cold; of unmitigated and burning sunshine for one fortnight, and more than polar frigidity for the next; of a constant transfer of moisture, by distillation like that *in vacuo*, from the point beneath the sun to the point the farthest from it; of a variable zone of running water; of the people themselves; of their manners, customs, and political institutions; of their peculiar physical construction; of their ugliness; of their want of ears, those useless appendages in an atmosphere so peculiarly modified; of their consequent ignorance of the use and properties of speech; of their substitute for speech in a singular method of inter-communication; of the incomprehensible connection between each particular individual in the moon, with some particular individual on the earth—a connection analogous with, and depending upon that of the orbs of the planet and the satellite, and by means of which the lives and destinies of the inhabitants of the one are interwoven with the lives and destinies of the inhabitants of the other; and above all, if it so please your Excellencies—above all of those dark and hideous mysteries which lie in the outer regions of the moon—regions which, owing to the almost miraculous accordance of the satellite's rotation on its own axis with its sidereal revolution about the earth, have never yet been turned, and, by God's mercy, never shall be turned, to the scrutiny of the telescopes of man. All this, and more—much more—would I most willingly detail. . . .

But Poe's plans were forestalled, he felt, by the publication, a few months after the first appearance of "Hans Pfaall," of Locke's "Moon Hoax" articles in the New York *Sun*. Poe even suggested to friends that the idea was stolen from him, and to the book version of "Hans Pfaall" printed in the 1840 *Tales of the Grotesque and Arabesque* he appended an extensive criticism of the plausibility of Locke's hoax and why no one should have been taken in by it in spite of its apparent seriousness. Later, however, with ironic justice, Poe wrote "The Balloon Hoax" about a crossing of the Atlantic in three days, which was published as an extra in Locke's own newspaper in 1844; and after the hoax was exposed, Poe said, "If, as some assert, the *Victoria* did not absolutely accomplish the voyage recorded, it will be difficult to assign a reason why she *should* not have accomplished it":

> The great problem is at length solved. The air, as well as the earth and ocean, has been subdued by science and will become a common and convenient highway for mankind. *The Atlantic has been actually crossed in a Balloon!* and this without difficulty—without any great apparent danger—with thorough control of the machine—and in the inconceivably brief period of seventy-five hours from shore to shore!

Earlier than this Poe's longest story, almost a novel, was published as a book in 1838 (its first few chapters had been serialized in the *Southern Literary Messenger* in 1837). *The Narrative of Arthur Gordon Pym of Nantucket* is an adventurous sea story which begins as Pym stows away; continues with mutiny, murder, shipwreck, storm, starvation, cannibalism, attack by savages; and concludes with Pym drifting in a hot sea with a companion and a captive savage in a frail canoe toward the South Pole. Strange white animals with scarlet teeth and claws float by the canoe, a fine white powder falls continually over them, and a range of vapor to the south begins to look like

> a limitless cataract, rolling silently into the sea from some immense and far-distant rampart in the heavens. The gigantic curtain ranged along the whole extent of the southern horizon. It emitted no sound. . . .
>
> Yet we were evidently approaching it with a hideous velocity. At intervals there were visible in it wide, yawning, but momentary rents, and from out these rents, within which was a chaos of flitting and indistinct images, there came rushing and mighty, but soundless winds, tearing up the enkindled ocean in their course.
>
> The darkness had materially increased, relieved only by the glare of the water thrown back from the white curtain before us. Many gigantic and pallidly white birds flew continuously now from beyond the veil, and their scream was the eternal "Tekeli-li!" as they retreated from our vision. . . . And now we rushed into the embraces of the cataract, where a chasm threw itself open to receive us. But there arose in our pathway a shrouded human figure, very far larger in its proportions than any dweller among men. And the hue of the skin of the figure was of the perfect whiteness of the snow.

Poe took his inspiration from many sources—sometimes ideas, plots, incidents, even descriptions themselves—and Poe's *Pym* probably was indebted to *Symzonia* (1820) by Captain Adam Seaborn (which was probably a pseudonym for Captain John Cleves Symmes of Ohio, who in 1818 issued a circular to institutions of learning in Europe and America stating that the earth is hollow and open at the poles). The hollow-earth theory provided a new "distant and unexplored land" in which strange people and stranger civilizations could be found by adventurers; Poe may have intended to continue his novel, or publish a sequel to it, taking his characters into the center of a hollow earth; "Ms. Found in a Bottle" probably was a fragment preliminary to *Pym*. Or he may have meant only to leave the novel unfinished and mysterious (the novel closes with a three-page note announcing the disappearance of Pym along with the two or three final chapters.

Various writers would attempt sequels, particularly Jules Verne in *The Sphinx of the Ice-Fields*.

"Mesmeric Revelation," published in *Columbian Lady's and Gentleman's Magazine* in 1844, projected Poe's views on the nature of God and the universe through the medium of a hypnotized man (compare Hawthorne's notebook entry: "Questions as to . . . Mysteries of Nature . . . to be asked of a mesmerized person"). It was "steam-engine time" for mesmerism, and writers were building it into their stories.

"The Facts in the Case of M. Valdemar," published in *The American Review* in 1845, describes the effort to keep a dying man alive through hypnotism; even though he dies, his body does not decay and he continues to communicate for seven months. "A Tale of the Ragged Mountains," published in *Godey's Lady's Book* in 1844, tells about a strange and fatal rapport, achieved through hypnotism, between a neurotic young man and a British officer who had died nearly fifty years before in an uprising in India.

Poe's fascination with science and the potential of technology is displayed in "The Thousand-and-Second Tale of Scheherazade," published in *Godey's*

Lady's Book in 1845. Scheherazade, still attempting to save herself from imminent execution, tells the king about Sinbad's visit to the future in which he encounters all the wonders of Poe's times, described as fabulous or magical by Sinbad but explained as realities in voluminous footnotes; the king, who has accepted the previous fantastic adventures of Sinbad, thinks Scheherazade's last story ridiculously impossible, and has her strangled.

The year Poe died he was still writing science fiction. His story "Mellonta Tauta," published in *Godey's Lady's Book* in 1849, is told in the form of a letter from a lady who takes a transatlantic trip in a powered passenger balloon in the year 2848 and describes the wonders of her times. This may be the first story of the future in which the significance of change occupies a central position. Poe's final science fiction story, "Von Kempelen and His Discovery," involved the transmutation of lead into gold. It was published in *The Flag of Our Union* in 1849.

While he was writing the stories that we now consider science fiction—much of which he considered minor or even, as in the case of *Pym*, "silly"—Poe was writing major poems, significant criticism, "tales of ratiocination" such as "The Gold-Bug" and "Murders in the Rue Morgue" that are father to detective fiction, and terror stories such as "The Fall of the House of Usher," "The Tell-Tale Heart," "The Black Cat," "The Pit and the Pendulum," and "The Masque of the Red Death." Even his terror stories, however, are imbued with his interest in abnormal psychology and could be read as a kind of science fiction.

Poe himself considered his best stories to be "Ligeia," "The Gold-Bug," "Murders in the Rue Morgue," "The Fall of the House of Usher," "The Tell-Tale Heart," "The Black Cat," "William Wilson," and "A Descent into the Maelstrom."

Poe had his own unique speculations about the physical nature of the universe. He presented them first as a kind of lyceum lecture and then cast them into the form of an essay published as a monograph in 1848 under the title of "Eureka: A Prose Poem." Poe described in a letter what he was trying to say:

General Proposition. Because nothing was, therefore all things are.

1. An inspection of the *universality* of gravitation—of the fact that each particle tends not to any one common point, but to every other particle, suggests perfect totality of *absolute unity* as the source of the phenomenon.

2. Gravity is but the mode in which is manifested the tendency of all things to return into their original unity.

3. I show that the law of the return—*i.e.*, the law of gravity—is but a necessary result of the necessary and sole possible mode of equable irradiation of matter through a *limited* space.

4. Were the universe of stars (contradistinguished from the universe of space) unlimited, no worlds could exist.

5. I show that unity is nothingness.

6. All matter springing from unity sprang from nothingness, *i.e.*, was created.

7. All will return to unity, *i.e.*, to nothingness.

"Eureka" received some criticism from scientists, but Poe did not think highly of scientists ("merely scientific men," he called them—"the most bigoted and the least capable of using, generalizing, or deciding upon the facts which they bring to light in the course of their experiments"), and a liberal reading of Poe's theories might find them similar to the speculations of some of today's cosmologists.

But Poe's contributions to science fiction had more effect than his contributions to scientific theory; he supplied method, theory, theme, skill, inspiration, and popularization. Sam Moskowitz points out in *Explorers of the Infinite* that "his greatest contribution to the advancement of the genre was the precept that every departure from norm must be logically explained *scientifically*."

One of Poe's most significant successors was a young Irish magazine writer with the romantic name of Fitz-James O'Brien. Born in Ireland in 1828, the son of a well-to-do lawyer, O'Brien pursued two careers—one as a writer, the other as a Bohemian—in which he achieved outstanding success. He began both early in life. He had youthful stories and poems published in Irish, Scottish,

Poe's conversation with a mummy

and British magazines; and he squandered an inheritance of £8,000 in less than three years, tried to elope with the wife of an English officer, and fled to the United States in 1852, three years after the death of Poe.

In the next ten years he wrote prolifically, selling most of his stories and verses to the leading magazines of the times; but he appeared unconcerned about money, coming or going. "Profligate, prodigal, dashing, versifying," as Bruce Franklin called him, O'Brien was welcomed into the best society, and enjoyed the company and admiration of other writers. He enlisted in the Union Army and was immediately wounded in a flamboyant duel with a Confederate officer. The wound was inadequately treated and he died of it. O'Brien was 33.

Most of O'Brien's work was minor and commercial; he would be forgotten today if it were not for a handful of brilliantly original stories of which most, if not all, were fantasy ranging into the surrealistic and science fiction.

His best-known story, a classic which pioneered the theme of the world in microcosm, was "The Diamond Lens" (*Atlantic Monthly,* 1858). The narrator, a young microscopist obsessed with the desire to create the most powerful microscope ever imagined, consults through a medium with the spirit of Leeuwenhoek, who instructs him how to construct the perfect microscope by using a 140-carat diamond across which a strong electrical current has been passed. By chance an acquaintance in the apartment above just happens to have a 140-carat diamond. The narrator murders to get it, constructs his lens, and peers through it:

Leeuwenhoek

> On every side I beheld beautiful inorganic forms, of unknown texture, and colored with the most enchanting hues. These forms presented the appearance of what might be called, for want of a more specific definition, foliated clouds of the highest rarity; that is, they undulated and broke into vegetable formations, and were tinged with splendors compared with which the gilding of our autumn woodlands is as dross compared with gold. . . .
>
> While I was speculating on the singular arrangements of the internal economy of Nature, with which she so frequently splinters into atoms our most compact theories, I thought I beheld a form moving slowly through the glades of one of the prismatic forests. . . .
>
> It was a female human shape. . . . I cannot, I dare not, attempt to inventory the charms of this divine revelation of perfect beauty. Those eyes of mystic violet, dewy and serene, evade my words. Her long, lustrous hair following her glorious head in a golden wake, like the track sown in heaven by a falling star, seems to quench my most burning phrases with its splendors. . . .

Gradually, however, the drop of water evaporates, and the world within it —and the lovely humanlike creature—shrivels and dies. The narrator faints, destroys the microscope in his fall, and later is considered mad.

Some of O'Brien's short stories had at least thematic influence on later science fiction and fantasy: "The Pot of Tulips" (1855), a ghost story featuring a return from the grave; "From Hand to Mouth" (1858), a surrealistic fantasy about disembodied but living eyes, ears, hands, and mouths which surround the narrator in his hotel room; "The Golden Ingot" (1858), about an old scientist who awakens to find a bar of gold in his crucible (his daughter has saved up her money and bought it for him); "The Lost Room" (1858), a realistic fantasy about a man who leaves his room on an errand and returns to find it filled with a pair of carousing couples whom he cannot evict; "The Wondersmith" (1859), another realistic fantasy about little wooden toy soldiers with poisoned weapons and an attempt by gypsies to kill all the Christian children at Christmas (the theme of tiny murderous people would be used much later in A. Merritt's classic novel of terror, *Burn Witch Burn!* and then the film based on it, *The Devil Dolls*); "What Was It? A Mystery" (1859), prototype for the story about the unexplained invisible creature whose existence challenges our sense of security (later to be followed by Guy de Maupassant's "The Horla" (1887), Ambrose Bierce's "The Damned Thing" (1893), H. P. Lovecraft's "The Colour Out of Space" (1927), and possibly every other story of invisibility including H. G. Wells's *The Invisible Man* (1897), which, like "What Was It?," suggested perfect transparency as the mechanism for invisibility); and "How I Overcame My Gravity" (1864), which speculated that the gyroscope might be used to achieve antigravity.

But O'Brien's most striking story and greatest achievement was "The Diamond Lens," and it had the greatest influence on later writers; Ray Cummings wrote several novels on the theme, beginning with *The Girl in the Golden Atom* (1919). In a story that appeals to every reader who ever imagined an atom as a miniature solar system or our solar system as a giant atom, "He Who Shrank" (1936), by Henry Hasse, describes a mad scientist who injects a new drug called Shrinx into his laboratory assistant and sends him shrinking eternally through one subatomic universe after another. Theodore Sturgeon used the concept of microscopic creatures as a means of collapsing time: a scientist in "Microcosmic God" (1941) introduces problems into the miniaturized world he creates in order to acquire the scientific solutions the tiny people develop over their accelerated generations. (Daniel Galouye played a clever variation on this theme in his *Simulacron X*.) And James Blish in *The Seedling Stars* (1957) produces a microscopic race of men through genetic manipulation.

Herman Melville

Herman Melville (1819–91), the famous American author of *Moby Dick* and other novels mostly related to the sea, was something of a naturalist, inspired by his early sea voyages and experiences in the islands of the South Pacific, but was skeptical of the significance of science; even though some of his novels could be classified as utopias or anti-utopias, they did not include scientific marvels. But Bruce Franklin located one story Franklin considered science fiction among Melville's nineteen shorter works—"The Bell-Tower" (1855); it involves a manlike automaton, which may be the first fully developed story in English about a robot, and "includes all the elements which were soon to become conventional —the automaton as destroyer; the creator as a being cut off from normal organic creation; society as a possible beneficiary, possible victim of the automaton."

Edward Everett Hale

Edward Everett Hale (1822–1909), Unitarian minister and popular author of his time best-known today for his short story "The Man Without a Country," used science fiction situations, like many of his contemporaries, when they came to mind. One story, "The Brick Moon," which was serialized in the October, November, and December issues of the 1869 *Atlantic Monthly* (a sequel, "Life in the Brick Moon," appeared in the February 1870 issue), was one of the first serious fictionalized considerations of an artificial satellite. In Hale's story a carefully constructed brick moon 200 feet in diameter was to be hurled into orbit, as an aid to navigation, by the use of two giant flywheels made from oak and pine hooped with iron. But the workmen who were living in the moon while it was under construction—along with their wives—went up with the moon when it accidentally rolled forward onto the flywheel mechanism. The rest of the story described the ingenious means by which the workmen and their wives raised food, communicated with earth, and survived.

Edward Bulwer-Lytton

Mrs. Mary Griffith's "Three Hundred Years Hence" (1836) was a utopian work that utilized a narrative device later popularized by Edward Bellamy in *Looking Backward* (1888) and H. G. Wells in *When the Sleeper Wakes* (1899): a sleeping man is accidentally buried by an explosion and avalanche; 300 years later he is unearthed and awakened and guided through the new civilization of Pennsylvania, New Jersey, and New York. The long sleep was not original with Mrs. Griffith, of course; Washington Irving used it in "Rip Van Winkle" (1819–20), and a midwestern lawyer named Paxton, in a verse entitled "A Century Hence" (1880), anticipated some of Bellamy's forecasts and referred to the ancient history of the plot:

> We've all read the mythical story of old,
>   How seven young sleepers withdrew,
> And hid in a cavern, where, weary and cold,
>   They slept a whole century through—
> Then rose to return to their whole habitation,
>   But found it dismantled and hoary;
> Their kindred were dead, and the new generation
>   Refused to give heed to their story.

Sir Edward Bulwer-Lytton (1803–73), English novelist and playwright who in 1842 had written *Zanoni*, an allegory attacking the mechanistic interpretation of life (and made use of an elixir of life, the occult "science" of the Rosicrucians, and the theme of a Chaldean alive through many centuries), nearly

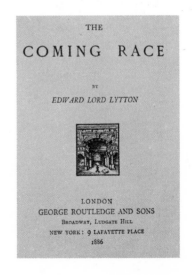

THE

COMING RACE

BY

EDWARD LORD LYTTON

LONDON
GEORGE ROUTLEDGE AND SONS
BROADWAY, LUDGATE HILL
NEW YORK: 9 LAFAYETTE PLACE
1886

LEFT: Samuel Butler

RIGHT: W. H. Hudson

LEFT: William Morris

RIGHT: William Dean Howells

thirty years later was inspired by the theory of evolution to write a utopian novel called *The Coming Race* (1871). His utopia was underground, where a race (called the Vril-ya, through their mastery of an all-penetrating electricity called Vril), had evolved from men above into an intellectual, self-controlled race surpassing ours in the same ways that we surpass savages.

Erewhon (1872) attacks what *The Coming Race* idealizes. Samuel Butler's narrator finds in the interior of New Zealand an advanced civilization which has discarded machinery because by a process of evolution machinery would develop consciousness, enslave man, and finally supersede him. In this connection we might compare Arthur Clarke's speculation that man is the organic, evolutionary bridge between the inorganic and the ultra-intelligent machine which may well be man's successor.

W. H. Hudson (1841–1922), like Butler, believed that the ideal life would be lived without machinery. Hudson's utopia, *A Crystal Age* (1887), described a race of future Englishmen who dress like ancient Greeks and till the soil; his narrator arrives in the future after having been stunned by a landslide. Edward Bellamy (1850–98) achieved fame and influence with his utopia, *Looking Back-ward* (1888). His narrator is hypnotized to cure his insomnia but the cure works too well; in a soundproof vault he sleeps more than a century. Socialist propaganda when it was written, the novel seems modest enough today; Bellamy applied the theory of evolution to industrial organization to prove that the inevitable result of the process—"industrial evolution which could not have terminated otherwise"—is state socialism. The book's secondary characteristics were more charming than its major thesis, and other writers, including Wells, would emulate its detailed wonders of future life.

William Morris (1834–96) wrote *News From Nowhere* (1890) to herald a new day when a revolutionary crowd would destroy machinery. William Dean Howells (1837–1920) combined satire and utopia in *A Traveler From Altruria* (1894); the satire entered through the way in which a visitor from Altruria reacts to American institutions and customs; the utopia from his descriptions of the socialistic state of Altruria, which resembles a curious marriage of Bellamy's mechanistic and Morris' artistic utopias.

In 1871 came the publication of another work, "The Battle of Dorking," which launched a related but distinct genre. *Blackwood's Magazine* published the short story, first anonymously, then in monograph form over the name of Lieutenant-Colonel Sir George Tomkyns Chesney. The story made a great deal of money—*Blackwood's* made a final settlement of nearly £280—but more significantly, sowed the seeds for a host of martial imitators, some of which, like *The War of the Worlds* and *The War in the Air*, fell within the mainstream of science fiction.

The genre might be called the prophetic (or cautionary) novel of future war (and the first representative of the genre might be the work already cited, the 1763 *Reign of George VI*). Its distinguishing characteristic is a richly detailed description of an imminent war, often fought with future weapons or tactics, which goes badly for the nation attacked. "The Battle of Dorking" tells how German infantry invade England and defeat a poorly prepared English army. It begins:

> You ask me to tell you, my grandchildren, something about my share in the great events that happened fifty years ago. 'Tis sad work turning back to that bitter page in our history, but you may perhaps take profit in your new homes from the lesson it teaches. For us in England it came too late.

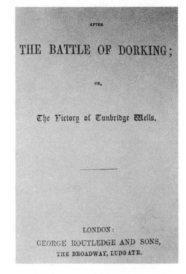

The purpose of "The Battle of Dorking" was to make dramatically clear the need for a complete reorganization of the British military system. What it did was cause alarm. It even drew a response from Prime Minister Gladstone, in defense of the British treasury:

> In *Blackwood's Magazine* there has lately been a famous article called "The Battle of Dorking." I should not mind this "Battle of Dorking," if we could keep it to ourselves, if we could take care that nobody belonging to any other country should know that such follies could find currency or even favour with portions of the British public; but unfortunately these things go abroad, and they make us ridiculous in the eyes of the whole world. I do not say that the writers of them are not sincere—that is another matter—but I do say that the result of these things is practically the spending of more and more of your money. Be on your guard against alarmism. Depend upon it that there is not this astounding disposition on the part of all mankind to make us the objects of hatred.

Many writers would imitate "Dorking," not only in English but in French, German, Scandinavian, Italian, and other languages, depicting the invasions of those countries and sometimes adapting other works to their particular geography, but none of them would have Chesney's impact.

None of these, neither the utopias nor the visions of wars to come, belong to the mainstream of science fiction. The utopias were concerned with making a point external to the dramatic problem of the book; the battle stories usually appealed to nationalistic fears or fervors outside the ambit of the work. In contemporary science fiction the demands of the story predominate.

But all of these, and other factors as well, had prepared the world for the first writer who would make science fiction his way of life—and in the process shape it, solidify a genre, and make a fortune. That man was Jules Verne. He had a master, Poe, who had shown him the way and the method. And the world was waiting.

CHAPTER 4
A VICTORIAN ENGINEER:
1828-1905

IN *Lives of the Engineers,* a five-volume book published in 1874, author Samuel Smiles set out:

to give an account of some of the principal men by whom this nation has been made so great and prosperous as it is—the men by whose skill and industry large tracts of fertile land have been won back from the sea, the bog, and the fen, and made available for human habitation and sustenance; who, by their industry, skill, and genius, have made England the busiest of workshops.

"Our engineers," Smiles wrote, "may be regarded in some measure as the makers of modern civilization."

The latter half of the nineteenth century was the half-century of the engineer. It was a time of building roads and railroads; of improving the steam engine and methods of agriculture, including the use of chemical fertilizer; of discovery of gold and commercial oil wells; of development of better processes for making steel, of the chemical industry, of electricity, and of invention.

Celluloid, the first plastic, was invented in 1870, and its uses seemed limitless. Manufacturers made it into collars and cuffs, billiard balls, motion-picture film. One of them tried to make a golf ball out of celluloid; when that failed he tried a celluloid ball filled with gutta-percha; and when that didn't work, a gutta-percha ball filled with celluloid.

Science could do anything.

The world meanwhile was changing in other, more disturbing ways. The Franco-Prussian war frightened the capitalistic world, not with the quick defeat of France but with its aftermath, the organization of the Paris Commune. 1871 brought the internal unification of Germany and Italy.

Motion pictures were invented in 1872, barbed wire in 1874 (making possible the fencing, and the farming, of the American West), and the telephone in 1876. *The New York Times* carried the following account:

Prof. A. Graham Bell's Discovery

Boston, Mass., Oct. 19, 1876—The account of an experiment made on the evening of Oct. 9 by Alexander Graham Bell and Thomas A. Watson is interesting, as being the record of the first conversation ever carried on by word of mouth over a telegraph wire. Telephones were placed at either end of a telegraph line owned by the Walworth Manufacturing Company, extending from their office in Boston to their factory in Cambridgeport, a distance of about two miles. The company's battery, consisting of nine Daniels cells, was removed from the circuit and another of ten carbon elements substituted. Articulate conversation then took place through the wire. The sounds, at first faint and indistinct, became suddenly quite loud and intelligible.

Was that the voice of the engineer announcing the shape of things to come?

Alexander Graham Bell

The four-cycle gas engine was invented in 1876, electric welding and the microphone in 1877, the incandescent lamp and the cash register in 1879, the high-speed internal combustion engine in 1880.

In 1881 Alexander II of Russia was assassinated by a member of a revolutionary group calling itself the People's Will.

The tuberculosis germ was discovered in 1882. The first plastic fiber, rayon, was invented in 1883. In 1884 came two inventions that made practicable the mass production of magazines and books: the linotype and the wood-pulp process for making paper. The first did away with the laborious handsetting of type; the second provided cheap and plentiful paper. Together they helped create the mass-circulation magazines, and then the pulp magazines upon which the development of science fiction would depend.

The steam turbine was invented in 1884. The first electric street railway was opened in Baltimore in 1885; that year Louis Pasteur prevented rabies with his new vaccine; and the motorcycle and the electrical transformer were invented. In 1886 the electrolytic process for producing aluminum was developed and the halftone engraving was invented. Halftone engraving allowed magazines to provide full-page photographic illustrations for $20 that would have cost them $200 as woodcuts. The illustrated magazine became common: *McClure's Magazine,* for instance, virtually doubled its circulation with Ida Tarbell's history of Napoleon, profusely illustrated with portraits, and then doubled it again with Lincoln reminiscences illustrated with hundreds of little-known photographs and paintings.

The disc-record Gramophone was invented in 1887, the pneumatic tire and the Kodak in 1888. Advertising was beginning to appeal to the people through the mass-circulation magazines, and one ad would proclaim: "If it isn't an Eastman and Walker it isn't a Kodak."

In 1889 the World's Fair in Paris displayed the Eiffel Tower (nearly 1,000 feet high) and the first automobile, a Benz.

Color photography was invented in 1891, as well as the oil-cracking process and the first practical submarine; the diesel engine came in 1892; the commercial adding machine and the coke oven in 1893. In 1894 Thomas A. Edison's Kinetoscope, for which he had been awarded a patent in 1891, was given its first public showing.

X rays were discovered in 1895 and the radio telegraph and the photoelectric cell were invented. In 1899 the first peace conference was held at The Hague and established the permanent court of arbitration; the Boer War broke out in South Africa.

This is the environment of invention and discovery into which Jules Verne was born.

Walt Whitman described "the greatness of nineteenth-century man," I. F. Clarke observes, "in phrases that are closely related to the epic fantasies of the new science described by Jules Verne":

> *His daring foot is on land and sea everywhere,*
> *he colonizes the Pacific, the archipelagos,*

Louis Pasteur

LEFT: Thomas Alva Edison

RIGHT: Advertisement for the first Kodak

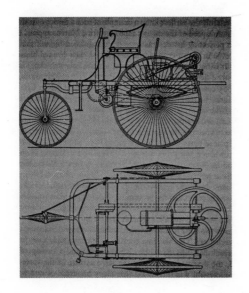

With the steamship, the electric telegraph,
the newspaper, the wholesale engines of war,
With these and the world-spreading factories
he interlinks all geography, all lands.

Clarke summed it up: "Whitman's verse is a programme for the series of books that Jules Verne poured out between 1863 and his death in 1905. . . . Before Verne the marvels of science had on occasions been incidental to stories of romance; but Verne gained a world-wide success for his ability to make technological achievements a subject for fiction."

Another critic, Benjamin Appel, speculates that Verne would have approved the religion predicted in *Memoirs of the Year Two Thousand Five Hundred* —a religion based on useful knowledge: "The first rite was to gaze at the stars through a telescope; the second, to look through a microscope." Verne was a man of his times; he not only accepted science and invention, he gloried in it.

Verne was born on February 8, 1828, in Nantes, France—actually on what was then an island, Ile Feydeau, about thirty miles from the mouth of the Loire. He was the son of a distinguished lawyer and was educated for the law, but he longed to be a writer and his father provided an allowance for a fling at the literary life in Paris. At first the stage attracted him; he wrote plays and librettos for opera, some of which were produced but none of which brought him great recognition or income. He also wrote half a dozen short stories; one of them, "Master Zacharius," a parable about a demon who appears in the form of a human clock to tempt the proud Swiss inventor of the clockwork escapement, convinced Pierre Verne not only of his son's genius but his piety. Pope Leo XIII later confirmed this opinion by commending the younger Verne for the purity of his writing.

The father was disappointed, then, when in 1857 his son decided to marry a young widow with two daughters and asked his father to buy him a share in a Paris stockbroker's business. Jules assured his father that he would continue to write, and he did, usually rising at five and writing until he went to the Exchange at ten. The theater still was his goal, however, and an operetta, a musical comedy, and a comedy were produced in 1859, 1860, and 1861.

Nevertheless, though Verne considered himself a failure as a writer, the major influences of his life were beginning to come together to create what would later be called science fiction. His early literary influences were James Fenimore Cooper, Sir Walter Scott, and what he called "the two Robinsons"—Defoe's *Robinson Crusoe* and Wyss's *Swiss Family Robinson* (he preferred the latter). Then he discovered Edgar Allan Poe, who was to become his literary master; in 1864 he wrote a critical article about Poe's works in which he expressed both his fascination with Poe's subjects and methods and his distaste for Poe's materialism, lack of faith, and dissipation:

Edison and an early motion picture camera

Jules Verne at thirty

65

Illustrations from *Five Weeks in a Balloon.* LEFT: "A Mysterious Rival." RIGHT: "A Dangerous Moment."

Here then is a summary of the principal works of the American romancer; have I gone too far in describing them as strange and supernatural? Has he not created in real earnest a new form of literature, a form emanating from the *excessive* sensitiveness of his brain, to use one of his own words?

In leaving on one side its incomprehensibility, what we have to admire in the works of Poe are the originality of his situations; the discussion of little-known facts; the observations of the more morbid faculties of man; the choice of his subjects; the personality, always strange, of his heroes; his own nervous and morbid temperament; his mode of expressing it by bizarre interjections. And yet, in the midst of these impossibilities, there sometimes appears a verisimilitude which grips the reader's credulity.

May I now be permitted to direct attention to the materialistic aspect of his stories; never do we feel within them any sense of providential intervention. Poe never seems to recognize this; he claims to explain everything by physical law, which he is ready even to invent if need be; we never feel in him that faith which might bestow upon him the incessant contemplation of the supernatural.

He creates his fantasy *coldly*, if I may express myself thus, and this wretched man is always an apostle of materialism. I imagine however that this is less due to his temperament than to the exclusively practical culture of the United States; he wrote, he thought and dreamed in American, this positivist of a man; this tendency being acknowledged, we can admire his work.

By his remarkable stories we can judge the state of overexcitement in which Edgar Poe lived; unfortunately his nature did not satisfy himself; and his excesses led him into the *terrible illness* of alcoholism which he had so well named and of which he died.

Verne's first venture into a new kind of writing began under the influence, perhaps, of Poe's "Balloon Hoax" and through his acquaintance with a daring aeronautical enthusiast, a professional photographer who worked under the pseudonym of Nadar (and whom Verne used as a basis for his characterization of Ardan in *From the Earth to the Moon* and *Round the Moon*). Nadar planned a series of balloon ascensions to raise money for the construction of a heavier-than-air flying machine, and Verne's interest in the project led him to write a nonfictional or semifictional book about the possible uses of balloons in exploration. It was his most ambitious work, and his disappointment at repeated rejections from publishers led him finally to throw it into the fire. His wife saved it, however, and insisted on his trying one more publisher. That publisher was Jules Hetzel, who would be Verne's publisher until Hetzel's death.

It was not the original manuscript that Hetzel published, however, but a book that Hetzel persuaded Verne was buried in that manuscript: a fictional account of the exploration of unknown Africa by a balloon. Hetzel liked the new book so much that he asked Verne to write two books a year for publication in a new magazine he was launching and then as books, and Verne signed a lifetime contract which provided what was then the comfortable payment of 20,000 frances a year (later adjusted upward as Hetzel prospered). This is what Verne had been waiting for, and he gave up his job at the Exchange with a dramatic farewell that one colleague later quoted from memory:

Boys, I'm leaving you. I've had an idea, the sort of idea, they say, which ought to come to everybody once a day, though it's come to me only once in my lifetime, the sort of idea which should make anybody's fortune. If it succeeds I shall have come across a gold-mine, and then I shall go on ceaselessly writing, while you fellows go on buying shares the day before they fall and selling them the day before they rise. I'm leaving the Exchange. Good evening, boys.

The book that started it all was *Five Weeks in a Balloon*, published in 1863. It was an immediate success, though it does not seem startling today and perhaps was not even startling in 1863, ninety years after the Montgolfier brothers made their first manned balloon ascension. However, in its complex detail—of the trip, of the balloon, and of its equipment—it was beyond the capacities of his times and certainly beyond the imaginings of Verne's readers. (Years later editor John Campbell would point out that "the reader wants the author to do one of two basic things—and prefers the author who does both. The author's function is to imagine for the reader, of course—but he must either (a) imagine in greater detail than the reader has, or (b) imagine something the reader hasn't thought of. Ideally, the author imagines something new, in greater detail.")

Verne imagined a balloon a bit better than the ordinary balloon: it included a furnace which heated the hydrogen in the hermetically sealed balloon when the passengers wanted to rise, and let it cool when they wished to descend so that they could take advantage of favorable winds. An English explorer, his manservant, and a Scottish hunter ascended from Zanzibar and soared across Africa. "As to where this will end," said the newspapers, "Providence only knows."

Five Weeks in a Balloon established a pattern for Verne's future novels: he would take something reasonably possible, often an idea pioneered by others, and through his power of research and invention, through his use of scientific explanation, and through his primary emphasis (unlike most of his utopian colleagues) on the entertainment value of the story itself, he would make his readers believe that indeed it could be happening or was about to happen.

Verne was no visionary. He worked close to the present, often putting together contemporary devices into new combinations or analogous developments yet to come. ("My electricity is not everybody's electricity," Captain Nemo explains, "and you will permit me to withhold further details.") Verne had come across a gold mine, and he would indeed go on ceaselessly writing.

Two books a year, year after year? It was a staggering program even for a disciplined writer with Verne's enthusiasm. But Verne would not fall far short: he started writing novels relatively late—he was 35—but he would continue for forty-two years and would write nearly eighty books.

A Journey to the Center of the Earth was published in 1864. It too was derivative. Symmes already had popularized the concept of a hollow earth; Poe had suggested that he was going to write about it in "Ms. Found in a Bottle" and *Arthur Gordon Pym;* and Baron Ludvig Holberg (1684–1754) already had written about *A Journey to the World Under-Ground* (1741) in which Nicholas Klimius falls through a cavern into the center of the earth, where he finds a sun surrounded by planets and, after three days as a satellite, is drawn to one of the planets by a giant bird. Typically, however, the detail with which Verne described the adventurous trip, in which a German professor, his nephew, and a guide travel through cavern after cavern ever deeper into the earth, and the storyteller's suspense with which Verne imbues it, made the story popular worldwide. The trip begins when the professor finds in an ancient Icelandic chronicle a scrap of parchment which is translated as:

Descend into that crater of Sneffels Yocul which the shadow of Scartaris touches

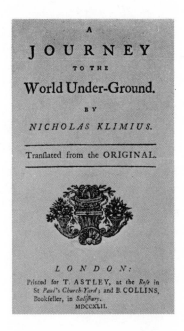

Illustration from *Journey to the Center of the Earth:* "A Singular Forest"

Strange creatures in the
center of the Earth

just before the calends of July, audacious traveler, and you will reach the centre of the earth. I have done it. Arne Saknussemm.

Eventually the explorers reach a subterranean sea and push themselves out into it with an improvised raft. They come upon "the most fearful of antediluvian reptiles, the world-renowned Ichthyosaurus or Great Fish Lizard" locked in battle with "the terrible enemy of its fearful rival, the Plesiosaurus, or Sea Crocodile."

At last have mortal eyes gazed upon two reptiles of the great primitive ocean! I see the flaming red eyes of the Ichthyosaurus, each as big, or bigger than a man's head. . . . These animals attacked one another with inconceivable fury. . . . They raised mountains of water, which dashed in spray over the raft, already tossed to and fro by the waves. Twenty times we seemed on the point of being upset and hurled headlong into the waves. . . . We at last reached a spot where the shore became extremely narrow. The sea almost bathed the foot of the rocks which were here very lofty and steep. . . . At last, under a huge overhanging rock, we discovered the entrance of a dark and gloomy tunnel. There, on a square tablet of granite, which had been smoothed by rubbing it with another stone, we could see two mysterious, and much worn letters, the two initials of the bold and extraordinary traveler who had preceded us on our adventurous journey.

"A.S.," cried my uncle; "you see I was right. Arne Saknussemm, always Arne Saknussemm! . . . Wonderful and glorious Genius, great Saknussemm, you have left no stone unturned, no resource omitted, to show to other mortals the way into the interior of our mighty globe."

Other authors would follow that way, most notably Edgar Rice Burroughs in his *Pellucidar* series.

Verne's next conquest was space. In 1865, probably inspired by Poe's "Hans Pfaall," Verne wrote *From the Earth to the Moon*, a story in which three men are shot in a projectile toward the moon from a cannon built on the coast of Florida. J. O. Bailey suggests that "Verne might have written a first-rate voyage to the moon if he had not idolized his 'master' Poe, misunderstood 'Hans Pfaall,' and written two exciting romances following it up in the spirit of its facetious enveloping plot rather than of its central story." Where Poe had caricatured the Dutch, Verne caricatured the Americans as hustling Yankees and joiners of such strange organizations as the Baltimore Gun Club, which existed to invent, develop, and test new weapons. This mythical club brought together a strange group, primarily composed of veterans of the Civil War, many of them shockingly mutilated, under the leadership of one Impey Barbicane, who renews their interest in weapons by proposing to fire a cannon shell at the moon.

The real hero of the book is the gigantic cannon they build. Verne describes with documentary realism how the plans are drawn up and the cannon con-

From the Earth to the Moon

structed, though with some lack of precision about the weight of the projectile and the amount of propellant.

"The problem before us is how to communicate an initial force of 12,000 yards per second to a shell of 108 inches in diameter, weighing 20,000 pounds. Now when a projectile is launched into space, what happens to it? It is acted upon by three independent forces: the resistance of the air, the attraction of the earth, and the force of impulsion with which it is endowed. . . .

"Now, up to the present time," said Barbicane, "our longest guns have not exceeded twenty-five feet in length. We shall therefore astonish the world by the dimensions we shall be obliged to adopt . . . for a projectile nine feet in diameter, weighing 30,000 pounds, the gun would only have a length of two hundred and twenty-five feet, and a weight of 7,200,000 pounds. . . . I propose to quadruple that length, and to construct a gun of nine hundred feet. . . ."

Funds to construct the *Columbiad* poured in from all nations, including France, Turkey and Peru. ("Russia paid in as her contingent the enormous sum of 368,733 roubles. No one need be surprised at this, who bears in mind the scientific taste of the Russians, and the impetus which they have given to astronomical studies.")

Captain Nicholl, an armorer, denounces the project, and Michael Ardan, an adventurous Frenchman, sends a message: "Substitute for your spherical shell a cylindrical-conical projectile. I shall go inside. . . ." And Ardan averts a duel between Nicholl and Barbicane by inviting them both to join him in the projectile and see whether it reaches the moon.

The moon advanced upward in a heaven of the purest clearness, outshining in her passage the twinkling light of the stars. She passed over the constellation of the Twins, and was now nearing the halfway point between the horizon and the zenith. A terrible silence weighed upon the entire scene! Not a breath of wind upon the earth! not a sound of breathing from the countless chests of the spectators! Their hearts seemed afraid to beat! All eyes were fixed upon the yawning mouth of the Columbiad.

Murchison followed with his eyes the hand of his chronometer. . . .

"Thirty-five!—thirty-six—thirty-seven!—thirty-eight!—thirty-nine!—forty! FIRE!!!"

Instantly Murchison pressed with his finger the key of the electric battery, restored the current of the fluid, and discharged the spark into the breach of the Columbiad.

An appalling, unearthly report followed instantly, such as can be compared to nothing whatever known, not even to the roar of thunder, or the blast of volcanic explosions! No words can convey the slightest idea of the terrific sound! An immense spout of fire shot up from the bowels of the earth as from a crater. The earth heaved up, and with great difficulty some few spectators obtained a momentary glimpse of the projectile victoriously cleaving the air in the midst of the fiery vapors!

"The Future Express" *From the Earth to the Moon*

Thrown off course by a near-miss with an earth-circling meteor, the projectile does not reach the moon but is left circling in an orbit around it, apparently forever.

Ever compulsive about tying up neatly any dangling threads, even those left by other authors, Verne provided a sequel, *Round the Moon* (1870), in which he brushed aside the ending of the earlier novel (the astronomers must have been mistaken when they thought they saw the projectile go into orbit) and returned the projectile to Earth where it splashed down into the Atlantic. But he made his impatient readers wait for five years while Ardan, Barbicane, Nicholl, and two dogs apparently circled the moon. Verne concludes:

And now will this attempt, unprecedented in the annals of travels, lead to any practical result? Will direct communication with the moon ever be established? Will they ever lay the foundation of a traveling service through the solar world? Will they go from one planet to another, from Jupiter to Mercury, and after awhile from one star to another, from the Polar to Sirius? Will this means of locomotion allow us to visit those suns which swarm in the firmament?

To such questions no answer can be given. But knowing the bold ingenuity of the Anglo-Saxon race, no one would be astonished if the Americans seek to make some use of President Barbicane's attempt.

Meanwhile Verne was working on other books. *Captain Hatteras*, a two-volume novel about the exploration of the North Pole, was published in 1866, and *The Children of Captain Grant* (also called *In Search of the Castaways*), which sent an exploring party around the world at a latitude because the longitude had been lost from the message, was published in 1868. And *Twenty Thousand Leagues Under the Sea* came out in 1870.

Most of Verne's novels can be classified under the general heading of what Bailey calls "the wonderful journey" or, as Verne himself labeled them, "voyages extraordinaires." *Captain Hatteras, Captain Grant,* and *Twenty Thousand Leagues Under the Sea* (which might have been called *Captain Nemo*) are typical.

The Children of Captain Grant, for instance, follows an exploring party led by Lord Glenarvon around the Earth at the thirty-seventh parallel, encountering an earthquake in the Andes, an attack by wolves on the pampas, a flood, treachery among Australian criminals, a shipwreck on the New Zealand coast, and capture by cannibals before the riddle of the messages (in English, French, and German) found in a bottle is correctly deciphered. Verne found in geography as much inspiration as he found in technology, and he wrote two travel books, an *Illustrated Geography of France* (1867–68) and *The Exploration of the World* (1878–80).

The favorite of many critics as well as readers, *Twenty Thousand Leagues Under the Sea* contained some of Verne's best ideas and characterization. Written shortly after Verne acquired an eight-ton shrimp boat and adapted it for pleasure cruising, *Twenty Thousand Leagues* is a Verne novel in which the characters are not completely subordinated to the apparatus; marvelous as is the submarine *Nautilus* (named after an experimental submarine developed by Robert Fulton), it is overshadowed by the brooding presence of Captain Nemo, its builder and commander: he is a complex individual aware of the potentialities of his discoveries, conscious of the power he holds, and filled with dark moods created in part by the mysterious tragedy of his past and in part by a consciousness of his own doom.

Professor Aronnax is asked to investigate a series of inexplicable events at sea involving sea monsters, and vessels striking uncharted reefs and being struck by "something sharp and penetrating." The professor, his Flemish servant, Conseil, and a "prince of harpooners," Ned Land, join an expedition to find the monster. When they find it and pursue it, at last it turns and rams them. In the shock of impact the professor and Ned Land are knocked overboard and Conseil jumps after them to help his master.

The monster is, of course, the *Nautilus,* which eventually picks them up. The misanthropic Captain Nemo ("I have done with society," he says, "for reasons which I alone can understand") agrees to keep them aboard for life if they will consent to being locked in their cabins whenever he wishes. The rest of the novel is a wonderful journey of undersea marvels they encounter in their voyage around the world, including a visit to the South Pole, a trip through an undiscovered tunnel under the Isthmus of Suez, hunting trips on the ocean floor, inspection of Spanish galleons and petrified trees and the heart of a volcano—all the wonders of nineteenth-century nature study, Bailey says, rather than the

LEFT: Drawing of Fulton's submarine *Nautilus*
RIGHT: Verne on the *Saint-Michel III,* 1880

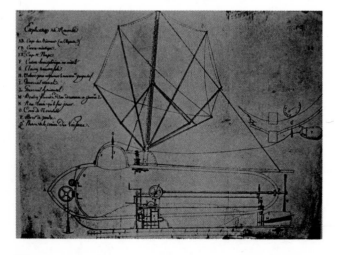

Illustrations from *Twenty Thousand Leagues Under the Sea.* ABOVE LEFT: "A Mysterious Visitor." ABOVE RIGHT: "The Secret of the Sea." BELOW LEFT: "Hunting Under the Sea." BELOW RIGHT: Illustration from *The Mysterious Island*

grotesqueries of earlier imaginary voyages. On one underwater exploration, Professor Aronnax sees, at the foot of an active volcano on the Atlantic sea floor:

There, before my eyes, ruined, destroyed, overturned, appeared a town, its roofs crushed in, its temples thrown down, its arches dislocated, its columns lying on the ground, with the solid proportions of Tuscan architecture still discernible upon them; farther on were the remains of a gigantic aqueduct; here, the encrusted base of an Acropolis, and the outlines of a Parthenon; there, some vestiges of a quay, as if some ancient port had formerly sheltered, on the shores of an extinct ocean, merchant vessels and war triremes; farther on still, long lines of ruined walls, wide deserted streets, a second Pompeii buried under the waters, raised up again for me by Captain Nemo.

Where was I? Where was I? I wished to know at any price. I felt I must speak, and tried to take off the globe of brass that imprisoned my head.

But Captain Nemo came to me and stopped me with a gesture. Then picking up a piece of clayey stone he went up to a black basaltic rock and traced on it the single word—

"ATLANTIS"

Although much of the story is a tour of marvels such as the magnificently baroque *Nautilus* itself or the natural world beneath the sea, or an explanation of how the scientific marvels work, it is sustained by the riddle of Captain Nemo and what he will do with his unique powers. After ten months Professor Aronnax, Ned Land, and Conseil escape near Norway while the *Nautilus* is being drawn toward the maelstrom (Poe's influence again?), and Aronnax, and the reader, are left without answers to the fate of the *Nautilus* and the motivations, nationality, or even the real name of Captain Nemo.

Again Verne kept his readers in suspense for five years, but just as he was likely to leave a novel with unanswered questions (like Edgar Rice Burroughs after him) so he invariably returned to tidy up. *The Mysterious Island,* a three-volume novel published in 1875, tidied up not only *Twenty Thousand Leagues Under the Sea* but *The Children of Captain Grant. The Mysterious Island* begins with five assorted northern prisoners (and the inevitable Verne dog) escaping from Richmond in a balloon and being blown far into the Pacific by a week-long storm. Finally they are dropped on a desert island. The castaways outdo Robinson Crusoe with their industry and inventions. The inventions, which recreate virtually every accomplishment of nineteenth-century technology, illustrate a second type of Verne's science fiction: the first was the wonderful journey, the second, the wonderful invention. The new Robinsons (an early draft of the novel was called *Uncle Robinson*) receive help from an unknown source (a chest containing just what the castaways need); they find on a neighboring island a mutineer marooned there by Captain Grant; they are besieged by pirates whose ship is inexplicably destroyed; and at last, in a cavern inside a volcano, the castaways find the *Nautilus* and the dying Captain Nemo. Captain Nemo reveals his past and the secret of his misanthropy: he had been Prince Dakkar, son of an Indian raja, educated in Europe to help lead his people back to a European level of civilization and to political freedom; he fought in the great sepoy revolt against the English rulers, and when it was put down he turned to science, built the *Nautilus,* and made the sea his kingdom as a means of obtaining revenge and financing battles for independence.

After Nemo's death the castaways, warned of the impending destruction of the island in a volcanic eruption, are rescued from a reef by the Glenarvon yacht, which has just completed its around-the-world search for the children of Captain Grant.

Earlier Verne's steady production had been interrupted by the Franco-Prus-

From *Around the World in Eighty Days*

Verne at the height of his success

From *Dr. Ox's Experiment*

From *The Giant Raft*

Illustrations from *Hector Servadac, or Off on a Comet.* LEFT TO RIGHT: "Walking or Flying," "Night View of Saturn," "Approach to Earth"

sian War, during which he organized a small coast-guard service. After a couple of minor works in 1871 and 1872, *Around the World in Eighty Days* appeared in 1873. It was not science fiction even in its own day, though it was a wonderful journey all the same. Published in weekly installments in journals and newspapers in several countries in 1872, the travels of the Englishman Phileas Fogg and his French servant Passepartout aroused such interest that some newspapers had the story telegraphed to them to avoid the long wait for the mail, and several steamship companies offered to pay Verne if he would use one of their ships to complete the Atlantic leg of Fogg's journey. Other consequences: reporters have attempted to duplicate or beat the time of the trip (and nearly one hundred years later humorist S. J. Perelman thought he could still capitalize on Verne's wonderful journey by retracing Phileas Fogg's footsteps); stage plays were adapted from it (the first, a none-too-faithful Paris production that Verne did not approve, liberated him from financial concerns), and the late Michael Todd turned it into an epic motion picture, one of the earliest super wide-screen productions with stereophonic sound and cameo roles by many well-known actors.

Dr. Ox's Experiment (1874) begins with an offer by a mysterious scientist to light a stolid Flemish town with "oxyhydric gas" at his own expense and ends in a farce as Dr. Ox pumps pure oxygen through the pipes and accelerates the pace of life not only for the people but for dogs, cats, horses, and plants. Offenbach helped adapt it into a musical comedy.

Hector Servadac, or Off on a Comet (1877) describes the collision of a comet with the Earth, a comet which carries off a portion of the Earth and its scattered inhabitants, including a French officer (Servadac) and his comic servant Ben Zoof, two Englishmen playing chess on a fragment of the Rock of Gibraltar, and a miscellaneous collection of other characters. With the comet they pass each of the known planets (with lectures by a handy astronomer), are saved from the cold of outer space by seeking refuge in volcanic caverns, and finally return to the Earth by balloon when the comet swings back close to Earth.

The Underground City, also called *Black Diamonds* (1877), returns to the marvels of electricity (in this instance incandescent lights, which were about to be invented by Edison). The novel describes the building of a mining town in a gigantic cave containing a coal lode and includes, besides some adventure and mystery, a discussion of everything science knew about coal.

The Five Hundred Millions of the Begum, also called *The Begum's Fortune* (1879), is Verne's closest approach to a utopian work. Will machinery be good or bad for mankind? he asks, and shows it working out both ways. A French scientist inherits 527 million francs through the fortunate marriage of a kinsman in India; a German scientist also claims the fortune. They end up dividing it and

From *The Master of the World*   From *The Purchase of the North Pole*   From *The Sphinx of the Ice Fields*

each builds a utopian city in Oregon: the Frenchman builds Frankville, complete with the latest conveniences of science, while the German constructs a German super-city called Stahlstadt, a fortress and industrial concentration camp, only thirty miles away. (The German's plans to destroy Frankville are foiled when his giant cannon blows up.)

The Steam House (1880) amounts to a fancy house trailer pulled by a mechanical elephant powered by steam; in the comforts of the trailer a group of Englishmen explore India, hunt big game, visit cities, ford rivers, and have narrow escapes from natives. The concept was not original with Verne. A dozen years earlier an American dime-novelist named Edward F. Ellis had written a story, published in Beadle's *American Novels*, entitled "The Steam Man of the Prairies." Another publisher of dime novels, Frank Tousey, distributed Harry Enton's *Frank Reade and His Steam Man of the Plains* in 1876; it would be followed by other Frank Reade steam books: *. . . and His Steam Horse, . . . and His Steam Team, . . . and His Steam Tally-Ho.* Then, as Sam Moskowitz relates, the man called the American Jules Verne, Lu Senarens, "retired Frank Reade to a farm (completely run by steam-driven mechanical tools)" and began a new series with *Frank Reade, Jr., and His Steam Wonder* (a locomotive and caboose which did not need tracks). All of these came before 1880. In fact Verne, who not only did not keep his debts a secret but publicly acknowledged many of them, sent a letter of admiration to the author of the Frank Reade, Jr., series, and it was forwarded to Senarens, then only 18.

The *Star of the South,* or *The Southern Star Mystery* (1884) deals with the artificial manufacture of diamonds. As in O'Brien's "Golden Ingot," apparent success in creating a diamond is traced to a servant's placing a real diamond in the crucible.

Robur the Conqueror (1886), also called *The Clipper of the Clouds*, is Verne's attempt to do for the airplane what *Twenty Thousand Leagues Under the Sea* did for the submarine, and the novels have much in common. "The future of aviation," Robur says, "belongs to the aeronef [heavier-than-air flying machine] and not the aerostat [dirigible balloon]." And when the science of the future produces the airplane, it "will greatly change the social and political conditions of the world." Robur's machine, the *Albatross*, is 112 feet long and shaped like a ship's deck; it is carried aloft like a helicopter by seventy-four screws mounted on thirty-seven slim uprights, and propelled by horizontal screws at front and rear driven by electricity (again, it "is not everybody's electricity") generated by a new kind of battery invented by Robur.

The *Albatross* takes aboard two captives, who represent conflicting opinions on how to build a dirigible, and tours the world to demonstrate the aeronef's superiority, "whale-shooting in the Pacific and cannibal-shooting in Africa," as J. O. Bailey describes it. It ends up partly wrecked on a barren island, where Robur's two captives destroy it with dynamite rather than let it continue to X island—where Robur intends to develop his science with the aid of a colony he will found, and eventually to conquer the world. The book ends, however, with the escape of Robur (Verne's symbol for future science) and his reappearance in a new airplane to laugh at those who do not believe in the new science. The airplane, he says, will be given to the world when the world is ready.

Nearly twenty years later, the year before Verne's death (1905), he brought Robur back in *The Master of the World*. But this is a different Robur, not the hero, not the symbol of advancing science, but the mad scientist, symbol for unleashed destructive power, who has developed a combination ship-submarine-airplane-automobile. Robur intends to terrorize the world but, in a fit of hubris, hurls his ship into an electrical storm, is struck by lightning, and falls into the sea.

The Purchase of the North Pole (1889) returns to the Baltimore Gun Club with a story about an invention that does not work because of a misplaced decimal point. Barbicane and Company buy the Arctic regions for two dollars a square mile because they have discovered coal under the ice cap. By loading a 400-million-pound cannon with a newly invented explosive, melimelonite, they hope to turn the earth, thereby warming the polar regions and exposing the coal. But when the cannon goes off, nothing happens.

In *The Castle of the Carpathians* (1892) Verne turns to the gothic: a deserted castle, believed to be haunted, in an isolated village in the Carpathians, is actually occupied by a scientist using mechanical devices to frighten the local citizens. The villain of the story is science. As in *The Master of the World* and *The Purchase of the North Pole*, the old Victorian engineer has turned querulous; he has begun to doubt his old faiths and to destroy his own icons.

The list of Verne's books seems inexhaustible: *Propeller Island* or *The Floating Island* (1895), *The Sphinx of the Ice Fields* (Verne's 1897 sequel to Poe's *The Narrative of Arthur Gordon Pym*, in which he tidies up after his master, discovering at the South Pole a giant lodestone in the shape of a sphinx which pulls all metal to it, including Pym's body, fastened to a musket), *The Lighthouse at the End of the World* (1905), and many others, including eight books published posthumously.

Verne as an old man

Having paid homage to Poe and to Defoe with *The Mysterious Island*, Verne turned to another hero, J. R. Wyss, and wrote a sequel to Wyss's *Swiss Family Robinson*, entitled *The Second Fatherland* (1900). Verne also reworked Dumas' *The Count of Monte Cristo* with a nonscience fiction book, *Mathias Sandorf* (1885). After 1870 and predominantly after 1878, Verne wrote more and more traditional fiction, such as *Michael Strogoff*, a novel of life in czarist Russia.

Most of his work was novel length, and some of it, particularly toward the end of his life when his pen grew weary, was never translated into English. His books and the plays made from them were his fortune, but he did write a few shorter works which were published in magazines. Later his work would be reprinted frequently in pulp magazines. Hugo Gernsback, in the first issue of *Amazing Stories*, announced, "Exclusive arrangements have already been made with the copyright holders of the entire voluminous works of all of Jules Verne's immortal stories. Many of these stories are not yet known to the general American public. For the first time they will be within easy reach of every reader through *Amazing Stories*."

Verne is important, I. F. Clarke says, "because his work represents the high tide of European delight in the marvels and possibilities of science."

He was, biographer Kenneth Allott points out, the almost archetypal expression of nineteenth-century romantic interest in science and technology. "In this respect," Professor Mark Hillegas wrote in *The Future as Nightmare: H. G. Wells and the Anti-Utopians*, "his greatest contribution was to establish in the public consciousness science fiction as a distinct mode of writing. Although he had only slight direct influence on Wells, his writings helped to create the readership for the much more important scientific romances and stories which Wells began writing in the 1890s."

Yet, as J. O. Bailey noted in *Pilgrims Through Time and Space,*

[Verne's] imaginary inventions and discoveries were not bold ones. Because he described many imaginary machines that were invented shortly afterwards, Verne has been called a prophet. He was, no doubt. But he limited his inventions, for the most part, to machines on which scientists were at the time experimenting. He saw that mechanical progress was in acceleration, that flying, submarine travel, and electric lights were just around the corner. When he described an invention not just around the corner (as he did, for instance, in the story of a trip to the moon), he wrote in a style to make fun of the whole thing. He only touched upon the social significance of his inventions. His importance, that is, his immense popularity in every nation and the impetus he gave to scientific fiction, is due rather to the use he made of invention as a means to a new kind of geographic story, voyage of wonders, and exuberant adventure.

Verne was not a great inventor of science fiction ideas nor of plots; it is not for this that he is honored as one of the fathers of modern science fiction. In fact, Verne disclaimed invention in a famous comment about the work of H. G. Wells:

I do not see the possibility of comparison between his work and mine. We do not proceed in the same manner. It occurs to me that his stories do not repose on a very scientific basis. No, there is no rapport between his work and mine. I make use of physics. He invents. I go to the moon in a cannon-ball discharged from a cannon. Here there is no invention. He goes to Mars [sic] in an air-ship, which he constructs of a metal which does away with the law of gravitation. Ça, c'est très joli, but show me this metal. Let him produce it.

Perhaps because his visions were less fantastic and more realizable, he may have influenced more men toward science and discovery than anyone in his generation. Poe was a literary influence, but Verne was a social influence; and with Verne, not Poe, begins the impact of science fiction on society. Igor Sikorsky, the developer of the first practical helicopter, became interested in the concept of an aircraft that could rise vertically when, as a boy in Russia, he had read *Robur the Conquerer* in translation; and speleologist Norman Casteret said that *Journey to the Center of the Earth* first put into his head the idea of cave exploration. Byrd, Beebe, Yuri Gargarin, Marconi, Santos Dumont, and many others have admitted to being inspired by Verne's novels. After a flight to the South Pole, Admiral Byrd said, "It was Jules Verne who launched me on this trip," and submarine developer Simon Lake began his autobiography with the words, "Jules Verne was in a sense the director-general of my life."

More important, Verne pioneered a genre: he defined science fiction, he made it exciting, he made it popular, he made it profitable, he made it respectable, he gave it identity. As I. F. Clarke points out, "Before Verne the marvels of science had on occasions been incidental to stories of romance; but Verne gained a world-wide success by his ability to make technological achievements a subject for fiction."

He did it by being a storyteller—but a storyteller in a new vein, in a new era; a storyteller of the future and the wonders that would be. His direct influence on future writers and their work would not be great; but because of him there was an audience for what they wrote—and a market.

In some respects it can be said that science fiction began with Verne—a century after the beginning of the Industrial Revolution—for Verne was the first successful science fiction writer in the sense that science fiction made him immensely popular and financially well-off.

We might paraphrase what Verne had to say about Robur. "And now who is this Verne? Verne is the fiction of the future. Perhaps the fiction of tomorrow. Certainly the fiction that will come."

Verne's tomb at Amiens

CHAPTER 5
THE BIRTH OF
THE MASS MAGAZINES:
1885–1911

THE MAJOR INFLUENCE on the evolution of science fiction as the nineteenth century surged toward the twentieth was the mass magazine. Until the nineteenth century, and particularly its last decade and a half, periodicals were either nonexistent or scarce and relatively expensive, and what was printed in journals of the eighteenth and early nineteenth centuries was intended for a small, educated, literate upper class.

The long chain of discoveries and events that led to the development of the mass magazine began in eleventh-century China with the invention of movable type, continued through Johann Gutenberg's invention of the printing press in 1450, and culminated in a series of nineteenth-century inventions such as the rotary printing press in 1846, the linotype and wood-pulp paper in 1884, and the halftone engraving in 1886. These coincided with one other critical development: universal primary education, which resulted in general literacy.

The ways in which technology and commerce are interrelated, with each other and with tradition and social change, is a subject whose complexities would require another book; however, the swift appearance of the mass magazine after the inventions of the 1880s was no coincidence. Again, it was steam-engine time.

In 1876 the United States celebrated its centennial with an exhibition in Philadelphia that featured the future more than the past: the most powerful steam engine in the world, a new device for writing letters called a typewriter, new steam-powered farm equipment, and a washable floor-covering called linoleum. The United States was the most industrialized nation in the world and had half the world's railway mileage. President James A. Garfield attributed the nation's increasing wealth to "a single mechanical contrivance, the steam locomotive."

Farms were becoming vastly more productive and efficient as farmers applied Chilean nitrates and then chemical fertilizers to their crops, and new machinery within a few decades reduced the labor of producing an acre of wheat from sixty-one hours to three hours.

Population doubled between 1870 and 1900, and the work week dropped from 12 hours a day to 10 hours while per capita income increased by 50 percent. For many Saturday was a half holiday, and Americans began to look for ways to spend their new leisure and their higher wages.

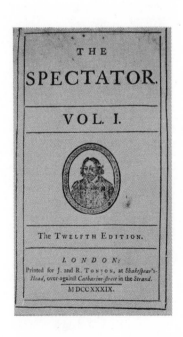

One of these ways was the popular magazine.

Magazines had been plentiful in America and England before the 1880s, but their prices were relatively high and their circulations were relatively low. Edgar Allan Poe wrote for—and edited—such magazines as the *Southern Literary Messenger, Burton's Gentleman's Magazine, Godey's Lady's Book, Graham's Magazine,* and a magazine he founded himself called *Broadway Journal;* but almost the only means of distribution was by mail, and such magazines considered themselves fortunate to accumulate a few thousand readers.

Then there were such general magazines as *Century* and the *North American Review, Harper's Magazine, Atlantic, Cosmopolitan Magazine,* and *The Saturday Evening Post.* The *Post,* which began publication with an issue dated August 4, 1821, was for many years more a weekly newspaper miscellany than a magazine. At the end of 1855 it carried such features as serials, news of military operations during the Civil War, and woodcut illustrations; and it advertised a circulation of between 80,000 and 90,000. It was a hand operation done by skilled workmen who set type letter by letter, carved pictures into wood blocks, and printed an issue sheet by sheet; it sold for $2 a year, raised to $2.50 in 1865.

But most magazines sold for twenty-five or thirty-five cents. The price may not seem excessive, but the average working man earned little more than one dollar a day. His alternative was the nickel weekly (in England priced sometimes at one pence, about two cents U.S.): they were devoted to entertainment and self-improvement, and ran an endless cycle of serials, sometimes three or four an issue.

The dime novel was another option. It was called a dime novel even though it often sold for five cents, and even though it was not a novel at all but a novelette, usually thirty-two pages. But it had a good action picture on the cover or title page and, inside, adventure, excitement, and a few original ideas, all set forth in pedestrian, often awkward prose.

Irwin Beadle was one of the earliest publishers of dime novels, with beginnings in the 1860s, but the great days of the dime novel were the 1880s and 1890s with *Beadle's Half-Dime Library, Beadle's Dime Library, Waverly Library, Beadle's Boys' Library,* and *Beadle's Pocket Library.* Some of Beadle's competitors published *Old Sleuth, Old Cap Collier, Wide Awake Library, Young Sleuth, Secret Service, Old King Brady, Pluck and Luck, Work and Win,* the *Frank Reade Library,* the *James Boys Weekly,* the *Wild West Weekly,* the *New York Weekly, Diamond Dick, Log Cabin Nugget, Buffalo Bill Stories,* and *Rough Rider Weekly.* In 1896 *Tip-Top Weekly* began presenting to American youth the incomparable character of Frank Merriwell. Almost as popular was the *Nick Carter Library.*

The Revolutionary War, the Civil War, and the Wild West were featured in the early dime novels; later they dealt with desperadoes and detectives, foreign adventures and polite young men seeking success, but it all added up to entertainment, and boys saved up their money to buy them and read them in the woodshed or under the covers at night because dime novels had a bad reputation. (One of the memorable moments of my own childhood occurred when my father showed me, stacked high on a closet shelf, some 150 Frank (and his less perfect and more likeable brother Dick) Merriwell novels he had saved—not the original dime novels but the later Street & Smith reprints—now, alas, moldered back into the wood pulp from which they came.

One subject for dime novels was science fiction, a kind of rudimentary, marvelous-invention sort of science fiction, but a science fiction which appealed to the perennial instincts and desires of men for entertainment, illumination, instruction, and explanation. And the man who wrote most of them was Luis Phillip Senarens (1863–1939). *Amazing Stories* called him (in 1928) the American Jules Verne, but his readers knew him only under a series of pseudonyms, the most common being "Noname." A Brooklyn boy, Senarens began writing novels for Frank Tousey's *Boys of New York* when he was only 14, and he had begun selling stories to children's publications two years before.

In 1879 Tousey turned to Senarens—then 16—to take over the Frank Reade series from Harry Enton. Like his French contemporary, Senarens went on ceaselessly writing until his death. Sam Moskowitz estimates that "in a bit more than thirty years, he wrote some forty million words and fifteen hundred individual stories under twenty-seven pseudonyms." In the 191 issues of Tousey's *Frank Reade Library*, Senarens conducted Frank Reade, Jr., and his friends on an exploration of almost every region of the Earth and involved them in fantastic adventures; later Senarens wrote more than fifty invention stories about Jack Wright for *Young Men of America.*

Senarens, Moskowitz notes, wrote about five kinds of inventions: aircraft, robots, submersibles, armored vehicles, and powered land and sea vessels; in the process he created "the single greatest mass of robot literature ever written by one man."

In anonymity and pseudonymity he helped found a branch of boys' literature which today illuminates the social climate of the times and the aspirations of its youth, and which may have contributed to the technological trends of succeeding periods as it responded to those of its own era. In the process, along with Jules Verne and others, he helped create an environment in which science fiction could grow into popular literature.

Most publications die because of economic reasons—they lose their audience or their costs climb faster than the price they can charge. The dime novels were killed by censorship. Attacks by church groups, incited by sermons, led to dealer boycotts, Moskowitz records. "Western, detective, and sea stories with their necessary violence, criminality, and piracy were bad enough, but stories of aircraft, submarines, robots, and tanks seemed to some segments of the population to be drawn from the dark pits of madness." The minds of the younger generation were threatened. The Tousey dime novels were discontinued in 1897. Frank Reade was brought back briefly in a weekly magazine in 1902, but the era of the dime novel was ending as the age of the pulp magazine began.

The place of the dime novel in the hearts of the nation's boys was taken

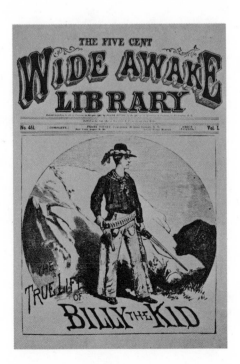
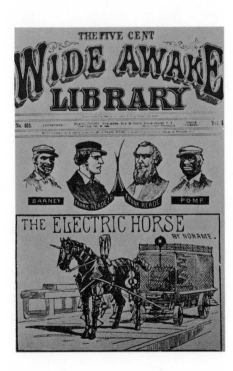

Early "dime novels" carried the stories of Luis Senarens ("Noname"), in which Frank Reade, Jr., ventured into remarkable areas

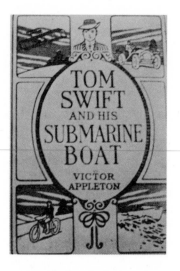

Like Frank Reade, Tom Swift invented wonderful gadgets that took him to strange places

by books such as those about the Rover Boys, and in the science fiction line by those about Tom Swift and others.

Now it was the turn of the mass magazines. The technological developments in printing which made the mass magazines possible were joined by others: the railroad, the automobile, and the truck which could transport magazines, a nationwide distribution system (American News) to get them out where people could buy them, general advertising to help pay the bills, and universal primary education to provide a reading public.

Compulsory primary schooling was a product of the post-Civil War era, when enthusiasm for the power of education swept across the nation. By the mid-1890s thirty-one state legislatures had made elementary-school attendance compulsory, and between 1870 and 1900 the number of high schools increased from 500 to 6,000, and the number of annual graduates from 16,000 to 95,000.

Low-priced magazines had been tried earlier in the century, but the time was not right. Some of the quality magazines—*Lippincott's, Century, Harper's, Cosmopolitan*—reduced their prices in the eighties from thirty-five to twenty-five or twenty cents, partially in response to the founding of *Scribner's Magazine* as a fully illustrated "quality magazine" at twenty-five cents; Frank Munsey priced *Munsey's Magazine* at twenty-five cents when it went from a ten-cent weekly to a monthly.

In the eighties, too, the *Ladies' Home Journal* became a publishing success story. It began in 1883 as a supplement to a farm family paper called *Tribune and Farmer* founded in 1879 by Cyrus Curtis. Within a year it had reached a circulation of 25,000 and it became an independent publication when Curtis traded the farm journal to his partner for the *Ladies' Home Journal* and the plant's type. By 1889 circulation was 440,000.

The Saturday Evening Post passed through a succession of hands, declining to 35,000 circulation in the late eighties. In 1897 it was sold to Curtis for $1,000 (and a year later traced its ancestry to Benjamin Franklin through the *Pennsylvania Gazette,* and added ninety-three years to its age). By the end of 1903, under the editorial direction of George Horace Lorimer, and with the aid of Curtis' formula—newspaper advertising, Ben Franklin's common sense, liberal amounts of popular fiction, club rates, and young salesmen competing for prizes and scholarships—the *Post's* circulation reached 600,000 on its way up.

Meanwhile, an English publisher named George Newnes had founded a weekly called *Tit-Bits* in 1881, and filled it with hundreds of short news items and clippings of interest. Its success (it still is published) led Newnes to found *The Strand Magazine* ten years later. A quality, copiously illustrated magazine printed on coated paper, *The Strand* frequently published short stories. Imitators began to appear immediately: *Ludgate Monthly, Pall Mall Magazine,* and *The Idler,* with *Pearson's Magazine* coming along about five years later.

In the United States, *The Strand* had an American edition which sold originally for twenty cents but cut its price to ten cents in 1895. S. S. McClure founded *McClure's Magazine* in 1893, after he considered issuing an American

S. S. McClure

Frank Munsey

Christmas, 1897   January, 1896 (Vol. 1, No. 1)   February, 1892

edition of *The Idler*. *McClure's* first popular success was Ida Tarbell's illustrated series on Napoleon, which doubled circulation and sent it toward its first 100,000. Tarbell's series on Lincoln pushed the magazine from 175,000 to 250,000. Fiction serials, scientific articles and articles about new discoveries, personality pieces—all helped to increase readership. Later, beginning in 1902, came its muckraking period, and circulation passed 500,000 during World War I.

The first number of *McClure's* carried two scientific articles: an interview with Thomas A. Edison about his current inventing work, and a piece about the future of science by Alexander Graham Bell; later would come articles about Pasteur's research, Roentgen rays, Marconi's invention of wireless telegraphy, horseless carriages, experiments in flying, and new developments in liquid air, radium, and other wonders.

Frank A. Munsey was one of the romantic figures of American capitalism. A Maine boy who set out to be a millionaire and succeeded through publishing, Munsey not only believed in the Horatio Alger myth, he wrote serials in that tradition for his own magazines and lived it himself. He went to New York in 1882 with plans for a boys' weekly to be called *Golden Argosy*. His next ten years were one financial gamble after another—a $10,000 advertising campaign and free distribution of 100,000 copies in 1886, and the next year a $95,000 campaign which raised circulation to 115,000 and debts even higher. In 1888 the title was shortened to *Argosy*, but six years later circulation had dropped to 8,000. Then in 1896 *Argosy* became the first all-fiction magazine, the first successful all-fiction "pulp." The pulps had been created and the pulps would dominate the fiction scene and direct the development of science fiction for more than half a century.

As a pulp magazine, *Argosy* was a success. A more spectacular success was *Munsey's Magazine*, which was founded in 1889 as *Munsey's Weekly* and sold for ten cents. It lost money. Munsey changed it to a monthly in 1891 and raised the price to twenty-five cents. It still lost money. During the panic of 1893, Munsey lowered the price to ten cents. The American News Company refused to distribute the magazine at Munsey's offer of three-and-a-half cents a copy. Munsey turned to direct-mail circulars and newspaper advertising for subscribers, and then founded his own Red Star News Company. As a ten-cent magazine *Munsey's* doubled its circulation each of the first three months and by 1895 had reached 500,000. With its advertising revenues of more than $300,000 a year, it helped carry other Munsey publications over difficult times.

June, 1893 (Vol. 1, No. 1)

Cosmopolitan cut its price to twelve-and-one-half cents a copy when *McClure's* appeared. *Peterson's Magazine* became a ten-cent magazine at the end of 1893; *Godey's* followed the next year. Frank Munsey estimated in 1903 that the couple of hundred ten-cent American magazines had 85 percent of all magazine circulation, but only four were big money-makers, his own *Munsey's* and *Argosy, Cosmopolitan,* and *McClure's.*

Much of their income came from advertising. *Munsey's Magazine* averaged 160 pages of text and 80 to 100 pages of advertising. Advertising in all publications increased 80 percent in the eighties and doubled between 1890 and 1905, with one-fourth of the increase going to magazines. The reason for the sudden jump in advertising was a change in the method of product distribution. Up to this time advertising had largely been limited to the retailer, and he had little interest in national advertising. Now manufacturers of proprietary medicines and cosmetics, then of sewing machines, pianos, organs, typewriters, books, and magazines, began to see the value of creating demand which could be passed back to the manufacturer from the local retailer.

Up to this time science fiction had existed in small literary magazines, like Poe's work, or in hard-cover books, like Verne's. Now it had a medium in which it could come into every home. The advantage was reciprocal: the magazines that brought it quickly found that science fiction was popular fare.

Six Sherlock Holmes stories were published consecutively in the *Strand* and started Sir Arthur Conan Doyle, who would make a significant contribution to science fiction as well as detective fiction, on his way to fame and fortune. Verne's "Dr. Trifulgus—A Fantastic Tale" appeared in 1892. Other science fiction writers would appear later in the pages of the *Strand.* One writer, M. P. Shiel, achieved his reputation through a series of future-war and apocalyptic novels such as *The Empress of the Earth* (published in book form as *The Yellow Danger*) which launched the theme of the "yellow menace" from Asia; *The Lord of the Sea;* and *The Purple Cloud,* in which almost everyone on earth is killed by a poisonous gas that comes out of the Earth.

The Pall Mall Magazine included among its contributors Rudyard Kipling, Israel Zangwill, Frank Stockton, and George Chesney, Sam Moskowitz records in his *Science Fiction by Gaslight,* which has helped preserve examples of the period's science fiction and the history of the magazines that published it.

The first few issues of *Idler* featured Mark Twain, Kipling, Zangwill, Doyle, and Bret Harte. One of the editors, Robert Barr, wrote a story about "The Doom of London," which created a subgenre of doom or castastrophe stories. The story, published in *The Idler* in 1892, reads today like a cautionary tale against air pollution:

M. P. Shiel

It was on a Friday that the fog came down upon us. The weather was very fine up to the middle of November that autumn. The fog did not seem to have anything unusual about it. I have seen many worse fogs than that appeared to be. As day followed day, however, the atmosphere became denser and darker, caused, I suppose, by the increasing volume of coal-smoke poured out upon it. The peculiarity about those seven days was the intense stillness of the air. We were, although we did not know it, under an air-proof canopy, and were slowly but surely exhausting the life-giving oxygen around us, and replacing it by poisonous carbonic acid gas. . . . The newspapers on the morning of the seventh were full of startling statistics, but at the time of going to press the full significance of the alarming figures was not realized.

Much of the science fiction in *The Idler* was reprinted in *McClure's Magazine* in the United States, but *McClure's* also first published original science fiction, including Kipling's story about regular passenger service by dirigible, "With the Night Mail."

Stories by a promising new writer began to appear in 1894, mostly in the *Pall Mall Budget*. In "The Stolen Bacillus" an anarchist makes off with a vial of deadly cholera germs, planning to start an epidemic. When he is chased, he decides to drink the contents himself, but it turns out that the vial really contained specimens of a bacterium which turns monkeys blue. "The Diamond Maker" tells how an experimenter has worked in secret for years to make diamonds from carbon, but now cannot dispose of them.

"The Flowering of the Strange Orchid" describes a "brown shrivelled lump of tissue" that comes into the hands of an amateur botanist to whom nothing has ever happened; it grows into a bloodsucking plant which almost does away with him. "In the Avu Observatory" relates the battle between an astronomer in Borneo and a giant batlike creature which flies into his observatory. "The Lord of the Dynamos" tells the story of a superstitious Eastern helper in a electric-railway generating station who makes a god out of the dynamos, accidentally sacrifices his tyrannical boss to that god, and then throws himself upon the naked terminals:

> So ended prematurely the worship of the Dynamo Deity, perhaps the most short-lived of all religions. Yet withal it could at least boast a Martyrdom and a Human Sacrifice.

"Aepyornis Island" is about an explorer who, while collecting specimens for a company, finds eggs 1½ feet long in a tarry saltwater swamp on an island near Madagascar. Through the treachery of his native helpers he gets set adrift in the broiling sun with the eggs of the extinct bird. Finally, when he reaches a desert island, one remaining egg hatches, grows into a flightless bird 14 feet tall, and becomes a pet, until it turns on the man, and he must kill it.

The young writer of these stories was H. G. Wells. The next chapter will be devoted almost entirely to his impact and continuing influence on science fiction. These early stories, however, illustrate several characteristics of the beginning writer which carry over into the mature author of best-selling, critically acclaimed novels: a preference for the uninvolved narrator, usually with the story told after the fact; stories based in science or natural history which reveal a scientific education and a mind alert for curiosa; and a philosophy suggesting a belief that man's dominion over the earth is an illusion, that there are perplexing mysteries today and many more to come, that there are dangers around man he does not suspect, and that man's pursuit of knowledge and invention follows a perilous path. These characteristics would be displayed more clearly in later stories.

H. G. Wells' "In the Abyss" appeared in August, 1896

"The Argonauts of the Air" (1895) describes two pioneer fliers being tossed out of their experimental airplane to their deaths. "The Remarkable Case of Davidson's Eyes" (1895) relates how "Davidson, stooping between the poles of the big electromagnet, had some extraordinary twist given to his retinal elements. . . ." For several weeks his eyes see only what is at first taken to be "a phantasmal world" and is finally realized to be Antipodes Island on the other side of the Earth from London.

"The Late Mr. Elvesham" (1896) involves an interchange of personality between an old man and a young man by means of a mysterious powder. In

From "The Star," in *Graphic*,
Christmas, 1897

May, 1897

From "A Story of the Stone Age,"
The Idler, May, 1897

"The Plattner Story" (1896) another strange powder blows a schoolteacher into what seems to be another dimension, perhaps the realm of the dead, where events on earth can be observed. "In the Abyss" (1896) describes a descent into the depths of the sea by a kind of prototypical bathyscaphe, which is captured briefly and worshipped by a reptilian race of intelligent manlike creatures living there. And "The Sea Raiders" (1896) tells about a brief attack along the English shores by a new variety of giant squid.

"The Crystal Egg" (1897), in some ways prefatory to *The War of the Worlds*, is centered on a piece of crystal through which can be seen a valley (apparently on Mars) inhabited by birdlike creatures who peer into similar crystals set on masts; the creatures have two sets of tentacles under the mouth. Also visible are wingless, tentacled creatures; clumsy, white bipeds that are chased and caught by the hopping Martians; and a gigantic mechanical apparatus which is seen advancing along the causeway beside the canal.

"The Star" (1897) describes the near-destruction of Earth by a large planetary body which wanders into the solar system from outer space, collides with Neptune and turns incandescent, and finally falls into the sun.

H. G. Wells, 1901

The Martian astronomers—for there are astronomers on Mars, although they are very different beings from men—were naturally profoundly interested by these things. They saw them from their own standpoint of course. "Considering the mass and temperature of the missile that was flung through our solar system into the sun," one wrote, "it is astonishing what a little damage the earth, which it missed so narrowly, has sustained. All the familiar continental markings and the masses of the seas remain intact, and indeed the only difference seems to be a shrinkage of the white discoloration (supposed to be frozen water) round either pole." Which only shows how small the vastest of human catastrophes may seem, at a distance of a few million miles.

"A Story of the Stone Age" and "A Story of the Days to Come," both published in 1897, represent the Janus head of science fiction—one face watches our primitive ancestors learning how to cope with their physical and social environment; the second, our descendants suffering from atavistic romantic impulses in an environment which has become completely subjugated by man, the city.

"The New Accelerator" (1901) describes the invention of a drug which speeds up all the bodily processes several thousand times, so that the person who takes it moves so swiftly he is invisible and everything else seems frozen in place. The story closes with the intention of the inventor and the narrator to make the drug available "at all chemists and druggists, in small green bottles" under the name of "Gibberne's Nervous Accelerator."

No doubt its use renders a great number of very extraordinary things possible;

October, 1895

for, of course, the most remarkable and, possibly, even criminal proceedings may be effected with impunity by this dodging, as it were, into the interstices of time. Like all potent preparations it will be liable to abuse. We have, however, discussed this aspect of the question very thoroughly, and we have decided that this is purely a matter of medical jurisprudence and altogether outside our province. We shall manufacture and sell the Accelerator, and, as for the consequences—we shall see.

"The Empire of the Ants" relates the story of a trip up the Amazon River to investigate stories of a plague of big poisonous ants. The expedition finds the ants organized, acquiring technology, and killing everything in their path. "By 1920," the story concludes, "they will be half-way down the Amazon. I fix 1950 or '60 at the latest for the discovery of Europe."

Wells's novels were more important and certainly more successful, but many of his short stories did in a few words what his novels did in many—they explored concepts that seemed as if they had never before been conceived by man, they dealt with the impact of unusual events or new developments on ordinary men, and most of them created thematic successions that can be traced through later science fiction.

The most significant event of the late nineteenth century for science fiction, however, was the publication of *The Time Machine*. It appeared in 1895 in five installments in *The New Review* and immediately created critical acclaim for Wells and new respect for the developing genre. Three years later Ford Madox Ford wrote, "I do not have to assure you that it did not take us long to recognize that here was Genius. Authentic, real Genius. And delightful at that."

Wells's work suddenly was welcome everywhere, and so were the stories of others who dealt in the area of the speculative and the future. *Pearson's Magazine* serialized anonymously George Griffith's *Angel of the Revolution*, which describes the repulse of an attack on England by a Russian air armada, another of the future-war novels pioneered by Chesney's "Battle of Dorking." *Pearson's* also published Griffith's "War in the Water," about a battle between two fleets of ironclads; Cutliffe Hyne's "London's Danger," about London's fire hydrants freezing during a cold winter, allowing fire to destroy London; Levin Carnese's "A Genius for a Year," about smart pills; and W. Bert Foster's "The Man Child," about a lost race of white Indians.

The Strand also was busy: it published Fred M. White's "The Purple Terror," about a carnivorous plant; Meade and Eustace's "Where the Air Quivered," about a mechanism for projecting a deadly jet of cyanide gas; and Grant Allen's "The Thames Valley Catastrophe," which describes an unexpected volcanic eruption that destroys London.

Pearson's published Griffith's "A Corner on Lightning," about a scientific plot to cut off the world's electricity; Weeks's "Master of the Octopus," which also focused on electrical power; Curtis's "The Monster of Lake LeMetrie," in which a man's brain is transplanted into the head of a prehistoric reptile; and Hyne's serial, *The Lost Continent*, an Atlantis story in which a man and a woman escape the sinking of the continent on an ark.

In the United States an unusual magazine would be born in 1895 and called *The Black Cat*. Its publisher, Herman D. Umbstaetter, sold it for five cents, published only short stories, and got them largely from amateurs through continuous contests. Umbstaetter claimed to have discovered such authors of later fame as Jack London, Rupert Hughes, Octavius Roy Cohen, and Ellis Parker Butler. A good number of the stories *The Black Cat* printed, though not all, were science fiction and fantasy.

Argosy, which placed its greatest reliance on the adventure story, also published science fiction frequently, stories such as Andre Laurie's serial *The Conquest of the Moon*, in which the moon is drawn down to the Sahara Desert by magnets; Frank Aubrey's *A Queen of Atlantis*; Griffith's *The Lake of Gold*; William Wallace Cook's *A Round Trip to the Year 2000, Cast Away at the Pole, Adrift in the Unknown, Marooned in 1492*, and *The Eighth Wonder*. In the first decade of this century, *Argosy* also began to publish stories of comic invention, which would become a kind of subgenre surviving into the late thirties and forties in stories by L. Sprague de Camp and Henry Kuttner, and into the sixties in motion pictures by Walt Disney.

Frank Munsey added *All-Story Magazine* in 1905, and it featured science

From Grant Allen's "The Thames Valley Catastrophe," *The Strand*, December, 1897

H. Rider Haggard

Cover of 1887 edition

fiction from its first issue. Some of its memorable publications include Garrett P. Serviss's *The Moon Metal* and *A Columbus of Space,* which featured atomic-powered spaceships on a trip to Venus.

Street & Smith created the *Popular Magazine* in 1904 as competition for *Argosy,* and serialized H. Rider Haggard's *Ayesha: The Further History of She* in 1905. It also ran stories of comic inventions and another subgenre, scientific detectives. In 1905 the *Monthly Story Magazine* began publication; two years later it was retitled *Blue Book.* It published the sea stories and fantasies of English author William Hope Hodgson, and some of the first stories of George Allan England, who later would be acclaimed one of the most popular and influential science fiction writers of his time after the publication, in *Cavalier,* of his *Darkness and Dawn* trilogy in 1912 and 1913.

The stories written and published during this period of science fiction's early history inevitably had their effects upon audience and upon authors who would emulate them or react to them, and many of them today seem relatively modern in concerns and effective in technique. But the two most important contributions of the period were the creation of the mass magazines and the introduction of H. G. Wells. The magazines provided a market for science fiction, and they would lead in time to the pulp magazines and then to the science fiction magazines themselves. The career of H. G. Wells spanned fifty years, and his influence would grow and diminish over that half-century. But the publication of *The Time Machine* was an announcement that the time machine that was science fiction had arrived; it could be literature and popular fiction too; it could predict; it could speculate; it could think seriously and expect serious consideration.

Each succeeding novel by Wells had its impact: *The Invisible Man,* which was serialized in *Pearson's Weekly* in 1897 and published in hard cover by *Pearson's* the same year, and *The War of the Worlds,* which was serialized in *Pearson's Magazine* earlier that year and then in newspapers and magazines throughout the United States.

Just as the Martians had conquered Earth, Wells had captured science fiction—and science fiction, for the moment at least, had captured the imagination of the world.

Two illustrations from Arthur Conan Doyle's *The Lost World*

CHAPTER 6
PROPHET OF PROGRESS: 1866-1946

POE PIONEERED the form and established the methods by which it could achieve its effects, Verne won it an audience, H. G. Wells demonstrated that it could be literature—thus might go the canon of the creation of the science fiction genre.

But neither life nor literature is so simple. Poe was not merely a pioneer; he was a literary artist trying to make a living. Verne was not merely a popularizer but a man of his time with an inventive mind who wrote out of his convictions of what was important and what he could do well. Wells was conscious of literary values but even more deeply concerned with his unique insights into people and society, and most of all concerned about personal success. And even these amplifications ignore the contributions of the Mary Shelleys, the Hawthornes, the O'Briens, the Hales, the Senarenses and a host of dime-novelists and writers for the early mass magazines, and even the Haggards and the Doyles, as well as the influences of history, technology, and scientific thought.

Other writers already had made or were to make significant contributions to the developing literature of scientific possibility, of rationalized fantasy, and of speculation about the past and the future—which one day would be called science fiction.

Mark Twain (1835–1910) published his time-travel novel, *A Connecticut Yankee in King Arthur's Court* (1889), predicted television (called the "tele-lectroscope") in a story called "From the 'London Times' of 1904" (1898), and included science fiction elements in *Extracts from Captain Stormfield's Visit to Heaven* (1909) and the long-suppressed *Letters from the Earth* with the unfinished novel *The Great Dark* about microscopic life in a drop of water.

H. Rider Haggard (1865–1925), whose perennially popular novel *She* was published in 1887, was a prolific author of fantasy and science fiction as well as historical romances, including the Allan Quatermain series of novels and stories, the novels about ancient Egypt, and others such as *When the World Shook* (1919).

Sir Arthur Conan Doyle (1859–1930) wrote not only Sherlock Holmes stories and his favorite historical novels, but a number of science fiction novels and stories, particularly those featuring the eccentric Professor Challenger which began with *The Lost World* (1912) and *The Poison Belt* (1913), as well as his non-Challenger work, *The Maracot Deep* (1929).

Ambrose Bierce (1842–1914), who disappeared mysteriously in Mexico after writing extensively about mysterious disappearances, wrote dozens of tales of horror between 1870 and 1896, collected in *Can Such Things Be?* (first edition, 1893); among them were several stories classifiable as science fiction, such as "The Damned Thing" and "Moxon's Master," one of the first robot stories.

Rudyard Kipling (1865–1936), the poet laureate of the British Empire, also contributed science fictional extrapolations in such stories as "Wireless" (1902), "With the Night Mail" (1905), and "Easy as A.B.C." (1912).

Several isolated novels were popular or influential, including Ignatius Donnelly's apocalyptic *Caesar's Column* (1890) and Stanley Waterloo's novel about the caveman, *The Story of Ab* (1897). A similar novel would be published by Jack London (1876–1916), *Before Adam* (1906). London was the author, as well, of such futuristic fiction as *The Scarlet Plague* (1915), the socialist propaganda novel *The Iron Heel* (1907), and the remarkable *The Star Rover* (1915), as well as numerous short stories.

The most revolutionary thought of the day was evolution, and the author who was the most inspired by it was H. G. Wells, who was born seven years after the first publication of Darwin's theory. The world was still trying to refute it or adapt to it throughout much of Wells's early life, and some critics interpret the scientific romances and utopias of Wells as a fictional working-out of the theory of evolution. If evolution is the survival of the fittest, if every living creature must adapt to the demands of his environment or die, what does it mean for the individual man and for the increasingly complex societies he builds? Will not men, too, be selected by their environment? Will they not change, adapt? Will other creatures not rise from obscurity to threaten man's dominion? And will not the social structures that man builds demand increasing specialization by individuals and the increasing surrender of individualism to society's needs?

Charles Darwin

The great struggle between traditional values and the new values suggested by the theory of evolution and the scientific and technological forces for change in the world reached full force in the late nineteenth century; it has continued ever since, its most recent skirmish the debate between C. P. Snow and F. R. Leavis, and their respective champions, under the impetus of C. P. Snow's 1959 lecture "The Two Cultures." That controversy, carried on throughout much of the early sixties, began with Snow's view that the scientific culture and the literary culture were tragically separated by a lack of understanding brought on by an even more fundamental failure of communication. "I believe," he said, "the intellectual life of the whole of Western society is increasingly being split into two polar groups." And he added that the literary culture was as illiterate in the basic scientific principles upon which modern society and its future depend as the scientific culture is illiterate in the basic documents of literature. He went on to describe literary intellectuals as "natural Luddites" who "have never tried, wanted, or been able to understand the industrial revolution, much less accept it." Leavis, a literary critic influenced by Matthew Arnold's conviction that literature is central to a civilization and that the function of the critic is to determine "the best that is known and thought in the world," sneered at Snow's position as "crass Wellsianism" representative of the encyclopedist movement of the twenties and thirties, and sought to demolish Snow's argument by attacking his reputation as a novelist.

Henry James

Martin Green, in "A Literary Defense of 'The Two Cultures,'" defined the spirit of the encyclopedist "summed up in Wells's three compilations, *An Outline of History, The Science of Life,* and *The Work, Wealth, and Happiness of Mankind*" as "a spirit of broad general knowledge, national and international planning, optimism about (or at least cheerful businesslike engagement with) the powers of contemporary science and technology, and a philistinism about the more esoteric manifestations of art and religion."

In Wells's day the debate over these values was between Wells and Henry James, the primary proponent in his day of Art and The Novel. Joseph Conrad (who, said Wells, "had gone literary with a singleness and intensity of purpose that made the kindred concentration of Henry James seem lax and large and pale") and James both publicly admired Wells's fiction. James was filled with "wonder and admiration" for Wells's early stories and scientific romances, spoke of reading *The First Men in the Moon* "à petites doses as one sips (I suppose) old Tokay," and of allowing *Twelve Stories and a Dream* "to melt, lollipopwise, upon my imaginative tongue," and Conrad wrote to Wells how much he liked his work, particularly *The Invisible Man:* "Impressed is *the* word, O Realist of the Fantastic!" and added, "It is masterly—it is ironic—it is very relentless—and it is very true."

Joseph Conrad

But James kept after Wells to work harder at the art of writing, to improve his description, his characterization, his subtlety, in spite of James's evident fascination with what Wells actually was doing. And Wells, in spite of his flirtation with the artistic, finally concluded:

That would have taken more time than I could afford. . . . I had a great many things to say and . . . if I could say one of them in such a way as to get my point over to the reader I did not worry much about finish. The fastidious critic might object, but the general reader to whom I addressed myself cared no more for finish and fundamental veracity about the secondary things of behavior than I.

And he went on to comment:

I was disposed to regard a novel as about as much an art form as a market place or a boulevard. . . .

And:

The larger part of my fiction was written lightly and with a certain haste.

When Conrad asked him to describe a boat in the ocean, Wells felt that

he wanted to see it with a definite vividness of his own. But I wanted to see it and to see it only in relation to something else—a story, a thesis.

Wells began his writing career preparing articles for newspapers, and that was how he finally saw himself:

In the end I revolted altogether and refused to play their game. "I am a journalist," I declared, "I refuse to play the artist! If sometimes I am an artist it is a freak of the gods. I am a journalist all the time and what I write *goes now*—and will presently die."

This conflict between the literary and the journalistic, the past and the future, the pessimistic and the optimistic, can be traced through the later history of science fiction down to the controversy created by the introduction in the sixties of what was called the New Wave.

In terms of practical application, the argument sums up as a statement by the scientific culture: "Things can be better if we apply our minds to the task." And the reply of the literary culture: "But they won't," and its unconscious extension to, "They can't."

In spite of Wells's acceptance of a brief life for his writing—writing which even today seems modern, direct, readable, and effective—his books have survived. Jack Williamson, in *H. G. Wells, Critic of Progress*, called him immortal.

The physical organism, under-sized and squeaky-voiced and generally inadequate, died in 1946. The serious literary artist had perished thirty years before, a martyr to great causes. Yet Wells himself lives on, in a multitude of conflicting images.

He is the forgotten author who was once the prophet of the masses. He is the craftsman of the short story who wrote "The Country of the Blind," the amateur statesman welcome in the White House and the Kremlin, the international pundit whose snap judgments sold for a dollar a word. He is the atheist who hated God, the evangelist of a deified Spirit of Man, the zealot who tried to write a new Bible. He is the cockney Don Juan, and the tenderly devoted husband revealed in the *Book of Catherine Wells*, and the loving father who wrote "The Magic Shop" to entertain his son. He is the facile popular journalist who learned from a book by J. M. Barrie how to write glittering trivia; he is the prodigal father of modern science fiction; he is the dedicated and inspiring teacher whose classroom finally included most of the world. He is the utopian optimist who campaigned for an "open conspiracy" to set up a new world order. But he is also the critical pessimist who challenged every theory of progress.

To understand Wells, Williamson thinks, one must consider him as a critic of progress. To understand his concern for progress—or, more broadly, his involvement in the educational, scientific, political, and historical currents of his times—we must understand his childhood and his education.

Wells was born in Bromley, Kent, a few miles from London, in 1866. His father was a gardener and the son of a gardener, who lost a series of jobs, Wells recalled, because "he did not like to be told things and made to do things." But it was as a gardener that Joseph Wells met a ladies' maid in the household; they married and bought an unsuccessful crockery shop called Atlas House, which Joe Wells helped support by his talents as a professional cricket

The mature H. G. Wells

Wells in 1911

player and the items of cricket equipment he included in the store.

Into this lower middle-class environment, with poverty lurking nearby, Herbert George Wells was born. His mother, Sarah, a devout believer in conventional religion and Victorian values, wanted nothing more than to "get on" in life and to see her children well-placed in some decent profession and "getting on." But, Wells recalls,

> Vast unsuspected forces beyond her ken were steadily destroying the social order, the horse and sailing ship transport, the handicrafts and the tenant-farming social order, to which all her beliefs were attuned and on which all her confidence was based. To her these mighty changes in human life presented themselves as a series of perplexing frustrations and undeserved misfortunes, for which nothing or nobody was clearly to blame—unless it was my father. . . .

Wells found his father's nonconformity as difficult to understand as his mother's acceptance, and the life they led and the future laid out for him was basically repugnant to his rebellious dreams and desires.

He attributed his escape to two broken legs—the first rescued him from a brief career as assistant in his mother's shop and introduced him to the splendor of books that his father brought him; the second ended his father's sporting career and led to his mother's returning, as housekeeper, to the estate at Up Park from which she had been married.

A third, more universal factor was the enactment of the Education Act of 1871, which organized the British and the National schools into a state system and supplemented them with Board schools. Wells attended two National schools and a grammar school, with brief attempts to apprentice him to a draper and then to a pharmaceutical chemist in between. At the grammar school, at the age of 15, he learned how to master a subject on his own through a system of national grants given teachers whose students could pass special examinations. Wells was quick and bright, and his teacher set him to learning a variety of subjects through what today is described as independent study.

After another two miserable years in a second attempt at draper's apprentice, he returned to his grammar school as a teacher-student, and did so well on the May special examinations that he received a "free studentship" to the Normal School of Science, South Kensington, which later became the Imperial College of Science and Technology and a part of the University of London. Its mission was to train teachers for science classes.

Wells as student, 1886

Wells continued as a student in London for three years, the first year as a student in biology under Thomas Henry Huxley, the champion of Darwinism, who carried on running debates with the great men of his times over the validity and meaning of Darwin's theories. That year may have provided the most critical influence on Wells's intellectual development; his next two years spent studying physics and geology were growing failures—he attributed them to inadequacies in teaching—which drove him from the school before he earned his degree. He would in later years say that he was "at home with biology, ill at ease, in a state of fundamental incomprehension, with the physical sciences."

> The biological course from which I came had been a vivid, sustained attempt to see life clearly and to see it whole, to see into it, to see its inter-connexions, to find out, as far as terms were available, what it was, where it came from, what it was doing, and where it was going.

And, of course, he learned it from a man for whom biology had become not a descriptive scheme but a science of process. Six years after Huxley's death in 1895, Wells wrote:

> I do not know if the students of to-day will quite understand how we felt for our Dean—we read his speeches, we borrowed the books he wrote, we clubbed out of our weekly guineas to buy the *Nineteenth Century* whenever he rattled Gladstone or pounded the Duke of Argyle. I believed that he was the greatest man I was likely to meet, and I believe that all the more firmly to-day.

This "yellow faced, square faced old man with bright little brown eyes," to whose lectures Darwin himself sometimes had come, saw in evolution no happy

Thomas Huxley

prospects for the future of mankind. By the 1880s Huxley had decided that the evolutionary process would never lead to moral or social improvement, for cosmic nature is the "headquarters of the enemy of ethical nature," and the only chance for social and ethical progress is the "checking of the cosmic process at every step." But Huxley was pessimistic about any major victories for the ethical in a period of social and economic injustice, when ambitious militarists were rationalizing wars of conquest with Darwin's theory of the survival of the fittest, when empire builders found in Darwin a natural sanction for their acquisitions, when Darwin seemed to nod at modern robber barons building fortunes out of the misery of others, when, indeed, it seemed that whatever succeeded was right.

Darwin himself ended his *Origin of the Species* on a note of hope:

> As all the living forms of life are the lineal descendants of those which lived long before the Cambrian epoch, we may feel certain that the ordinary succession by generation has never once been broken, and that no cataclysm has desolated the whole world. Hence we may look with some confidence to a secure future of great length. And as natural selection works solely by and for the good of each being, all corporal and mental endowments will tend to progress toward perfection.

Williamson believes that this view of progress, Wells, with his complex of conflicting drives to escape his middle-class origins and the convictions stemming from those origins, came to question. Before he could reach that point, however, he had to "get on"—a process which took him first to a teaching job in a Welsh school, where a playground accident smashed a kidney and where he discovered a lung condition, then to a private school called Henley House in London, and finally to a relatively prosperous situation as teacher in a thriving University Correspondence College created by the system of degree by examination.

Able at last to marry, Wells wed a cousin, Isabel, whom he had come to know and love while he attended the Normal School of Science. But they were incompatible temperamentally and sexually, and he went to live, without marriage for a couple of years, with a student, Catherine, whom he came to call Jane. During this period, as well, he earned his own bachelor of science degree by examination from the University of London, wrote a textbook on biology for the University Correspondence College, and began contributing articles to magazines.

His first article, "The Rediscovery of the Unique," which Wells later described as "ill-written but ingenious," was published in the July 1891 *Fortnightly Review.* A second metaphysical speculation, the "Universe Rigid," found its way into type at the *Review* before the editor, the famous, soon-to-be notorious Frank Harris, read it and summoned the author for an explanation. But the young Wells's feeble explanation was inadequate, and the article never was printed. Two years later, while reading a book by J. M. Barrie called *When a Man's Single,* Wells "hit quite by accident upon the true path to successful freelance journalism." The secret was to find his subjects in the observations, thoughts, and experiences of every reader, and to put them in language that those average readers could understand:

Wells as young man, 1892

> Why had I never thought in that way before? For years I had been seeking rare and precious topics. *Rediscovery of the Unique! Universe Rigid!* The more I was rejected the higher my shots had flown. All the time I had been shooting over my target. All I had to do was to lower my aim—and hit.

So he lowered his aim and began hitting all the time. He gave up his correspondence teaching responsibilities and began a life geared around the writing of articles like "On Staying at the Seaside" and "The Man of the Year Million."

In 1893 Wells had earned £380 13s. 7d. In 1894, the year he carried off Catherine Robbins, he earned £583 17s. 7d. In 1895 his income was £792 2s. 5d.; in 1896, £1,056 7s. 9d. at a time when a pound was worth $4 and the salary of a member of Congress was $5,000; and it kept expanding in that fashion for a number of years. The careful records were the product of his second wife's bookkeeping, but the concern with "getting on" was common to both. "In those days," Wells recalls, "I was full of mercenary *go;* 'price per thousand' and 'saleable copy' were . . . present in my mind."

This ambitious young middle-class rebel could not have turned to writing for a living at a better time:

THE
PALL MALL GAZETT
An Evening Newspaper and Review.

July 4, 1885

The last decade of the nineteenth century was an extraordinarily favorable time for new writers and my individual good luck was set in the luck of a whole generation of aspirants. Quite a lot of us from nowhere were "getting on." . . . The habit of reading was spreading to new classes with distinctive needs and curiosities. . . . An exceptional wave of intellectual enterprise had affected the British "governing class." . . . Such happy minor accidents as the invasion of England by the Astor family with a taste for running periodicals [the *Pall Mall* magazines] at a handsome loss, contributed also in their measure to the general expansion of opportunity for new writers. New books were being demanded and fresh authors were in request. . . .

But it was not by articles alone that Wells was "getting on." In 1894 Lewis Hind, editor of the weekly *Pall Mall Budget,* which had been split off the parent *Gazette,* suggested that Wells use his "special knowledge of science" in a special series of short stories to be called "single sitting" stories. For these he would be paid five guineas each. The first was "The Stolen Bacillus," but, he recalls, "I presently broadened my market and found higher prices were to be got from the *Strand Magazine* and the *Pall Mall Magazine.*"

W. E. Henley, editor of the *National Observer,* asked for an article, and Wells dug up his "peculiar treasure, my old idea of 'time travelling,'" from the *Science Schools Journal* and sent him a couple of papers. "He liked them and asked me to carry on the idea so as to give glimpses of the world of the future." An idea that ultimately was carried through at least seven versions, five of them published, became a series of articles for the *Observer.*

The version from the *Science Schools Journal,* which Wells had helped found while at the Normal School, Wells later categorized as "an experiment in the pseudo-teutonic Nathaniel Hawthorne style." It was entitled "The Chronic Argonauts" and the time traveler was called Nebogipfel. While the articles were running, the magazine was sold, Henley was removed as editor, and the articles were stopped. But for Wells it seemed that everything happened for the best—broken legs, injured kidneys, lost markets—for Henley, his head "bloody but unbowed," found another magazine to edit, the *New Review,* and asked Wells to rewrite the "Time Traveller" articles as a serial story. Wells rewrote it "from end to end," and it brought him instant recognition as a major literary figure working on the frontiers of a new form. It also brought him—perhaps almost as important—£100 for the serial, £50 advance from Methuen for the book rights; at the same time another publisher was going to bring out a book of his articles for an advance of £10. "Fairly Launched at Last," Wells called that chapter of his life story, *Experiment in Autobiography.*

For *The Time Machine* Wells had not only mined his past fictional production but his knowledge and speculations about evolution. Some of them he had summed up in an 1894 article in the *Pall Mall Gazette* called "The Extinction of Man":

Scene from George Pal movie *The Time Machine,* starring Rod Taylor

What has usually happened in the past appears to be the emergence of some type of animal hitherto rare and unimportant, and the extinction, not simply of the previously ruling species, but of most of the forms that are at all closely related to it. Sometimes, indeed, as in the case of the extinct giants of South America, they vanished without any considerable rivals, victims of pestilence, famine, or, it may be, of that cumulative inefficiency that comes of a too undisputed life.

No; man's complacent assumption of the future is too confident. We think, because things have been easy for mankind as a whole for a generation or so, we are going on to perfect comfort and security in the future. We think that we shall always go to work at ten and leave off at four and have dinner at seven forever and ever. But these four suggestions [the evolution of the ant and the cephalopod are two of them, foreshadowing two concepts of evolutionary competitors that Wells later would turn into fiction, "The Empire of the Ants" and "The Sea Raiders"] out of a host of others must surely do a little against this complacency. Even now, for all we can tell, the coming terror may be crouching for its spring and the fall of humanity be at hand. In the case of every predominant animal the world has seen, I repeat, the hour of its complete ascendance has been the eve of its entire overthrow.

In *The Time Machine,* Wells's original Nebogipfel became the rather ordinary Time Traveller (most of the characters are named, in a quaint style that would survive in occasional stories like "The Girl in the Golden Atom" (1919) for the next quarter-century, by their occupations, "the Psychologist," "the Medical Man," "the Provincial Mayor") and the concept of time traveling by means of a machine was made credible by a description of the machine, a demonstration of a model, and the Time Traveller's impressions of the process. The Traveller describes time as another dimension: "There is no difference between Time and any of the three dimensions of Space except that our consciousness moves along it," and follows it with several pages of examples and implications. He describes a model and its disappearance:

The thing the Time Traveller held in his hand was a glittering metallic framework, scarcely larger than a small clock, and very delicately made. There was ivory in it, and some transparent crystalline substance. . . .

We all saw the lever turn. . . . There was a breath of wind, and the lamp flame jumped. One of the candles on the mantel was blown out, and the little machine suddenly swung round, became indistinct, was seen as a ghost for a second perhaps, as an eddy of faintly glittering brass and ivory; and it was gone—vanished! Save for the lamp the table was bare.

A bit later the Traveller shows his skeptical friends the Time Machine itself:

Parts were of nickel, parts of ivory, parts had certainly been filed or sawn out of rock crystal. The thing was generally complete, but the twisted crystalline bars lay unfinished upon the bench beside some sheets of drawings, and I took one up for a better look at it. Quartz it seemed to be.

Toward the end of the book, the machine is described in a bit more detail after its return from the Traveller's first trip:

There in the flickering light of the lamp was the machine sure enough, squat, ugly, and askew; a thing of brass, ebony, ivory, and translucent glimmering quartz. Solid to the touch—for I put out my hand and felt the rail of it—and with brown spots and smears upon the ivory, and bits of grass and moss upon the lower parts, and one rail bent awry.

The process of traveling through time is described by the Traveller:

"I am afraid I cannot convey the peculiar sensations of time travelling. They are excessively unpleasant. There is a feeling exactly like that one has upon a switchback—of a helpless headlong motion! I felt the same horrible anticipation, too, of an imminent smash. As I put on pace, night followed day like the flapping of a black wing. . . ."

Two illustrations from *The War of the Worlds,* 1898

The Traveller spends much of his time in the future with a group of delight-ful childlike people called the Eloi, who turn out to be the degenerated de-scendants of the upper class; under the earth he finds factories tended by tro-glodytic Morlocks who contribute goods to the care of the Eloi but also use them for food. At the end the Time Traveller journeys forward to the ultimate fate of the Earth itself in the slow death of the Sun and the solar system.

Williamson believes that Wells expressed in *The Time Machine* his belief that progress has two cosmic limits: first, by eliminating challenges, progress itself results in degeneration; and second, Earth must finally be destroyed by natural forces (and, by extension, if man should escape Earth, the universe will meet its ultimate heat death, entropy).

The War of the Worlds (1898) also included an element of evolutionary philosophy: man as one species evolving in competition with others now faces superior aliens. The Martians are symbols of progress which has gone far beyond man; man is helpless before what, in another sense, looms as his ultimate sci-entific fate. Ironically, the defeat of the Martians is brought about by a com-peting species of life against which their very past successes have left them defenseless: bacteria.

Wells the writer, while he looked at the future with a kind of horrified dread, enjoyed the detailed destruction he plotted in his imagination. As he planned the novel, he recalled in his autobiography, "I wheeled about the district mark-ing down suitable places and people for destruction by my Martians." And he wrote to a friend:

I'm doing the dearest little serial for Pearson's new magazine, in which I completely wreck and destroy Woking—killing my neighbors in painful and eccentric ways—then proceed via Kingston and Richmond to London, which I sack, selecting South Kensing-ton for feats of peculiar atrocity.

Every science fiction writer, I suppose, has visited some such apocalyptic destruction upon familiar surroundings, as I did to the University of Kansas in the beginning of my novel *The Burning* and at the end of *The Immortals.*

Between the publication of *The Time Machine* and *The War of the Worlds,* Williamson believes, Wells took up the question of what he considered to be the human limits to progress, in *The Island of Dr. Moreau* and *The Invisible Man.* In *The Island of Dr. Moreau* (1896) Wells shows the conflict between ethical nature and the cosmic process within man himself, as Dr. Moreau attempts to make men out of animals through vivisection and pain. The process is sym-bolized by the law the Beast People chant:

"*Not to go on all-Fours; that is the Law. Are we not Men?*"
"*Not to suck up Drink; that is the Law. Are we not Men?*"
"*Not to claw Bark of Trees; that is the Law. Are we not Men?*"
"*Not to chase other Men; that is the Law. Are we not Men?*"

But Moreau and his benevolent, doomed assistant Montgomery are killed, in part through the chance that brought the stranger, Prendick, to the island, and the animals quickly revert to beasts. There is no hope for them—and by exten-sion for man—in Moreau's pure reason, in Montgomery's benevolence, or in Prendick's enlightened humanitarianism.

In *The Invisible Man* (1897) Wells demonstrates how selfish individualism must yield to society in the name of progress, even though Wells sees nothing particularly praiseworthy in society. Griffin, the man who makes himself invisi-ble through the use of chemicals, is the scientist as individual, his mastery of nature a tool of selfish personal power, Williamson thinks. But Griffin also illus-trates the paradox that only the individual can initiate change; society is con-servative and acts always to preserve the status quo. Wells reminds us, however, that the changes created by such antisocial instruments as Griffin are not neces-sarily good.

Another analysis, focused on the practical problems of the working writer, might point out that Wells is saying, as he says in almost every story of inven-tion, "You want something wonderful (like invisibility)? Like everyone who wishes for great powers, you will be sorry." It was a principle of story construc-tion that later writers of science fiction would find particularly useful: every

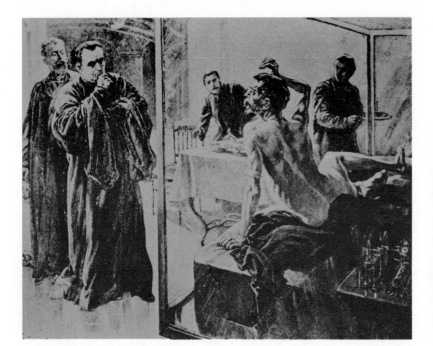

new ability, every invention, carries along with it a price; you gain something and you lose something.

In *When the Sleeper Wakes* (1899) Wells made a more systematic study of the trends of progress through a novel about a man who, like Bellamy's hero of *Looking Backward,* wakes after two centuries. He finds that the accumulated income from unearned legacies has made him the nominal owner of half the earth, but the real power is in the hands of a council of trustees. Graham is awed by technological progress:

> His first impression was of everwhelming architecture. The place into which he looked was an aisle of Titanic buildings, curving spaciously in either direction. Overhead mighty cantilevers sprang together across the huge width of the place, and a tracery of translucent material shut out the sky. Gigantic globes of cool white light shamed the pale sunbeams that filtered down through the girders and wires. Here and there a gossamer suspension bridge dotted with foot passengers flung across the chasm and the air was webbed with slender cables. A cliff of edifice hung above him, he perceived as he glanced upward, and the opposite façade was grey and dim and broken by great archings, circular perforations, balconies, buttresses, turret projections, myriads of vast windows, and an intricate scheme of architectural relief.

But he is astonished to find how little has been done for the common man. The rich are useless, conspicuous consumers and the poor have been forced into the Labour Company. The theme of the book, according to Williamson, is the relative and ambivalent nature of progress.

In *The First Men in the Moon* (1901) Wells, Williamson says, shows how specialization brought about by progress reaches its ultimate expression. In form, Wells's moon voyage is similar to the long tradition we have already traced through Lucian, Kepler, Godwin, Atterly, and Verne. But his expressed concern was "to look at mankind from a distance and burlesque the effects of specialization." His heroes, Cavor and Bedford, get to the moon in a round spaceship built by Cavor and propelled by an antigravity material called Cavorite. On the moon they find an advanced society which has gone to the ultimate limits of progress in the division of labor; the Selenites have carried specialization even further than the social insects: thinkers are almost all brains; machine tenders, almost all hands. Cavor, the selfless seeker after knowledge, at first regards the lunar society with admiration which later becomes mixed with horror.

Williamson views these five novels, along with some short stories, as a process in which Wells was testing progress. Williamson's theory is ingenious and persuasive—and we should not forget the potency, particularly for Wells, of Darwin's theories—but in the end perhaps a reading of Wells's five "scientific romances" as criticisms of progress, though they may be helpful in thinking about the works, is *too* ingenious. In his autobiography, Wells reads his life in other ways: "The main story is the development, the steady progressive growth of a modern version of the world and the way in which the planned reconstruction of human relationships in the form of a world state became at last the frame and test of my activities."

As Wells looked back from the vantage point of 1934:

> World forces were at work tending to disperse the aristocratic estate system in Europe, to abolish small traders, to make work in the retail trades less independent and satisfactory, to promote industrial co-ordination, increase productivity, necessitate new and better informed classes, evoke a new type of education and make it universal, break down political boundaries everywhere and bring all men into one planetary community. The story of my father and mother and all my family is just the story of so many individual particles in the great mass of humanity that was driving before the sweep of these as yet imperfectly apprehended powers of synthesis. . . . An outburst of discovery and invention in material things and of innovation in business and financial method, has, we realize, released so much human energy that, firstly, the need for sustained toil from anyone has been abolished, secondly, practically all parts of the world have been brought into closer interaction than were York and London three centuries ago and, thirdly, the destructive impulses of men have been so equipped, that it is no longer possible to contemplate a planet in which unconditioned war is even a remote possibility. We are waking up to the fact that a planned world-state governing the complex of human activities for the common good, however difficult to attain, has become imperative, and that until it is achieved, the history of the race must be now inevitably a record of catastrophic convulsions shot with mere glimpses and phases of temporary good luck. We are, as a species, caught in an irreversible process. No real going back to the old, comparatively stable condition of things is possible; set-backs will only prolong the tale of our racial disaster. We are therefore impelled to reconstruct the social and economic organization until the new conditions are satisfied.

By 1900 Wells found himself free from his old concerns about poverty and failure. He was sought after for his fiction and his society; he was meeting other writers, other kinds of thinkers, and great men in all kinds of careers. *The Island of Dr. Moreau* was so grim that it had a difficult time finding a publisher, but *The Invisible Man* ran serially in *Pearson's Weekly* and *The War of the Worlds* in *Pearson's Magazine* in England and in *Cosmopolitan* in the United States, as well as in syndication in American newspapers in late 1897 and early 1898, frequently with the locales of the destruction changed to fit the individual city, as they would be in Orson Welles's famous Mercury Theater dramatization in 1938 and in the 1953 George Pal motion picture. Its impact led to the commissioning of a sequel from Garrett P. Serviss, an astronomer and popular science writer, entitled *Edison's Conquest of Mars,* in which Thomas Alva Edison assembles the great minds of earth to build a space fleet armed with disintegrator rays to destroy the Martians before they can mount a second attack on earth.

The Strand and *Cosmopolitan* published *The First Men in the Moon* simultaneously in 1900–01. *Pearson's* and *Cosmopolitan* serialized the next big Wells science fiction novel, *The Food of the Gods,* in 1903–04; it described the invention of a special food which caused men (and, by accident, some insects and rats as well) to grow into giants, and their subsequent confrontation with the little people. A British newspaper outbid *Strand* and *Pearson's* for the serial rights to *In the Days of the Comet* (1906), a novel in which a comet passes close to the earth and the interaction of gases creates a new gas which completely changes human nature and creates a utopia.

Meanwhile, almost as soon as they were serialized the novels were being published in hard covers, and the short stories were being gathered together into collections. For the rest of his active writing career Wells, like Verne before him, would produce nearly two books a year.

But he was not confining his writing to science fiction. *Love and Mr. Lewisham* was published in 1900 and a series of other novels about modern life followed. Wells's writing career has been divided into three periods: the scientific romances (1895–1900), the comedies (1900–10), and the novels of ideas

Wells with Mr. & Mrs. George Bernard Shaw in 1902

A sequel to *War of the Worlds* by Garrett P. Serviss, 1947

(after 1910). Wells had become involved with the Fabian Society, whose discussions and debates about the road to a socialist utopia he had attended as a student at the Normal School, and he credits the Fabians with having "done much to deflect me from the drift toward a successful, merely literary career into which I was manifestly falling." It was in this stage that he turned to his utopian novels and his encyclopedist works in which he interpreted man's evolutionary progress in all its phases as a movement toward a unified world.

Undervalued for many years after his death and even in the last years of his life, in his early period he was compared to Robert Louis Stevenson or H. Rider Haggard or Jules Verne, in his comedies to Dickens, in the journalism of his last period to Defoe. (Such comparisons, Wells suggested, were created out of "the medieval assumption that whatever is worth knowing is already known and whatever is worth doing has already been done. . . . Anybody fresh who turned up was treated as an aspirant Dalai Lama is treated, and scrutinized for evidence of his predecessor's soul. So it came about that every one of us who started writing in the nineties, was discovered to be 'a second'—somebody or other.")

The new appreciation of Wells began in 1957 with the publication of an article by his (and Rebecca West's) son, Anthony West, in which West called George Orwell and St. John Ervine "the new obscurantists" who upheld a false image of Wells as "a mind led away to folly and despair by the nineteenth-century progressive fallacy and by a blind faith in science." West conceded that Wells had an optimistic phase, beginning about 1900, when success had brought him out of the rural and proletarian worlds in which he had grown up and into contact with men of wealth and intelligence who were also men of good will. However, Williamson suggests that in his early scientific romances Wells had eased his own tension, that he used the early fiction to discharge the buried emotions in conflict with his role in society and found in the ritual of social conformity an individual freedom of thought and behavior. Williamson notes with some astonishment how the unconventional Wells was able to get on with people, keeping the affections of his parents and brother, ending his unfortunate first marriage without bitterness, and conducting his extramarital affairs without losing his second wife.

Still from the Alexander Korda movie, *The Shape of Things to Come*, 1936

This optimistic period after 1900 produced the utopias which gave the name "Wellsian" to a vision of a world filled with super-gadgets and mechanical wonders, run by an elite of scientists and engineers for the good of the people—much like the ending of the 1936 motion picture made from his 1934 novel *The Shape of Things to Come.*

But Wells considered the writing of utopias to be the major function of a man concerned with the groupings of people working together that we call societies —that is, of a sociologist. In 1906 Wells read a paper to the Sociological Society entitled "The So-Called Science of Sociology" in which he denied that Herbert Spencer and Auguste Comte had created a new and fruitful system of human inquiry, and denied even that a science of sociology was possible. Everything in the universe, he said, is unique (remember the "Rediscovery of the Unique"?), and sociologists cannot deal with people in sufficiently large numbers to make possible the kind of generalizations, say, that physicists make about atoms. Instead, Wells suggested, sociology "must be neither art simply, nor science in the narrow meaning of the word at all, but knowledge rendered imaginatively, and with an element of personality; that is to say, in the highest sense of the term, literature." One literary form recognized as valuable to sociology, Wells said, is historical fiction. Another, utopian fiction, is usually neglected and is more important. "I think, in fact, that the creation of utopias—and their exhaustive criticism—is the proper and distinctive method of sociology."

I figure to myself a similar book, a sort of dream book of huge dimensions, in reality perhaps dispersed in many volumes by many hands, upon the Ideal Society. This book, this picture of the perfect state, would be the backbone of sociology. It would have great sections devoted to such questions as the extent of the Ideal Society, its relations to racial differences, the relations of the sexes in it, its economic organisations, its organisation for thought and education, its "Bible"—as Dr. Beattie Crozier would say—its housing and social atmosphere, and so forth.

"To a very great extent," Mark Hillegas wrote in *The Future as Nightmare:*

Two illustrations from the
1908 edition of *The War in
the Air*

H. G. Wells and the Anti-Utopians, "Wells devoted the rest of his life to writing
—and criticizing—this dream book."

In 1902, before the Royal Institution, Wells distinguished between two kinds
of minds. The first, oriented to the past, regards the future "as sort of black
nonexistence upon which the advancing present will presently write events."
That is the legal mind, always referring to precedents. The second kind of
mind, oriented to the future, is constructive, creative, organizing. "It sees the
world as one great workshop, and the present as no more than material for the
future, for the thing that is yet destined to be." Finally, Wells predicted what
might be accomplished if the future-oriented mind were given freedom to
express itself:

All this world is heavy with the promise of greater things, and a day will come, one day
in the unending succession of days, when beings who are now latent in our thoughts
and hidden in our loins, shall stand upon this earth as one stands upon a footstool and
shall laugh and reach out their hands amidst the stars.

According to the standards of the later anti-utopian writers, Wells's first
books could be considered "anti-Wellsian." But after that phase had been completed, Wells launched into writing his dream book, into describing his ideal
state, in novels like a *Modern Utopia* (1905), *The War in the Air* (1908), *The
World Set Free* (1914), *Men Like Gods* (1923), and *The Shape of Things to
Come* (1934). For Wells, the shape of things to come—and the bogies against
which the anti-utopian writers who followed him would react—involved a massive, civilization-destroying war (sometimes with atomic weapons, as in *The
World Set Free,* which makes him one of the first writers to deal with the
question of atomic bombs) followed by a beneficent reign of scientists and
engineers.

Other elements in Wells's dream book: massive cities, sometimes roofed with
glass, while the countryside is relatively deserted and sometimes is tilled by
machine; travel by ship to the moon; the abolition of the home; education of
children in crèches; improvement of medicine and increase in longevity; the
freeing of mankind from labor by the perfection of machines; free, rapid movement from place to place; the withering away of government; a great central
index to all the world's inhabitants, so that the state is kept informed of each
individual's location; regulated parenthood; eugenics; the World State.

A Modern Utopia, which Wells attributed to his early fascination with Plato
("Plato ruled over the making of that book"), is an example of Wells's concepts
of citizenship: a class of samurai, an order of "voluntary nobility," are similar to
Plato's Guardians in *The Republic* and can be traced on to Heinlein's citizen-
soldiers in *Starship Troopers.* In the samurai resides all political power: they

From *Modern Utopia,* 1905

are the only administrators, lawyers, practicing doctors, and public officials of almost every sort, and the only voters. They exist—compare Plato and Heinlein —because Wells believed that the intricacy of utopian organization demanded more powerful and efficient methods of control than the democratic process allowed. The order of samurai is open to any adult over 25 who is in a reasonably healthy and efficient state, and who has passed the exit examination of a college or upper school. If he joins the order, he must follow the "Rule," which forbids such things as alcohol, drugs, smoking, betting, usury, games, trade, and servants. He must wear the plain dress of the order and keep himself in good health and physical condition, and he must keep his mind alert by reading a certain number of new books a year. He must be chaste but not celibate, though if he marries he may remain in the order only if his wife at least follows the woman's "Lesser Rule." Finally, each year he must spend at least seven consecutive days alone in a wild, solitary place developing his inner resources.

C. S. Lewis

It was against this vision of a beneficent reign of scientists and engineers following world cataclysm, and in the context of the disillusion of World War I, the excesses of communism, the failure of capitalism in a worldwide depression, World War II and its accompanying brutalities and civilian warfare and genocide, that the anti-utopias were written: E. M. Forster's "The Machine Stops" (1909); Evgennii Zamyatin's *We* (1924); in a sense Karel Capek's *R.U.R.* (1921); Aldous Huxley's *Brave New World* (1932) and *Ape and Essence* (1946); C. S. Lewis's *Out of the Silent Planet* (1938), *Perelandra* (1943), and *That Hideous Strength* (1945), which, Kingsley Amis points out, were attacks on utopia from a conservative Christian right instead of a disillusioned left; Ayn Rand's *Anthem* (1938) and *Atlas Shrugged* (1957); George Orwell's *1984* (1947); Franz Werfel's *Star of the Unborn* (1946); Gore Vidal's *Messiah* (1953); Evelyn Waugh's *Love Among the Ruins* (1953); Anthony Burgess's *A Clockwork Orange* (1962) and *The Wanting Seed* (1963); and others.

The anti-utopia returned to the mainstream of science fiction with *The Space Merchants* (1953), by Frederik Pohl and Cyril Kornbluth, serialized in *Galaxy* as *Gravy Planet* in 1952. About the same time came Kurt Vonnegut's *Player Piano* (1952). They were soon followed by Arthur Clarke's *Childhood's End* (1953); Pohl's "The Midas Plague" (1954), Ray Bradbury's *Fahrenheit 451* (1954) which actually was published originally as a short novel called *The Fireman* in 1951, and a variety of Robert Sheckley stories and novels such as *The Status Civilization* (1960) and many others.

George Orwell

The utopia meanwhile had almost disappeared, although B. F. Skinner's *Walden Two* (1948) and Aldous Huxley's *Island* (1962) may represent the beginning of a new cycle.

The influence of Wells on the writers who followed him was summed up by George Orwell in 1945:

> Thinking people who were born about the beginning of this century are in some sense Wells's own creation. How much influence any mere writer has, and especially a "popular" writer whose work takes effect quickly, is questionable, but I doubt whether anyone who was writing books between 1900 and 1920, at any rate in the English language, influenced the young so much. The minds of all of us, and therefore the physical world, would be perceptibly different if Wells never existed.

His influence lingers on in the persistent reactions to his utopian visions. Whether he shaped them himself or reflected the visions of his times, he made them current, gave them form, and dramatized them, even though in the end, like Verne, he denounced them in a despairing book called *Mind at the End of Its Tether.*

Before then, however, he had turned to other writings, to his contemporary novels of life and manners and to nonfiction, such as the *Outline of History* (1919), which sold more than 2 million copies between 1919 and 1934; *The Science of Life* (1930), with his son, G. P. Wells, and Julian Huxley; and *The Work, Wealth and Happiness of Mankind* (1931). These three books formed a trilogy aimed at showing what the world and mankind were like and how business and science fitted into the scheme of things.

His autobiography suggests that he felt most pleased with such contemporary novels as *Kipps* (1905), *Tono Bungay* (1909), *Mr. Britling Sees It Through*

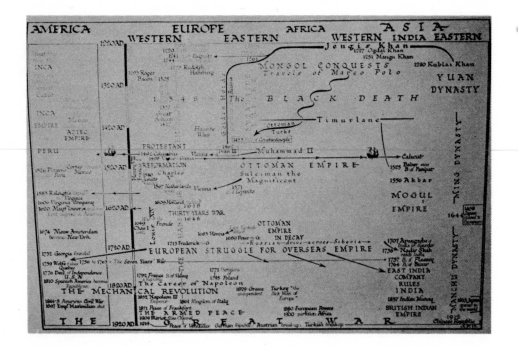

From *Outline of History*

(1915), and *Joan and Peter* (1918), but his science fiction, in particular his earlier scientific romances, have outlasted them. His influence on science fiction, moreover, has been greater than his influence on intellectual history. In a sense the science fiction writers of the forties and fifties and at least part of the sixties were the children of Wells. They were writers who in their youth had been unable to find sufficient science fiction in magazines to satisfy their thirst for fantasy and their hunger for the future. They had searched the dim, book-lined corridors of public libraries for anything that resembled science fiction, and they had dug out the old books by Jules Verne, H. Rider Haggard, Sir Arthur Conan Doyle, and H. G. Wells—particularly H. G. Wells. And the ideas shaped the writers.

Wells had these ideas by the hundreds—ideas which, in the best tradition of science fiction, seemed as if they had never been thought before: time travel by mechanical means, creation of artificial men, invisibility through chemical transparency or induced by speed of movement, attack on earth by extraterrestrials, world-controlling wealth through compound interest, antigravity, biologically controlled specialization, superman, duplicate or parallel worlds, the destruction of life by cosmic accident, the impact of the airplane and the tank on warfare, the atomic bomb and worldwide destruction, improvement of the species by alien influence, man-eating plants, attack by creatures from the sea, conquest by ants, displaced vision, the hatching of extinct eggs, wandering bodies from space which threaten earth, interplanetary television receivers, prehistoric people. . . .

The list seems endless. In a sense Wells became the father of modern science fiction because of his productivity; in a sense because of the originality of his ideas; in a sense because of his example—he made science fiction both a popular and a literary success. As Raymond Chandler was to say about Dashiell Hammett, ". . . an art which is capable of [*The Maltese Falcon*] is not 'by hypothesis' incapable of anything. Once a detectve story can be as good as this, only the pedants will deny that it *could* be even better."

Wells shifted the focus of science fiction from the individual to society. Although his stories were customarily narrated through the limited viewpoint of a single individual, that person was almost always an ordinary individual representative of his class or his society; through his thoughts and reactions we obtain in part the social implications Wells wished to impart. Science fiction would revert from time to time to romance and the romantic hero of unusual abilities or stature, but it would never be quite the same.

And Wells developed theories about writing and techniques that he could pass on to other writers:

The thing that makes such imaginations interesting is their translation into commonplace terms and a rigid exclusion of other marvels from the story. Then it becomes human. How would you feel and what might not happen to you, is the typical question, if for instance pigs could fly and one came rocketing over a hedge at you. How would you feel and what might not happen to you if suddenly you were changed into an ass and couldn't tell anyone about it? Or if you suddenly became invisible? But no one would think twice about the answer if hedges and houses also began to fly, or if people changed into lions, tigers, cats, and dogs left and right, or if anyone could vanish anyhow. Nothing remains interesting where anything may happen.

And:

For the writer of fantastic stories to help the reader to play the game properly, he must help him in every possible unobtrusive way to *domesticate* the impossible hypothesis. He must trick him into an unwary concession to some plausible assumption and get on with his story while the illusion holds.

And the ideas Wells held about the world and the way he tried to change the world to suit them seemed to sum up for many years the attitude of the science fiction writer and reader:

Most individual creatures since life began have been "up against it" all the time, have been driven continually by fear and cravings, have had to respond to the unresting antagonisms of their surroundings, and they have found a sufficient and sustaining interest in the drama of immediate events provided for them by these demands. Essentially, their living was continuous adjustment to happenings. Good hap and ill hap filled it entirely. They hungered and ate and they desired and loved; they were amused and attracted, they pursued or escaped, they were overtaken and they died.

But with the dawn of human foresight and with the appearance of a great surplus of energy in life such as the last century or so has revealed, there has been a progressive emancipation of the attention from everyday urgencies. What was once the whole of life, has become to an increasing extent, merely the background of life. People can ask now what would have been an extraordinary question five hundred years ago. They can say, "Yes, you earn a living, you support a family, you love and hate, but—*what do you do?*" . . .

In studies and studios and laboratories, administrative bureaus and exploring expeditions, a new world is germinated and develops. It is not a repudiation of the old but a vast extention of it, in a racial synthesis into which individual aims will ultimately be absorbed. We originative intellectual workers are reconditioning human life.

Of his own efforts in this respect, Wells said:

I have found the attempt to disentangle the possible drift of life in general and of human life in particular from the confused stream of events, and the means of controlling that drift, if such are to be found, more important and interesting by far than anything else. I have had, I believe, an aptitude for it. . . .

Wells meeting with Molotov in Russia

Wells himself denied that he had been influenced by his most distinguished science fiction predecessor, and he resisted being called the English Jules Verne, just as Verne had resented the way in which the young Englishman had usurped the position he had created for himself with a pedestal of books. Wells wrote:

There's a quality in the worst of my so-called "pseudo-scientific" (imbecile adjective) stuff which differentiates it from Jules Verne, *e.g.*, just as Swift is differentiated from Fantasia—isn't there? There is something other than either story writing or artistic merit which has emerged through the series of my books. Something one might regard as a new system of ideas—"thought."

Wells traced his influences to Swift. In the history of the many-versioned *Time Machine*, he wrote, "A cleansing course of Swift and Sterne intervened before the idea was written again for Henley's *National Observer*."

What Wells did was important. What he thought was influential. But what may be more significant than either was what, by his example, he showed was possible.

And it is the possible of which science fiction is made.

CHAPTER 7

THE RISE OF THE PULPS: 1911–1926

As THE NINETEENTH CENTURY became the twentieth, the United States was ready for progress and the romance of progress and for the fiction that would sum up these dreams as meaningful human adventures.

Senator Chauncey Depew of New York said, "There is not a man here who does not feel 400 percent bigger in 1900 than he did in 1896, bigger intellectually, bigger hopefully, bigger patriotically." And Senator Mark Hanna of Ohio said, "Furnaces are glowing, spindles are singing their song. Happiness comes to us all with prosperity."

And Henry James said of that time, "The will to grow was everywhere written large, and to grow at no matter what or whose expense."

In France Jules Verne was still turning out his two books a year, although his hand and his powers of invention were growing weary, and in England H. G. Wells had just completed his anti-utopian novels, with their gloomy view of progress, and was beginning his comedies. H. Rider Haggard was writing his novels of adventure placed in remote corners of the world or the past, Sir Arthur Conan Doyle was trying to escape Sherlock Holmes by writing historical novels, and M. P. Shiel was developing his novels of future war and catastrophe.

But the mood of the United States was Vernian. Wages were low but rising, and prices were not exorbitant: eggs were a penny apiece, butter was twenty-four cents a pound, sirloin steak sold for the same, and a turkey dinner cost twenty cents. Everywhere machinery was being introduced to do old things better or to do things that no one had ever done before: ride in an automobile or a subway, see a motion picture.

If Americans were optimistic and self-confident at the turn of the century, they had good reason. Over the past 100 years, the nation had expanded from five million people in a few Eastern states to 76 million spread across a continent. A nation of farms had become the world's leading industrial power with literate, productive workers educated in a newly built system of public education. Every fact and figure produced by a recently completed census suggested an even more glorious future.

The promise, in most of its outline, was not an illusion: each year brought new discoveries and inventions, and each technological advance provided new impetus for accelerating change and subtly altered day by day the ways in which people thought about their lives, their societies, their political structures, their communities, their families, and themselves.

In 1900 came the invention of cellophane, the dirigible, and the caterpillar tractor; in 1901, the mercury vapor lamp—and President McKinley was assassinated by an anarchist. In 1902 the radio telephone was invented; in 1903, the Wright brothers flew the first heavier-than-air machine. Just nine days before,

Samuel Langley, the secretary of the Smithsonian Institution, had failed to launch a flying machine from the roof of a houseboat on the Potomac; it had cost the War Department $50,000 and Langley five years of effort. Almost everybody was sure that man would never fly. Not until 1908, in fact, was there a general awakening to the fact that man was flying, and then the air became filled with men.

In 1904 came the invention of the vacuum-tube diode and the signing of the Entente Cordiale by England and France, which became the Triple Entente when Russia signed in 1907.

In 1905 an obscure Swiss patent-office examiner named Einstein announced a new theory of physics called relativity.

In 1906 the vacuum-tube triode was invented and Britain launched the *Dreadnaught*, the first large battleship. In 1907 came the invention of the helicopter, Bakelite, and the vacuum cleaner.

In 1909 Robert Peary reached the North Pole. In 1911 Roald Amundsen reached the South Pole; and the combine, air conditioning, and the gyrocompass were invented. In 1913 came the invention of the hot filament x-ray tube and the multimotored airplane.

In 1914 the Panama Canal was opened, World War I began, and the tank was invented, bearing a strong resemblance to the description in a 1904 H. G. Wells story in the *Strand* called "The Land Ironclads."

They were essentially long, narrow, and very strong steel frameworks carrying the engines, and borne upon eight pairs of big pedrail wheels, each about ten feet in diameter, each a driving wheel and set upon long axles free to swivel round a common axis. This arrangement gave them the maximum of adaptability to the contours of the ground. They crawled level along the ground with one foot high upon a hillock and another deep in a depression, and they could hold themselves erect and steady sideways upon even a steep hillside. The engineers directed the engines under the command of the captain, who had look-out points at small ports all round the upper edge of the

Albert Einstein in his twenties

The Wright brothers first flight at Kitty Hawk, December 17, 1903

In his 1903 *Strand* story, "The Land Ironclads," Wells described a vehicle remarkably like the modern tank

adjustable skirt of twelve-inch iron-plating which protected the whole affair, and who could also raise or depress a conning-tower set about the port-holes through the centre of the iron top cover. The riflemen each occupied a small cabin of peculiar construction, and these cabins were slung along the sides of and before and behind the great main framework, in a manner suggestive of the slinging of the seats of an Irish jaunting-car. . . .

Although Wells was incorrect in extrapolating from the seagoing warships of his time—his "land ironclads" were 80 to 100 feet long and contained a substantial crew—rather than the truck or tractor, he was right about the tank's revolutionary effect on warfare, and in his autobiography he criticized the reluctant, unimaginative use of it in World War I.

In 1915 came the invention of the radio-tube oscillator and the arc searchlight, and in 1916, stainless steel.

In 1917 the Communist Revolution broke out in Russia.

In 1918 an armistice ended World War I, and the mass spectroscope and the automatic electric toaster were invented. In 1920 the League of Nations was established in Geneva. In 1922 the Union of Soviet Socialist Republics was created, Mussolini became premier of Italy, and radar was invented. In 1923 Hitler was imprisoned after the Beer Hall Putsch and wrote *Mein Kampf*, and the iconoscope scanner and the bulldozer were invented.

In 1924 Lenin died and Stalin won the power struggle that followed.

World War I with its trench warfare had stripped battle of any remaining glamor (except in the air, where a kind of romantic knighthood had a brief new flowering) and had ended the easy optimism of the twentieth century's first decade; that disillusion would breed a lost generation and an entire genre of anti-utopias.

But all that was still in the future. Also in the future, for the United States at the turn of the century, were six decades of remarkable expansion interrupted by periods of wartime and economic dislocation. The expansion would fuel a basic belief in progress into which the dislocations would insert moments of uncertainty and self-doubt. By 1960 population would increase by more than 100 million over the 76 million of 1900, high-school graduates from 100,000 to nearly 2 million, college enrollments from 238,000 to more than 3 million, life expectancy from 47.3 years to 69.7 years, the average wage from 22 cents per hour for a 59-hour week to $2.26 an hour for a 39.7-hour week, and the gross national product from under $17 billion to more than $500 billion.

In 1900 people in the United States had good reason for looking at the future with optimism; they knew the world was changing, but change looked like a friend bringing gifts rather than a thief coming to steal away their inheritance. Years later, in *The Lonely Crowd*, Riesman would speak of "inner-directed" and "other-directed" people and societies, but the American people were becoming future-directed.

Teddy Roosevelt summed up some of the spirit of that time, a spirit that would seep into science fiction as well. H. G. Wells visited Roosevelt in 1906, and the President brought up *The Time Machine* to disagree with its pessimism. Wells recalled their conversation: "If one chose to say America must presently lose the impetus of her ascent, that she and all mankind must culminate and pass, he [Roosevelt] could not conclusively deny that possibility. Only he chose to live as if this were not so." And he continued, as Wells remembered:

Theodore Roosevelt

"Suppose, after all," he said slowly, "that should prove to be right, and it all ends in your butterflies and morlocks. *That doesn't matter now.* The effort's real. It's worth going on with. It's worth it. It's worth it—even so."

This kind of environment encouraged the further development of science fiction. Jules Verne had proved that people were eager to read about future wonders and wonderful voyages; H. G. Wells had demonstrated that science and the future could be the subject of literature; and the magazines had proved that they could be printed and distributed economically even at a dime a copy, that the public was eager for fiction, and that part of the mix of fiction desired by a sizable share of the reading public was fiction about science, adventures in strange worlds, wonderful journeys, and cautionary tales about possible catastrophes and possible future societies.

The pulps had been created in 1896, as Frank Munsey's *Golden Argosy* evolved into *Argosy*, 192 pages of fiction for a dime. That was just a dozen years after the invention of pulp paper, a rough-surfaced printing medium which yellowed quickly (it contained within itself the acid of its own destruction), shredded readily, and did not reproduce pictures well, but which had one outstanding virtue: it was cheap. It was made from wood shredded to fibers and then reduced to pulp by chemicals, then pressed and dried on a mesh mold.

For much of their history the pulp magazines had covers that extended past the body of the magazine, and ragged edges caused by the pages being slit or torn rather than trimmed. The result may have been visually interesting, but produced a cover easily bent or torn and edges that constantly showered readers with small flakes of paper. One could immediately single out the reader of pulp magazines by the garish cover of the publication he was reading, or (if he had torn the cover off or hidden it behind another magazine) by the snow of paper flakes on his clothing.

Circulation of *Argosy* doubled when it changed to an all-fiction policy. For four years it remained about 80,000 and then took off, reaching a half-million by 1905. Munsey made $237,000 from the magazine in 1904, $300,000 in 1907. Matthew White, Jr., who had become the editor in 1889, remained in that position until 1928.

The popularity of science fiction was making itself evident with the publication of H. G. Wells's stories and serials, particularly *The War of the Worlds* and *The First Men in the Moon* in *Cosmopolitan*, and science fiction began to appear with some frequency in *Argosy*. One example is William Wallace Cook's *Round Trip to the Year 2000*, which ran serially from July to November 1903, and featured a revolt by mechanical robots called "muglugs." Sam Moskowitz speculates that if the novel had possessed more literary merit, we might today be referring to robots as "muglugs." Fortunately, the world waited for Karel Čapek's 1921 play, *R.U.R.* (Rossum's Universal Robots), in which Čapek took the word robot from the Czech word *robota*, which means involuntary service or work.

Street & Smith, which had built up a publishing empire based on dime novels and magazines for boys, began issuing *Popular Magazine* in 1903 as a boy's magazine under the editorship of experienced dime-novel editor Henry Harrison Lewis; but in 1904, under editor Charles Agnew MacLean, it changed to "adventure fiction" and increased its pages from 96 to 194. In its second year it obtained the American serial rights to H. Rider Haggard's *Ayesha* (the sequel

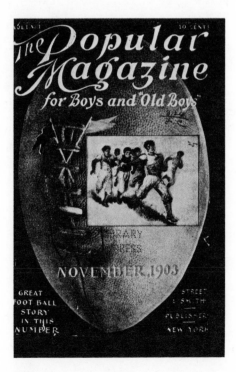 

LEFT: November, 1903
(Vol. 1, No. 1)

RIGHT: January, 1905
(featuring *Ayesha*)

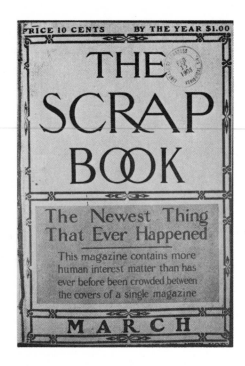

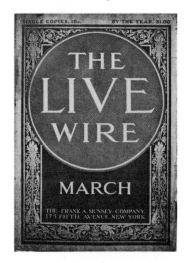

to *She* for which the world had waited for eighteen years), and during its run *Popular Magazine's* circulation increased from 70,000 to nearly 250,000.

Munsey brought out a new pulp magazine, *All-Story*, in 1905. Robert H. Davis, who had come to work for *Munsey's Magazine* the year before as fiction editor, was in charge. He would remain until 1926, the year after Munsey's death, and would become famous as an editor and a discoverer of new talent. Within a year the magazine had a printing of 250,000.

The Monthly Story Magazine, which came out in 1905, reached greater fame when it became the *Blue Book* in 1907.

In 1906 Street & Smith brought out new competition, the *People's Magazine*, and Munsey started *The Scrap Book*, with Robert Davis as editor and Perley Poore Sheehan as managing editor. *The Scrap Book* proposed to publish a wide variety of short items, perhaps modeled after *Tit-Bits*, and even offered to buy scrapbooks. In 1907 Munsey experimented with publishing the magazine in two sections—the second section all fiction—for twenty-five cents, but the next year it went back to its previous form.

In 1906 Munsey also published the first specialized pulp magazine, the *Railroad Man's Magazine*, which was filled with railroad stories; the second specialized magazine, the *Ocean*, which offered 192 pages of sea stories for a dime, came out in 1907 but lasted only a year. *The Live Wire* was published by Munsey in 1908 to exploit the original concept of *The Scrap Book*, but was merged with that magazine within a few months. In 1908 the fiction section of *The Scrap Book* assumed the title of *Cavalier*, and shortly thereafter *Cavalier* became a separate magazine; Bob Davis, of course, was editor (*The Scrap Book* lasted through 1911).

The slick magazines were paying reasonably good rates for their fiction: many paid five cents a word, and established authors negotiated their own rates. Davis had an agreement with O. Henry to pay ten cents a word for each story he accepted if it was submitted first to *Munsey's Magazine*. But in the pulps the customary rates were one-half to one cent a word, and the Munsey magazines were almost the only ones which paid upon acceptance. A full-length serial often brought the author only $400; Garrett P. Serviss, who had written *Edison's Conquest of Mars* some years before, received $400 from *The Scrap Book* for his 65,000-word novel *The Sky Pirate*.

In another novel, *A Columbus of Space*, serialized in *All-Story* in 1909, Serviss described a spaceship powered by atomic energy derived from uranium and a Venus whose clouds parted only once in a lifetime to reveal a huge, burning sun which drove the Venusians mad. If that concept seems familiar, readers may be remembering the more definitive form that appeared in 1941, when Isaac Asimov developed into the classic "Nightfall" an idea suggested by John Campbell from a quotation by Ralph Waldo Emerson: "If the stars should appear one night in a thousand years, how would men believe and adore, and preserve for many generations the remembrance of the city of God."

Short Stories, which was founded in 1890 to publish classics and translations, was bought by Doubleday in 1910 and converted into a 160-page pulp. In 1910 and 1911 all Munsey magazines were having circulation problems. Munsey's reaction was to order pulp action-covers and inside illustrations for his three pulp magazines. Moskowitz, who has recorded a history and anthology of the Munsey magazines in his *Under the Moons of Mars*, suggests that another favorite circulation remedy was to increase the quantity of science fiction.

The Scrap Book was combined with *Cavalier* in 1912. Serviss's masterpiece, *The Second Deluge*, was published in *Cavalier* in 1911; the novel described a new worldwide flood caused when the earth passed through a small nebula composed of water. The earth was left under oceans six miles deep, but a second Noah, astronomer Cosmo Versal, had predicted the event and built a gigantic ark. Later the novel was published in hard covers and reprinted in *Amazing Stories* in that magazine's first year, in *Amazing Stories Quarterly* in 1933, and in *Fantastic Novels* in 1948.

Another author who became, with Serviss, one of the two most popular science fiction authors of his time was George Allan England. His four-part novel, *The Elixir of Hate*, was published in *Cavalier* in 1911. It involved a man who swallowed a scientist's elixir of life and kept growing younger, a theme that would become, in the hands of F. Scott Fitzgerald, "The Curious Case of Benjamin Button," a 1920 story in which a man is born 70 years old and gradually grows younger until he ends up as a baby in a crib.

George Allan England

When *Cavalier* merged with *The Scrap Book* it became a weekly and featured a new novel by England, the first of a trilogy that would become his most famous work, *Darkness and Dawn*. The first 50,000-word novel tells about an engineer and his secretary, who awaken after many centuries in a state of mysterious suspended animation to find themselves in the ruins of New York City:

> The Jersey shore, the Palisades, the Bronx, and Long Island all lay buried in dense forests of conifers and oak, with only here or there some skeleton mockery of a steel structure jutting through.
>
> The islands in the harbor, too, were thickly overgrown. With a gasp of dismay and pain, Beatrice pointed out the fact that Liberty no longer held her bronze torch aloft. . . .
>
> Fringing the water-front, all the way round, the mournful remains of the docks and piers lay in a mere sodden jumble of decay, with an occasional hulk sunk alongside.
>
> Even over these wrecks of liners, vegetation was growing rank and green. All the wooden ships, barges, and schooners had utterly vanished. . . .

The novel continues with their adventures as they seek food, shelter, and the remnants of civilization. Its publishing history includes serialization in the *New York Evening Mail* in 1912 as *The Last New Yorkers*, hard-cover publication—along with its two sequels, *Beyond the Great Oblivion* and *The Afterglow*—as *Darkness and Dawn*, a 1940 reprinting in *Famous Fantastic Mysteries*, and another hard-cover publication in 1965.

Reader's sections, for editorial comments and letters to the editor, had been part of the *Popular Magazine* almost from its start. One was added to *Argosy* in 1911, to *Cavalier* in 1912. Later that year *Cavalier* tried to organize its readers with the founding of what Bob Davis called the "Cavalier Legion" and offered a free button bearing a green star in a red circle and the slogan "Good Fiction, Good Fellowship." Two years later Arthur Sullivant Hoffman, editor of *Adventure*, would create a similar organization whose name would be taken over by veterans in 1919—the American Legion.

Edgar Rice Burroughs, 1912

Even as a weekly, *Cavalier* retained its circulation of approximately 75,000. *Argosy* had a solid circulation in 1911. But the future of *All-Story* was uncertain. Then, on August 24, 1911, an unknown writer sent to managing editor Thomas

Newell Metcalf 43,000 words of an uncompleted novel entitled *Dejah Thoris, Martian Princess,* and asked that if accepted it be printed over the name of "Normal Bean." The author was Edgar Rice Burroughs, a 35-year-old failure at a dozen different enterprises and occupations.

But Burroughs thought he could write pulp fiction and sell it. "If people were paid for writing rot such as I read I could write stories just as rotten," he recalled in 1929. "I knew absolutely that I could write stories just as entertaining and probably a lot more so than any I chanced to read in those magazines."

When Metcalf asked Burroughs to finish the story for him, Burroughs, then living in Chicago, asked about rates of payment, saying that his sole motive for writing the story was his need for the money, that there was no sentiment involved, "although I became very much interested in it while writing."

The novel was serialized as *Under the Moons of Mars,* by (because of an artist's error) "Norman Bean." For the 65,000-word serial, *All-Story* paid Burroughs $400. It was a bargain, for Burroughs began writing, as some writers do, at the top of his form. In *Under the Moons of Mars* were all the characteristics that later would make him rich and famous: the mysterious circumstances, the unfettered imagination, the persistent action, the unabashed coincidences, the Victorian code which governed the behavior of his heroes—all of them flawed but in their totality weaving tapestries of far-off romantic adventure that had never before been displayed.

Under the Moons of Mars (published in book form as *A Princess of Mars*) still is the favorite of many Burroughs' fans. It begins with John Carter, who has just discovered a fabulous gold mine, fleeing from pursuing Indians and hiding in a cave. He falls into a strange sleep which leaves him paralyzed while some mysterious creature moans behind him. Then he finds himself freed from his own body and walks onto the ledge outside the cave to look at the night sky. One large red star in particular attracts his attention:

—it was Mars, the god of war, and for me, the fighting man, it had always held the power of irresistible enchantment. As I gazed at it on that far-gone night it seemed to call across the unthinkable void, to lure me to it, to draw me as the lodestone attracts a particle of iron.

My longing was beyond the power of opposition; I closed my eyes, stretched out my arms toward the god of my vocation and felt myself drawn with the suddenness of thought through the trackless immensity of space. There was an instant of extreme cold and utter darkness.

And the next chapter begins:

I opened my eyes upon a strange and weird landscape. I knew that I was on Mars; not once did I question either my sanity or my wakefulness. I was not asleep, no need for pinching here; my inner consciousness told me as plainly that I was upon Mars as your conscious mind tells you that you are upon Earth. You do not question the fact; neither did I.

Burroughs' Mars was implausibly strange: green savages 15 feet tall, with four arms, equipped with swords and firearms, riding 10-feet-tall, eight-legged beasts, and inhabiting magnificent ruined cities on the edges of the dead sea bottoms. Along canals flowing with life-giving water lived a more civilized but still warlike race of man-sized and man-shaped red men, who had flying machines and other remnants of what was a greater civilization before Mars began to die, and who maintained the atmosphere plant that provided all Mars with air to breathe. In subsequent adventures John Carter discovers, in inaccessible areas at the poles, hidden civilizations of the three legendary original races of Mars, white men, black men, and yellow men, plus strange ruins and artifacts and astonishing flora and fauna, most of it bloodthirsty, including great white apes and plant men. In one adventure after another, usually in pursuit of his lost love or even a friend, he emerges victorious as the greatest fighting man on Mars.

There are many elements of the pseudo-scientific, invention-by-analogy sort of paraphernalia, and there are touches of the downright ridiculous—the Martians, for instance, reproduce by eggs that are incubated to maturity, but John Carter not only woos and wins his Martian princess (who has what Burroughs delicately refers to as a "bosom"), they also have a son ("not a day passed

Burroughs as a cowboy
in Idaho, 1891

February, 1912 (contained
Under the Moons of Mars)

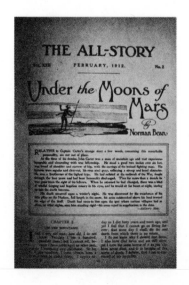

when I was in the city that Dejah Thoris and I did not stand hand in hand before our little shrine planning for the future, when the delicate shell should break"). But Burroughs usually attempted to achieve some measure of verisimilitude. His "Barsoom" bears a general relationship to the concept of Mars popularized by Percival Lowell in his books *Mars and Its Canals* (1906) and *Mars as the Abode of Life* (1908), although Professor Richard D. Mullen has demonstrated that Burroughs used no more of Lowell than he might have learned from a casual reading of newspapers and popular magazines, and even then his Barsoom and its customs varied considerably through eleven books. And Burroughs used a Poe-like device to lend conviction to his narration, a device that he would use for almost all his later books: the hero tells his story to Burroughs or through Burroughs by various means—in the John Carter books through the manuscripts or notes that Carter makes on his periodic returns to Earth; in the David Innes books of the Pellucidar series through personal narration in a Saharan oasis and then by telegraphy; in the Carson Napier Venus series through telepathy. He discarded the narrative method in the Tarzan series, after the first book, as an unnecessary encumbrance.

Burroughs' readers ignored or forgave his flaws: in return he gave them a good story filled with invention and adventure told by a courageous hero battling incredible odds for the love of a beautiful woman. For many an earthbound reader it was the stuff of daydreams, and Burroughs recalled how he had daydreamed many of the fantastic stories he later set down. But his reputation had not yet been built in 1912 when *Under the Moons of Mars* ran serially. Metcalf had suggested that Burroughs write a historical novel. Burroughs obediently wrote *The Outlaw of Torn*, which Metcalf rejected three times. Then, on June 4, 1912, Burroughs submitted a new novel called *Tarzan of the Apes*. *All-Story* bought it for $700 and published it complete in the October 1912 issue (now a prime collector's item).

Both of Burroughs' first published novels brought forth a remarkable response from readers, including letters of praise and threats of violence against Burroughs and Metcalf if they did not produce sequels—for both novels end with typical Burroughs cliff-hangers: *Under the Moons of Mars* concludes with all of Mars dying because of the failure of the atmosphere plant and John Carter returned unwillingly to his Earth body, not knowing whether he had saved Mars, and Dejah Thoris, with his heroics; *Tarzan* ends with the noble ape-man concealing the proof of his parentage, renouncing the Greystoke estate so that it will go to Cecil Clayton, and giving up Jane Porter so that she can marry Cecil.

Inexplicably, Metcalf rejected the sequel to *Tarzan*, called *Ape Man*, but serialized *The Gods of Mars*, second in the Mars series, beginning in January 1913. In this novel John Carter, mastering the process of projecting his astral self (though in the flesh) to Mars, discovers the white and black races and the terrible truth behind the Martian religion, which induces Martians (who live to be 1,000) to go on a final pilgrimage down the River Iss to death.

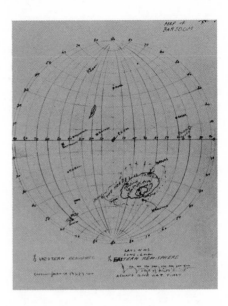

Map of "Barsoom"

Burroughs in 1916

In 1912, *All-Story* ran the novel that was to begin it all: *Tarzan of the Apes.* At left is the original manuscript and pen.

On February 6, 1913, the first story in the Pellucidar series arrived, a short novel called "The Inner World." It was built around a concept we have seen more than once before, the concept of a hollow Earth. Pellucidar is a savage world lit by Earth's molten core; it is at an earlier stage of evolutionary development than Earth; cavemen coexist with dinosaurs; and the dominant form of life is a species of winged reptile. David Innes reaches the inner world by accident, while testing a "mechanical subterranean prospector" invented by eccentric Abner Perry:

> Roughly, it is a steel cylinder a hundred feet long, and jointed so that it may turn and twist through solid rock if need be. At one end is a mighty revolving drill operated by an engine which Perry said generated more power to the cubic inch than any other engine did to the cubic foot. . . . We passed through the doors into the outer jacket, secured them, and then passing on into the cabin, which contained the controlling mechanism within the inner tube, switched on the electric lights.

The Return of Tarzan,
June, 1913

The "iron mole" works perfectly except for one minor detail: it cannot be steered. It plunges vertically down through the earth 500 miles and breaks through, when Innes and Perry think they are doomed, into Pellucidar. One possibly unique concept Burroughs introduces is the variability of time where no common measure for it exists. Perry comments, "I am rapidly coming to the conviction that there is no such thing as time—surely there can be no time here within Pellucidar, where there are no means for measuring or recording time."

Meanwhile Archibald Lowry Sessions, editor of Street & Smith's *New Story Magazine*, had purchased *Ape Man* for $1,000 and published it as *The Return of Tarzan*. Sheepishly, Metcalf wrote Burroughs to ask if he would set a price for first look at all future stories. Burroughs asked for five cents a word. Metcalf offered two cents, and Burroughs, who was a good enough businessman to make a fortune but careful enough never to turn down a sale or price himself higher than his market would pay, accepted—for 1913. At that price his next work, "The Cave Girl," earned him $600.

In 1913 Sessions bought *The Outlaw of Torn* for *New Story* for $500 but offered $3,000 for a new Tarzan novel. Street & Smith's magazines—*Popular, People's, New Story, Top-Notch*—were doing well, and so were the Munsey pulps, and they were publishing a great deal of science fiction. Sam Moskowitz records that in 1913 *All-Story* published fourteen science fiction stories, four of them novels, in twelve issues, for a total of almost half a million words. Among them was Burroughs' *The Man Without a Soul* (book title: *The Monster Men*) about the creation of synthetic life, for which Burroughs received $1,165. The October issue carried in its reader's department "A Martian Glossary" of terms used in Burroughs' Martian stories; in December *All-Story* began publication of *The Warlord of Mars*, in which John Carter chases his kidnapped princess from the south pole to the north pole of Mars. This brought Burroughs nearly $1,200.

In 1914 Metcalf offered Burroughs two-and-a-half cents a word and wanted 50,000 words a month. The reason: *All-Story* was going weekly.

Still Burroughs' security was not assured. *New Story* had turned down *The Mucker,* a novel of character and regeneration and adventure. Burroughs had completed number three in the *Tarzan* series, *The Beasts of Tarzan.* Metcalf offered $2,000; Sessions reneged on his $3,000 offer and suggested $2,000. Burroughs accepted $2,500 from Metcalf.

All-Story Weekly began to publish its backlog of Burroughs stories: a novelette about a caveman who awakens into the present from a long sleep, "The Eternal Lover"; *The Mad King,* a Graustarkian novel; "The Inner World," which was published under the title of "At the Earth's Core"; and *The Beasts of Tarzan.* Metcalf, however, lost his job (the loss of *The Return of Tarzan* had always rankled in the Munsey organization) when *All-Story* was combined with *Cavalier,* and Bob Davis continued as editor.

Moskowitz estimates that by 1914 Burroughs was earning $20,000 a year from magazine sales alone; that seems a bit high since Moskowitz's figures for Burroughs' earnings during his first two-and-a-half years of writing total less than $10,000. But it was good money for a pulp-magazine writer, particularly in those days, and book sales were just beginning. In 1914 A. C. McClurg of Chicago

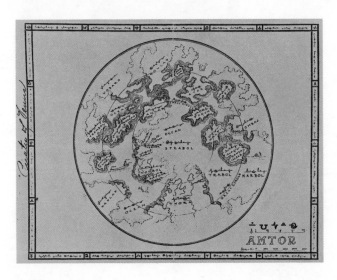

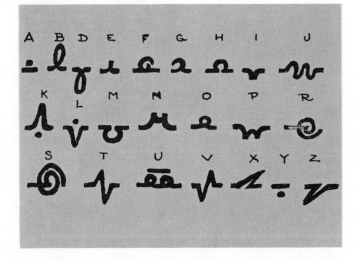

published *Tarzan of the Apes*; it sold a million copies in its initial hard-cover edition and many more in cheaper reprints by A. L. Burt and Grosset & Dunlap.

In 1931 Burroughs founded his own publishing company in Tarzana, California, and reissued as one-dollar reprints ten of the Tarzan series for which he owned the book rights, plus the entire Mars and Venus series (in which Carson Napier sets off for Mars in a rocket ship he builds for the purpose but is thrown off course by the moon and lands on Venus). Before his death in March 1950 at the age of 75, Burroughs had made, according to his own estimate, a fortune of more than $10 million. He had written fifty-nine books published during his lifetime, twenty-four of them featuring Tarzan. He claimed sales of 35 million hard-cover copies in North America alone: about 15 million for Tarzan books, about 20 million for the others. In addition, we might include the income and the impact upon popular culture of several generations of film Tarzans, reprints in magazines and newspapers, radio dramatizations, cartoon strips and magazines, and the paperback revival of the early sixties.

Burroughs was a phenomenon even in his own time; inevitably he produced imitators as well as more legitimate successors. One of the first was Charles B. Stilson, whose trilogy about Polaris and a fantasy land located in a volcanic valley in the Antarctic was published in *All-Story* beginning in December 1915 with *Polaris of the Snows*, and followed by *Minos of Sardanes* and *Polaris and the*

Burroughs even drew maps of the planet "Amtor" (*left below*) and devised an alphabet

Burroughs in a number of
activities: Riding a favorite
horse, 1928; talking with the
first movie Tarzan, Elmo
Lincoln, 1918; and working
in his office at Malibu

Goddess Glorian. The adventures of Polaris begin with the death of his crippled father, who urges his son to leave the snows of Antarctica where he has been raised, and go "North! North! To the north, Polaris. Tell the world—ah, tell them —boy—The north! The north! You must go, Polaris!" He kills polar bears with his spear and a knife; rescues a girl who has come with a party to discover the South Pole, and who find themselves on a broken ice floe being carried in a current back to the South. "Ah, all is lost, now!" the girl gasps.

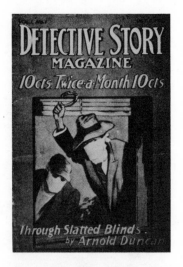

October 15, 1915 (Vol. 1, No. 1). One of the first of the specialized pulps

> Then the great spirit of the man rose into spoken words. "No, lady," he called, his voice rising clearly above the shrieking and thundering pandemonium. "We yet have our lives."

That philosophy would echo through the scientific romance. "I am still alive," Tarzan says at a moment of imminent destruction. "I still live," says John Carter.

J. U. Giesy, who wrote a long series of short stories about a scientific detective named Semi-Dual, wrote a trilogy of novels about the adventures of a young physician who has studied the occult religions and mastered the art of astral projection. He roams the earth, explores the moon, and finally projects himself toward Sirius, the Dog Star, where he finds himself captured in the fury of a sun:

> Directly beneath him, as it appeared, the Dog Star rolled, a mass of electric fire. Mountains of flame ran darting off into space in all directions. Between them the whole surface of the sun boiled and bubbled and seethed like a world-wide caldron. Not for a moment was there any rest upon that surface toward which he was sinking with incredible speed. Every atom of the monster sun was in motion, ever shifting, ever changing yet always the same. It quivered and billowed and shook. Flames of every conceivable color radiated from it in waves of awful heat. Vast explosions recurred again and again on the ever heaving surface. What seemed unthinkable hurricanes rushed into the voids created by the exploding gases.

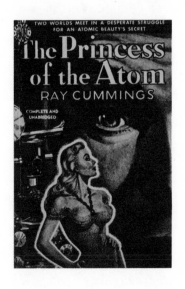

Ray Cummings

Blown outward from the sun, Jason Croft finally makes his way to a planet of Sirius, "one of the Dog Star's pack," and finds there a Romanlike race of human beings and—what else?—a beautiful girl with whom he immediately falls in love. *Palos of the Dog Star Pack* was published in *All-Story Weekly* in 1918 and followed by *Mouthpiece of Zitu* and *Jason, Son of Jason.*

Austin Hall produced several effective stories for *All-Story,* including "Almost Immortal" in 1916 and "The Rebel Soul" in 1917; both of them dealt with the transference of the spirit from one body to another. Homer Eon Flint wrote *The Planeteer* and *King of Conserve Island;* published in *All-Story* in 1917 and 1918, they dealt with overpopulation in the twenty-third century, the shifting of the earth to an orbit near Jupiter, and life, technology, and conquest in the future. Together Hall and Flint collaborated on a classic novel of mystery leading to a long-delayed revelation about the existence of another world on a separate plane. It was called *The Blind Spot.* The first appearance of the blind spot came in a bare room of a deserted house:

> But just then the old lady's lean fingers clinched into his arm; her eyes grew bright; her mouth opened and she stopped in the middle of her drone. Jerome grew rigid. And no wonder. From the middle of the room not ten feet away came the tone of a bell, a great silvery voluminous sound—and music. A church bell. Just one stroke, full toned, filling all the air till the whole room was choked with music. Then as suddenly it died out and runed into nothing. At the same time he felt the fingers on his arms relax; and a heap at his feet. . . .

The Blind Spot was serialized in *All-Story* in 1921; Austin Hall wrote a sequel, *The Spot of Life,* which appeared in *Argosy* in 1932.

Other writers were providing romantic adventures in strange places or on other worlds. Ray Cummings' "The Girl in the Golden Atom" was published in *All-Story* in 1919. It began much like O'Brien's "Diamond Lens," with the Chemist developing a vastly more powerful microscope through which he peers into a scratch on his mother's gold wedding ring and sees a microscopic world, and in it—a beautiful girl. He discovers a drug that will shrink him to whatever size he wishes and one that will expand him, and he sets off, upon his mother's ring, toward adventure and love:

> "I found myself now, as I looked about, walking upon a narrow, though ever

A. Merritt

broadening, curved path. The ground beneath my feet appeared to be a rough, yellowish quartz. This path grew rougher as I advanced. . . ."

Eventually, continually growing smaller, he climbs and slides down to the world at the bottom of the scratch where he finds forests and his beautiful girl, Lylda, whose people he rescues from destruction by growing larger and stamping out their attackers. The Chemist returns without Lylda, to make certain that the way is safe, but when he goes back into the golden atom for her, he does not return—at least not until the full-length sequel, *The People of the Golden Atom*, published by *All-Story* the following year.

There were many others: Victor Rousseau with the *Sea Demons* in 1916 and the *Messiah of the Cylinder* in 1917; Francis Stevens (pseudonym for Gertrude Bennett) with *The Nightmare* in 1917, *Labyrinth* in 1918, *Citadel of Fear*, and *Heads of Cerberus* in 1919; Garrett Smith with *After a Million Years* in 1919; and Murray Leinster, who would write and sell millions of words of science fiction in the next five decades under his pen name and his real name, Will F. Jenkins, with "The Runaway Skyscraper" in 1919, about the Metropolitan Tower in New York being carried back in time, and "The Mad Planet" in 1920, about the destruction of civilization by a vast increase in carbon dioxide in the air and the effort of a primitive young man to survive in a world dominated by giant flora and fauna.

In 1917 *All-Story* introduced a new writer who would rival Burroughs in popularity, if not in productivity or commercial instincts. There was good reason for all three: A. (for Abraham) Merritt had a romantic imagination and a poetic style to match, but he also was the 33-year-old associate editor of Hearst's Sunday magazine section, *The American Weekly*. His first story was "Through the Dragon Glass"; his second publication was an *All-Story* serial in 1918, *The People of the Pit*. The same year saw the publication of a novelette called "The Moon Pool," which created such a sensation that Bob Davis offered Merritt $2,000 for a sequel. The story describes the fate of an exploring party investigating mysterious ruins on an island in the Pacific and their living death through a strange energy creature which lives inside one of the structures and draws its strength from the moon. It lives in a circular pool of pale blue water, perhaps twenty feet in diameter, surrounded by a lip of glimmering silvery stone. Seven glowing shafts of light shine down upon it, each a different color: pink, green, white, blue, amber, amethyst, silver.

"Through the water tiny gleams of phosphorescence began to dart, sparkles and coruscations of pale incandescence. And far, far below I sensed a movement, a shifting glow as of something slowly rising. . . .

"It had grown milky, opalescent. The rays gushing into it seemed to be filling it; it was alive with sparklings, scintillations, glimmerings. . . .

Reprinted in *Famous Fantastic Mysteries*, 1939

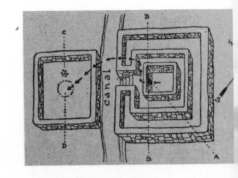

From "The Moon Pool"

"So I stood while the pool gleamed and sparkled; the streams of light grew more intense and the mist glowed and strengthened. I saw that its shining core had shape— but a shape that my eyes and brain could not define. . . . It was neither man nor woman; it was unearthly and androgynous. . . .

"Over the head of the misty body there sprang suddenly out seven little lights. Each was the color of the beam beneath which it rested. I knew now that the dweller was—complete! . . .

"There was the rush past me and as the dweller paused, straight into it raced Edith, arms outstretched to shield me from it! . . .

"She stopped and reeled as though she had encountered solidity. And as she faltered it wrapped its shining self around her. The crystal tinklings burst forth jubilantly. The light filled her, ran through and around her as it had with Stanton. . . .

"I dragged myself to the brink. Far down I saw a shining, many-colored nebulous cloud descending; caught a glimpse of Edith's face, disappearing; her eyes stared up to me filled with supernal ecstasy and horror. . . ."

The Conquest of the Moon Pool was serialized in 1919, and Merritt would

The Ship of Ishtar began
November 8, 1924

The Snake Mother began
October 25, 1930

carry on two careers for the next fifteen years, writing in his spare time and ultimately becoming editor of *American Weekly*. Among his later novels of romance, mystery, and lush descriptions: *The Metal Monster, The Face in the Abyss, The Snake Mother, The Ship of Ishtar, Seven Footprints to Satan, Dwellers in the Mirage, Burn Witch Burn, Creep, Shadow!* and the uncompleted *Fox Woman* (completed by Hannes Bok).

Merritt's books would be published in hard covers by Putnam and later reprinted by Liveright, and his works would be reprinted by Avon and kept in print in paperback—seven novels and one short-story collection selling more than 4 million copies by 1959, with *Seven Footprints to Satan* selling 1 million alone and five of his books still selling well in hard covers. At least one novel, *Burn Witch Burn,* was made into a motion picture ("The Devil Dolls" with Lionel Barrymore), and his stories were reprinted again and again, in the early *Amazing Stories,* for instance, and then in the late thirties and early forties in *Famous Fantastic Mysteries* and *Fantastic Novels;* and *The Ship of Ishtar* was acclaimed, fourteen years after its publication, as the most popular story *Argosy* had ever printed.

Meanwhile the pulp-magazine field was changing: *Argosy* went weekly in 1917 and began increasing its publication of fantasy and science fiction. The first crime-story magazine, *Detective Story Monthly,* was published by Street & Smith in October 1915; two years later it would be joined by *Mystery Magazine* and later by many others. *Western Story* magazine created the western pulp in 1919; *Love Stories* created a new popular genre in 1921. It was the beginning of a move toward the specialized pulp fiction magazine begun by *Railroad Magazine. The Thrill Book,* which might have been the first science fiction and fantasy magazine, was launched by Street & Smith in 1919 as a semi-monthly but lasted only sixteen issues.

The magazines were raising their prices: the World War I paper shortage had evolved into a period of increasing paper costs, and the labor movement, which reached a peak of unrest between 1914 and 1917, was steadily raising printing costs. But it was a bad time for price increases: World War I had been followed by a recession and motion pictures were becoming a popular alternative to the pulp magazine. For their July 1920 issues, *Argosy* and *All-Story* merged into *Argosy All-Story Weekly.*

At the time of the merger, Frank Luther Mott estimated, in his *History of American Magazines, Argosy All-Story* had a circulation of 500,000 and maintained 400,000 into the twenties. One reason for the merger was to cut costs and still maintain the ten-cent price. Merging made it possible to reduce the editorial staff; Bob Davis left and started a literary agency. Although Burroughs would sell novels and stories in later years to *Argosy,* as well as to other adventure magazines (particularly *Blue Book*) and science fiction magazines, when Davis left Burroughs was told by an assistant editor, "We are overstocked."

It was the end of an era.

Out of it had come a new kind of fiction, the scientific romance. Not the scientific romance of H. G. Wells, who had emphasized the scientific, but the scientific romance with the emphasis on the romance. From this period, more than any other, pulp fiction got its reputation as escape literature, a reputation that would be difficult for the mystery, the western, and particularly science fiction to live down.

Burroughs, the embodiment of all that was good and bad of that period, still retains in his books the quality with which he began in 1911—the ability to captivate the young. When his books became available in paperback beginning in 1962, my children were as enthralled by them as I had been at their age—and again the books sold millions of copies.

Burroughs demonstrated once more the popular appeal of science fiction—though a different, adventure-oriented kind of science fiction—just as Jules Verne had done in his time and Wells had done in his. Burroughs had carried the pulps through a difficult time—if not alone at least in significant part.

Now the field was ready for the specialized magazines, and a young publisher of radio and invention publications was dreaming about a magazine that would predict in detail the delightful, thrilling future in store for us through scientific progress.

CHAPTER 8
THAT AMAZING DECADE: 1926-1936

IN THE LAST DECADE of the nineteenth century, the low-priced monthly magazines demonstrated that the growing middle class of the nation would buy magazines in quantity. In the first two decades of the twentieth century, the pulp magazines demonstrated a sufficient demand for fiction to support a variety of cheap monthly and even weekly magazines. Now the twenties were to feel the narrowing currents of specialization which were producing assembly lines, the division and subdivision of professions and disciplines, hobbies, entertainments, fads, fashions, increasing college attendance and proliferating programs of instruction, and the genre pulps, including science fiction and fantasy.

The decade of the twenties began in a mood of prosperity: the gross national product had doubled in the previous ten years and now was more than $71 billion, and the ordinary citizen was sharing some of the abundance of the maturing industrial society: Americans bought some 10 million cars between 1910 and 1920. The use of electric power and the internal-combustion engine created a revolution as great as that created by the use of steam in the 1750s.

Part of the reason for general prosperity in 1920 was the engineering genius and social invention of a self-taught engineer. His impact upon the nature of our society and the world was far greater than we recognize. Think what a science fiction story could have been written in 1880 about "an imaginary vehicle that can move without horses by some internal source of power; a horseless carriage, in other words." In fact, Isaac Asimov has already thought about it and come up with not one story but three, which distinguish among adventure science fiction, gadget science fiction, and social science fiction. He has even made up a word for his horseless carriage; he calls it an automobile.

Writer X spends most of his time describing how the machine would run, explaining the workings of an internal-combustion engine, painting a word-picture of the struggles of the inventor, who after numerous failures, comes up with a successful model. The climax of the yarn is the drama of the machine, chugging its way along at the gigantic speed of twenty miles an hour, possibly beating a horse and carriage which have been challenged to a race. This is gadget science fiction.

There were, of course, many such stories written in the late nineteenth century. They were called dime novels. In the early twentieth century they would have been called *Tom Swift and His* . . .

Writer Y invents the automobile in a hurry, but now there is a gang of ruthless crooks intent on stealing this valuable invention. First they steal the inventor's beautiful daughter, whom they threaten with every dire eventuality but rape (in these adventure stories, girls exist to be rescued and have no other uses). The inventor's young assistant goes to the rescue. He can accomplish his purpose only by the use of the newly perfected automobile. He dashes into the desert at an unheard-of speed of twenty miles an hour to pick up the girl who otherwise would have died of thirst if he had relied on a horse, however rapid and sustained the horse's gallop. This is adventure science fiction.

And this, of course, would have been the approach of Jules Verne, and the approach of a hundred science fiction motion pictures.

Writer Z has the automobile already perfected. A society exists in which it is already a problem. Because of the automobile, a gigantic oil industry has grown up, highways have been paved across the nation, America has become a land of travelers, cities have spread into the suburbs—and what do we do about automobile accidents? Men, women, and children are being killed by automobiles faster than by artillery shells or airplane bombs. What can be done? What is the solution? This is social science fiction.

And this is what Asimov and many contemporary writers have been doing since 1939—but that is a story for a later chapter. As Asimov comments, "It is easy to predict an automobile in 1880; it is very hard to predict a traffic problem." That is the science fiction writer's challenge. (Robert Heinlein has suggested that a greater science fiction accomplishment would have been to predict the change created by the automobile in the nation's courting habits.)

Henry Ford

The hero of the science fiction story that was never written about the automobile was Henry Ford. He was no mysterious Robur, no confident Barbicane, no doom-ridden Captain Nemo, even though the bare outline of his early life would have fit the early Verne's ideas of the engineer-inventor. But Verne never dealt in detail with the social implications of his inventions; his storytelling instincts turned him toward adventure and the individual.

No science fiction writer could have created the complex, contradictory character that Ford really was (Aldous Huxley, in his 1932 novel *Brave New World*, recognized through his invented vocabulary some of the implications of the assembly line—Before Ford, After Ford, in the Year of Our Ford, "Ford's in his flivver; all's well with the world"—but he did not deal with the man himself).

The Model T

Henry Ford came out with the Model T, the flivver, in 1908 and advertised it as "The Universal Car." Until then automobiles had been so expensive that only the rich could afford them. The new "tin lizzie" sold for $850. In 1916 the price dropped to $360 when Ford perfected the technique of the assembly line. It was a triumph of the engineering mind: rather than hire or train skilled mechanics and artisans to take parts to an immobile chassis, why not take unskilled workers, teach them to do one task, and move the work past them—let them put one piece onto a vehicle as it came by. The concept revolutionized industry and as much as anything else, perhaps, created our economy of abundance (although today, with the old battle of scarcity won, some industries are experimenting with the artisan's method of manufacturing to improve worker morale and increase his satisfaction with his job).

Ford became a billionaire, even though he kept lowering his prices rather than raising them. That was another social invention. "Every time I lower the price a dollar, we gain a thousand new buyers," he said. If it were not for the fact that Ford had no use for reading and the search for knowledge ("Books muss up my mind," he said), he might have learned the low-price, high-volume lesson from the example of Frank Munsey and the dime magazines.

But Ford was not finished with his social engineering. In 1914 he more than doubled the wages of his workers to $5 a day and reduced the nine-hour shift to eight hours; he also speeded up the assembly line and hired efficiency experts to stand behind workers with stop watches. It worked: Ford company profits doubled within two years. Moreover, more money went into the pockets of Ford workers—and by example into the pockets of other workers—that enabled them to buy Fords.

Specialization was beginning to prove itself in the most meaningful way: it paid off.

The United States emerged from World War I with new industrial capacity and an advantage in world trade. After the economic crisis of 1920–21, manufacturing began to rise rapidly; by 1929 it had increased more than 80 percent over 1913. In 1925 President Coolidge said, "The business of America is business."

Wall Street's optimism spread across the nation. Fortunes were being made in the stock market as prices rocketed. The warnings of a few prophets of doom such as Roger Babson were ignored. Installment purchases—another social invention—multiplied during the decade of the twenties; "buying on time" conquered the old Puritan fear of debt.

Prohibition, the noble experiment, began in 1920 and helped create an atmosphere of widespread disrespect for the law and may have created organized crime: were racketeers and rumrunners and hijackers any worse than the ordinary citizen who went to his speakeasy for a drink of bathtub gin or smuggled Scotch? Even President Harding's cronies succumbed to the lawless, grafting, get-your-share spirit of the times.

A new industry of entertainment was developing out of Tom Edison's invention: the experimental nickelodeons of the first two decades were changing into great new palaces of entertainment. Going to a movie became an experience in opulence, and motion-picture stars, ten times larger than life, were being created to fill the giant screens.

Radio, which had been in the air since Marconi invented the radio telegraph in 1895, became a practical method of communication in the twenties; KDKA, Pittsburgh, announced the returns of the Harding-Cox presidential elections in 1920 and went on to become the first regularly scheduled broadcaster of news, church services, and music. By the end of the decade 618 stations were in business, and networks were regularly broadcasting across the nation. (And if any aliens were watching from afar, the process began the perceptible brightening of the Earth's "radio image" which would signal the birth of another technological civilization in the galaxy.)

During the twenties newspapers discovered the selling power of scandal and sensation, sex and violence: the New York *Daily News* became the nation's first tabloid in 1919; five years later it had the nation's largest circulation, 750,000. Five years later it was joined by the *Daily Mirror* and the *Evening Graphic*, which soon became known as the "Pornographic."

Magazines were specializing, too. The old mass-market giants—*The Saturday Evening Post, Collier's, The Literary Digest*—were still growing. But new magazines were being created to please more discriminating tastes or satisfy more peculiar desires: in *American Mercury* editors Henry L. Mencken and George Jean Nathan were criticizing the nation's bourgeois tastes and traditions; *Time* was offering the first weekly news summary; *The New Yorker* was appealing to the sophisticate in purchases and entertainment; and Bernarr Macfadden's *True Story Magazine* was paying writers good rates for their "true confessions" that tantalized nearly 2 million readers.

The first issue of *Amazing Stories* (April, 1926) and its founder, Hugo Gernsback

In the middle of the decade, on April 5, 1926, Hugo Gernsback added another specialized publication to the newsstands of the nation. The magazine was *Amazing Stories*, and it was the world's first science fiction magazine.

The editorial in the first issue said:

Amazing Stories is a *new* kind of fiction magazine! It is entirely new—entirely different—something that has never been done before in this country. Therefore, *Amazing Stories* deserves your attention and interest.

One more evidence of the way in which the world had changed: novelty had become a significant selling point.

The new magazine exhibited no indecision about what it would publish: scientifiction. Gernsback had invented the word to describe the contents of his new magazine, and his first editorial went on to define what he meant.

By "scientifiction" I mean the Jules Verne, H. G. Wells, and Edgar Allan Poe type of story—a charming romance intermingled with scientific fact and prophetic vision.

(The tradition of defining science fiction as "what I mean when I point at it" got an early start.) Indeed, the words "AMAZING STORIES—SCIENTIFICTION" appeared together on the spine of the magazine beginning with the third issue and continued for years afterwards. It was a compromise between Gernsback's commercial instincts and his ideals, and it would torment science fiction for generations. When readers would write to complain about the garish covers (by Frank R. Paul), the large size, the quality of the paper (although it did have trimmed edges from the first issue), and even the title of the magazine, Gernsback explained that a magazine had to call attention to itself on the crowded newsstands, that of 150,000 copies printed (by October 1927) only 5,250 went to subscribers, and that although *scientifiction* described the stories better than *amazing*, *Amazing Stories* appealed more to the masses. "Anything that smacks of science," Gernsback wrote, "seems to be too 'deep' for the average type of reader." He recalled an earlier experiment which might have resulted in a science fiction magazine in 1924. He had mailed 25,000 letters soliciting subscriptions to a new magazine to be called *Scientifiction,* and the response was discouraging. Gernsback thought the title frightened many potential readers.

Finally, Gernsback defended the title *Amazing Stories* as appropriate to the kind of stories he wished to publish: "The formula in all cases is that the story must be frankly amazing; second, it must contain a scientific background; third, it must possess originality."

Underlying Gernsback's basic desire to sell magazines and make money was his desire to promote understanding of science and technology through fiction; the fiction was a kind of candy coating for a pill of instruction. His first editorial went on:

For many years stories of this nature were published in the sister magazines of *Amazing Stories*—"Science and Invention" and "Radio News."

Not only do these amazing tales make tremendously interesting reading—they are also always instructive. They supply knowledge that we might not otherwise obtain—and they supply it in a very palatable form.

As if to illustrate further what he meant by "scientifiction," Gernsback published in his first issue stories by all three of the authors he had pointed at— Verne, Wells, and Poe: Verne's *Off on a Comet*, Wells's "The New Accelerator," and Poe's "The Facts in the Case of M. Valdemar." The names of all three were printed in large type on the cover, and, as a matter of fact, it would be a rare issue in the next year and a half that did not have the names of at least Verne and Wells on the cover. (For years the masthead of the magazine carried a drawing of Jules Verne's tomb at Amiens "portraying his immortality.")

What did *Amazing Stories* publish? For the first three issues, it was entirely reprints, and reprints formed the greatest proportion of the contents for the first year. They were largely familiar favorites: Verne's *A Journey to the Center of the Earth*, "Dr. Ox's Experiment," *The Purchase of the North Pole*, and "A Drama in the Air"; Wells's "The Crystal Egg," "The Star," "The Man Who Could Work Miracles," "The Empire of the Ants," "In the Abyss," *The Island of Dr. Moreau,* and *The First Men in the Moon;* Poe's "A Mesmeric Reve-

Gernsback's editorial defining "scientifiction"

lation," and "The Sphinx"; O'Brien's "The Diamond Lens"; Locke's "The Moon Hoax"; Murray Leinster's "The Runaway Skyscraper" and "The Mad Planet"; Garrett P. Serviss's "The Moon Metal" and *A Columbus of Space,* and stories by such pulp-magazine authors as Austin Hall, George Allan England, and A. Hyatt Verill.

Following the pattern set by the pulp magazines of earlier days, *Amazing Stories* always included at least one serial, sometimes two, and reached a peak of four in its October 1926 issue.

With all the reprints, it is not surprising that Gernsback found it necessary to include in his third issue's editorial, "Some of our readers seem to have obtained the erroneous idea that *Amazing Stories* publishes only reprints. . . . That is not the case." He presented an appeal that would be echoed in later science fiction magazines: new writers wanted, no previous experience necessary but must have fertile and original mind. The next issue starred two new stories on the table of contents, one, translated from the German, written by Curt Siodmak, who would later go on to a distinguished career as fantasy screenwriter and novelist (*Donovan's Brain* and *Hauser's Memory* are two novels that became motion pictures).

As a matter of fact, Gernsback's first editorial had made clear his interest in new fiction:

> Many great science fiction stories destined to be of an historical interest are still being written, and *Amazing Stories* will be the medium through which such stories will come to you. Posterity will point to them as having blazed a new trail, not only in literature and fiction, but in progress as well.

The first science fiction magazine could have happened earlier. With a different title or perhaps a bit more courage or conviction on Gernsback's part, *Scientifiction* might have appeared in 1924 or 1925. Even earlier, *The Thrill Book,* edited by Harold Hersey for Street & Smith in 1919, aimed at the publication of "different" stories, but they were not directed at the tastes of the rising new scientists, technologists, and devotees of progress that Gernsback identified, and the magazine lasted only sixteen issues. *Weird Tales,* founded in 1923 and edited for many years by Farnsworth Wright, stuck steadfastly with fantasy fiction until forced to include some science fantasy (where, in a spectrum, fantasy and science fiction become indistinguishable) to meet competition and to accommodate the submissions of a *Weird Tales* regular like H. P. Lovecraft.

The father of the science fiction magazine, and thereby of much of what

Weird Tales began with the March, 1923, issue and carried some science fiction from time to time

developed into modern science fiction, was born August 16, 1884, in Luxembourg. According to his biographer, Sam Moskowitz, Gernsback's father was a well-to-do wine wholesaler, and the boy's earliest education was from private tutors. Later he attended the Ecole Industrielle of Luxembourg and the Technikum in Bingen, Germany.

Sam Moskowitz relates a charming story about Gernsback that ought to be true, describing how the nine-year-old Hugo was so overcome by reading a German translation of Percival Lowell's *Mars as the Abode of Life* that he fell into a fever and raved about strange creatures, fantastic cities, and masterfully engineered canals. Unfortunately for legend, Lowell's book was not published until 1908.

No matter the accuracy of the recollection, Moskowitz, who knew Gernsback and became his editor for a short-lived science fiction magazine in 1953, depicts Gernsback as a man who would never be satisfied with what is known. He was the prototype for one kind of science fiction reader, the kind who turns to science fiction out of his impatience to enjoy the wonders of the future, a person who not only is not disturbed by change but eager to anticipate what is going to happen so that he can enjoy it now. In his pursuit of change and the future, Gernsback joyfully discovered Verne and Wells.

Telephones and other forms of electrical communication were just coming into use in Gernsback's youth. At the age of 13 he installed an intercom system in a Luxembourg Carmelite Convent. He was also working on inventions, particularly a battery similar to the Ever-Ready layer battery, but France and Germany refused him patents. He decided that the United States was the land of opportunity and the future, so he packed up his battery and emigrated with his accumulated savings—some $200 when he landed in New York in February 1904.

Gernsback's battery proved impractical to mass-produce. He tried getting a job, but that didn't work out. He went into partnership to build and sell batteries to car manufacturers, but his partner intercepted the checks. After recovering the money from his partner's father, Gernsback began manufacturing batteries for a large New York City distributor of motor-car equipment. The depression of 1907 brought the loss of his Packard contract and the dissolution of his company.

But it was a period of hope: when one business failed, start another, and sooner or later, like Horatio Alger, you will find success in business. Gernsback formed another partnership, this time with a telegraph operator who roomed at the same boarding house on 14th Street, to import electrical equipment into the United States. The Electro Importing Company became the first mail-order radio house. Among its early offers was a Gernsback-designed home radio set—which both sent and received (since no commercial stations were in existence)—for

Gernsback as a young man

With model of early sending and receiving set

$7.50. The Telimco Wireless also was sold in department stores. In 1957 a replica was placed in the Henry Ford Museum in Dearborn.

I met him only once—at the World Science Fiction convention held in Chicago in 1952—and thought him a strange mixture of personal reserve and aggressive salesmanship. Jack Williamson described him once as a "successful businessman who was interested in gadgets and liked science fiction." In an era of showmen, Gernsback was a showman. He promoted his Telimco Wireless in 1908 by building the first walkie-talkie and hiring a man to carry it on his shoulders in downtown New York.

Meanwhile he began to publish—first a radio catalog in 1905 and then the first radio magazine, *Modern Electrics*, in 1908. He also opened the first radio store, introduced the word "television" in an article "Television and the Telphot" in *Modern Electrics*, formed a society of 10,000 wireless radio amateurs, issued *The Wireless Blue Book*, published the first book on radio broadcasting (*The Wireless Telephone*, in 1910), and predicted radio networks.

And, in 1911, he began writing *Ralph 124C 41+* in serial form for *Modern Electrics*. The roster of its scientific predictions was included in Chapter 1—in a 1958 edition the late Fletcher Pratt called it "a book of prophecy" whose very method, "that of supplying the people of the future with technical inventions that are the logical outgrowths of those currently in use or logically developed from currently accepted principles," has become fundamental in science fiction— but its most remarkable bit of prescience may have been Gernsback's description of radar:

> *A pulsating polarized ether wave,* if directed on a metal object can be reflected in the same manner as a light-ray is reflected from a bright surface or from a mirror . . . if, therefore, a polarized wave generator were directed toward space, the waves would take a direction as shown in the diagram, provided the parabolic wave reflector was used as shown. By manipulating the entire apparatus like a searchlight, waves would be sent over a large area. Sooner or later these waves would strike a space flyer. A small part of the waves would strike the metal body of the flyer, and these waves would be reflected back to the sending apparatus. Here they would fall on the Actinoscope, which records only reflected waves, not direct ones. From the actinoscope the reflection factor is then determined. . . . From the intensity and the elapsed time of the reflected impulses, the distance between the earth and the flyer can then be accurately calculated.

The paragraph cited is not only a fair sample of the book's technological predictions but a fair sample, as well, of its contents. The title translates into words as "one to foresee for one," and the original magazine version not only contained lengthy descriptions of tomorrow's marvels and how they came to be developed (and sometimes footnotes citing contemporary research as justification) but diagrams as well.

The plot itself is little more than a rationale for a guided tour of Ralph's world; it provided Gernsback with the opportunity, through Ralph, to lecture the reader about the technological promise implicit in the world of 1911, although the latter part of the novel is enlivened by the kidnapping of Ralph's girl friend, his pursuit of her toward Mars, and her restoration to life, through Ralph's genius. Ralph was an unusual person, even in the year 2660:

> His physical superiority, however, was as nothing compared to his gigantic mind. He was *Ralph 124C 41+*, one of the greatest living scientists and *one of the ten men on the whole planet earth permitted to use the Plus sign after his name.*

Some of these characteristics would persist in science fiction for years, some even down to the present: the guided tour, the detailed explanation of how machines work, the unsophisticated ways of getting background information across to the reader. But no one would quite come up to Gernsback's standards for popularizing science and its potential, or match his efforts to turn readers toward scientific careers.

In 1912 Gernsback sold *Modern Electrics* and started *Electrical Experimenter*. In 1915 he began writing "Baron Munchausen's New Scientific Adventures," which took the Baron to Mars and provided descriptions of the life, inventions, and philosophy of the Martians. Science fiction stories by other writers began to appear in *Electrical Experimenter*, authors developed by Gernsback at

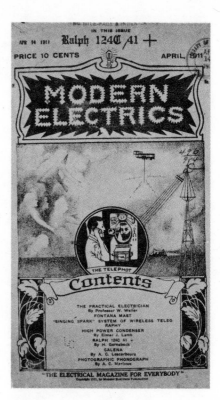

Ralph 124C 41+ began in April, 1911

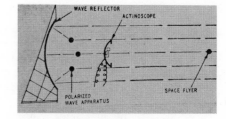

Radar diagram from *Ralph 124C 41+*

first and then authors who had made their reputations in other publications, such as Ray Cummings and George Allan England. When *Electrical Experimenter* became *Science and Invention* in August 1920, Gernsback frequently ran two stories an issue and another story in his companion magazine, *Radio News.*

Gernsback's intuition that there were others like him and that those who were interested in reading about the frontiers of science and technology would also be interested in imaginary adventures into strange new worlds (the most important one was the future) was supported by the response of his readers. Now that there was a magazine to record the phenomenon, the correlation of interests among science fiction readers could be isolated and identified. In 1949 *Astounding Science Fiction* would conduct a readers' survey which would reveal that 93 percent of its readers were male, that the average reader was a college graduate just under 30 with a professional or technical position, and that he had been reading the magazine about eight years.

In August 1923, with a backlog of science fiction stories, Gernsback published a special "Scientific Fiction Number" of *Science and Invention;* it included six science fiction stories and a cover painting of a man in a space suit.

Amazing Stories was greeted by readers as the answer to what had been until then an unrecognized need. One of Gernsback's early discoveries was the enthusiasm and dedication of the science fiction reader, his inborn fannishness waiting to be expressed. It was as if some forgotten Diaspora had scattered a nation so thoroughly that not one citizen knew another, but now, through *Amazing Stories,* each had discovered his Zion, and they could gather together in spirit in a new ghetto to practice their forgotten rites. Hints of this almost religious relationship had appeared in the readers' columns of earlier pulp magazines, but no one had interpreted them correctly.

The third issue of *Amazing Stories,* for June 1926, documented Gernsback's reaction:

> One of the great surprises since we started publishing *Amazing Stories* is the tremendous amount of mail we receive from—shall we call them "Scientifiction Fans"?— who seem to be pretty well oriented in this sort of literature. From the suggestions for reprints that are coming in these "fans" seem to have a hobby of their own of hunting up scientifiction stories, not only in English, but in many other languages.

In the first issue Gernsback had indicated the possibility of a department entitled "Readers' Letters," but it would not start for almost a year, and when it did it was called "Discussions." The department became a meeting place for fans and perhaps the origin of modern science fiction fandom, as well as a forum for discussing the fiction that was being published and for working out new lines of development or rejecting old ones. Through the readers' columns in *Amazing* and later magazines, the opinions of individual readers became a consensus, and, although they were not always successful in obtaining trimmed edges, better paper, more appropriate titles, less garish covers, or stories by this favorite author or that, the letter writers and the fans wielded an influence on the development of science fiction far beyond their actual numbers. Seminal editors and authors, it is true, would have the greatest influence on the evolution of the genre, but through the letter columns and fandom not only would certain stories, themes, and authors be blessed and cursed, but many potential writers would become aware of science fiction and would begin their own private process of creation.

Fandom was a unique response to fiction—nothing like it had ever been seen before, and perhaps its like will never be seen again. The western story and the mystery story might have their aficionados, but their readers would not claim kinship by reason of their reading tastes nor come together for local, regional, national, and even international meetings to discuss their passion. Their affection, if it went beyond casual interest, would be centered usually on a single writer, such as Ian Fleming, or even a single character, such as Sherlock Holmes (who has his own fandom, the Baker Street Irregulars). Science fiction would have that, too, with its cults of Edgar Rice Burroughs fans (the Burroughs Bibliophiles, with their journal *ERBdom,* and the Dum-Dum Society), Conan the Barbarian fans, Tolkien fans, and, more recently, water brothers

August, 1923

taken from Heinlein's *Stranger in a Strange Land*. But each of these separate fan groups would relate in some way to science fiction as a genre. In fan literature and at conventions there would be serious discussions of Fandom As a Way Of Life, discussions so frequent and so serious that communication on the subject required only the acronym "fiawol." (Fandom has developed its own vocabulary of acronyms, neologisms, and portmanteau words.)

Of fans and fandoms, more later; for now the important fact was the reception given the new magazine, the near-manic enthusiasm of the relatively few fans and the more temperate response of the many readers. The readers' column contained suggestions for starting a "young men's science club" (*Amazing* offered itself as an official club organ) and later carried reports of a Science Correspondence Club, which mentioned an officer in the club named Raymond A. Palmer. A letter in the October 1927 issue came from an 18-year-old young man named John (Jack) Williamson from Elida, New Mexico. A year later his first science fiction story, "The Metal Man," would be published in the December 1928 issue of *Amazing*, and he would go on to become one of the major, and most adaptable, authors of science fiction. Recently he recalled the excitement with which he discovered *Amazing*:

> I grew up on a sort of semi-desert farm in southeastern New Mexico. The weather was dry. Farm prices were low. I wanted to be a scientist, but I had no opportunity to get the training to get into it. When I came across my first copies of the old *Amazing Stories* it was like discovering a fantastic new world. It was something I could get into. It was better than real science because it had all sorts of implications for the future as well as today. And the experiments worked.

One of the things the readers wanted was more—more stories, more magazines. By the third issue Gernsback was writing about the possibility of semimonthly publication; he included a coupon in that issue so that readers could vote upon the question (also in that issue was a coupon with which to order the hardcover edition of *Ralph 124C 41+*, and a few issues later Gernsback would offer a free Auto-Strop razor with every one-dollar, five-month subscription to *Science and Invention* or *Radio News*). Gernsback announced the results of the reader poll in the September 1926 issue: 498 readers voted for monthly publication, 32,644 for semimonthly. (Such bits of information lead me to question some of the other details of Gernsback's career; a response of more than 33,000 readers to a questionnaire is so incredible that it must be considered a bit of exaggeration for public consumption.) However, *Amazing* never went semimonthly, perhaps out of the concern expressed by some readers that twenty-five cents a month was within their resources but fifty cents would be excessive.

Gernsback did the next best thing. He published a companion magazine, an annual, in 1927. It featured a new novel by Edgar Rice Burroughs, *The Master Mind of Mars*. A printing of 100,000 copies was virtually sold out, even at fifty cents a copy. In 1928 the annual became a quarterly and sold well. Gernsback pointed out in the quarterly that, combined with *Amazing Stories*, it came close to fulfilling his readers' wish for semimonthly publication; the quarterly had twice the number of pages as the monthly (at twice the price) and contained mostly new stories.

In *Amazing*'s October 1927 issue Gernsback offered as an excuse for not improving the quality of the paper that in spite of its printing of 150,000 copies, the magazine was not yet on a paying basis. From a good businessman, the statement was hard to believe; the editorial costs were low—he used many reprints which must have cost almost nothing, and he paid only one-half cent a word or less for new stories—and the price of the magazine was relatively high for the period.

By then new authors were beginning to appear regularly. Gernsback had performed a major service to science fiction and to science fiction readers by reprinting the hard-to-find stories and novels of Verne and H. G. Wells, but the readers were beginning to want new visions, and the ones who had been brought up on pulp action were beginning to chafe a bit at literary dawdling. A letter in the October 1927 issue criticized H. G. Wells for using "too many words to describe a situation," and Gernsback, always sensitive to reader requests, began to de-emphasize both the reprints and the names of his childhood favorites

From *Skylark of Space,*
August, 1928

From an early Buck Rogers story

on the cover. Two months later the name of Wells was not on the cover, even though his "Country of the Blind" was among the contents.

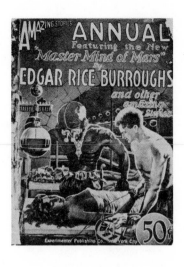

By the end of the second year of publication, new authors were being developed and new names were appearing on the cover. The issue of August 1928 featured a serial by a new author, *Skylark of Space* by E. E. Smith, Ph.D. The same issue contained a story entitled "Armageddon—2419 A.D.," by Philip Nowlan, in which a character named Anthony Rogers is put into suspended animation by a radioactive gas in an abandoned mine and wakes up 500 years later in an era of jumping belts, ray guns, and interplanetary warfare. The story, of course, became the basis for the comic strip "Buck Rogers."

In addition to Nowlan and "Doc" Smith, who would rise to fame with galactic plots and super-science, other new writers were appearing: David H. Keller, M.D., who pioneered psychological science fiction stories; John W. Campbell, Jr., who started as a writer of super-science and worlds to wreck and went on as a writer to create sociological science fiction under the name of Don A. Stuart and, as the long-time editor of *Astounding Science Fiction* (now called *Analog*), to create much of what we knew in the forties and fifties as modern science fiction; Stanton A. Coblentz, poet and satirist; Fletcher Pratt, who would become a distinguished naval writer and sometime editor; Harl Vincent; Jack Williamson; Edmond Hamilton; and Miles J. Breuer, M.D.

Gernsback was fond of listing the scientific credentials of his writers; he himself was listed on the masthead as F.R.S. (presumably "Fellow of the Royal Society"), and his elderly managing editor, a son-in-law of Thomas Edison, was T. O'Conor Sloane, M.A., Ph.D.

By this time Gernsback had a substantial publishing house which included a physical-culture magazine, *Your Body;* a couple of joke books, *Tid Bits* and *Cookoo Nuts;* a wide variety of single-issue publications; and a few hard-cover books. He also operated radio station WRNY in New York, which in 1928 started "daily television broadcasts"—the face of the performer was televised after each radio program—which could be received by only a few hundred crude experimental sets. The October 1928 issue of *Amazing Stories* advertised the second issue of Gernsback's *Television,* which included an article on how to build your own television receiver.

Sam Moskowitz relates a melodramatic story of envy and legal shenanigans which resulted in the collapse of Gernsback's first publishing empire: Bernarr Macfadden, the physical culturist who had built a publishing empire of his own, saw a potential rival in Gernsback and offered to buy Gernsback's million-dollar corporation. Gernsback turned him down. On February 20, 1929, three creditors sued Gernsback for payment, and, according to New York law at that time, three creditors could force bankruptcy. The Experimenter Publishing Company was sold, with Teck Publications taking over *Radio News* and *Amazing Stories,* and Gernsback's creditors were paid $1.08 for each $1 owed: *The New York Times* called it "bankruptcy deluxe."

Sam Merwin, Jr.

Undismayed, Gernsback quickly founded the Stellar Publishing Company, and offered subscribers to *Science and Invention* an opportunity to receive *Everyday Mechanics;* subscribers to *Radio News, Radio-Craft;* and subscribers to *Amazing Stories, Science Wonder Stories.* Eight thousand subscriptions came in; Gernsback was back in business; his publishing empire was reconstituted.

Amazing Stories was sold in 1939 to the Ziff-Davis Publishing Company and in the early sixties to Ultimate Publishing Company.

In his editorial in the first issue of *Science Wonder Stories,* June 1929, Gernsback invented the term "science fiction." Unlike second thoughts in general, it was the most successful term ever used to describe the genre, although recent attempts have been made to find some other word or words by those who feel that "science fiction" is too restrictive or not sufficiently descriptive. One contemporary alternative is Robert Heinlein's 1947 suggestion, "speculative fiction."

Raymond A. Palmer

Other magazines soon joined Gernsback's constellation: *Air Wonder Stories, Scientific Detective Monthly, Science Wonder Quarterly*—and then all the Gernsback science fiction magazines merged into *Wonder Stories,* the first all-slick science fiction magazine, at least in the quality of its paper.

But the stock market crash which preceded the Depression was only months

June, 1929 (Vol. 1, No. 1)

July, 1929 (Vol. 1, No. 1)

June, 1930 (Vol. 1, No. 1)

Spring, 1930 (Vol. 1, No. 3)

Fall, 1930

away. The Depression would be a great period for the genre magazines; all sorts of detective magazines, western magazines, and adventure magazines rainbowed the news dealers' stands, including a number of magazines created to narrate the adventures of a single character or group of characters: *Doc Savage, The Shadow, The Phantom, G-8 and His Battle Aces, The Spider, Secret Agent X, Operator #5,* and the pulp science fiction hero *Captain Future.* But money was scarce, and in 1936 Gernsback sold *Wonder Stories* to Standard Magazines, where it would be edited as *Thrilling Wonder Stories* by Leo Margulies and later, along with *Startling Stories,* by a series of editors. (One, Samuel Merwin, used to liven the lengthy readers' letter section with comic comments by Sergeant Saturn, until such capers were discarded in the late forties as inconsistent with science fiction's newfound respectability as the prophet of the atomic bomb.)

Amazing Stories and *Fantastic Stories* later would come under the editorship of a long-time fan, clever little Ray Palmer, who would print (and perhaps help originate) the famous Shaver Hoax stories, and writer Howard Browne, who

Magazine rack in the thirties

would turn them briefly into well-paying slicks aiming, unsuccessfully it seems, at a new market. Sometime fan, agent, and writer Ted White has been the most recent (and, in the opinion of some critics, perhaps the best) editor of *Amazing* and its sister publications.

Gernsback never completely turned his back on science fiction, even though at times it seemed as if science fiction had forgotten Gernsback. He experimented in 1939 with three issues of *Superworld Comics*, but he was ahead of his time. Meanwhile *Radio-Craft* metamorphosed into the successful *Radio Electronics,* and a new magazine, *Sexology,* added a new chapter to the Gernsback publishing history.

Gernsback made one last farewell performance as a publisher of science fiction, perhaps inspired by the World Science Fiction Convention held in Chicago in 1952, where he was guest of honor and gave a speech. It was reminiscent of an October 1927 *Amazing Stories* editorial in which he urged patent reform so that authors could apply for provisional patents on the devices they predict (quoting Columbia Professor Michael Papin: "To discover the need for an invention, and to specify it, constitutes 50 percent of the invention itself"). Then in March 1953 a new magazine appeared on the newsstands, *Science Fiction Plus,* with Sam Moskowitz as managing editor and with that speech as one feature. It was a large-format magazine like the original *Amazing Stories,* but it was printed on coated stock, carried no advertisements, and featured five-color covers and two-color interior illustrations. The first issue, among other material, contained an article billed as a story by Gernsback on "The Exploration of Mars," which described a trip to Mars by "Grego Banshuck" and three other anagrams of Hugo Gernsback (the picture of Grego is a picture of Gernsback in a space helmet), and an article on "The Cosmatonic Flyer" by Greno Gashbuck. There were less Gernsback-oriented issues that followed, but it lasted for only seven issues, and by the end it was being printed on pulp paper.

The radio-electronics industry presented Gernsback with the silver Hugo Gernsback Trophy in 1953, for fifty years of service to the radio electronic art; however, his most lasting tribute may be the awards presented each year by the fans attending the World Science Fiction Convention to the works they consider the best science fiction of the year. Among Oscars and Emmies, Grammies and Edgars (after Edgar Allan Poe), there is, as well, a Hugo.

Amazing Stories carried the caption:

Extravagant Fiction Today .... Cold Fact Tomorrow

That was Gernsback's vision, a vision summarized in his formula: "The ideal proportion of a scientifiction story should be 75 percent literature interwoven with 25 percent science." The vision may have been narrow, but it got science fiction launched into a new era. Gernsback died on August 19, 1967, but what he created lives on. Even if the science fiction magazine itself should pass from the newsstands, his contribution would still continue: Gernsback provided a focus for enthusiasm, for publication, for development. He may not have shaped modern science fiction—that honor we will reserve for others—but he provided a place for science fiction to be shaped.

Looking back upon the place, it may have been a ghetto, but it was a golden ghetto, a place of brotherhood and opportunity and wonder. Before Gernsback, there were science fiction stories. After Gernsback, there was a science fiction genre.

March, 1953 (Vol. 1, No. 1)

Gernsback's anagrams

A Gernsback Christmas card

CHAPTER 9
THE EXPANDING
UNIVERSE: 1930-1940

THE THIRTIES began with the United States doubting itself, even questioning its own survival, and ended with an optimistic look at a future of increasing technological miracles. It began in the Depression, so aptly named, and ended in hope and renewed vigor, even though that hope was shadowed by the beginnings of war in Europe.

With the thirties, the center of science fiction clearly was in the United States. The creation of the science fiction magazines had focused the interests of science fiction readers on a developing medium with an evolving message, and new writers were being created out of the readership. *Amazing Stories* had passed into the hands of Teck Publications, but Gernsback was creating *Wonder Stories* in its many metamorphoses, and a new magazine was formed in January 1930, *Astounding Stories of Super Science*, edited by Harry Bates and published by Clayton Magazines, which also published westerns, adventure, detective, and love story magazines.

The first issue of *Astounding Stories* included stories by Ray Cummings, Murray Leinster, and Victor Rousseau, and an editorial by Harry Bates describing the kind of stories that would be included in future issues. It said, in part:

> Tomorrow, more astounding things are going to happen. Your children—or their children—are going to take a trip to the moon. They will be able to render themselves invisible. They will be able to disintegrate their bodies in New York and reintegrate them in China—and in a matter of seconds.
>
> Astounding? Indeed, yes.
>
> Impossible? Well television would have been impossible, almost unthinkable, ten years ago. . . .

Even more important than the appearance of a new magazine was its new word rate: two cents a word, on acceptance. That was magnificence compared with the customary half-cent a word paid by *Amazing Stories* on publication (though frequently publication was long-delayed) and by *Wonder Stories* after publication. The situation later was recalled by H. L. Gold as "a fraction of a cent a word payable upon law suit." Jack Williamson remembers getting a lawyer at the Fiction Guild to collect for him.

But the primary fact of the thirties, for science fiction as well as the nation and the world, was the state of the economy. World War I, with its inhumanity, its prolonged trench warfare, its indiscriminate bombings and shellings, and its poison gas, had destroyed a naïve faith that man had outgrown all that, that he was destined to improve himself and his society for the foreseeable future. America's exposure to the ugly facts of modern warfare was mercifully brief; the nation itself was virtually untouched by it. But now the economy of the nation

January, 1930 (first issue)

had gone awry. Social and economic theories had been developed to explain how society and the economy were supposed to operate, but suddenly they no longer explained what was happening. Natural forces were out of control and nobody could do anything about it.

The individual citizen felt as if the Earth itself were disappearing beneath his feet (as in fact it was for the Dust Bowl farmer), as if nature had turned against him, as if the gods had forsaken him, as if he were a victim of life instead of its master. Technology was useless; science had no answers.

Incomes plummeted like brokers diving out of skyscrapers, and so did prices. Between late October and mid-November of 1929, stocks lost more than 40 percent of their total valuation, a drop of $30 billion; General Electric stock dropped from $1600 to $600 by the end of 1930; Union Cigar went from $113.50 to $4.00. In 1932 a coal miner earned $723 a year; a steelworker, $422.87 a year; a public-school teacher, $1,227; and a college teacher, $3,111. At the University of Kansas, faculty salaries were reduced 10 percent for 1932–33, and the following year salaries stood at 15 to 25 percent below what they had been two years before.

Prices were low, too, of course. Sirloin steak cost twenty-nine cents a pound; pork chops, twenty cents; butter, twenty-eight cents; and bread, five cents a loaf. A modern six-room house in Detroit was advertised for $2,800; an English cottage in Seattle, with eight rooms, three baths, and a ballroom for $4,250. A washing machine cost $47.95; a gas stove, $23.95; a woman's wool dress, $1.95; a man's suit, $10.50; and a Pontiac coupe, $585.00.

The President was Herbert Hoover, and he worked hard at measures to ease the economic slump. But he believed that "economic depression cannot be cured by legislative action or executive pronouncement."

The election of Franklin Delano Roosevelt brought the New Deal, the distribution of relief funds, and the beginnings of "recovery" and make-work programs, which may not have solved the economic problems but which alleviated misery and helped provide a reassurance that something was being done about the Depression.

Even the pace of invention seemed to slow during the thirties. The twenties ended with a flurry: in 1928 the invention of the television-image pickup tube, the differential analyzer computer, and the electric shaver; in 1929 the perfecting of the rocket engine by R. H. Goddard and the discovery of penicillin; and in 1930 the invention of the cyclotron. Two significant gaps occurred in the steady progress of technological development; nothing important was invented until nylon and synthetic rubber in 1935, xerography in 1938, and the betatron, FM broadcasting, and the electron microscope in 1939.

It seemed as if economic and political events had drained the intellectual and scientific vitality of the nation. But perhaps the rapid pace of invention during the previous two centuries had solved the easy problems; and the subtle things that men were now beginning to do with molecules, atoms, subatomic particles, and electronics required a return to basic research.

But if technology was coasting, basic science was not. Atoms, which Isaac Newton had described as "solid, massy, hard, impenetrable, moveable particles" and nineteenth-century physicists still regarded as small, solid objects, became small, massive nuclei surrounded by shells of electrons, through the research of Lord Rutherford and others. They used X rays and magnetic fields at first, and these probes gradually developed into increasingly sophisticated and powerful atom smashers, which produced a bewildering profusion of subatomic particles from what was once considered indivisible. Particle physics became one of the glamor sciences as it produced new results, new insights, and even new applications such as atomic energy; but it also became more abstruse, with its antiparticles and antimatter.

Meanwhile Max Planck's quantum theory presented a picture of energy in packets (1900) which Einstein applied to photoelectric effect and the specific heat of solids. Einstein went on to add to his 1905 special theory of relativity a 1911 paper on the equivalence of gravitation and inertia and his general theory in 1916; he won the Nobel Prize in physics in 1921. In 1924 Louis Victor de Broglie expanded Einstein's wave-particle duality to a dualism between energy and matter. No longer were energy and matter to be considered sep-

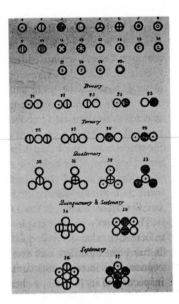
Dalton's symbols

Albert Einstein

September, 1940 (Rogers)

arate and inviolable. The old physics was rapidly breaking apart, and mechanical causality in the old Newtonian sense, which visualized the universe wound up and working like a clock, received a blow from which it might never recover when Werner Heisenberg in 1927 announced his uncertainty principle; it theorized that one cannot know simultaneously the position and velocity of a particle; and thus, as physicist P. W. Bridgman would speculate later, nature has placed limits to man's knowledge.

While knowledge at the subatomic level was becoming smaller, fuzzier, and less certain, the universe was becoming larger, older, and more profusely populated with habitable planets. The origin of the Earth, the sun, the other planets, and ultimately the universe itself, once the province of myth and religion, became permanently a matter for science when Galileo and Copernicus began substituting observation for faith. Newton established in his monumental 1687 work, *Principia*, the laws of gravitation and of motion, which provided theory and method for calculating the positions of stars and planets.

Comte de Buffon

In 1755 Kant speculated about an infinite system of galaxies in the universe, with suns and planets condensing out of rotating gaseous disks. A different origin for the planets had been suggested ten years earlier by a French naturalist named Buffon: a collision between the sun and a comet knocked off bits of the sun which became the planets. The distance between stars is such that if Buffon's theory is correct, planets are accidental and few in the universe; if Kant's is right, planets would be the rule and innumerable. These opposing views, modified through the generations, vied for the allegiance of astronomers and cosmologists for two centuries. Kant's theory of cloud condensation, as modified by Laplace, was popular until James Clerk Maxwell pointed out in the nineteenth century the impossibility of the planets having sufficient matter to be drawn together by gravitational attraction in the face of the sun's immense pulls; there was, as well, a problem of angular momentum. So Buffon, as modified by Chamberlin and Moulton and then Jeans and Jeffries, returned to favor, and the uniqueness of Earth made man once more seem alone in the universe. In the forties the pendulum swung back toward a view of the planets being formed when cold bits of matter like meteorites came together with dust and gas and water; they stuck together because the mixture itself was sticky, later being heated by internal radioactivity and the lighter gases being driven off by the solar wind.

Immanuel Kant

The incredible size of the universe and even of our own galaxy, the Milky Way, was unsuspected even by those who, like Galileo, Kant, Wright, and Herschel, could see the myriad stars and the nebulae which might, some thought, be distant galaxies. The discovery and analysis of Cepheid variables—stars which brighten and darken regularly—led to a 1918 announcement by Harlow Shapley of a galaxy 30,000 light-years thick and 300,000 light-years wide, ten times bigger than previous estimates; later the size was reduced to about 25,000 by 100,000. Our sun, meanwhile, was demoted from a central position in our galaxy to a peripheral spot in one of the spiral arms, just as in past centuries the Earth had been demoted from its position in the center of the solar system. In 1924 at Mount Wilson, Edwin P. Hubble finally proved the existence of other galaxies and demonstrated that our own was no more central in the universe than was our sun in the galaxy or our Earth in the solar system. The existence of billions of galaxies like our own was suspected, and some of them were a billion light-years away. Moreover they were getting farther away.

Einstein's model universe was static, but his equations required a situation without equilibrium—an expanding universe. Hubble noted in 1929 that the stars —and galaxies—farthest from Earth were receding from Earth faster and with a speed which could be estimated from the extent to which their spectrums were shifted toward the red. The universe was not only bigger and more populated with stars, and perhaps with planets, than anyone had ever supposed, but it was getting bigger all the time.

Close at hand were the political activities which were dicing with man's immediate future: totalitarianism was growing in Europe, with the Nazi takeover of Germany in 1933 and the beginning of a series of aggressive actions to redress World War I losses, which would culminate in 1939 with the start of World War II. But science fiction writers had their eyes fixed on more-distant vistas. They

James Clerk Maxwell

were reading Sir James Jean's *The Universe Around Us* (1929) and *The Mysterious Universe* (1930), and their vision had turned cosmic. The letter columns of *Amazing Stories* referred frequently to Einstein, with the editor confessing that he didn't understand everything that he would like to know about Einstein's theories; those were the days when it was popular to repeat that only half a dozen persons in the world understood Einstein.

And *Amazing Stories* ran *The Skylark of Space* serially in 1928. Its author, Edward E. Smith (1890–1965), would be known to several generations of science fiction fans as "Doc" Smith because of his Ph.D. from George Washington University. (Earned in food chemistry, the degree led Smith into full-time professional positions as a doughnut-mix specialist.) He was born in 1890 in Wisconsin and raised in Washington and Idaho.

E. E. Smith and
John Campbell

Smith wrote the 90,000-word novel in 1915, 1916, 1919, and 1920 in collaboration with the wife of a former classmate, Mrs. Lee Garby. He had difficulty selling it until *Amazing Stories* offered $75.

Edmond Hamilton (born 1904) had a two-part novel called *Crashing Suns*, which began in *Weird Tales* the same month. Its vision, like Smith's *Skylark*, was galactic. Perhaps the turn toward larger space was a reaction to the materialism of the era (the Depression was still a year away), perhaps it was stimulated by the growing astronomical discoveries and cosmological speculation, or perhaps the time was ready—it was "galactic time," the universe was expanding in the imaginations of men, and a generation of readers and writers responded.

The new era did not open pretentiously:

Petrified with astonishment, Richard Seaton stared after the copper steam-bath upon which he had been electrolyzing his solution of "X," the unknown metal. For as soon as he had removed the beaker the heavy bath had jumped endwise from under his hand as though it were alive. It had flown with terriffic speed over the table, smashing apparatus and bottles of chemicals on its way, and was even now disappearing through the open window. . . .

That was the opening paragraph of *The Skylark of Space*. The scene continued with Seaton, Smith's brilliant scientist-hero, realizing, "I have liberated the intra-atomic energy of copper! Copper, 'X,' and electric current. . . . We'll explore the whole solar system! Great cat, what a chance! . . ."

Melodramatic though the plot may have been—it involved attempts by an arch-villain named Marc "Blackie" Duquesne to steal the secret of the atomic propellant and his actual theft of Seaton's fiancee—juvenile though the romantic episodes and dialogue, with its strained invention of future slang, actually were, readers reacted with great enthusiasm to the concept of the hero as inventor and his interplanetary adventures. The editor of *Amazing Stories* felt the same way:

Perhaps it is a bit unethical and unusual for editors to voice their opinion of their own wares, but when such a story as "The Skylark of Space" comes along, we just feel as if we must shout from the housetops that this is the greatest interplanetarian and space flying story that has appeared this year. Indeed, it probably will rank as one of the great space flying stories for many years to come. The story is chock full, not only of excellent science, but woven through it there is also that very rare element, love and romance. This element in an interplanetarian story is often apt to be foolish, but it does not seem so in this particular story.

We know so little about intra-atomic forces, that this story, improbable as it will appear in spots, will read commonplace years hence, when we have atomic engines, and when we have solved the riddles of the atom.

You will follow the hair-raising explorations and strange ventures into far-away worlds with bated breath, and you will be fascinated, as we were, with the strangeness of it all.

Doc Smith went on to write two sequels and other series of novels in which miracle workers with bus bars and test tubes, new kinds of mental controls, giant muscles, and battle-axes would solve insoluble problems concerning the life and deaths of worlds, solar systems, and galaxies.

Skylark Three appeared in *Amazing Stories* in 1930. *The Spacehounds of IPC* introduced alien intelligences and the ion drive in 1931. *Triplanetary* brought in "inertialess" vessels and the "inertialess" drive. Science fiction, if it was going to paint its pictures on a galaxy-wide canvas, had to make an end

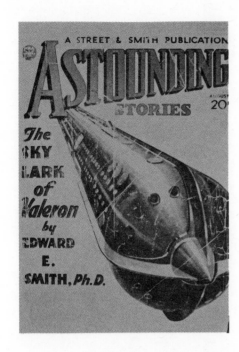

Skylark of Valeron ran in
the issues of August and
September, 1934
(Both covers by
Howard V. Brown)

The SKYLARK Part
One
of
VALERON
by EDWARD E. SMITH, Ph.D.
Illustrated by Elliot Dold

Two illustrations from the
August, 1934, issue
(Elliott Dold)

run around the limiting factor of the speed of light; Smith's concept was that
Einstein's theories set no limit to the velocity of *inertialess* mass, and he men-
tions in one novel a speed of ninety parsecs (a parsec is 3.26 light-years) per
hour.

The Skylark of Valeron returned to the Skylark series and introduced Doc
Smith to the readers of *Astounding* in 1935. By then *Astounding* had been purchased from Clayton Magazines by Street & Smith and was edited by F. Orlin
Tremaine, who was seeking to distinguish the magazine by getting and publishing stories with bold new ideas which he labeled "thought variants." Tremaine
promoted Smith's new serial, increased the magazine's contents by 25,000
words, and saw circulation grow.

In 1936 Smith planned a 400,000-word novel—Smith's writing scope, like his
scene, was vast—divided into four segments. This was his major work, his Lensman series, which appeared over the next ten years in *Astounding: Galactic
Patrol* (1938), *Grey Lensman* (1939), *Second Stage Lensman* (1941), and

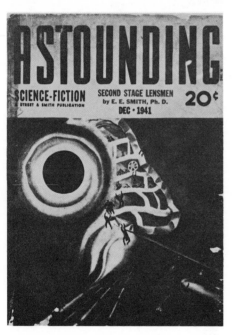

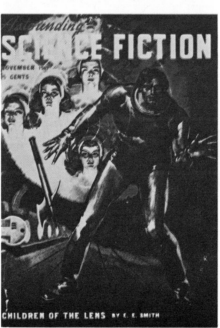

A few *Astounding* issues in which "Doc" Smith's ambitious Lensman series appeared. ABOVE LEFT: October, 1939; RIGHT: November, 1939; BELOW LEFT: December, 1941; RIGHT: November, 1947 (All covers by Rogers)

Children of the Lens (1947). Together they make up an epic about the long battle between good and evil, between Arisians (using Lensmen of various alien origins) and Eddorians (with their black-hearted henchmen). The backdrop is the entire universe, and what is at stake is not merely survival but the survival of good. The novels are filled with apparatus, not only inertialess vessels but Q-guns, tractor beams, screens, wall shields, needle rays, projectors, space axes, thought screens, mental force, thionite (the worst of all known habit-forming drugs), and the lens, a counterfeit-proof bracelet and telepathic communication device. The scene in which Kimball Kinnison, hero of the series, first puts on his lens provides as good a sample as any:

The forearm was wrapped in thick insulation, molds and shields snapped into place, and there flared out an instantly suppressed flash of brilliance intolerable. Then the molds fell apart, the insulation was removed, and there was revealed the LENS. Clasped to Kinnison's brawny wrist by a bracelet of imperishable, almost unbreakable, metal in which it was imbedded, it shone in all its lambent splendor—no longer a whitely inert piece of jewelry, but a lenticular polychrome of writhing, almost fluid, radiance which proclaimed to all observers in symbols of ever-changing flame that here was a Lensman of the Galactic Patrol.

Despite their flat characters and their Victorian conversations and relationships, the novels appealed to developing fandom; the sweep of the action, the scope of the concepts, the black and white of the conflict, and the massiveness of the books themselves created science fiction's epic, and if the writing was inadequate, epics have seldom been judged by the quality of their writing.

Virtually all of Smith's novels were published in hard covers by the specialized book publishers who sprang up out of fan enthusiasm after World War II. In fact, the original motivation of the fan presses seemed to be the immortalization of Doc Smith; they wanted to make his works available to a generation of readers who had grown up deprived of his imagination. But a more complete account of the fan presses will be presented in Chapter 11.

Meanwhile other authors were responding to the vision of an inhabited galaxy where men in spaceships could roam among the stars and work wonders with their understanding of the basic laws of the universe.

E. E. Smith

Early book publication of several E. E. Smith novels by the fan presses after World War II

Edmond Hamilton, an Ohio farm boy who grew up to pit galaxies against each other, already had clashed suns in 1928. The next year, in a *Weird Tales* novelette, he began the publication of a series of stories which would describe a future in which a galaxy of populated worlds would be organized into a Council of Suns, and order would be kept and the Council's edicts enforced by an Interstellar Patrol.

The Interstellar Patrol marked the beginning of a consensus future history for humanity that Don Wollheim would call "science fiction's cosmogony of the future." By this time Hamilton was well-launched into a career that earned him the title of "world-wrecker" or, alternatively, "world-saver," in which he would toss planets and suns around like beach balls. He began sending stories to magazines the same year *Amazing Stories* was founded, 1926, but much of his production in the early years, including all he wrote in the first three years, went to *Weird Tales*.

Hamilton was prolific—every pulp writer trying to make a living from selling words for one-half cent to a penny had to be prolific or starve—and stories came pouring out of his typewriter. In addition to his planet-pitching prowess, Hamilton was profligate with ideas. Among the concepts he developed or popularized were: Charles Fort's concept that earth is property (compare Eric Frank Russell's 1939 *Unknown* serial *Sinister Barrier* and Fortean themes in the work of H. P. Lovecraft and the *Amazing Stories* Shaver Hoax stories); aerial cities (compare Swift's *Laputa* and James Blish's *Cities in Flight*); aliens in metal bodies (compare the Professor Jameson stories by Neil R. Jones); impenetrable darkness as a weapon (compare Murray Leinster's "The Darkness on Fifth Avenue"); matter transmitters (compare Alfred Bester's *The Stars My Destination* and Harry Harrison's recent series of stories collected into *One Step From Earth*); war between micro- and macro-universes; speeded-up evolution (compare Wells's *The Island of Dr. Moreau* and Theodore Sturgeon's "Microcosmic God," among others); metal-roofed planets (compare Asimov's *The Caves of Steel* and a novel I wrote with Jack Williamson, *Star Bridge*); an army of historic warriors recruited by time machine (compare Van Vogt's "Recruiting Station"); and Earth as a living creature (compare Haggard's *When the Earth Screamed* and Nelson Bond's "And Lo! the Bird").

In 1939 Leo Margulies, editorial director of Standard Magazines, attended the first World Science Fiction Convention, and was so impressed by the enthusiasm and dedication of the attendees that he told the audience, "I didn't think you fans could be so damn sincere." His response was a new pulp magazine aimed at teen-agers, to be called *Captain Future*. Ed Hamilton would write all but three of the twenty-one novels and novelettes which appeared in the magazine. They were written to a formula: a super-scientist with three aides—a robot, an android, and a beautiful girl—would undertake and complete in each

Edmond Hamilton
in the 20s . . .

and in the 70s

From *Weird Tales*, September, 1928

Julius Schwartz, Edmond Hamilton, Jack Williamson

Mort Weisinger

Leo Margulies and
Manly Wade Wellman

episode a crusade to bring a villain to justice; in the process the hero would be captured—and escape—exactly three times.

Unlike Doc Smith, who would improve what he did but be unable to do anything else, Hamilton adapted to changing times. He had difficulty living down his reputation as a galactic wheeler-dealer, as one of the pulpier of the pulp writers, but he began writing sociological science fiction in 1932, some years before there was any appreciable market for it, and he would go on to write the science fiction called for by changing tastes. And he would see *Captain Future* come back to trouble him, when the Captain underwent a rebirth in paperback in 1969–70, and, worst of all, without further payment to Hamilton.

Jack Williamson is another writer whose career has extended from the twenties to the seventies, six decades. When A. Merritt's *The Moon Pool* was serialized in *Amazing* in 1927, Williamson began to write stories strongly influenced by Merritt's romantic imagination and lush prose, using science fiction as a doorway into another world from the arid New Mexico farm he knew. His subsequent stories contributed to the expanded vision that characterized the thirties, including unique concepts such as the Heaviside layer supporting life, a tiny artificial planet suspended in a laboratory, a beautiful woman flying about in space asking entry into a spaceship, and a matter-transmitter for space travel.

He sold stories to all the science fiction magazines and to *Weird Tales,* too. His typewriter was catholic: it did not produce a single kind of fiction, and Williamson never established a reputation built around one character or one kind of writing. Instead, he learned how to write—apprenticing himself for a

Spring, 1944 (Bergey)

Edmond Hamilton . . .   and Jack Williamson . . .   on the Mississippi, 1931

Jack Williamson in 1943 . . .   and in 1960   Williamson with Frederik Pohl, 1971

The Legion of Space

*A full book-length serial
of Super-science
Crashing into the unknown future
of the Universe*

by JACK WILLIAMSON

Illustrated by Howard V. Brown
In Six Parts. Part One.

Title page and illustration
from *Astounding*,
April, 1934 (Brown)

LEFT: May, 1936 (Brown)
RIGHT: May, 1938
(Schneeman)

Dr. Miles J. Breuer (drawing)

period to Miles J. Breuer, whose work he admired—and he was willing to adapt himself to the changing ideas of the times and of the magazines: he attempted characterization by giving a hero a lisp or a stutter or a characteristic mannerism or habit of speech; and if this seems like a modest contribution, it was sufficient among the cardboard heroes of the period to give Williamson a reputation which he later learned how to deserve.

In 1933 he began writing a space epic which would become better-known than anything else he ever wrote: *The Legion of Space* was published in 1934, *The Cometeers* in 1936, and *One Against the Legion* in 1939, all in *Astounding Stories*. They could be summed up as the Three Musketeers in space plus Shakespeare's Falstaff, in the reincarnation of Giles Habibula, seeking to discover the secret of AKKA, the ultimate weapon which will determine the fate of mankind, and which turns out to be little more than a ten-penny nail. The trilogy would be among the first books reprinted by the fan presses after World War II.

Meanwhile the nature of science fiction was changing, and Williamson was changing with it: in his early days he had provided a bridge between the writers of the scientific romance and the new scientifically based stories that Gernsback wanted. In 1942 he began another group of stories describing in naturalistic detail the lives of asteroid miners who hunted the contraterrene (c.t.) or antimatter boulders scattered through the asteroid belt. Eventually the stories, originally published in *Astounding Science Fiction* in 1942, 1943, and 1949 would be published as books: *Seetee Shock* (1950) and *Seetee Ship* (1951). Out of them would come a New York *Daily News* comic strip which Williamson would plot: "Beyond Mars."

Williamson had still other metamorphoses: his sociophilosophical story "The Equalizer" in 1947 was followed by one of the most successful and memorable robot novelettes ever written, *With Folded Hands . . .* Its conclusion is one of science fiction's most dramatic statements of the conflict between man and machine. The home town of the hero, a robot salesman, has been visited by an improved type of robot which calls itself a humanoid. It is centrally controlled from a massive computer on a distant planet, and its utopian mission is to serve and obey, and guard man from harm. But the humanoids can do everything

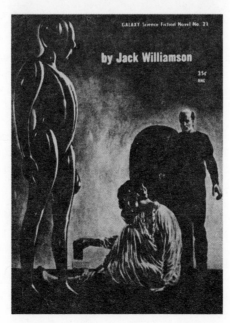

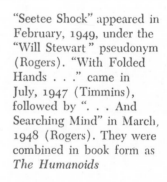

"Seetee Shock" appeared in February, 1949, under the "Will Stewart" pseudonym (Rogers). "With Folded Hands . . ." came in July, 1947 (Timmins), followed by ". . . And Searching Mind" in March, 1948 (Rogers). They were combined in book form as *The Humanoids*

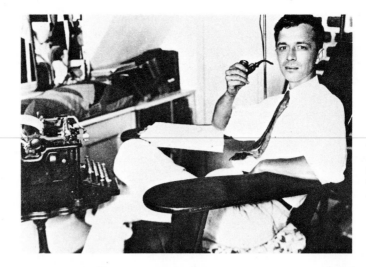

William Fitzgerald
Jenkins, better
known to science
fiction fans as
"Murray Leinster,"
in the 1920s, 1930s,
1940s, 1950s and
1960s.

better than man can do, including his arts and skills and creations. At the end there is nothing for man to do: he cannot even be unhappy because the humanoid surgeons have learned how to perform lobotomies:

"No, there's nothing the matter with me," he gasped desperately. "I've just found out that I'm perfectly happy under the Prime Directive. Everything is absolutely wonderful." His voice came dry and hoarse and wild. "You won't have to operate on me."

The car turned into the shining avenue, taking him back to the quiet splendor of his home. His futile hands clenched and relaxed again, folded on his knees. There was nothing left to do.

The ellipsis in *With Folded Hands* . . . contained a sequel, . . . *And Searching Mind,* published in book form as *The Humanoids.*

For a few years in the fifties Williamson had a writing block which he managed to break through with collaborations, chiefly with Frederik Pohl, with whom he wrote a series of three "Undersea" juveniles and other novels. Besides the sharing of effort, Williamson said once, collaboration helped give him "a sense of audience, a sharper sense of direction" and "made it easier to find a mask, or a voice, or a persona for the story." He felt, he said, as if he were writing it for his collaborator, and that made it flow easier.

Other things were occupying him in the fifties as well: as if to bring off one last metamorphosis, he earned his Ph.D. in English and added a career as a university teacher to his accomplishments. He called it "rejoining the establishment."

Another writer who was so adaptable that he was never stereotyped has had the longest career of all: William Fitzgerald Jenkins, born in 1896, who began writing science fiction for *Argosy* with the "Runaway Skyscraper" in 1919. The undisputed dean of science fiction writers has had fiction published in six decades, much of it under the pen name of Murray Leinster. Among his memorable stories are: "First Contact," which presents the dramatic problem of the first meeting between earthlings and aliens, only this one is in the Crab Nebula, far from Earth, and it illustrates how even the most difficult of problems can be solved pragmatically with sufficient good will and ingenuity; "The Strange Case of John Kingman," about a man who has been locked up in an asylum for 162 years, the discovery that he is an alien, and the attempt to cure him of his paranoia; "A Logic Named Joe," dealing with the problems inherent in a central, home-linked computer; "Proxima Centauri," about an interstellar spaceship that is a self-sufficient world; "Sidewise in Time," which introduced a new concept of time in parallel tracks (somewhat like J. W. Dunne's serial universes, in which the nature of the world depends upon the outcome of historical events), and what happens when these time tracks coexist for a period; "The Ethical Equations," which describes how a new equation for ethical behavior is applied to a drifting alien spaceship; and others such as "If You Was a Moklin," "De Profundis," and his "Med Service" series.

But these represent only a small portion of his production; as much or more of his hundreds of stories went to slick markets under his real name, Will Jenkins. He also was an inventor, coming up with several serious inventions including a workable front-projection method for motion picture and advertising backgrounds.

He wrote adventure fiction, technological fiction, and when that began to be antiquated by new tastes and new developments, he turned to the sociological and psychological impact of future change.

Such was the mainstream of science fiction in the thirties. But it was not all of it: in addition to the first year or so of *Amazing Stories*, reprinting continued in other magazines—Wells, Verne, the various scientific romances of Edgar Rice Burroughs and A. Merritt and others, certain instant "classics," reader favorites. . . . Then there were new stories by pulp writers such as Arthur J. Burks, who wrote 10,000 words a day and sold most of them to western, detective, and adventure pulps as well as to some science fiction magazines. Other writers introduced during this period include S. Fowler Wright, who began writing for *Weird Tales* in the late twenties; Raymond Z. Gallun (1929); Eric Temple Bell (who wrote under the name of John Taine) and Ralph Milne Farley (1930); John Beynon Harris (who would become better known under the name of John Wyndham, beginning in 1950), Harry Bates, and Manly Wade Wellman (1931), Donald Wandrei, Otto Binder (who would write some stories with his brother Earl under the name of Eando Binder), and Thomas Gardner (1932); John Russell Fearn (who would have an English science fiction magazine named after one of his pseudonyms, Vargo Statten, 1933); and Henry Hasse and Russell Winterbotham (1936).

H. P. Lovecraft (1890–1937) specialized in horror stories, although he was a lover of science fiction and provided science fiction frameworks for some of his

Arthur J. Burks

Stanley Coblentz

S. Fowler Wright

Raymond Z. Gallun

John Taine

Manly Wade Wellman

Arthur K. Barnes

John Wyndham

Dr. David H. Keller

Ralph Milne Farley

STANDING: L. Sprague de Camp, John D. Clark, Julius Schwartz, Mort Weisinger, Jack Williamson, Ed Hamilton, Otis Adelbert Kline. KNEELING: Otto Binder, Manly Wade Wellman, Frank Belknap Long, Jr.

Henry Hasse

H. P. Lovecraft

Henry Kuttner, C. L. Moore, Robert Bloch and friend

Clark Ashton Smith

Donald Wandrei

Robert Bloch

Frank Belknap Long

Carl Jacobi

Stanley Weinbaum

Thomas Gardner

August Derleth

works. Most of his stories were published in *Weird Tales.* He developed his own mythos, "Cthulhu," which was inspired by his reading of Lord Dunsany in 1919. Other writers were attracted to his consistent portrayal of a world in which unseen, ancient powers, exiled from Earth long ago, were struggling to return. A few writers even began to use the Lovecraft myths of R'lyeh, the great stone city under the sea; the terrible *Necronomicon,* written in the Middle Ages by the mad Arab Abdul Alhazred; and Miskatonic University, located near Lovecraft's native Providence—these figured in several of Lovecraft's books or stories, such as: *The Call of Cthulhu, The Colour Out of Space, The Dunwich Horror, The Whisperer in Darkness, At the Mountains of Madness, The Shadow Over Innsmouth,* and *The Shadow Out of Time.* He had a significant influence on a number of fantasy writers through his prolific correspondence as well as his published work: Clark Ashton Smith, Donald Wandrei, Robert Bloch, Henry Kuttner, C. L. Moore, Frank Belknap Long, and Carl Jacobi. He was admired by the late August Derleth (1909–71), and Arkham House was created to reprint his work and the works of his followers. But his influence on science fiction was small, as was true of most fantasy until relatively contemporary times; however, science fiction did have some influence on fantasy, particularly through Street & Smith's *Unknown* (companion magazine to *Astounding*), which was published from 1939 to 1942.

Stanley Weinbaum (1902–35) burst into science fiction with "A Martian Odyssey" in 1934. It presented one of the earliest believable portraits of an alien, an ostrichlike Martian creature named Tweel or Trrrweerrlll.

"The Martian wasn't a bird, really. It wasn't even birdlike, except at first glance. It had a beak all right, and a few feathery appendages, but the beak wasn't really a beak. It was somewhat flexible; I could see the tip bend slowly from side to side; it was almost a cross between a beak and a trunk. It had four-toed feet, and four-fingered things—hands, you'd have to call them, and a little roundish body, and a long neck ending in a tiny head—and that beak. It stood an inch or so taller than I. . . ."

Tweel not only was intelligent, but possibly more intelligent than man. As the narrator pointed out:

"I couldn't pick up a single idea of his and he learned six or seven words of mine. And do you realize what complex ideas he put over with no more than those six or seven words? The pyramid-monster—the dream-beast! In a single phrase he told me that one was a harmless automaton and the other a deadly hypnotist. . . ."

Damon Knight called Weinbaum "the most inventive science fiction writer since Wells." Weinbaum specialized in fantastic yet believable aliens; he wrote light romantic travelogues of the solar system; and he wrote other fiction which seemed unlike anything that had ever been written before, stories like "The Adaptive Ultimate," "Proteus Island," and "The Black Flame." He died of throat cancer at 33, fifteen months after his science fiction career began.

The science fiction mainstream was now flowing with increasing vigor through the magazines, and other writers were turning to themes that had become associated with science fiction—writers such as Olaf Stapledon, Aldous Huxley, and Philip Wylie.

July, 1938 (Finlay)

Stapledon (1886–1950) was a philosopher with a doctorate from the University of Liverpool. His second book (his first was the 1929 *A Modern Theory of Ethics*) broke over science fiction and part of the intellectual world like a shattering cascade of ideas. J. B. Priestly called it a masterpiece. Hugh Walpole said it was "as original as the solar system." Arnold Bennett said, "There have been many visions of the future but none in my experience as strange as *Last and First Men*." Brian Aldiss said of it, in the preface to a later edition, "One cannot call it a novel, for it is much less that than a meditation."

Speak of a cosmic viewpoint: Stapledon took for his subject the future history of man himself, with side trips into science, sociology, culture, sexuality, psychology, and philosophy, from 1930 through the next 2 billion years, through the rise and fall of civilizations and the eventual evolution of competitive creatures and then of man himself, through migrations to Venus and finally to Neptune where, on the edge of extinction, mankind is spraying countless artificial human spores into space to be carried by solar radiation toward the most promising region of the galaxy.

In a sentence echoing the ideas of Edmund Crispin (quoted in Chapter 1), Aldiss remarks about the book: "Man is the hero of the chronicle; men are of little account." About halfway through the book Stapledon began a chapter, "We have now followed man's career during some forty million years. The whole period to be covered by this chronicle is about two thousand million."

Two thousand million years later: man on Jupiter, in all his final flower and glory, is doomed by a sudden and unexpected increase in the sun's radiation, and the Last Men begin to sow the universe with artificial human seed.

One among them preaches a great and moving message of the meaning of mankind, a message which speaks for much of science fiction:

Great are the stars, and man is no account to them. . . . Too soon, seemingly, he comes to an end. But when he is done he will not be nothing, not as though he had never been; for he is eternally a beauty in the eternal form of things.

Man was winged hopefully. He had in him to go further than this short flight now ending. . . . Instead, he is to be destroyed. He is only a fledgling caught in a bush-fire. . . . The music of the spheres passes over him, through him, and is not heard.

Yet it has used him. . . .

But does it really use him? Is the beauty of the Whole really enhanced by our agony? And is the Whole really beautiful? And what is beauty? . . .

But one thing is certain. Man himself, at the very least, is music, a brave theme that makes music also of its vast accompaniment, its matrix of storms and stars. Man himself in his degree is eternally a beauty in the eternal form of things. It is very good to have been man. And so we may go forward together with laughter in our hearts, and peace, thankful for the past, and for our own courage. For we shall make after all a fair conclusion to this brief music that is man.

Olaf Stapledon

Other books followed: *Last Men in London* (1932) described a visit to our era through the time-spanning power of the Last Men's minds, by one of the doomed Last Men on Neptune. After another philosophical book (*Waking World*, 1934), Stapledon produced *Odd John: A Story Between Jest and Earnest* (1935), one of the earliest and best of the superman novels (we might compare J. D. Beresford's *The Hampdenshire Wonder*, 1911; in certain ways, H. G. Wells's *The Food of the Gods*, 1904, and *Star-Begotten*, 1937; Philip Wylie's *Gladiator*, 1930; A. E. Van Vogt's *Slan*, magazine version 1940, book 1946; and many others).

The Star Maker (1937) covered the entire history of the universe from its creation to its end; it considered the function of the creator of the universe and the relationship between two subgalactic races, the Echinoderms and the Nautiloids, described galactic civilizations and galactic wars, and finally visualized an end to war and a utopia out of which developed a telepathic Cosmic Mind in which every mentally developed creature participated. Even suns and nebulae were found to be intelligent beings.

There were other books of philosophy, but Stapledon's final major science fiction book was *Sirius: A Fantasy of Love and Discord* (1944) about a super-dog who develops intelligence equal to or possibly higher than that of a human.

Aldous Huxley (1894–1963) brought new life to the anti-utopia in 1932

Philip Wylie

with his satire on life in a machine-dominated society, *Brave New World*. The book has inspired more arguments among science fiction fans and critics ("Well what about *Brave New World*?" "But that isn't science fiction; that's good!") than any other book, with the possible exception of George Orwell's *1984* (1949). Both books illustrated the continuing interest of satirical and literary writers in the techniques and future histories of the science fiction writers, which would develop into more significant and broader use in the sixties. But their influence on science fiction was limited to the educational impact on a few writers and readers of the exposure to the techniques and ideas of the literary culture. Satires, utopias, and anti-utopias are not quite science fiction, although they are allied genres which sometimes overlap science fiction. Satires, utopias, and anti-utopias differ from science fiction in that what they are about and what they say about it refers to something else, usually something contemporary, that they wish to criticize or praise, and almost always to the detriment of the story's verisimilitude, or appearance of reality. Science fiction takes its speculations seriously—or if not always seriously, at least as reasonable possibilities; the science fiction future is important for its own sake.

Philip Wylie (1902–71) was an able popular writer who used science fiction for his own purposes. He came from a family of writers. He discovered science fiction early but also discovered James Joyce and the literary experimenters, and later in his life was torn between his desire to write literary prose and his urge to expound ideas, motivations that customarily, though not always, work in opposite directions.

In 1927 Wylie wrote *Gladiator*, although it would not be published until 1930, following publication of two novels of manners. The following year he wrote *Murderer Invisible*, and Universal, which had purchased the film rights to Wells's *Invisible Man*, also bought Wylie's book and incorporated some elements from it in the motion picture. That led to a screenwriting assignment for Wylie on Wells's *Island of Dr. Moreau*, which appeared as *Island of Lost Souls*, starring Charles Laughton.

The Savage Gentleman appeared in 1932. Although Wylie continued to work on screenplays, he also produced stories for the slick magazines, including *Redbook*, whose editor was Edwin Balmer. With the help of friends at the California Institute of Technology, Wylie took plot ideas suggested by Balmer and wrote *When Worlds Collide*. The novel, a sensation when it was serialized in *Blue Book* in 1932, was syndicated in newspapers and issued immediately in hard covers. Later it would become one of George Pal's epic motion pictures. In 1933 the sequel appeared, *After Worlds Collide*, and it was received with almost as much enthusiasm. Then Wylie went on to other projects: an experimental novel titled *Finnley Wren* (1934), which established his literary reputa-

When Worlds Collide, by Philip Wylie and Edward Balmer, appeared in September, 1932. Below are illustrations by Joseph Franké

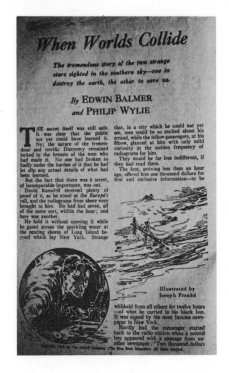

tion, and *Generation of Vipers* (1942), which established his vituperative powers and shattered a variety of American icons, including "momism."

Wylie continued to write prophetic fiction, including a 1945 atomic-bomb story, "The Paradise Crater," which was censored by Military Intelligence. Finally in 1950 came his last big science fiction book, *The Disappearance*. Just before his death, he turned his own television script—about a Los Angeles killed by smog and man—into a novel, *L.A. 2017*.

Other writers of the period would turn out stories for the slick magazines but would rarely appear in the science fiction magazines. Among these writers were Charles G. Finney, Pat Frank, Jack Finney, Gerald Kersh, and a number of others. Still others would divide their efforts between slicks and science fiction magazines, such as Murray Leinster, Nelson Bond, and for a time Robert Heinlein. And some, such as Ray Bradbury, would graduate from the science fiction magazines into the slicks and books.

The thirties also marked the appearance of writers who would produce a few stories suggestive of a potential they would not reach until later. One such writer was Clifford Simak (born 1904), a full-time newspaper man and part-time writer who would spend most of his working life as an editor for the Minneapolis *Star*. He started writing science fiction in the thirties, with stories such as "World of the Red Sun" in the 1931 *Wonder Stories*, "Mutiny on Mercury" in 1932, and later "The Voice in the Void," "The Hellhounds of the Cosmos," "The Asteroid of Gold," and an off-beat story called "The Creator," which appeared in a semiprofessional magazine in 1935.

Clifford Simak

The thirties also provided transitional writers. The most important, it turned out, was John W. Campbell. More clearly than any other he marked the transition between the Depression and hope, between cosmic vision and personal insight, between the scientific romance or romanticized science and modern science fiction.

Campbell began his writing career as a student at the Massachusetts Institute of Technology. Born in 1910 in Newark, New Jersey, the son of an electrical engineer, Campbell was a prototype for the precocious youngster who turns to science fiction to make up for his own social inadequacies, who makes science fiction a career or a religion because reality is both disappointing and dull. Campbell found science fiction early: first Edgar Rice Burroughs, then *Argosy*, *Weird Tales*, and the first issue of *Amazing Stories*. He was particularly impressed by the cosmic imagination displayed in Doc Smith's *Skylark of Space*, and much of Campbell's early writing was cosmic in scope, though carefully detailed scientifically.

John W. Campbell

He was still under 20 when he sold two stories to *Amazing*, and his first two published stories, in 1930, typically were about a super calculating machine. His first story appeared the same month the first issue of *Astounding Stories of Super Science* was published.

By 1934, when Campbell's galactic novel *The Mightiest Machine* was serialized in *Astounding*, he and Doc Smith were being called the two greatest science fiction authors. Meanwhile he had dropped out of M.I.T.—not, as the ironic legend reports it, because he had failed physics, but because he couldn't cope with German—and got his degree, majoring in physics, a year later from Duke University. He worked briefly as a salesman of Fords, then exhaust fans, then gas heaters. But he continued to write. In 1933 he wrote a story called "Twilight" about the stagnation and degeneration of the human race, which was carefully tended by faithful automatic machinery:

Twilight—the sun has set. The desert out beyond, in its mystic, changing colors. The great, metal city rising straight-walled to the human city above, broken by spires and towers and great trees with scented blossoms. The silvery-rose glow in the paradise of gardens above.

And all the great city-structure throbbing and humming to the steady gentle beat of perfect, deathless machines built more than three million years before—and never touched since that time by human hands. And they go on. The dead city. The men that have lived, and hoped, and built—and died to leave behind them those little men who can only wonder and look and long for a forgotten kind of companionship. They wander through the vast cities their ancestors built, knowing less of them than the machines themselves.

Summer 1930 (Morey)

In 1934 Campbell sold the story to F. Orlin Tremaine, the new editor of *Astounding*. A far different story than anything Campbell had written before, it seemed to call for a new name, and Campbell adopted the pseudonym of Don A. Stuart from the maiden name of his wife. That story and the later stories to be published under the name of Stuart ("Atomic Power," "Blindness," "The Escape," a series of stories called "The Teachers," "Night," "Frictional Losses," "Forgetfulness," "Out of Night," "Cloak of Aesir," and "The Elder Gods") helped create a new kind of science fiction in which the exterior problem was only a means of getting at a deeper problem of psychology, philosophy, or sociology, mixed with personal and racial tragedy and all arranged neatly along an effective story line.

For me the Stuart stories reached their peak in 1938 with the publication of "Who Goes There?" It describes the discovery, by a group of scientists at an Antarctic camp, of an alien creature that has been frozen deep in the ice for millions of years. It thaws and comes to life; by the time it has been destroyed, it has eaten some of the animals and begun to imitate them down to the structure of the cells themselves. The problem it poses is this: has it also eaten one or more of the scientists? If it has, is there a test that can distinguish monster from human? And can it be found before it escapes the frozen wastes to repopulate the world with itself? The resemblance between the story and the motion picture ostensibly based upon it, *The Thing* was purely coincidental.

With "Who Goes There?" Campbell's career as a writer, for all practical purposes, was over at 28. In September 1937 he had been hired to edit *Astounding*, and the nominal supervision of Tremaine would end in May 1938 when Tremaine left Street & Smith. As an editor, Campbell would continue the process begun by his Stuart stories, the process of changing science fiction into something new and more effective, more serious and more significant.

But that is the next chapter in science fiction's development.

Meanwhile, the United States had climbed out of its Depression. The economy and the people were moving again, hoping again, looking to the future again as a place of hope and fulfillment. The 1939 World's Fair in New York was its symbol, and the symbol of the World's Fair was the 700-foot-tall needle-like Trylon and the 200-foot-in-diameter globe called the Perisphere. They were straight out of science fiction, and the most popular exhibit of the fair was General Motors's "Futurama," with Norman Bel Geddes' depiction of the American landscape in 1960. Everyone who had been to the fair wore a G.M. button bearing the legend, "I have seen the future."

America had seen the future, and it liked what it saw.

Hope for the future had begun to create what eventually would be recognized as a science fiction world.

October, 1936 (Morey)

Button from 1939 World's Fair. BELOW: Two scenes from General Motors' "Futurama" exhibit at the Fair

CHAPTER 10
THE ASTOUNDING
EDITOR:
1938-1950

THE DOZEN YEARS between 1938 and 1950 were *Astounding* years. During these years the first major science fiction editor began developing the first modern science fiction magazine, the first modern science fiction writers, and, indeed, modern science fiction itself.

The editor was John W. Campbell; the magazine was *Astounding Stories,* a name which soon became *Astounding Science Fiction* and then, later, *Analog Science Fact & Fiction* as the magazine evolved. We noted in the last chapter Campbell's ascension into the science fiction heavens as a writer of galactic epics to rival those of Doc Smith, and his development, as Don A. Stuart, into one of the first of the modern writers who would focus their concerns on society and the philosophical, economic, psychological, and sociological aspects of change.

John W. Campbell

Now, as editor of the leading science fiction magazine—a pulp magazine, to be sure, but Campbell did not think of it as a pulp magazine and few of its writers and readers felt that the meanness of the form diminished the value of the contents—Campbell had the opportunity to translate his vision of science fiction into reality through the work of other writers. His fiction writing was almost finished; he would turn his talents largely to the writing of editorials and blurbs, an occasional article, and voluminous letters.

Creating a new kind of magazine was not an easy job. *Astounding* paid the best rates in the field, but in the late thirties that was only a cent a word and occasionally a bit more. Other science fiction magazines advertised rates of a penny a word but often paid less for longer stories and did not always pay until

Shortly after Campbell became editor of *Astounding,* new magazines began appearing on the newsstands. A few are shown in the pages that follow (artists' names in parentheses)

February, 1939 (Vol. 1, No. 3) (Wesso)

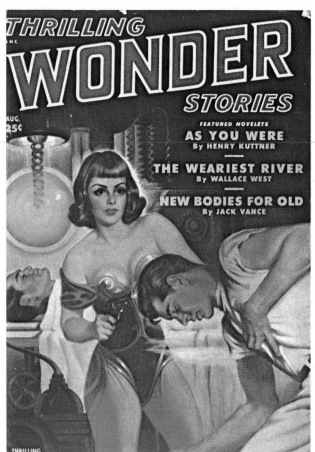

August, 1950 (Bergey)

September-October, 1939 (Vol 1. No. 1) (Unknown)

February, 1940 (Vol. 1, No. 1) (Binder)

May, 1940 (Vol. 1, No. 2) (Mayorga)

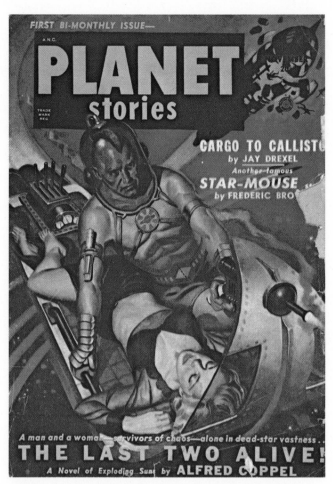

November, 1950 (first issue: Winter, 1939) (Unknown)

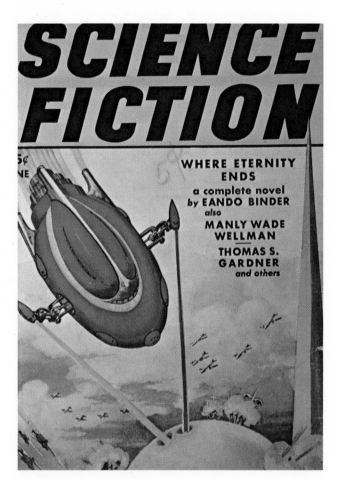

June, 1939 (Vol. 1, No. 2) (Paul)

Summer, 1940 (Vol. 1, No. 1) (Binder)

January, 1950 (first issue: July, 1940) (Lawrence)

March, 1941 (Vol. 1, No. 1) (Morey)

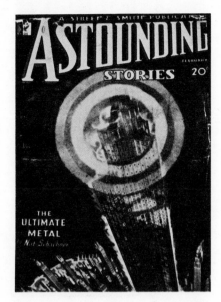

February, 1935 (Howard V. Brown)

February, 1938 (Brown)

November, 1938 (Brown)

January, 1940 (Schneeman)

December, 1946 (Alejandro)

April, 1965 (Schoenherr)

publication; the confession magazines, which demanded considerably less of a writer, paid two or three times as much. A penny a word was enough to interest the dedicated writer, but seldom the serious literary artist, and only a few writers could sell enough or write fast enough to make writing science fiction a full-time career. The majority were part-time writers who worked full-time at other occupations, which probably produced writers who were less skilled but more involved with what they were writing.

Campbell made the best of it. The main current of science fiction always has adopted a philosophy of pragmatism; when change is your subject and the implications of change your theme, you do not want to blind your eyes or blind your mind with prejudices about what is good or right or true. Pragmatic science fiction says that what is good or right or true is what works. John Campbell was in the middle of the current longer than anyone, and he worked with what he had without, I suspect, ever sighing over unreachable possibilities.

In his editorial for the December 1946 issue, entitled "Our Monthly Contest," Campbell appealed for new writers, for part-time writers:

The war is over, many men are back, including tens of thousands of professional

During Campbell's editorship, *Astounding Stories* became *ASTOUNDING Science Fiction,* then *Astounding SCIENCE FICTION,* and finally *ANALOG Science Fiction— Science Fact,* as the emphasis on content shifted over the years

technicians. Many readers of Science Fiction recently servicing radar, sonar, and similar equipment, engineers at home who were doing research on such devices, are now free to carry on civilian operations again.

I'd like to point out that Astounding Science Fiction pays cash money for stories; that we need stories constantly; that we are found with beaming smiles and great joy when a new, unknown author shows up with a bell-ringer, and that we need new authors.

It works like this: each month we run a contest, open to all comers. We pay up to $2,000 first prize for a long novel, and about $300 goes out every month for a novelette. For a short story, we pay from $75 to $150, depending on length.

You do not have to be an old-time author to sell stories; our regular buying is a wide-open, everybody-welcome contest.

Many of our top authors today sold us the first story submitted—the first story ever submitted anywhere.

We do *not* want stories "like" those of present authors; we want new angles, fresh ideas, a different, new, and interesting approach.

While this contest is, in the nature of things, open to all comers, in practice only regular readers of Science Fiction are apt to make the grade. Of those readers, past experience indicates professional technical people have a better chance of becoming permanent top rankers.

We have no staff writers; every author is a free-lance.

We don't recommend writing for Science Fiction as a full-time career, but it's a handy source of income for auxiliaries. You can buy a new radio with a short story, or a really fine camera. Or if you're really patient, you can buy a car with a couple of novelettes, or a short serial. With a long serial you can get the down payment on a house—if you can find a house!

Incidentally, most of the authors, once they get started, tend to find that writing a story is something like reading one—it can be as surprising to find which way your characters take you as to find which way another author's plot twists! . . .

March, 1939 (Vol. 1, No. 1) (Scott)

Campbell, it is clear, not only was willing to make do with part-time writers, he welcomed them—particularly those with technical information, scientific training, and the ability to see their dramatic implications.

He had to triumph over other problems. Hardly had he got well started when World War II intervened. Science fiction, like other nonmilitary activities, was forced to certain makeshifts for five years as writers went off to military service or related fields, and the paper shortage killed off magazines. *Unknown*, *Astounding*'s offbeat sister fantasy magazine, expired after a meteoric three-year career.

The measure of how well Campbell succeeded in surmounting war-related problems resides in the stories selected by the Science Fiction Writers of America for the Science Fiction Hall of Fame: out of twenty-six stories in the book published between 1934 and 1963, seven were originally published in *Astounding* between 1941 and 1945. And those years are part of what has come to be known among long-time science fiction readers as science fiction's "golden age."

Nevertheless, the war years must have created difficulties in filling the magazine with the kind of stories Campbell wanted. The full impact of the revolution Campbell had created was delayed until after the war, and then, as the above editorial illustrates, Campbell began searching for new writers to supplement those returning or to replace those who would never return—either because five years had turned them to occupations other than writer or, like Heinlein, because they were moving on to better-paying markets.

In 1937, however, when Campbell took over the editor's chair at *Astounding* (it was not much of a chair, nor an office; even in 1952, when I first visited him, the office was tucked away in a dark corner of what seemed to be mostly a warehouse), his problem was how to communicate his vision of the new science fiction to writers who could translate it into effective stories. (Campbell himself did not view it in such grand terms: what he wanted to do, he recalled later, was to make *Astounding* a good science fiction magazine, and he wanted to learn how to be an editor.)

Out of the past Campbell had retained a few writers he could count upon: one of his early heroes, E. E. Smith, who would continue his Lensman epic begun with *Galactic Patrol* in September 1937; Jack Williamson, who would adapt to new demands and respond to new challenges; Murray Leinster, who

L. Ron Hubbard

would provide material when he had time from his writing for the slicks; and Clifford Simak, who was inspired to return to science fiction writing by Campbell's appointment. Others would be attracted to *Astounding* and the new fantasy magazine, *Unknown,* including the prolific L. Ron Hubbard, who later would desert science fiction to become the Moses of a new religion, Scientology, which developed out of his every-man's psychiatry, Dianetics. Three new major writers came into prominence in 1937 and 1938: Eric Frank Russell, L. Sprague de Camp, and Lester del Rey.

But the golden age began in 1939, with the introduction of A. E. van Vogt, Theodore Sturgeon, and Robert A. Heinlein, who all began their careers in *Astounding;* and the appearance of a new writer whose first story appeared in *Amazing* but who also turned quickly to *Astounding:* Isaac Asimov. Asimov's first story, in the March 1939 *Amazing,* was "Marooned off Vesta." His first story for *Astounding* was "Trends," in July 1939. In the same issue appeared A. E. van Vogt's "Black Destroyer." Robert Heinlein's first story, "Lifeline," appeared in the August 1939 issue. Theodore Sturgeon's "Ether Breather" appeared in the September 1939 *Astounding.*

Asimov, Heinlein, and Sturgeon all would produce stories infinitely superior to their first, but Van Vogt was introduced at the top of his form; of course he had the advantage of seven earlier years writing true confessions, love stories, radio plays, and trade-paper articles. But all four were following two of Campbell's first suggestions, as described in Anthony Boucher's mystery *roman à clef, Rocket to the Morgue,* where Campbell is called Don Stuart:

Grant your gadgets, and start your story from there. In other words, assume certain advances in civilization, then work out convincingly just how those would affect the lives of ordinary individuals like you and me. . . . In other words, to sum it all up in a phrase of Don's: "I want a story that would be published in a magazine of the twenty-fifth century."

Such editorial requirements involved less overt descriptions, and more information carried by implication, as Austin Carter (Robert Heinlein) points out in *Rocket to the Morgue:*

For instance, in one story of René Lafayette's there is a noble amount of whisky drinking, and the name of the whisky is Old Space Ranger. And that one phrase paints an entire picture of a civilization in which interplanetary travel is the merest commonplace.

Some of Campbell's interests in psychology and sociology, philosophy and political science, that he had exhibited in the stories he wrote under the name of Don A. Stuart, would be reflected in the stories he received. He was an untiring and unrelenting disseminator of ideas, some of them his own and some gathered from other writers with whom he was in constant correspondence or conversation.

Campbell became the focus of what may have been the liveliest speculation going on at the time, and his irreverent science fiction viewpoint transformed everything into material for his magazine—or magazines, with the addition

Theodore Sturgeon

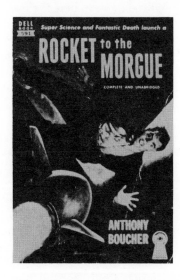

Isaac Asimov

A. E. van Vogt

Robert Heinlein

of *Unknown* in 1939. His lunches with writers became contests of imagination and logic, with every idea turned on its head and inside out until the writer had his story virtually written by the time he left the table. With writers at a distance, Campbell would answer their inquiries and story suggestions with immediate, long, analytical letters—some running five to ten pages single-spaced—filled with challenging concepts that often forced the entire revision of a story. The late Mark Clifton, who turned out a series of stories about psychic powers for Campbell in the fifties, told about their voluminous correspondence; it slowed down, Clifton said, only when he wrote the editor that he could write letters or he could write stories but he couldn't do both.

Campbell also wrote his ideas into editorials, the more controversial and shocking the better. To read the editorials or the letter column, "Brass Tacks," was to receive a preview of the magazine for six or twelve months ahead, because these were the ideas then being discussed over the Campbell lunch table or in letters, and writers not in the immediate Campbell circle would turn the editorials themselves into drama. One famous issue (November 1949) was created out of a reader's letter which pretended to be written to rate the stories in an issue yet to be printed.

Campbell's position in the field, at the head of the best-paying, highest-circulation magazine, gave him the advantage of preeminence: writers looked to him as their primary market, wrote their ideas to him and accepted his suggestions, sent him their stories first, and often rewrote them to his order. He also had the good fortune to become a science fiction editor when science fiction was responding to an upswing in popularity. *Marvel Science Stories* came out in 1938. *Amazing Stories* was purchased by Ziff-Davis in 1938 and, under the editorship of Raymond A. Palmer and with a policy of elementary science fiction for younger readers, began a climb in circulation that soon would push *Amazing* ahead of *Astounding* (Palmer claimed a high of 185,000, but that was before the day of official circulation figures). Campbell didn't worry; he believed that readers would graduate from *Amazing* to *Astounding*.

Science fiction received some unexpected advertising on Halloween, 1938, when Orson Welles's Mercury Theater of the Air produced its radio adaptation of H. G. Wells's *War of the Worlds*, and thousands of listeners across the nation panicked in the belief that the Martian invasion was real. How much the incident added to science fiction's readership is debatable, but pulp-magazine publishers being the straw-clutchers they are, the magazine field responded.

Other new magazines were splashing the newsstands with their primary colors. Standard Magazines, which had bought *Wonder Stories* from Gernsback in 1936 and changed its title to *Thrilling Wonder Stories*, brought out a companion magazine, *Startling Stories*, in 1939, and in 1940 added *Captain Future*. The misleadingly titled *Famous Fantastic Mysteries* would be published in 1939 by Munsey's Publishing Company to reprint the great old scientific romances from the Munsey pulps—A. Merritt, George Allan England, Austin Hall, Charles B. Stilson, Victor Rousseau, Homer Eon Flint, and Ray Cummings. Those romantic writers not only brought back golden memories to old pulp-magazine fans, they found thousands of new readers who were equally captivated.

Other magazines were started: Frederik Pohl, a member of a New York fan club called the Futurians, which produced an unusual number of editors and writers for science fiction, became the teen-aged editor of two new science fiction magazines, *Astonishing Stories* and *Super Science Stories*. Produced with a low budget by Popular Publications, these magazines lived on stories rejected by *Astounding* and on the early work of other Futurians and friends: Pohl himself; Cyril Kornbluth, with whom he would later collaborate; Donald Wollheim; Richard Wilson; and James Blish. *Planet Stories* was started in 1939 as a science fiction adventure magazine. *Fantastic Adventures* was created in 1939 as a companion magazine to *Amazing*. Several others were launched in hope and survived for several years or sometimes only several issues: Blue Ribbon Publications' *Science Fiction* and *Future Fiction*, 1939–43, which were edited first by Charles Hornig and then by Robert W. Lowndes; *Comet Stories*, 1940–41; *Science Fiction Quarterly*, 1940–43; *Dynamic Stories*, two issues in 1939; *Fantastic Novels* (1940–41 and 1948–50) and *Stirring Science Stories* and *Cosmic*

Stories. These last two had an editorial budget of exactly nothing, but nevertheless lasted four and three issues respectively, and provided a starting place for the young Donald A. Wollheim's editing career.

Four magazines were being published when 1938 began. By 1940 the total had climbed to eighteen. Recovery from the Depression? Perhaps. The "I have seen the future" impact of the 1939 New York World's Fair? Perhaps. The war in Europe with all its excitement and its continual reminders of the future and the certainty of change? Perhaps. A publishers' bandwagon? Perhaps. Campbell's influence? Perhaps. Or perhaps it was only our old friend, steam-engine time.

Many differing views have been expressed regarding Campbell's influence on the field. Asimov has written:

> What, specifically, did Campbell do? First and foremost, he de-emphasized the nonhuman and nonsocial in science fiction. Science fiction became more than a personal battle between an all-good hero and an all-bad villain. The mad scientists, the irascible old scientist, the beautiful daughter of the scientist, the cardboard menace from alien worlds, the robot who is a Frankenstein monster—all were discarded. In their place, Campbell wanted businessmen, space-ship crewmen, young engineers, housewives, robots that were logical machines.
>
> He got them.
>
> Again the dividing line is not sharp. Science fiction with real character existed before Campbell, notably in the stories written by Stanley G. Weinbaum in his short, meteoric career. . . .
>
> The importance of Campbell is that he was not content to let Weinbaums spring up accidentally. He looked for them. He encouraged them. It is that which makes the years 1938–1945 the "Campbell Era."

Elsewhere Asimov has said that Campbell wanted stories in which the science was realistic, stories which represented the scientific culture accurately. Both views are illustrated in Campbell's own "Who Goes There?" The problem is how to tell alien monsters from humans among a group of scientists isolated in the Antarctic, and the characters go about solving it in a doggedly scientific manner even though they, and the readers, recognize the urgency of solving the problem before spring and the possible escape of the monster to take over the world.

Such differences in approach created modern science fiction: up to this time science fiction had been largely a medium for heroes, larger-than-life characters placed in strange, ultimately demanding circumstances. Such stories would not disappear—they would be found in adventure fiction, in romantic survivals, in teen-age fiction—but the central stories of science fiction would be populated by men of their own times, accepting the strangeness of their situations as commonplace realities. Nonprofessional prophets tend to forget this basic fact about human nature: every generation grows up with and accepts as natural its own

A group of science fiction personalities in the 1950s: (left to right) Randall Garrett, Sam Moskowitz, Isaac Asimov, Donald Benson and John W. Campbell

Ross Rocklynne   Eric Frank Russell   L. Sprague de Camp   Henry Kuttner

problems. Incautious seers fall into what might be called the "future fallacy": because the future would be alien and perhaps horrible or incomprehensible to us, they assume that it would be equally alien, horrible, and incomprehensible to those who live there.

Donald Wollheim, in his book *The Universe Makers,* would register his dissent from the popular view that Campbell created modern science fiction. Calling Campbell "a victorious Vernian," Wollheim attributed the success of Campbell and *Astounding* to the fact that Campbell had only one magazine (not including *Unknown*) to produce each month while his competitors had to contend with four or six or eight. Campbell "had the time to do a better job than usual, to give more attention to each story, to avoid the mistakes that the pulp-trained editors of *Wonder* and *Startling* and *Planet Stories* and *Amazing* were making. Campbell had the time and understanding that they did not have."

Wollheim offered an explanation for what he called the "enigma of John W. Campbell" by describing Campbell as "a living fossil," "the last pulp editor still in business." "It must be a frustrating thing for one man, so talented, to find himself in such a perpetual and isolated role." Wollheim thinks that Campbell was a would-be scientist.

To begin with, Campbell was aware, more so than most, of the dynamic era of science that was opening up after the war. He was aware of the potentials of science-fiction thinking for the working scientist when funds for research started to become virtually unlimited during the war and even more so afterward. He himself was a mine of new concepts—concepts which he gave freely to his writers and which sparkled and bounced through the pages of his magazine—he surely must have been charged with the need to join in that research, to partake of the wonders being discovered, to contribute his share and have his share of glory. But this was not to be. He was stuck where he was. He tried at one time to launch a general science magazine, even managed to get control of one for two or three numbers, but it proved a washout. So it was *Astounding* which had to be his workshop, his laboratory, his platform for glory.

Certainly the wistfulness of middle age, summed up in the phrase "might have been" affects most men—but I find it difficult to discount Campbell's accomplishments on such grounds. In an interview shortly before his death on July 11, 1971, Campbell told me, "Nobody was looking for a young physicist when I got out of school in 1933."

"Do you ever wish that they had been looking for a young physicist?" I asked.

"I think I'm lucky," Campbell said. "I've had more fun this way. I've had more opportunity to meet people than I would have had in that more-limited field. I've been able to communicate, which is fun for anybody. No, I've had more fun this way!"

Wollheim considers Campbell an enigma because of his later enthusiasms: L. Ron Hubbard's Dianetics, beginning in 1950; "psi" powers and a crusade against the unscientific banning of psychic data from the laboratory; sociology, contemporary evolution, racial differences, politics. . . . Science fiction, because it is a literature of change, has been more intrigued by the future than the past,

Schedule 1
(Form 1040A)

Department of the Treasury—Internal Revenue Service

**Interest and Ordinary Dividends
for Form 1040A Filers** (L)

1998

OMB No. 1545-0085

Name(s) shown on Form 1040A

Your social security number

Part I

Interest

(See pages 24 and 56.)

Note: *If you received a Form 1099–INT, Form 1099–OID, or substitute statement from a brokerage firm, enter the firm's name and the total interest shown on that form.*

1 List name of payer. If any interest is from a seller-financed mortgage and the buyer used the property as a personal residence, see page 56 and list this interest first. Also, show that buyer's social security number and address.

Amount

	1	

2 Add the amounts on line 1. | 2 |

3 Excludable interest on series EE U.S. savings bonds issued after 1989 from Form 8815, line 14. You **must** attach Form 8815 to Form 1040A. | 3 |

4 Subtract line 3 from line 2. Enter the result here and on Form 1040A, line 8a. | 4 |

Part II

Ordinary dividends

(See pages 24 and 56.)

Note: *If you received a Form 1099–DIV or substitute statement from a brokerage firm, enter the firm's name and the ordinary dividends shown on that form.*

5 List name of payer

Amount

	5	

6 Add the amounts on line 5. Enter the total here and on Form 1040A, line 9. | 6 |

For Paperwork Reduction Act Notice, see Form 1040A instructions.

Cat. No. 12607V

1998 Schedule 1 (Form 1040A)

Printed on recycled paper

*U.S.GPO:1998-435-060

and it has attracted more liberals than conservatives. But Campbell's middle-aged enthusiasms began to appeal to a kind of offbeat conservative, particularly those with a mechanistic approach to psychology and sociology, who believed —or wanted to believe—in new religions, new philosophies, and strange, undiscovered powers. Science fiction liberals always have mistrusted their own true believers even more than conservatives, possibly because science fiction readers have persistently been lumped with psychic mediums and flying-saucer fanatics.

But the attempt to analyze writers—particularly craftsmen, such as science fiction writers at their best tend to be, rather than self-limiting stylists—from what they write or what they say about it has basic pitfalls, because writers may be intrigued by the dramatic possibilities of ideas in which they do not believe or about which they suspend their disbelief long enough to write a story or a novel. I choose to believe that Campbell found the ideas of his middle age fascinating—and perhaps temporarily fell under their spell, including that of Dianetics—but also found them useful material for science fiction. When he began urging writers to consider the dramatic possibilities of "psi" powers, he said that some older themes like atomic power and destruction and even space flight had been used up and science fiction needed a new infusion of ideas.

Campbell's late political and sociological attitudes I would rather attribute to his iconoclasm: political liberalism has as great a tendency to harden into doctrine as conservatism, and perhaps a greater tendency to excommunicate the heretic who questions, and Campbell always found rigidity of mind a tempting windmill. If anything, liberalism's current willingness to sacrifice long-term goals for short-term social ameliorations seems as alien to main-current science fiction as conservatism's unwillingness to change at all; and any *doctrine* is more alien than either.

Wollheim considers Campbell not so much the father of modern science fiction as the midwife:

For it seems to me that what happened is that the golden days of the forties, which are credited to Campbell's magazine, the days when a flood of really good writers began to show up with style and skill and ingenuity, represented something a little different. They were actually the first generation of writers who had grown up on science fiction, had been grounded and, as it were, schooled in science fiction and hence were able to utilize this in advancing further. Science fiction builds upon science fiction—and in the fact that magazines had been publishing s-f under that label since 1926 lay the reason why this generation of writers reached their twenties in time to write for Campbell when he, who was also a first-generation writer raised in the same school, was waiting and looking for better stuff. Campbell became an editor when the field itself came of age. Because he himself had mastered the field as it stood and because he himself, as an author, had fought to build upon what had been, he was able to recognize and assist those of his own generation.

Before that, in the late twenties and through the thirties, the men who wrote for the three or four science-fiction pulps—*Amazing, Wonder, Astounding*—had had their groundings in the general pulps. Their source of original foundations had been such magazines as *Argosy, Blue Book,* or worse. Such newcomers to s-f as began to show up in the pulps were very young—high school students, college freshmen—I sold my first

Fritz Leiber, Clifford Simak, Lester del Rey

Alfred Bester

William F. Temple

Fritz Leiber

James Blish

Richard Wilson

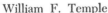

story to *Wonder Stories* when I was eighteen. Very few of us had any real grounding in science. Campbell himself sold a group of interstellar novels before he had his college diploma. And he went into editing directly afterward.

So what he found was the first fresh flood of developed science-fiction thinkers, men like Heinlein, Simak, and Asimov who had not been tarred with the old pulp styles and who were already sufficiently advanced in modern scientific study as to be aware that mechanistic universes à la Ray Cummings, George Allan England, and Homer Eon Flint were already passé.

Perhaps. But John Campbell was not a pulp editor: he did not think of himself as working with something less-enduring than the centuries; and the writers he introduced did not think of themselves as writing less than their best, or of writing down to any audience or to any lesser standards. With convictions like these, the medium was unimportant; Michelangelo's sculpture would have been just as great, though more perishable, if carved in soap.

One could sense a growing community among science fiction writers after Campbell became editor of *Astounding*, a community that had made tentative ingatherings after *Amazing* was founded and during the early and middle thirties, but one that now was developing a consciousness of mission and a consensus about how to write science fiction, which Campbell and *Astounding* helped to create, to develop, and to display. Campbell, by precept and editorial and blurb and responses in the letter section, helped shape a canon: scientific accuracy; logical development; askew viewpoints; novel, let's-turn-this-idea-inside-out-and-see-if-it-still-looks-the-same propositions; and last—this if anything was his weakness—narrative skill.

Surely Campbell did not *create* Asimov, Heinlein, Sturgeon, and Van Vogt; the only writers Campbell created were Campbell and Don A. Stuart. And if he had not been editor of *Astounding*, the others probably would still have written science fiction. But equally probably they would not have written the same stories in the same ways, and they might not have developed in the same directions or with the same persistence. Obviously, though, other influences were at work.

New magazines and new writers seem to appear simultaneously. Three new authors who contributed substantially to the field had their first science fiction stories published in 1937: L. Sprague de Camp, Henry Kuttner, and Eric Frank Russell. Five more appeared in 1938: Lester del Rey; Alfred Bester; L. Ron Hubbard; William F. Temple; and Robert Bloch, who had been published in *Weird Tales* for several years but would never be published in Campbell's *Astounding*, although he would have several stories in its companion fantasy magazine, *Unknown*. Another five appeared in 1939: Asimov, Heinlein, Sturgeon, Van Vogt, and Fritz Leiber. Another five in 1940: James Blish, Leigh Brackett, Cyril Kornbluth and Fred Pohl under pseudonyms, and Richard Wilson. Four in 1941: William A. P. White under his writing and editing pseudonym of Anthony Boucher, Ray Bradbury, Damon Knight, and Wilson Tucker. And there were four in 1942: Harry Stubbs under his pseudonym of Hal Clement, E. Mayne Hull (Mrs. A. E. van Vogt), Emil Petaja, and George O. Smith (the

Leigh Brackett, Mrs. Edmond Hamilton

first Kuttner story under the pseudonym of Lewis Padgett also appeared this year).

Those were the years in which new magazines exploded upon the newsstands. Many of them also imploded in 1941, 1942, 1943, and 1944 because of shortages of paper or purchasers, and only seven magazines (including *Weird Tales*) carried science fiction readers through the war years. The war years also brought forth few new writers. James Schmidt's first story was published in 1943; and the Kuttners (Henry and his wife, C. L. Moore) helped Campbell carry on, writing under the pseudonyms of Lewis Padgett and Lawrence O'Donnell (whose first story appeared in 1943). A. Bertram Chandler was introduced in 1944; Jack Vance and Bryce Walton in 1945; in 1946, as the war ended, Arthur C. Clarke, William Tenn (Phil Klass), and Margaret St. Clair; and in 1947, Poul Anderson, Alfred Coppel, H. B. Fyfe, and T. L. Sherred. That was the year *The Avon Fantasy Reader,* edited by Wollheim, began publication as a reprint periodical; and a magazine called *Fantasy Book* began to print the first of six issues scattered over three years. In 1948 three new writers appeared: Charles L. Harness, the mysterious Peter Phillips, and Judith Merril. In 1949 the only new writers introduced were Roger Dee, Katherine MacLean, and someone named Gunn.

In 1949 the eruption of new magazines began—a story that will be told in the next chapter—and a surge of new writers began to fill them with stories: ten major new writers in 1950, twelve in 1951, seventeen in 1952; then, as a decline set in for magazine publication, twelve in 1953, seven in 1954, three in 1955, four in 1956, three in 1957, and one in 1958; as magazines again began to wend their way toward the place where old magazines go to die, two in 1959, three in 1960, two in 1961, four in 1962, and four in 1963.

Such similar patterns in the emergence of new magazines and new writers suggest the possibility that the conditions producing new science fiction magazines also produce new science fiction writers. Certainly the opening of new markets encourages new writers, and new writing. Clifford Simak, for instance, turned to his wife in 1937, when he learned that John Campbell had been named editor of *Astounding,* and said, "I can write for Campbell. He won't be satisfied with the kind of stuff that is being written. He'll want something new." And, after a fallow period of five years, Simak began writing again—first a series of short stories, and then, at Campbell's suggestion, a 1939 serial called *Cosmic Engineers.* Simak speculates that if Campbell had not been named editor of *Astounding,* he might never have written science fiction again.

In 1949, when Tony Boucher and J. Francis McComas created *The Magazine of Fantasy and Science Fiction,* those writers who could write the kind of

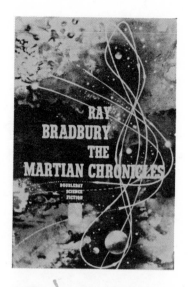

Ray Bradbury

Hal Clement

May, 1949 (Orban)

April, 1953 (Van Dongen)

George O. Smith

E. Mayne Hull, Mrs.
A. E. van Vogt

Emil Petaja

James Schmidt

Henry Kuttner and C. L. Moore (Mrs. Henry Kuttner)

A. Bertram Chandler

Margaret St. Clair

Poul Anderson

Alfred Coppel

T. L. Sherred

Charles L. Harness

literary stories Boucher and McComas preferred suddenly had the incentive to write them and the opportunity to have them published; before 1949 few had been written and fewer published.

Similarly, when *Galaxy* came out in 1950 under the editorship of Horace Gold, those writers who had *Galaxy*-type stories to tell suddenly found a market for them, and the second rank of magazines that sprang up around the feet of the giants was pleased to have the overflow, just as Fred Pohl, with *Astonishing Stories* and *Super Science Stories* in 1940, was pleased with the Heinlein and Asimov stories rejected by *Astounding*.

In my case, although my early ambition had been to write for *Astounding* (I sold Campbell my third story, "Private Enterprise," and eventually five other stories), I discovered that *Galaxy* stories were more like those I wanted to write, and I found the editor more receptive to the stories I submitted. And for a time *Galaxy* paid better, too. Unlike Simak, if I had been forced to depend upon

Wilson Tucker

Astounding as my market, I would have stopped writing science fiction, or I would have written much differently.

Perhaps, however, the emergence of new authors must be attributed to a variety of circumstances: new editors, new magazines, the evolution of science fiction, mutual stimulation, scientific and sociological inputs, changing world conditions—in other words, our old friend "steam-engine time."

Whatever the reason, few groups of writers have hit science fiction with the impact of Asimov, Heinlein, Sturgeon, and Van Vogt. In sheer quantity or totality of influence, other years—1952, for instance—may have been more productive, but Asimov, Heinlein, Sturgeon, and Van Vogt (keep saying it and it sounds like a Notre Dame backfield) not only were major talents but were quickly recognized as such.

They are among the reasons the forties have become known as the golden age of science fiction: Sturgeon was finding his unique voice and working out his individual themes; Van Vogt was creating the mythology of science, writing stories of science as magic or magic as science; Heinlein was developing his consistent "future history" of the next two centuries and creating definitive treatments, theme after theme; and Asimov was writing the distant future history of man as he ventured out into space, created an empire, and found that empire disintegrating and new civilizations springing from it. At the same time Asimov was creating his classic robot stories and novels, which did much to establish science fiction's thinking about man and machine; and, like Heinlein, he was also writing classic science fiction short stories that did not fit into the pattern of his other work.

A river of stories like no stories ever written before flowed into the science fiction magazines and swept away old concepts and old pretensions. Writers were examining all the old assumptions of science fiction and asking, in their stories: Are the assumptions valid? Are they true only in part, or in certain restricted circumstances? Or are they false in terms of the laboratory or the universe, the individual or the human race?

After "Black Destroyer," "Discord in Scarlet," and "Vault of the Beast," Van Vogt wrote his first novel, *Slan*, about telepathic mutants with tendrils who are hunted down like dangerous beasts. The 1940 *Astounding* serial was an immediate sensation: as one example, fans in Battle Creek, Michigan, conceived a cooperative housing development for fans to be called Slan Center, and a group of them actually moved into an eight-room house called the Slan Shack. In 1941 Van Vogt began the series of stories centered around the weapon shops ("The Seesaw," "The Weapon Shop," *The Weapon Makers*, and *The*

Katherine MacLean

A. E. van Vogt

January, 1946 (Timmins)

May, 1947 (Rogers)

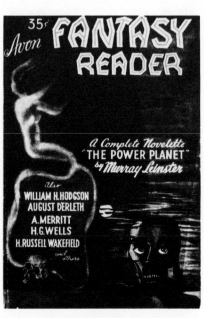

No. 1, 1947 (Unknown)

Weapon Shops of Isher) which bear the legend "the right to buy weapons is the right to be free."

Van Vogt had begun to find his style. James Blish called it "the extensively recomplicated story," and its best example was the 1945 serial *The World of Null-A*. The effect was created—or enhanced—by the method of writing Van Vogt described in a 1947 essay:

> Think of it in scenes of about 800 words. This is not original with me, but I have followed that rule religiously ever since I started to write. Every scene has a purpose, which is stated near the beginning, usually by the third paragraph, and that purpose is either accomplished, or not accomplished by the end of the scene. . . .
>
> There is one more point to bring out here. Ideas follow the 800 word scene. By this is meant that you cannot write 800 words about nothing. Having started a scene you must think of ideas to fill it out to the required length. In other words, if you find that you have solved your scene purpose at the end of 300 words, then something is wrong. The scene isn't properly developed. There are not enough ideas in it, not enough detail, not enough complication. . . .
>
> Ever since I started writing for the science fiction field, it has been my habit to put every current thought into the story I happened to be working on. Frequently, an idea would seem to have no relevance, but by mulling over it a little, I would usually find an approach that would make it usable. . . .

In 1946 Van Vogt began another series of stories about a decadent empire which has spaceships but worships the atom, a series that culminated in the 1950 *Astounding* serial *The Wizard of Linn*. Two years earlier *Astounding* would serialize the sequel to *World of Null-A*, titled *Players of Null-A*. But Van Vogt's *Astounding* period was almost over: some excellent short stories and novelettes would be published before 1950, but increasingly his fiction was appearing in lesser magazines, and *The Weapon Shops of Isher* was published in *Thrilling Wonder Stories* in 1949. Beginning in 1948 Van Vogt became increasingly involved in Hubbard's Dianetics and wrote almost no science fiction; in the late sixties he returned to writing science fiction again with a plan which began with writing ten novels, of which several already have been published.

Van Vogt's stories did not attempt to present a rational picture of the world nor a foretaste of progress to come; they dealt with the themes of science fiction as if they were fairy tales (as Robert Sheckley would do later, as well as turning fairy tales into science fiction): invincibility, indestructibility, teleportation, telekinesis, telepathy, transformation, superman. . . . One of his techniques was to use the familiar names of science but interpret them literally; in a Van Vogt story both individuals and apparatus have abilities commensurate with men's dreams. Thus when Van Vogt introduced a "games machine" in the *World of Null-A*, the reader gradually learned that it was a computer given human communication abilities and advanced to near godlike omniscience; and when the hero turns to a lie detector, the machine says, "You are lying."

Van Vogt's heroes are individuals isolated by their society or their own strange talents, usually undiscovered. They journey through a world of confusion and insuperable difficulties trying to discover why they are different or why the world has singled them out for mistreatment, but they are sustained by their inner certainty of moral superiority or great powers or latent powers which they must discover, develop, and master. They are at their most typical in such characters as Jommy Cross, the slan of *Slan;* Gilbert Gosseyn, the double-brained superman of *The World of Null-A;* and Michael Slade, the superman with the third eye in "The Chronicler" (book version: *Siege of the Unseen*). Many of Van Vogt's heroes suffer from amnesia, most from a condition difficult to distinguish from paranoia, but the action and ideas pour out in a profusion sufficient to keep the reader so engrossed that he has no time for questions. The confusion of the characters is matched by the confusion of the reader; the secret powers are the stuff of secret dreams—and may be the only kind powerful enough to cope with the confusion of contemporary society and its problems.

Later writers, such as Charles L. Harness and James Blish would use Van Vogt's methods and produce better-constructed stories, but none of them would match the impact and success of Van Vogt's early work. Take the magic of the opening lines from *Slan:*

Vol. 1, No. 1, 1947 (Milo)

October, 1940 (Rogers)

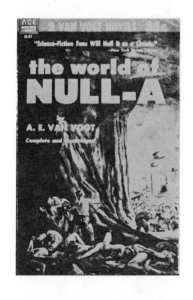

His mother's hand felt cold, clutching his. Her fear as they walked hurriedly along the street was a quiet, swift pulsation that throbbed from her mind to his. A hundred other thoughts beat against his mind, from the crowds that swarmed by on either side, and from inside the buildings they passed. But only his mother's thoughts were clear and coherent—and afraid.

"They're following us, Jommy," her brain telegraphed. "They're not sure, but they suspect. We've risked once too often coming into the capital, though I did hope that this time I could show you the old slan way of getting into the catacombs, where your father's secret is hidden. Jommy, if the worst happens, you know what to do. We've practiced it often enough. And, Jommy, don't be afraid, don't get excited. You may be only nine years old, but you're as intelligent as any fifteen-year-old human being."

September, 1962 (Emshwiller)

Later writers also would take the myths of science and explore them for their logical developments and human significance, and they, perhaps, would benefit most of all.

Sturgeon may have been the most gifted writer of the group. He pursued his own sensitive path through a variety of themes and plots, seeking his own voice, his own philosophy, and a market for what he wanted to write. In terms of career and impact he was handicapped by a reluctance to deal with story at the longer lengths; he was a short-story writer, and the novelists, with their magazine serials and book publications, made their reputations and fortunes more quickly and easily.

Sturgeon's early stories, though marked by his imagination and his flare for language, were competent and relatively conventional. There is, to be sure, a certain irony in the use of the word "conventional" to describe such a story as the 1941 "Microcosmic God," in which an unusual scientist named Kidder creates a microscopic race of beings who live a generation in eight days and provide him with answers to scientific and technological problems through their accelerated metabolism:

This quotation is from a paper that one of Kidder's high-speed telescopic cameras discovered being circulated among the younger Neoterics. It is translated from the highly simplified script of the Neoterics.

"These edicts shall be followed by each Neoteric upon pain of death, which punishment will be inflicted by the tribe upon the individual to protect the tribe against him.

"Priority of interest and tribal and individual effort is to be given the commands that appear on the word machine.

"Any misdirection of material or power, or use thereof for any other purpose than the carrying out of the machine's commands, unless no command appears, shall be punishable by death.

"Any information regarding the problem at hand, or ideas or experiments which might conceivably bear upon it, are to become the property of the tribe.

"Any individual failing to cooperate in the tribal effort or who can be termed guilty of not expending his full efforts in the work, or the suspicion thereof shall be subject to the death penalty."

Such are the results of complete domination. This paper impressed Kidder as much as it did because it was completely spontaneous. It was the Neoterics' own creed, developed by them for their greatest good.

Theodore Sturgeon

Another typical example of the early Sturgeon was a 1944 *Astounding* novelette called *Killdozer!* in which an alien intelligence animates a bulldozer and is fought by a courageous, quick-thinking machine operator.

In fantasy stories published in *Unknown* and elsewhere, Sturgeon's ability and originality showed through more quickly: "It," in 1940, described a mass of rotting vegetation that came to life in the woods; "The Ultimate Egoist" in 1941 told about a man who believed that he kept the universe in existence by believing in it—and proved himself right; and there was "Shottle Bop," also in 1941, with this memorable blurb on the cover: "The sign on the window said 'Shottle Bop—We sell things in bottles'; but the things in the bottles were—things!"

Sturgeon's first novel did not appear until *Fantastic Adventures* published *The Dreaming Jewels* in 1950, and Sturgeon did not find a more suitable market for his stories until the founding of *The Magazine of Fantasy and Science Fiction* and *Galaxy* in 1949 and 1950. Earlier, however, he had begun to try to

deal with science fiction in his own definition of human terms, with "Thunder and Roses," a 1947 *Astounding* novelette about a United States destroyed by a sneak atomic attack, which refuses to retaliate and thereby doom the entire world; and "Maturity," also in 1947, which considered the human tragedy of the superman.

In the fifties he turned to themes that were even more unusual: the Gestalt approach to superhuman powers, which eventually was published as *More Than Human;* and sex in all its varieties, such as *Venus Plus X* (1960) and *Some of Your Blood* (1961). Some of Sturgeon's explorations in personal statement, such as those that turn upon physical abnormality or human taboos, may be unsatisfying or unsuccessful as stories, but they seem typical of the attempts of Sturgeon and the times to liberate themselves, and his pioneer work has indeed been liberating. Because of Sturgeon other writers have been freer to write what they wished to write and able to find a market for it.

Asimov's fiction, on the other hand, seemed to be aimed at explication and codification, almost like the popularizations of science to which he turned in 1958, with such success that he has been called the most able science writer, and by all odds the most prolific, in this generation. A university professor of biochemistry who now retains only a nominal relationship to the academic world, Asimov has a witty, retentive mind, and his writing exhibits his logical ability to clarify and his imaginative ability to invent—in nonfiction, it is through example and simile; in fiction, via plot and metaphor. He has claimed little knowledge of the techniques of fiction writing, but since he is not afflicted with false modesty—nor true modesty either—he has said that lack of information may only be by comparison to his encyclopedic knowledge of everything else. His stories are skillful, though his prose may occasionally betray its professorial origin.

Asimov's influence—at the time, he has said, he was never aware of being anything but a minor writer—began in 1941 with his first robot story for Campbell, "Reason." Asimov said that Campbell codified the three laws of robotics after the story was accepted; Campbell demurred that they were implicit in the story:

1 a robot may not injure a human being, or through inaction allow a human being to come to harm;

2 a robot must obey the orders given it by human beings except where such orders would conflict with the First Law;

3 a robot must protect its own existence as long as such protection does not conflict with the First or Second Law.

Isaac Asimov

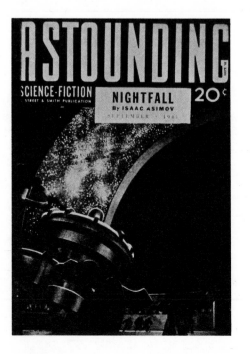

LEFT: September, 1941 (Rogers) RIGHT: Illustration from *Astounding*, September, 1941 (Koliker)

LEFT: June, 1942 (Rogers)

RIGHT: April, 1945 (Timmins)

LEFT: January, 1948 (Rogers)

RIGHT: November, 1949 (Rogers)

From the laws Asimov was able to derive a series of effective stories dealing with a conflict between or among the laws and other writers now would be forced to consider the logical development of robots (and, by extension, other machine-man interrelationships) rather than toy with the irrational, traditional dread of Frankenstein's monster. No longer was it enough to build; writers now were compelled to build logically, as a prudent man would, and the problems they would consider would be those, and only those, that prudence could not foresee.

By extension, science fiction itself became more logical. The scientific mind was saying to the science fiction writer: enough of old myths and romantic notions; there is romance and drama and, yes, myth too, in science and the scientific culture and the uncertainties of tomorrow.

"Nightfall," Asimov's 1941 *Astounding* story, was another expression of this spirit. It took the poetry of Emerson and said, in effect, "poetry be hanged—if men saw the stars only once every thousand years, it would be because there were six suns in the sky constantly shining, and darkness and the stars would so terrify men that they would go mad."

In 1942, impressed by Gibbon's *Decline and Fall of the Roman Empire*, Asimov began to shape a future to his own logic. With a novelette entitled *Foundation*, Asimov launched a series of novelettes and novels in which he traced a future history of man's empire in space and the development of a science called "psychohistory," by which man could make reasonable forecasts of the future. H. G. Wells had said forty years earlier that a science of sociology was impossible because sociologists could not deal with people in sufficiently large numbers to make predictions feasible. Asimov projected his history into a future in which mankind has colonized his galaxy. His psychohistory, therefore, could work on vaster numbers; Asimov defined it as:

that branch of mathematics which deals with the reactions of human conglomerates to fixed social and economic stimuli. . . . Implicit in all these definitions is the assumption that the human conglomerate being dealt with is sufficiently large for valid statistical treatment. . . . A further necessary assumption is that the human conglomerate be itself unaware of psychohistoric analysis in order that its reactions be truly random.

In the three books later published in book form as *Foundation* (1951), *Foundation and Empire* (1952), and *Second Foundation* (1953), Asimov explored the logical consequences of psychohistory, with its ability to foretell the future if almost no one knows about it, and the two "foundations" set up by Hari Seldon, the inventor of psychohistory, to speed the rebuilding of the human galactic empire after its collapse and shorten the dark ages to follow from 30,000 years to a millennium. In *Foundation* Seldon, put on trial, sums up the historical situation and the goals of his foundation:

Q. Is it not obvious to anyone that the Empire is as strong as it ever was?

A. The appearance of strength is all about you. It would seem to last forever. However, Mr. Advocate, the rotten tree-trunk, until the very moment when the storm-blast breaks it in two, has all the appearance of might it ever had. The storm-blast whistles through the branches of the Empire even now. Listen with the ears of psychohistory, and you will hear the creaking.

Q. (uncertainly) We are not here, Dr. Seldon, to lis—

A. (firmly) The Empire will vanish and all its good with it. Its accumulated knowledge will decay and the order it has imposed will vanish. Interstellar wars will be endless; interstellar trade will decay; population will decline; worlds will lose touch with the main body of the Galaxy.—And so matters will remain.

Q. (a small voice in the middle of a vast silence) Forever?

A. Psychohistory, which can predict the fall, can make statements concerning the succeeding dark ages. The Empire, gentlemen, as has just been said, has stood twelve thousand years. The dark ages to come will endure not twelve but *thirty* thousand years. A Second Empire will rise, but between it and our civilization will be one thousand generations of suffering humanity. We must fight that.

Q. (recovering somewhat) You contradict yourself. You said earlier that you could not prevent the destruction of Trantor; hence, presumably, the fall;—the *so-called* fall of the Empire.

A. I do not say now that we can prevent the fall. But it is not yet too late to shorten the interregnum which will follow. It is possible, gentlemen, to reduce the duration of anarchy to a single millennium, if my group is allowed to act now. We are at a delicate moment in history. The huge, onrushing mass of events must be deflected just a little,—just a little—It cannot be much, but it may be enough to remove twenty-nine thousand years of misery from human history.

Q. How do you propose to do this?

A. By saving the knowledge of the race. The sum of human knowing is beyond any one man; any thousand men. With the destruction of our social fabric, science will be broken into a million pieces. . . . *But,* if we now prepare a giant summary of *all* knowledge, it will never be lost. . . . All my project; my thirty thousand men with their wives and children, are devoting themselves to the preparation of an "Encyclopedia Galactica." . . . By the time Trantor falls, it will be complete and copies will exist in every major library in the Galaxy.

(Is it possible, the thought stirs, that Isaac Asimov, with his more than 150 books, is trying single-handedly to write that *Encyclopedia Galactica*?)

In these three books Asimov also established a future history of man

The later Asimov

October, 1953 (Emshwiller)

expansion into the galaxy, and the later breakdown of communication, that would find general acceptance in the main current of science fiction and provide a framework and inspiration for a thousand later stories, which would fill in that framework with details. Galactic empires had been described before, from E. E. Smith and Edmond Hamilton through Olaf Stapledon, but Asimov predicted a *human* galactic empire. The hubris was daring; the opportunities for fiction were multiplied. The concept of aliens in the universe would not be discarded—they too have meaningful statements to make about the human condition—but the pride in being human, the responsibilities of humanity, shone through Asimov's fiction. The historical parallels to his novels are clear; what Asimov added was a scientific consideration of them and a multiplication of the impact of events which made the consequences of stupidity staggering. For those who recognized the parallels, moreover, it was as if Asimov were saying, "What if the Romans had prepared and distributed broadly across their empire volumes containing all their knowledge and that of the Greeks and Egyptians and all previous civilizations? Would the Dark Ages have lasted for a thousand years?" Or, as Arthur Clarke pointed out, the ancient Greek computer found in an undersea wreck might have been built 500 years ago, and "if that culture had continued in a linear way—well, by this time we would have been at Rigel, because that thing was only five hundred years from the spaceship in linear development." The *Foundation* trilogy has seldom been out of print since the books were first published.

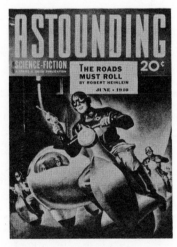

June, 1940 (Rogers)

Asimov himself filled in some of the details of his future history with such books as *Pebble in the Sky* (1950), *Tyrann (The Stars Like Dust)* in *Galaxy* (1951), *The Currents of Space* in *Astounding* (1952), his robot detective novels *The Caves of Steel* (in *Galaxy*, 1953) and *The Naked Sun* (in *Astounding*, 1956), and *The End of Eternity* (1955). He then turned to writing juveniles under the name of Paul French, and then left his position (except for a nominal lecture or two) as associate professor at Boston University to spend all his time writing. By then, however, his writing was the more profitable science-popularizing work for juveniles and adults typified by *The Intelligent Man's Guide to Science*. Asimov returned to writing some science fiction in 1971, and produced a major new novel, *The Gods Themselves*, in 1972.

Robert Heinlein also developed a future history. But, in his early writing at least, he limited his foresight to the next two centuries. Although he would not restrict himself completely to that future history—in his later work his range was almost as broad as Asimov's, but his galaxy was sometimes dominated by an alien federation in which mankind was sometimes a member—Heinlein's more limited initial scope was appropriate. For the first part of his writing career he set himself the task of filling in the future immediately at hand, and he constructed a carefully detailed scenario of the future in which the stories themselves, those not yet written as well as those already completed, were placed in time. The time chart on which they were set down was published in the *Astounding* issue for May 1941, in an editorial entitled "History to Come," and again when his stories were published in hard covers by the specialized fan press and in paperback by Signet.

Heinlein's work as a writer exhibited his ability to learn as he went along.

More important, he seemed capable of coming up with ideas that never had been thought before or of revitalizing old ideas with new treatments. He would write the definitive treatment of more science fiction themes than any writer since H. G. Wells, and perhaps because—unlike Wells—he had no apparent philosophy to promote, his stories often seemed to exhaust the possibilities implicit in their concepts.

But Heinlein's greatest early contribution was his future history—not the history itself, although it would have its value in stimulating fan discussion and later even the ideas of some outside the boundaries of science fiction, but the manner in which he approached his task. Heinlein was fascinated by social history, the way in which our society will develop, particularly as it is affected by invention and technology. The most effective way to discuss social history is to describe societies in action and men and women in conflict with their societies or protecting them from outside assault. Heinlein had to develop new ways of describing societies; readers were becoming weary of lengthy asides, either by an author or by one of his characters, and exposition had to be inserted in the midst of the story without slowing it down, particularly if the focus of the story was going to be on a character who was a part of his society, not a stranger to it.

Campbell would describe the difference in a 1946 anthology:

In older science fiction—H. G. Wells and nearly all stories written before 1935—the author took time out to bring the reader up to date as to what had happened before his story opened. The best modern writers of science fiction have worked out some truly remarkable techniques for presenting a great deal of background and associated material without intruding into the flow of the story. This is no small feat, when a complete new world must be established at the same time a story is being presented.

Campbell was describing, more than anyone else, Heinlein. Heinlein could be said to have brought the techniques of naturalism to science fiction. He used sensory detail to establish a scene, but this scene was placed in the future and the details he used also established a society; the process created in the reader a feeling not of wonder but of reality. He gave the reader the conviction that this was the future that lay ahead, else how could he evoke it so casually and describe it so minutely. And if this was the future, the reader was forced to take it seriously.

In one compelling example, a 1949 novel called *Gulf*, Heinlein described an ultra-competent, courageous, extra-intelligent adventurer who, sent on a secret mission, became involved in a confusing web of conspiracy and thwarted a public attack on his life. At the same time, with a few casual references within the flow of the story, he created a society of the future in which man has a colony on the moon, tube cars, instantly printed newspapers, pneumatic mail service, and strip teasers, alcohol, narcotics, and call girls available in every drug store —all described in the first six pages:

He decided to unload. He stepped suddenly off the sidewalk into the entrance of a drugstore and stopped just inside the door to buy a newspaper. While his copy was being printed, he scooped up, apparently as an afterthought, three standard pneumo mailing tubes. As he paid for them he palmed a pad of gummed address labels.
A glance at the mirrored wall showed him that his shadow had hesitated outside but was still watching him. Gilead went on back to the shop's soda fountain and slipped into an unoccupied booth. Although the floor show was going on—a remarkably shapely ecdysiast was working down toward her last string of beads—he drew the booth's curtain.
Shortly the call light over the booth flashed discreetly; he called, "Come in!" A pretty and very young waitress came inside the curtain. Her plastic costume covered without concealing.
She glanced around. "Lonely?" . . .

The alloying of pulp action techniques, naturalism, and science fiction theme seldom has been achieved so skillfully.

After Heinlein, writers would build societies with more thorough concern for interlocking details presented skillfully and subtly. But Heinlein made another contribution of equal value: he blazed trails where science fiction had never traveled before. After conquering the science fiction magazines through the early

Robert Heinlein with
Irving Pichel, director of
Destination Moon

At a banquet: SEATED, LEFT TO RIGHT: Robert Silverberg, Dr. Janet Lepson, Judy-Lynn Benjamin del Rey. STANDING: Isaac Asimov, Mr. and Mrs. John W. Campbell, Lester del Rey

forties, he attacked the slick magazines after the war with a series of carefully written visions of the immediate future; science fiction would never again be systematically excluded from those magazines as it had been before, except for a few carefully neutered exceptions. Then in 1947 Heinlein wrote his first juvenile book, *Rocket Ship Galileo,* and with its publication by Scribner's launched a new and remunerative career which, he later said, brought him more income each year on each juvenile book than the total income from any of his adult science fiction novels. More important to science fiction, other writers would follow the path he had opened, and together they would create in juvenile readers a potential market for adult science fiction when they grew up. Out of a class of 150 college students in science fiction as literature, 79 reported that they had read juvenile science fiction.

With the adaptation of some elements of *Rocket Ship Galileo* into the successful 1950 film *Destination Moon* (the movie also launched a science fiction film career for producer George Pal), Heinlein helped create a Hollywood market for serious science fiction and an atmosphere in which science fiction could be considered as serious fare for motion pictures.

And finally, with the publication of the phenomenally successful *Stranger in a Strange Land* in 1961, Heinlein anticipated the youth movement and the flower children, and when they discovered the book and the kind of message it contained, science fiction's banner was raised over a new and unexplored area; Heinlein led writers into a strange land in which they could tackle major new themes—such as religion, sex, new and unusual societies—and expect to have their speculations considered seriously. Along with a few other books, *Stranger in a Strange Land* and the motion picture *2001: A Space Odyssey* would introduce millions of people—primarily young people—to science fiction and help create a wide new audience. In the early forties science fiction fans were building "Slan Shacks"; in the sixties, young people, many of them not science fiction readers, were forming water brotherhoods.

July, 1950

Wherever science fiction writers would venture in the next three decades, they would find themselves walking in paths worn by one of these four writers; wherever new writers ventured they would find in the dust of a distant moon footprints marking the place where Asimov, Heinlein, Sturgeon, or Van Vogt had stepped before them; and because these four had been there the way would be easier and other writers could move on further into the unknown.

It would not be easy: to pick up an exciting idea and then to recognize that the definitive treatment has already been written by Sturgeon, Van Vogt, Asimov, or, most often, Heinlein, is discouraging in a field where continual novelty is demanded. After these four would come much repetition, much working out of smaller detail, much exploring of territory already staked out, but without these four the territory would have been infinitely smaller.

The way—or the ways—had been prepared for the postwar expansion that lay ahead.

CHAPTER 11

THE BIG BOOM: 1940-1955

WORLD WAR II loomed over the forties like a mushroom-shaped cloud. The world worked and sacrificed and watched the movements of fleets and armies, and nothing else mattered. Life continued, but only as a poor secondary activity—and yet enhanced, in a contradictory way, by a proximity to great events.

Magazines felt it too. Fiction was dominated by war stories and escape stories, and even science fiction became involved.

The weapons of war and the problems of war and peace once more became a major subject for science fiction: Mars, which had figured in hundreds of stories as a planet of mystery from which a savage invasion of Earth might be launched or to which some terrestrial rocket might go in search of truth or adventure, returned as a god of war. L. Ron Hubbard's 1940 novel *Final Blackout,* serialized in *Astounding,* described a world ravaged by long battles descending finally into savagery in which the only hope is a strong man like "the Lieutenant." The novel may have owed something of its extrapolation to Wells's *The Shape of Things to Come,* but its grim tone and its emphasis on character were far different. *Final Blackout* could have been published as an effective antiwar mainstream novel (a hard-cover edition was published in 1948 by one of the fan presses).

November, 1950 (Pattee)   July, 1942 (Rogers)   April, 1960 (Rogers)

Atomic weapons had been part of the science fiction arsenal since H. G. Wells and Philip "Buck Rogers" Nowlan, but in the total warfare of World War II their use became believable. In a 1941 *Astounding* novelette Robert Heinlein, writing under the pseudonym of Anson MacDonald (since the story fell outside his "future history"), produced his most prophetic vision. The United States, the story predicted, would be drawn into World War II, would develop an atomic weapon to end the war, and would enforce upon the world a "pax Americana." The weapon, it is true, was not a bomb but radioactive dust; many of the details and much of the analysis of the strategic situation, however, were amazingly prophetic and radioactive dust might have made just as effective a weapon. Radioactive wastes still represent a major disposal problem. Heinlein called his story (and his method of atomic control) "Solution Unsatisfactory"; John Campbell pointed out in a 1946 anthology that the official solution of the United States, secrecy, was even more unsatisfactory and suggested that if those in position to make political decisions about atomic weapons had begun thinking about the matter in 1940 we might have come up with a better answer.

Heinlein's reputation and that of science fiction do not rest upon the accuracy of their prophecies, however, but upon the effectiveness of their dramatization of the problems they can see or foresee. Other atomic-weapon or atomic-energy stories would be printed so frequently that critics would discount atomic bombs as "mere science fiction," and would dismiss science fiction because it dealt with such implausible subjects as atomic bombs. In fact, the atomic-doom story became dated within one or two years after the end of World War II and was almost impossible to place in a science fiction magazine—or to avoid in mainstream publications. One atomic-bomb story, Cleve Cartmill's "Deadline," when it was published in the March 1944 issue of *Astounding*, brought agents of Military Intelligence to the author and the editor asking who on the Manhattan Project had been talking. At one point a character says:

> "U-235 has been separated in quantity easily sufficient for preliminary atomic-power research, and the like. They got it out of uranium ores by new atomic isotope separation methods; they now have quantities measured in pounds. By 'they,' I mean Seilla research scientists. But they have *not* brought the whole amount together, or any major portion of it. Because they are not at all sure that, once started, it would stop before all of it had been consumed—in something like one micromicrosecond of time."

And a bit later in the story the character describes the actual bomb, which is a bit too small, a bit too light, and not quite workable—but it is not too far off:

> "Two cast-iron hemispheres, clamped over the orange segments of cadmium alloy. And the fuse—I see it is in—a tiny can of cadmium alloy containing a speck of radium in a beryllium holder and a small explosive powerful enough to shatter the cadmium walls. Then—correct me if I'm wrong, will you?—the powdered uranium oxide runs together in the central cavity. The radium shoots neutrons into this mass—and the U-235 takes over from there. Right?"

Unlike the outcome of Philip Wylie's *Blue Book* story, Campbell persuaded the agents that to suppress atomic-energy stories, in light of what had been published previously, would be more of a giveaway to enemy agents than to let them continue.

Campbell pointed out that everything necessary to predict an atomic weapon, even an atomic bomb, was available in scientific literature prior to 1939. All science fiction writers had to do was read the right journals. In 1946 Campbell would write that science fiction exists in the gap between the discovery of a scientific fact in the laboratory and its engineering application.

Other stories about atomic power appeared. Heinlein's "Blowups Happen," published in the September 1940 *Astounding*, speculated that an atomic power plant might always be too dangerous for Earth (shades of contemporary protests!) and that it might be necessary to place an atomic facility in space and ship the energy back in another form. Lester del Rey, in another display of prescience, wrote "Nerves," published in the September 1942 *Astounding*, about an accident in an atomic plant:

> "Just what will happen if it all goes off?" he asked.
> Jenkins shrugged, biting at his inner lip as he went over a sheaf of papers on the

From *Astounding*, September, 1940 (Schneeman)

desk, covered with the scrawling symbols of atomics. "Anybody's guess. Suppose three tons of the army's new explosives were to explode in a billionth—or at least, a millionth—of a second? Normally, you know, compared to atomics, that stuff burns like any fire, slowly and quietly, giving its gases plenty of time to get out of the way in an orderly fashion. Figure it one way, with this all going off together, and the stuff could drill a hole that'd split open the whole continent from Hudson Bay to the Gulf of Mexico, and leave a lovely sea where the Middle West is now. Figure it another, and it might only kill off everything within fifty miles of here. Somewhere in between is the chance we count on. This isn't U-235, you know."

When the news came on August 6, 1945, of the destruction of Hiroshima by an atomic bomb, every science fiction reader everywhere knew what it meant and knew the implications of the event. We already had lived through the experience many times in our imaginations. The atomic era had begun. I heard the radio broadcast in a hotel in Miami where I was attending a Navy school for advanced line-officers training, and I remember wondering whether a chain reaction had been started within the Earth itself and, if it had, how long would it take to eat its way to the United States. Many stories, including Cartmill's "Deadline," had mentioned the possibility. It points out that the explosion of a pound of U-235 would release as much energy as 100 million tons of TNT, and would be so concentrated that surrounding matter might be set off. Henry Kuttner, writing under the pseudonym of Lawrence O'Donnell, published "Clash by Night" in 1943, describing how Earth had been turned into "a star—all that remained of earth since atomic power had been unleashed there two centuries ago. The scourge had spread like flame, melting continents and leveling mountains."

First publication: 1943

In retrospect our fears seem ridiculous, but at the time of the first nuclear-bomb test at Alamogordo one nuclear scientist was plagued by the same possibility. As Robert Jungk reported the occasion in *Brighter Than a Thousand Suns*, "Carson Mark, one of the most brilliant members of the Theoretical Division, actually thought—though his intelligence told him the thing was impossible—that the ball of fire would never stop growing till it had enveloped all heaven and earth."

But that big boom, the cause of so much tragedy, guilt, and recrimination, announced not only the birth of the atomic age but the beginning of the science fiction age. From that moment on thoughtful men and women recognized that we were living in a science fiction world. In what other world could atomic bombs—and atomic energy—be a reality? Other events still to happen would confirm that realization in the minds of the observant.

So it seemed to postwar publishers as well. As suddenly as the explosion of the atomic bomb, that time was upon the world that everyone had summed up in the phrase, "When the war is over. . . ." To science fiction it meant another big boom. Fans, magazine publishers, even some book publishers became convinced that this was the time to put more science fiction into print. Again it was "steam-engine time" for science fiction.

The late Fredric Brown paid tribute to this state of mind in a 1948 novel published in the September 1948 *Startling Stories,* later published in book form by Dutton and Bantam, *What Mad Universe?* A science fiction editor is blasted into an alternate universe by the explosion of a rocket, and he discovers it to be a science fiction fan's dream:

From *Startling Stories,* September, 1948 (Bergey)

"You were thinking about your science fiction fan, Joe Doppelberg, and you were wondering what kind of universe he would dream about, what kind of universe he would really like. And this is it.

"That doesn't mean that this isn't a real universe, as real as your own. It was; it existed. But it is *the* universe out of infinite universes which happens to be the one exactly like what you were thinking of at the time of the flash—thinking of, that is, as the universe Joe Doppelberg would dream up."

What do they read in that universe? Science fiction. Only they don't call it science fiction there:

In a world where interplanetary and interstellar war and purple moon monsters were actual fact, cold reality, then stories about such things would be *adventure* stories, and not science fiction at all.

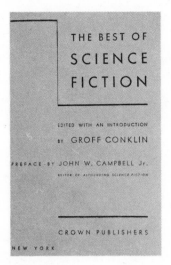
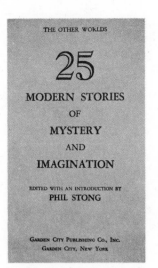

Two 1946 anthologies Title page A 1942 anthology Title page

The first publishing breakthrough came in the form of anthologies which capitalized on the golden age of science fiction. One day some scholar may pin down the dates when Groff Conklin and Healy & McComas first thought of putting together their big collections, but I like to think, until I learn better, that it occurred to each of them when they heard the news of the atomic bomb, and after the human shock faded away they began to realize that the unprecedented explosion had been the kicks and screams of a new age being born.

The results, at least, are clear: 1946 saw two major publishers bring out two big science fiction anthologies within a few months of each other. The first was Groff Conklin's *The Best of Science Fiction,* published by Crown. The second was *Adventures in Time and Space,* edited by Raymond J. Healy and J. Francis McComas for Random House. They had a few predecessors: a 1937 collection, apparently aimed at a teen-aged audience, *Adventures to Come,* edited by J. Berg Eisenwein and published by McLoughlin Brothers; *The Other Worlds,* edited by Phil Stong and published in 1942 by Garden City; an important breakthrough with *The Pocket Book of Science Fiction,* a paperback collection in 1943, and *Portable Novels of Science,* published by Viking in 1945, both edited by Donald Wollheim. But it was the two big anthologies of 1946 that were published in steam-engine time, and both became best sellers. *Adventures in Time and Space,* perhaps because of the Random House imprint, continues to be available over the years in a Modern Library edition. Both books earned good reviews and called new attention to science fiction as a genre deserving a retrospective study. Both also had good introductions, the Conklin book the better of the two with its more thorough historical analysis and a preface by John Campbell. It marked a beginning for serious literary consideration.

What was being considered was largely "modern science fiction," Campbellian science fiction, for the books were made up mostly of stories originally published in *Astounding* and in the years 1937 to 1945. Of the thirty-five stories in *Adventures in Time and Space,* for instance, thirty-two were from *Astounding* and all but four of these had been purchased by Campbell (one of those four was Campbell's own "Forgetfulness"). The pioneer anthologies helped spread science fiction's popularity as well, giving new readers an opportunity to sample a well-culled selection and providing aspiring writers with a how-to-do-it handbook of examples.

Anthologies became a regular feature of science fiction publishing: Groff Conklin began producing them on what seemed an annual basis, accumulating five by 1951. For several years August Derleth brought out one a year, beginning in 1948, for Pelligrini and Cudahy. Everett F. Bleiler and T. E. Dikty began editing *The Best Science Fiction Stories of the Year* in 1949; it did not achieve the success of more recent best-of-the-year collections, but it lasted for about ten years. Judith Merril, whose 1950 Bantam Books collection called *Shot in the Dark* returned to the paperback anthology pioneered by Wollheim for Pocket Books, entered the best-of-the-year sweepstakes in 1956 with books first published in

Edited by Donald Wollheim (1945)

Judith Merril

A group of post-war anthologies

First volume: 1949

First volume: 1956

Terry Carr

Donald A. Wollheim

hard covers by Gnome Press and reprinted by Dell Books, and later published in paperbacks by Dell alone.

In 1952 Tony Boucher wrote, "It's doubtful if any specialized field can lay as much proportionate stress on the anthology as science fiction does today. Probably within a few years the output will simmer down, as with the mystery, to a few standard annuals and an occasional collection based on unusual research or a novel idea."

For various reasons, possibly related to the unusual nature of science fiction and the science fiction reader, Boucher has proved to be a better editor than a prophet. Anthologies continued to pour out in an accelerating stream, and in recent years that stream has broken into new riverbeds.

Best-of-the-year anthologies now are being issued by several different publishers: Doubleday (for the first six volumes) and recently Harper and Row publish the stories selected as the best of the year by the Science Fiction Writers of America, under the title of Nebula Award stories; Harry Harrison and Brian Aldiss edit their selections as an annual volume for Putnam, and Donald Wollheim and Terry Carr did a selection for Ace Books until both left Ace; now both do their thing separately. Fred Pohl did a best-of-the-year book for Ace, which Forrest Ackerman took over. Lester del Rey edits another, and the end is nowhere in view.

Other editors are combing the old magazines for unanthologized and forgotten masterpieces (few are left); and still others are anthologizing the already anthologized. Groff Conklin was the most untiring anthologist of all, turning in the fifties and sixties to anthologies organized around particular themes and

Best-of-the-year collections

Huckster rooms at the Noreascon, the World Science Fiction Convention in Boston, 1971. A trading center for fans, collectors and dealers.

The costume ball at the 1971 Boston Noreascon, where fans of all shapes and sizes displayed costumes based on science fiction characters.

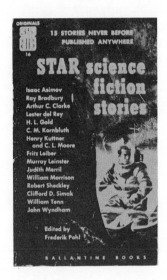
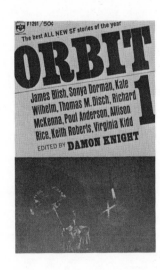
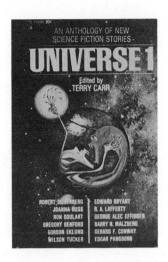

working at projects up to the time of his death. Robert Silverberg may have become even more prolific as an editor in this field, both in the theme and general anthology. Silverberg quoted an earlier anthologist, Frederik Pohl, as saying he finally gave up the profession because it was too easy. Now Roger Elwood has made a career out of science fiction anthologization.

In the last few years anthologies containing critical material have been aimed at the high-school and college student: Silverberg's *Mirror of Infinity* for Harper & Row; Dick Allen's *Science Fiction: The Future* for Harcourt, Brace, Jovanovich; Richard Ofshe's *Sociology of the Possible* for Prentice-Hall; and Isaac Asimov's *Where Do We Go From Here?* for Doubleday, with others soon to be published.

And with a volume entitled *New Tales of Space and Time*, Raymond J. Healy, whom we just met as co-editor of *Adventures in Time and Space*, pioneered a new type of anthology—the "anthology" of previously unpublished stories. By commissioning or soliciting original stories and offering better payment (or the promise of better payment through a share of half the royalties; the editor customarily takes the other half) and fewer editorial taboos, the original anthology succeeded in producing better and sometimes different stories. Sales were good enough to create a trend that would result in theme volumes, novelettes, or short novels created around a single world, a single theme, or even a single opening situation, and finally maturing into a fully developed alternative to the magazines in the form of annual or semiannual series (see Chapter 12).

A shorter-lived publishing phenomenon was the fan-based specialty press. To understand the unique creation of a publishing business built almost exclu-

Damon Knight

sively on love for a particular genre, we must take another look at the development of a unique aspect of science fiction, the fan.

When the appearance of the first science fiction magazine brought forth letters to the editor praising this story or criticizing that one, suggesting an old favorite, a new concept, or a greater mission, Gernsback immediately recognized the letter writers for what they were—fans. Robert Lowndes, a fan turned writer and editor, later wrote that "even when the Sloane *Amazing* was at its lowest ebb, it still received mail by the sack." Soon the letter writers began writing to each other.

The first result in 1930 was the creation of the Science Correspondence Club, dedicated to "the furtherance of science and its dissemination among the laymen of the world and the final betterment of humanity." Gernsback's belief that the major function of science fiction was to create scientists found disciples. The club had a publication, *The Comet*. Then fans in larger metropolitan areas began to get together. The first was New York's Scienceers, a bit later in 1930, who also had the ostensible purpose of discussing the science in science fiction, but who were more concerned about the fiction than the science in their publication, *The Planet*. Soon three New York fans issued what Moskowitz calls "the first true fan magazine," the *Time Traveller*.

Other fan publications followed: *The Science Fiction Digest*, another product of New York fans with the help of staff from elsewhere, came out in 1932, as did *Science Fiction*, a publication of two Cleveland fans; the *Fantasy Fan* was born in Jersey City in 1933 and produced the first fan-into-editor transformation when Gernsback saw it and picked the 17-year-old Charles D. Hornig as editor of *Wonder Stories*. Other publications followed: *Unusual Stories, Marvel Tales, Astonishing Stories, The Phantagraph, The Science Fiction Review, The Science Fiction Critic, The Planeteer, Fantasy News, Science Fiction Times, Fantasy Advertiser, Spaceways, Fanfare, Le Zombie, D'Journal, Vampire, Fanews, Fantascience Digest, The Fantasy Fan, Cosmos, Hackneyed Tales, Cosmic Call, The Scientifictionist, New Fandom, Voice of the Imagi-Nation, Shangri-L'Affaires, Snide, The Acolyte*, and a thousand others.

Many of them were hectographed, a process that was cheap but unattractive and limited to reproduction of about fifty copies. Mimeographing brought better-looking publications and longer runs and thicker journals. The best magazines—even some of the earliest—were printed.

The tradition of amateur journalism was already old when science fiction fans discovered it. Lovecraft, who became a member of the United Amateur Press Association in 1914 and a member of the National Amateur Press Association in 1917 and later president of both, once said, "What amateur journalism has given me is life itself." In 1937, under the leadership of Donald Wollheim, science fiction formed its first APA, the Fantasy Amateur Press Association (FAPA), to collect and distribute to no more than fifty members (no more than two dozen fan magazines were being published, they had circulations of twenty to thirty-five, and anyway the hectographed magazines were limited to about fifty copies) regular bundled mailings of their own publications. Later the less exclusive Spectator Amateur Press Society (SAPS) entered fandom.

LEFT: Big Name Fan Forrest J. Ackerman at 1971 Noreascon

RIGHT: A group of fan publications

Fans and writers at the first World Science Fiction Convention in 1939. STANDING LEFT TO RIGHT: Morojo, Julius Schwartz, Otto Binder, Mort Weisinger, Jack Darrow. SEATED: Forrest J. Ackerman, Ross Rocklynne, Charles D. Hornig, and newly arrived author Ray Bradbury

Fan magazines, though more expensive to publish and mail, continue to be major outlets for fan enthusiasm: *Locus* is an example of the weekly or biweekly mimeographed publication which carries news of professional and fan activity; *Luna*, a printed bimonthly primarily devoted to news items and reviews of professional magazines and books, with an occasional article; and *Riverside Review*, a quarterly which approaches the status of a scholarly journal. In addition, there is the professional journal of the Science Fiction Research Association, *Extrapolation*; that of the British Science Fiction Foundation, *Foundation*; *Science Fiction Studies* published at Indiana State University; *Algol*, *Science Fiction Review*, and two publications produced by the Science Fiction Writers of America, *The SFWA Bulletin*, which contains articles and news about science fiction including some public business of the organization, and *The Forum*, an internal publication of SFWA business, articles, and letters.

In 1973 Dr. Fredric Wertham, who much earlier had ripped the comic magazines for their *Seduction of the Innocent*, published a paean of praise for the new and free form of expression and what it had created in *The World of the Fanzines*.

Published communications—articles, letters, criticisms, and comments—have played a major part in the history of the fan magazine and in the development of science fiction itself.

Meanwhile, back in the time when the magazines were developing, clubs had begun to form, partially in response to the discovery of fellow science fiction fans in the letter columns of the science fiction magazines (many fans became well-known or even famous among their fellow fans for the frequency of their appearance in letter columns of professional and then fan magazines, and became known as letter hacks or, as the developing science fiction cant would write it, letterhacks). Another major push toward organization was Gernsback's announcement, in a 1934 *Wonder Stories*, of the creation of the Science Fiction League, "a noncommercial membership organization for the furtherance and betterment of the art of science fiction." Clubs sprang up in Brooklyn, Los Angeles, Philadelphia, Chicago, New York City, Queens, and other areas, some of them unlikely and the clubs short-lived. Fans who did not live in metropolitan areas had to content themselves with fan magazines or extensive correspondence, although some would venture long distances, often hitchhiking, to see other fans or attend conventions.

Conventions—the ingathering of fans at periodic intervals to discuss their avocation—began in Philadelphia in 1936 with a handful of fans from New York meeting with a similar number in Philadelphia at the home of one of the Philadelphia members. The first "world" convention was held at Caravan Hall in mid-Manhattan in 1939; about 200 attended. Subsequent world conventions were held in Chicago in 1940, in Denver in 1941, and in Los Angeles in 1946, after a wartime suspension.

Later conventions—in Philadelphia (1947), Toronto (1948), Cincinnati (1949), Portland (1950), New Orleans (1951)—began to confirm or create traditions: conventions named with such portmanteau words as NyCon and Denvention from the beginning, professional guests of honor (fan guests were added in 1967), a system of awards launched in Philadelphia in 1953 and becoming the present Hugo system at Cleveland in 1955, and a Trans-Atlantic Fan Fund (TAFF) in 1954 to bring a fan from overseas each year to attend the convention. But attendance was relatively low until the Chicago convention in 1952 reached 1,000. Attendance dropped again—ranging between 300 and 850—until New York reached 1,500 in 1967 and fans began complaining that conventions were getting too big. In 1957 the convention finally honored the "world" in its name by going to London, which it did again in 1965. With the 1970 convention in Heidelberg, Germany, a plan was approved to share the convention with the rest of the world every fourth year or so. Melbourne, Australia, put on the 1975 convention, and the 1976 convention was awarded to Kansas City. By this time, the number of fans attending—Washington, D.C., had 4,500 in 1974— became a major concern.

Why do the fans go to all the trouble?

The fans themselves ask the same question. Some of them answer with "fiawol," which is fanese for "fandom is a way of life"; others, unable to find a satisfactory answer, "gafiate"—get away from it all. First must come some kind of admiration, affection, or love for science fiction or an allied genre, such as fantasy, horror, or sword and sorcery; some fans get turned on by comic strips or comic magazines or motion pictures. Second comes the pleasure of the collector, which probably is little different from the thrills of the collector of stamps or baseball cards or barbed wire, except that a science fiction collection provides at least one additional experience: it can be read. Third comes the social experience of meeting with other collectors, other fans, directly or by correspondence; fourth, self-expression through publication of articles, letters, or magazines. At this stage the fan may tend to make fandom itself the center of his activity and forget or ignore science fiction; many fan magazines have little or nothing to do with the professional field. Fifth comes the possession of arcane knowledge, like that of a secret society or lodge, which becomes reinforced by the creation and evolution of a secret language, a jargon, a cant. Below is an abbreviated glossary taken from a history of fandom written by Harry Warner, Jr., *All Our Yesterdays:*

Boskone—Boston conference; pun involving New England fan gatherings and E. E. Smith's fiction.

Carbonzine—Fanzine that is reproduced by carbon paper.

Chainzine—Something like a carbonzine, but sometimes it doesn't even use carbon paper; each recipient in a designated list adds to it and mails it to the next person.

Chicon—Worldcon in Chicago.

Clubzine—Fanzine published by a fan club.

Degafiate—To resume fanac after gafiation.

Faan—Usually a fan who has lost most of his interest in science fiction and is now mainly interested in other fans and faans; occasionally a particularly enthusistic fan.

Fanac—Fan activity; something that a science fiction fan does while pursuing his hobby.

Fanzine—Fan magazine; amateur publication, sometimes free and sometimes sold for a price, published and written by fans without expectation of profit.

Fiawol—Fandom is a way of life; the philosophy that fandom is important enough to dominate life, antonym to fijagh: fandom is just a goddamned hobby.

Filthy pro—Semi-affectionate term for someone who makes money from science fiction.

Fringefan—Someone who is just barely a fan, or sometimes an individual who is not a fan at all but enjoys the company of fans.

Mailing comments—Reactions, reviews, and comments inspired by the contents of an apa mailing, a sort of postal conversation.

Mundane—Everything and everyone except fanac, fans, and their literature.

Neofan—Newcomer of fandom.

Prozine—Professional magazine; normally, one that publishes science fiction, weird fiction, or fantasy fiction.

Sercon—Serious, constructive, sometimes compliment, sometimes insult, depending on the intent.

Harry Warner, Jr.

A history of fandom

Sam Moskowitz

Another fan history

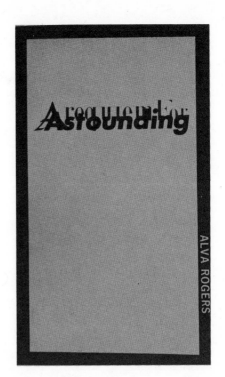

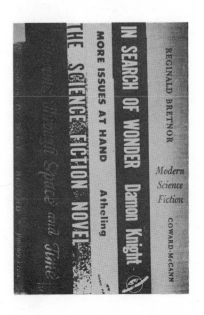

Subzine—Subscription fanzine; contrasted to those given away, or to apazines distributed only to apa members.

Trufaan—Particularly active and loyal faan.

Zine—Magazine.

Finally, fandom offered the opportunity available in any organization or social group, the chance to seize and wield power, to be important, to be recognized. In the early days of fandom, at least, annual polls would acclaim a "top fan," "number-one fan," or "fan of the year," honors matched today, perhaps, by the lionization at conventions of fan guests of honor; other accolades go or have gone to fanzines, fan writers, fan artists, fan poets, and others.

Power struggles began occurring almost simultaneously with the formation of fan groups, at first over the relatively serious grounds of whether a group should be primarily engaged in scientific experimentation or in the admiration, analysis, and promotion of science fiction; or over the issue of activism, whether fans should work toward the creation of a better world, which to some fans smacked of communism. Other issues focused on which individuals or groups would control a particular club or organization or put on a convention. At least one complete book, Sam Moskowitz's grandly titled *The Immortal Storm*, records those power struggles in astonishing detail. The importance to Moskowitz of success in this social structure is evidenced in his own recorded history of his drive to become the leading fan through publications, articles, the founding of a manuscript bureau to provide articles for fan magazines, conventions, and clubs. His battle for supremacy over the Futurians, which culminated for Moskowitz in the success of the first world convention in New York (and the exclusion from it of several Futurians), was related in language of this sort:

But again stark drama was preparing her lines for recitation, and what was to follow, coupled with the coincidence of simultaneous events, was to deal catastrophe to fandom as a whole. Ragnarok had caught the entire fan world napping!

The Immortal Storm may be the only book, someone has remarked, in which World War II comes as an anticlimax. Even Warner's *All Our Yesterdays*, a much more soberly presented history, suffers a bit from the realization that this is a microcosm indeed—as Moskowitz comments about a period in 1937, "Active fans then numbered less than fifty—the Fantasy Amateur Press Association could have included *every* fan of importance."

At its least, science fiction fandom is a fascinating sociological phenomenon deserving serious study; at best, it became an evolutionary force for progress in science fiction: criticizing, testing, discarding, contributing. Out of science fiction fandom came practically the only useful criticism published (later collected in such volumes as Damon Knight's *In Search of Wonder* and William Atheling's (James Blish) *Issues at Hand* and *More Issues at Hand*). Out of fandom also came the first bibliographical works and indexes: Everett F. Bleiler's *The Check-list of Fantastic Literature* and *Indexes to the Science Fiction Magazines* by Donald B. Day, the M.I.T. Science Fiction Society, and the New England Science Fiction Association.

Out of fandom came collections of the perishable pulp magazines and early books which now are in great demand among scholars and libraries and command substantial prices. A 1970 price list offered copies of *Astounding* from the early forties for $2 each, and older copies, if available, would be much costlier. Even in the forties, an A. Merritt collection was valued at $2,000, the first issue of *Amazing* at $8, and other issues from the twenties at $2 to $6 a magazine; today complete runs of some magazines are being priced at $25,000 and copies of 1930 *Astoundings* at $25 each. Even letters, memorabilia, and fan magazines and other publications bring surprising prices: a set of Lovecraft letters to Clark Ashton Smith was offered in 1971 for $10,500; booklets by Lovecraft (one of only ten pages) were listed at prices from $450 to $575; and fourteen issues of *The Science Fiction Critic*, an early fan magazine published from November 1935 to July 1938, were advertised for $65.

Out of fandom came editors conscious of what was wrong with earlier magazines and filled with a sense of mission: Hornig, Weisinger, Wollheim, Pohl, Palmer, Boucher, Lowndes, Merril, Knight, Blish, Shaw, and others. And out of fandom came new authors: Pohl, Blish, Knight, Kornbluth, Arthur Clarke, Isaac Asimov, Robert Bloch, P. Schuyler Miller, John Christopher (C. S. Youd), Ray Bradbury, and more recently Robert Silverberg, Harlan Ellison, Alexei Panshin, and many others. Equally as many writers and editors came into the field from outside fandom, many of them to make an impact as great or even greater, but the influence of fandom on professional science fiction has been substantial.

E. E. Smith's Lensman series, leather-bound

In the immediate postwar period the impact was on the publishing business. The specialty press was created, to be sure, in 1939 with Arkham House, founded by August Derleth and Donald Wandrei to bring together the writings of H. P. Lovecraft and later expanded to include other writers. It published the first book edition of Van Vogt's *Slan* and the first collection of Ray Bradbury's stories, *Dark Carnival*, as well as a significant list of others. Arkham's pattern would be followed by other specialty publishers, most of them less knowledgeable about printing, publishing, and distribution. Thomas P. Hadley of Boston published Doc Smith's *Skylark of Space* and sold out an edition of 1,000 copies through a single ad in *Astounding*. Hadley's partner, Lloyd A. Eschbach, founded Fantasy Press, and took over the mission of reprinting Doc Smith; among the accomplishments of Fantasy Press was the publication of the six volumes in E. E. Smith's Lensman series, bound in leather and boxed under the general title of *The History of Civilization*. Fantasy Press would also produce

Forrest J. Ackerman and part of his collection

More of the Ackerman science fiction collection

the first classic volume about science fiction writing, *Of Worlds Beyond,* in 1947.

The other publishers—Shasta, Fantasy Publishing Company, Gnome, Avalon, New Era, F.F.F.—rushed to printers to publish favorite authors and then to expand into other kinds of rescue operations on pulp classics and finally to solicit new books. But they had little hope for success, and some died as they gave birth to their only book. Their ability to sell two or three thousand copies of an obscure title, however, proved to commercial publishers that a limited but loyal public was willing to buy almost anything that was offered—the kind of public that in the thirties and forties, with their thousands of lending libraries, made mystery publishing virtually failure-proof.

Science fiction publishing differed from the publishing of other genre literature such as westerns and mysteries in its continuing timeliness. In a lead article for *Saturday Review,* Fletcher Pratt reported in 1949 that one regular publisher, interested in experimenting inexpensively with science fiction, offered to take some of a specialist publisher's remainders for a reissue under the name of the larger house. "Remainders?" was the reply. "Listen, when one of our books gets down to where it would be a remainder it becomes a rare book and we charge double for it." Arkham House needed four years to sell a limited edition of 1,268 of Lovecraft's *The Outsider and Others,* but as soon as the edition was exhausted dealers began to charge from twenty dollars to as much as one hundred dollars for a copy.

But the discovery of science fiction by the commercial publishers, with their large presses, better distribution, capital out of which to offer authors advances, and promises of royalties, was the end of the specialized presses; in their success was the seed of their destruction, even though some survived into the middle fifties. Henry Holt actually had started publishing science fiction in 1941 with several *Unknown*-type fantasy novels by L. Sprague de Camp and by De Camp in collaboration with Fletcher Pratt.

Simon and Schuster became involved in 1947 with the publication of Van Vogt's *The World of Null-A,* and went on to publish Williamson's *The Humanoids, Seetee Shock,* and others. Frederick Fell and Doubleday and Dutton got into the business in 1949, with Frank Belknap Long's *John Carstairs: Space Detective,* Heinlein's *Waldo & Magic Inc.,* and Fredric Brown's *What Mad Universe?* And Scribner's began an immensely profitable series of Heinlein juveniles with *Rocket Ship Galileo* in 1948 and *Space Cadet* in 1949. Then Winston launched a series of juveniles in 1951 with Del Rey's *Marooned on Mars.* Other hard-cover publishers got into the juvenile business: Harcourt Brace began publishing Andre Norton's juveniles in 1952, beginning with *Star Man's Son,* and Doubleday followed soon after. Eventually many science fiction writers—Gordon Dickson, Robert Silverberg, Isaac Asimov under the name of Paul French —would write science fiction in juvenile form; they referred to these books as annuities, since they continue to sell slowly but steadily year after year and the publishers keep them in print.

After a few years the tide of books reached its flood and started to ebb. A steady trickle came from Simon and Schuster and a few other main-line publishers, but Doubleday became the principal publisher and purveyor of science fiction in hard covers.

In the paperback field, the name was Ace Books. Under the editorship of Donald Wollheim, Ace got involved with science fiction early and published hundreds of science fiction and fantasy books in its back-to-back double volumes and more traditional formats. The other paperback firms were more cautious: New American Library picked up Heinlein early; Bantam Books signed up a good list of authors; and Ballantine Books, when it was founded in 1952, began an aggressive campaign to find or commission new manuscripts. Gold Medal Books and Ballantine were the beginning of a movement toward paperback originals that eventually would turn the paperback industry around, switching its primary emphasis from reprinting to creation. At its start the paperback industry had lived off hard-cover publishers; now the paperback publishers asserted their equality. The big money was in the volume sales of paperback publishing, particularly after the demise of the rental library, and hard-cover publishers began to live off paperback reprints. Traditionally they retained half the author's paperback royalties, a contractual arrangement that at first made good sense,

An Ace double volume

since paperback publishers selected their reprints from among hard-cover publications, and the hard-cover publisher therefore performed a significant service. Later, when more money was returned from paperback sales than original hard-cover publication, the arrangement became a kind of subsidy for the hard-cover publisher. The average mystery, western, or science fiction novel would earn well over twice as much in paperback royalties as from its hard-cover publication. Gradually the authors realized what was happening: original paperback publication was more profitable for them than hard-cover originals, even if later reprinted. Moreover, paperbacks made up a bigger market; it would accept and publish more books, and it would even, upon occasion, keep books in print.

Ballantine Books also launched two other innovative concepts: paying its authors a sufficiently large advance to enable them to write full-time, and providing simultaneous hard-cover and paperback publication—the hard-covers for libraries and review, from which the paperback is largely excluded, and the paperback for income. Both programs proved too expensive, but recently other firms have launched joint hard-cover and paperback publication—Delacourt and Dell Books, and Putnam and Berkley are two examples—although today hard-cover publication precedes paperback, and the advantage to the author lies in not sharing paperback royalties with the hard-cover publisher.

In recent days, since the hard-cover potential for science fiction has been enhanced by the sales of such novels as Michael Crichton's *The Andromeda Strain* and *The Terminal Man*, Ira Levin's *Rosemary's Baby* and *One Perfect Day*, and William Peter Blatty's *The Exorcist*, the trend toward original paperback publication has been slowed by authors willing to gamble paperback royalties against a possible good sale in hard-covers and the reviews, reputation, and library sales that go with hard-cover publication. The success of a few books has stimulated the interest of hard-cover publishers in science fiction and increased their willingness to promote science fiction titles. To this can be added the trend toward the auctioning of paperback reprint rights, which has often resulted in higher advance payments than the author could obtain for an original manuscript. A more recent trend is for paperback publishers to arrange for hard-cover publication.

The addition of Ballantine Books (and two good friends of science fiction in Ian and Betty Ballantine) as well as other paperback publishers was a major asset to science fiction. But the biggest boom in the early fifties was in magazines. Three new magazines—*The Magazine of Fantasy* (which became *The Magazine of Fantasy and Science Fiction* with its second issue), *Other Worlds,* and *A. Merritt Fantasy*—were started in 1949. *A. Merritt* would last only six issues; *Other Worlds,* created by Ray Palmer after he left *Amazing* under mysterious circumstances, would last through 1957 when it degenerated into a flying-saucer magazine, but *The Magazine of Fantasy and Science Fiction* would become one of the three major magazines in the field.

Ten new magazines would begin publication in 1950: *Fantasy Fiction Stories, Fantastic Story Quarterly, Worlds Beyond, Out of This World, Galaxy Science Fiction* and *Galaxy Novels, Future Science Fiction* (1950–60), *Imagination* (1950–58), *Marvel Science Stories* (revived for six issues after nine years), and *Two Complete Science-Adventure Books* (1950–54). The first four would be short-lived; *Worlds Beyond,* a promising magazine edited by Damon Knight, lasted for only three issues. The others would have more respectable durations, and *Galaxy* would become the third of the three major magazines. Its editions of novels would last through 1960.

Four magazines were created in 1951: *Science Fiction Quarterly* (an old name but a new magazine, 1951–58), *Authentic Science Fiction* (1951–57), *Suspense* (four issues), and *Ten Story Fantasy* (four issues). The British created *Worlds of Fantasy* and *Tales of Tomorrow* in 1950, *Wonders of the Spaceways* and *New Worlds* in 1951, *Nebula* in 1952, and *Vargo Statten* in 1954.

For a sampling of the new science fiction magazines of the 1950's, see pages 195 through 208.

The pace picked up again in 1952, with seven new magazines: *If*, which became one of the better second-rank magazines, later was sold to the Galaxy group; *Fantastic*, a companion magazine to *Amazing*, still is published; the more ephemeral *Science Fiction Adventures* (1952–58), *Dynamic Science Fiction* (1952–54) which published the first third of my thesis about science fiction, perhaps the only master's thesis ever serialized in a science fiction magazine—or a pulp magazine of any kind; *Space Science Fiction* (eight issues) edited by Lester del Rey; *Space Stories* (five issues); and *Fantastic Science Fiction* (two issues).

The deluge descended upon the newsstands in 1953: *Science Fiction Plus*, started as a slick magazine by Sam Moskowitz for Hugo Gernsback, lasted only seven issues; *Orbit Science Fiction*, only five; *Rocket Stories*, only three; *Vortex Science Fiction*, only two; *Fantasy Magazine*, which became *Fantasy Fiction* after its first issue, only four; *Science Stories* and *Cosmos Science Fiction*, also only four; *Tops in Science Fiction*, only two; but *Spaceway* stumbled into 1955, *Universe Science Fiction* obtained a brief reprieve by combining with *Other Worlds* in 1955, *Beyond Fantasy Fiction*, companion fantasy magazine to *Galaxy*, unfortunately barely lasted into 1955; *Avon Science Fiction and Fantasy Reader* (*Avon Science Fiction Reader* and *Avon Fantasy Reader* combined; two issues) and *Fantastic Universe* and *Science Fiction Stories* continued until 1960.

The meteoric careers of the new science fiction magazines—a bright flash and then oblivion—were enough to sober even the most euphoric science fiction editors and prospective publishers. Although 1953 was a boom year for new magazines, more magazines were being killed than born, including such an old favorite as *Famous Fantastic Mysteries*. The next year, 1954, saw the birth of *Imaginative Tales* (1954–58) and the birth and death of *Science Fiction Digest*, and the death of many more, including the venerable *Weird Tales*. In 1955 *Infinity Science Fiction* arrived on the stands, but three long-time favorites disappeared from them: *Planet Stories*, *Thrilling Wonder Stories*, and *Startling Stories*.

Satellite Science Fiction and *Super Science Fiction* began publication in 1956 and stopped in 1959. *Saturn*, begun in 1957, lasted five issues, and a second magazine named *Space Science Fiction* saw two issues; *Venture Science Fiction*, launched in 1957 under the editorship of Robert Mills as a companion magazine to *The Magazine of Fantasy and Science Fiction*, survived for nearly two years and would be reincarnated for another brief life span a decade later. *Vanguard*, edited by James Blish, would have a single issue in 1958; the British brought forth a magazine called *Science Fiction Adventures* that year. The

The Lost World (1925)

Metropolis (1926)

King Kong (1933)

King Kong

King Kong

The Invisible Man (1933)

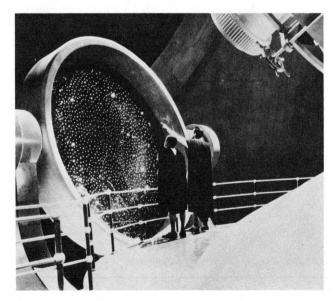

Things to Come (1936)

Things to Come

Destination Moon (1950)

When Worlds Collide (1951)

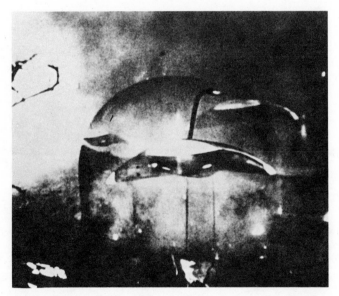

War of the Worlds (1953)

Forbidden Planet (1956)

The Time Machine (1960)

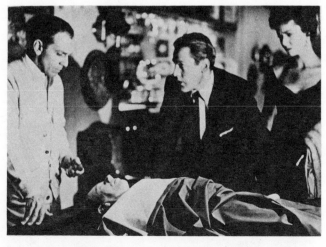

The Invasion of the Body Snatchers (1956)

publication of another new science fiction magazine would not be attempted until *Galaxy* publications brought out *Worlds of Tomorrow* in 1963.

What was happening?

Although it may not have been conceived in quite these terms, the late forties and early fifties had seemed like the birth of a science fiction world, not only in books and magazines but in motion pictures as well. John Baxter, who has written a book called *Science Fiction in the Cinema*, traces the boom in science fiction films to the success of George Pal's science fiction movie, the semidocumentary *Destination Moon*—based distantly on *Rocket Ship Galileo* by Heinlein, who also would have a hand in the script (Chesley Bonestell, astronomical artist and science fiction cover painter, would create the moon sets). Without discounting the follow-the-leader impulses of film makers, however, science fiction film production probably was responding to the same historical and psychological impulses that helped create the boom in magazines and books.

Good science fiction films, bad science fiction films—they seem to have little influence on the reading of science fiction, perhaps because the good ones usually have been lost in a welter of exploitation monster movies and cheaply made space adventures. Why there have been so few motion pictures which are both good films and good science fiction is a continuing puzzle to science fiction fans. Those that qualify might be shown in a film series of a dozen or so motion pictures: *The Lost World* (1925) and *Metropolis* (1926) for historical interest and then *Frankenstein* (1931), *King Kong* (1933), *The Invisible Man* (1933),

The Village of the Damned (1960)

The Day of the Triffids (1963)

Fahrenheit 451 (1966)

From the Earth to the Moon (1964)

Barbarella (1967)   Planet of the Apes (1967)

Things to Come (1936), Destination Moon (1950), When Worlds Collide (1951), The War of the Worlds (1953), Forbidden Planet (1956), An Invention for Destruction (also called The Fabulous World of Jules Verne, 1957), The Time Machine (1960), and 2001: A Space Odyssey (1968).

Pictures in the second rank, otherwise good films which are so-so science fiction or are marred in one way or another, would include: The Day the Earth Stood Still (1951), The Invasion of the Body Snatchers (1956), The Village of the Damned (1960) and its sequel The Children of the Damned (1963), The Day of the Triffids (1963), From the Earth to the Moon (1964), Robinson Crusoe on Mars (1964), The Tenth Victim (1965), Fahrenheit 451 (1966), Fantastic Voyage (1966), Barbarella (1967), Planet of the Apes (1967), and the other adaptations of the work of H. G. Wells and Jules Verne.

Other films which might be included because of their subject matter but have a different basic appeal include: Lost Horizon (1937), 1984 (1956), Dr. Strangelove (1964), and A Clockwork Orange (1971).

One explanation for the failure of films to capture the special qualities of science fiction may lie in the difference between the view of the science fiction fan and that of John Baxter, film industry spokesman, about Things to Come, the 1936 production based on H. G. Wells's 1933 novel The Shape of Things to Come. For many years I thought it the only good science fiction film ever made, not only because of its dramatic, rational vision of the future but because of its concern for the rule of reason over brute instincts, of its depiction of the role of science in the life of men, and of its faith in the role of man in the universe. Baxter says, "Wells marred it deeply with his simple-minded and often shoddy pamphleteering, but frequently the material is saved by a piece of magic in the design, a clever performance or some neat construction." Damon Knight observes that books like The Shrinking Man and The Power—and presumably the films based on those books—are not science fiction but "anti-science fiction." To which Baxter replies, "Science fiction supports logic and order, sf film illogic and chaos. Its roots lie not in the visionary literature of the nineteenth century, to which science fiction owes most of its origins, but in older forms and attitudes, the medieval fantasy world, the era of the masque, the morality play and the Grand Guignol."

Which is descriptive but does not answer the question: why cannot motion pictures deal adequately with science fiction? Science fiction, like Things to Come, says that man can create a better future by the use of his mind, by shedding old taboos. The science fiction film replies, in the hallowed tradition of "there are things man was not meant to know" and "he dared to dabble in

Arthur C. Clarke

George Pal

Miriam Allen DeFord

Gordon Dickson

Ward Moore

Richard Matheson

Chad Oliver

Mack Reynolds

Frank Robinson

Harry Harrison

Zenna Henderson

Dean McLaughlin

Kris Neville

Alan Nourse

Edgar Pangborn

E. C. Tubb

A. J. Budrys

Mildred Clingerman

192

Cleveland, 1955. CLOCKWISE FROM BOTTOM: Mildred Clingerman, Mark Clifton, Judith Merril, Mr. and Mrs. Frank Riley (Rhylich) and their two children, James Gunn

Ted Cogswell

Philip K. Dick

Daniel Galouye

Randall Garrett

Ron Goulart

Frank Herbert

Robert Sheckley

Theodore Thomas

Raymond Banks

Marion Zimmer Bradley

Joe L. Hensley

Anne McCaffrey

James White

Robert F. Young

God's domain," that we must trust our emotions and our traditions, that reason is cold, cruel, sterile, and joyless, and that science is antihuman. The audience of a traditional science fiction film (only here given the distasteful abbreviation "sci-fi") knows that the scientist will be unwise and reckless if not downright foolish, will endanger not only himself and his loved ones but probably the rest of humanity, and will be punished at the end.

Television tends to be much the same only more so: because of the demands of a weekly schedule, series tend to be infinitely repetitive, which is deadly to the very spirit of science fiction; the anthology shows tend to be promising but uneven and about as good as the knowledge and strength of the person in charge. In fact, the same statement could be made about science fiction films: the two truly outstanding science fiction films of all time, to my mind, are *Things to Come*, which H. G. Wells helped script and influenced even beyond that; and *2001: A Space Odyssey*, in which Arthur C. Clarke played a similar role of scriptwriter and consultant. And the films produced or directed by George Pal are almost all on my list of good films.

What Hollywood studios, writers, directors, and producers turned to, when they didn't know anything about science fiction, was monsters. Monsters they knew, and monsters they gave the public until the public might be forgiven if it thought that monsters and science fiction were synonymous. What Baxter thinks of monsters might be deduced from the following comment: "Fantasy and reality interpenetrate in *Creature from the Black Lagoon* (1954), a film that fulfills every promise Arnold made in *It Came from Outer Space*."

In the fifties the monster movies came to be so omnipresent Bob Bloch speculated that the failure of science fiction magazines was due to the disillusionment of the potential science fiction reader; they were being turned off science fiction by the monster movies just as they once had been turned away from the science fiction magazines by the bug-eyed monsters on the covers. John Campbell, on the other hand, after the beginning of spaceflight wondered if the desires of the science fiction reader for scientific and technological speculation were being satisfied simply by reading his daily newspaper.

I believe that other factors were at work. First, there was a time lag: the general public might be living in a science fiction world but it did not have to like it or even admit it; a new generation had to grow up with atomic bombs, television, spaceflight, and the uncertainty brought on by constant change, and to discover that conventional literature did not concern itself with these basic facts of their existence, or if it mentioned them it was only to deplore or despair. Their parents, on the whole, rejected science fiction first as unreal and then as unpleasantly real; the children found it their kind of literature.

Publishers looked upon science fiction as just one more bandwagon to jump upon. Most of them were poorly financed and unprepared to endure a period of losses while the magazine was establishing itself and finding its audience. Amid the wild burgeoning of new titles and competition for space on the crowded newsstands, a number of worthwhile magazines had little chance. The audience was limited until the postatomic generation grew into teen-agers. Some twenty, thirty, forty magazines were competing for the same readers. Even the hard-core fan could never read that many.

Some observers have blamed television for science fiction's troubles in the middle and late fifties. Television was coming into its own, and television viewing was still a national habit, even for many of the literate, and may have helped kill the large general magazines such as *The American Magazine, Collier's,* and *The Saturday Evening Post;* certainly its grasp on the advertising dollar had a major impact. What irony if television, predicted by science fiction authors since Gernsback's *Ralph 124C 41+*, should assassinate its prophets!

But the most important factor in the magazine situation, particularly for the smaller magazines, is and always has been circulation. In the fifties circulation became an increasing problem. New magazines were being created in other

November, 1949 (Vol. 1, No. 1) (Malcolm Smith)

December, 1949 (Vol. 1, No. 1) (Lawrence)

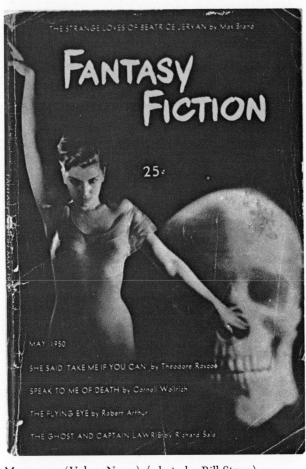

May, 1950 (Vol. 1, No. 1) (photo by Bill Stone)

Spring, 1950 (Vol. 1, No. 1) (Bergey)

December, 1950 (Vol. 1, No. 1) (Calle)

July, 1950 (Vol. 1, No. 1) (Unknown)

May-June, 1950 (Vol. 1, No. 1) (Bergey)

1950 (No. 1) (Stone)

October, 1950 (Vol. 1, No. 1) (Bok)

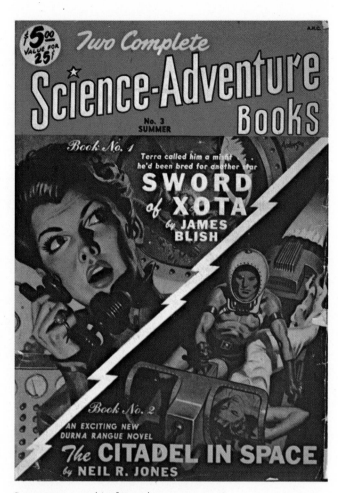

Summer, 1951 (Anderson)

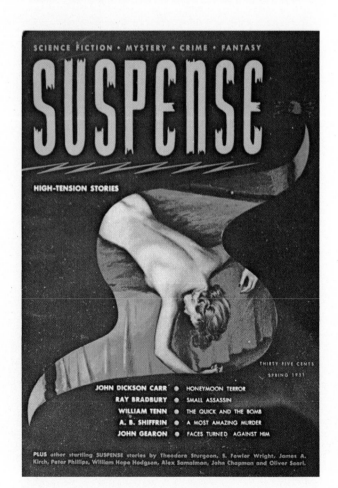

Spring, 1951 (Vol. 1, No. 1) (Unknown)

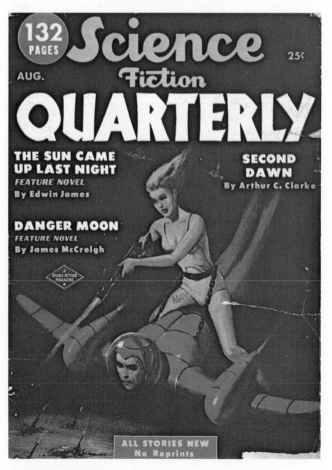

August, 1951 (Vol. 1, No. 2) (Morey)

Spring, 1951 (Vol. 1, No. 1) (Unknown)

March, 1952 (Vol. 1, No. 1) (Key)

Summer, 1952 (Vol. 1, No. 1)
(Phillips and Summers, photo by Roy)

November, 1952 (Vol. 1, No. 1) (Van Dongen)

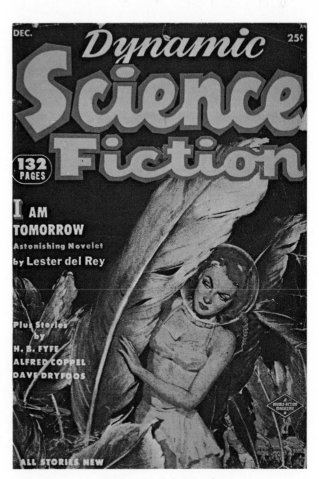

December, 1952 (Vol. 1, No. 1) (Ross)

August, 1952 (Vol. 1, No. 1) (Morales)

October, 1952 (Vol. 1, No. 1) (Emshwiller)

May, 1952 (Vol. 1, No. 1) (Orban)

1953 (Vol. 1, No. 1) (Unknown)

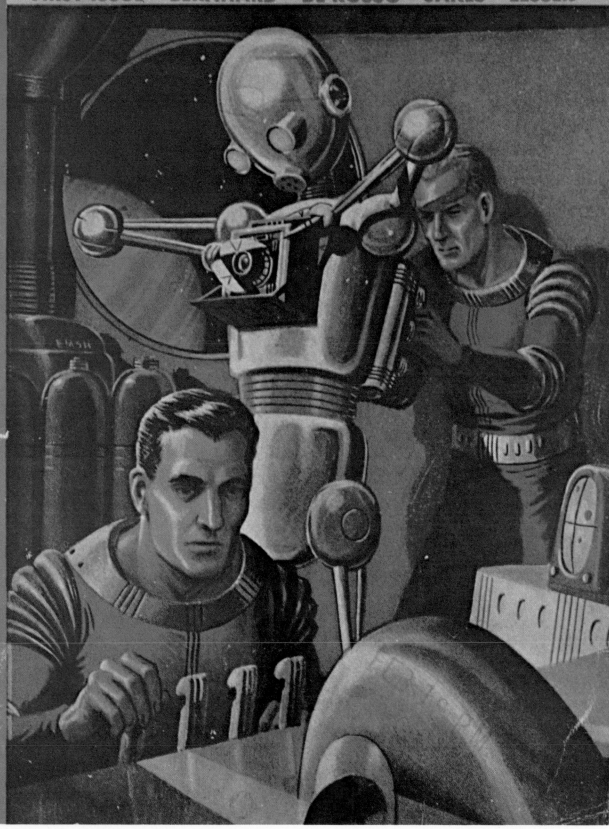

ROCKET STORIES

FIRST ISSUE • BERNHARD • DE ROSSO • JAKES • LESSER

APRIL 1953 35c

April, 1953 (Vol. 1, No. 1) (Emshwiller)

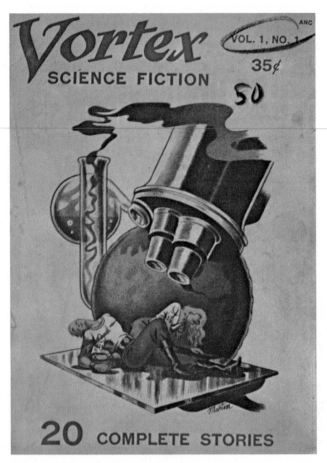

May, 1953 (Vol. 1, No. 1) (Martin)

February, 1953 (Vol. 1, No. 1) (Bok)

October, 1953 (No. 1) (Bok)

September, 1953 (Vol. 1, No. 1) (Schomburg)

CITADEL OF LOST SHIPS

Spring, 1953 (Vol. 1, No. 1) (Unknown)

December, 1953 (Vol. 1, No. 1) (Hunter)

June, 1953 (No. 1) (Malcolm Smith)

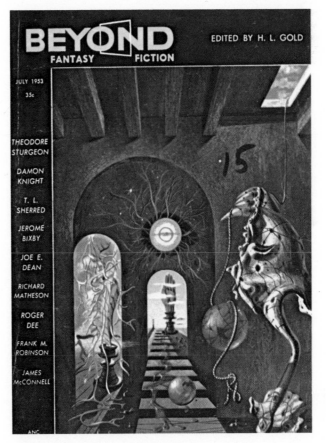

July, 1953 (Vol. 1, No. 1) (Powers)

June, 1953 (Vol. 1, No. 1) (Schomburg)

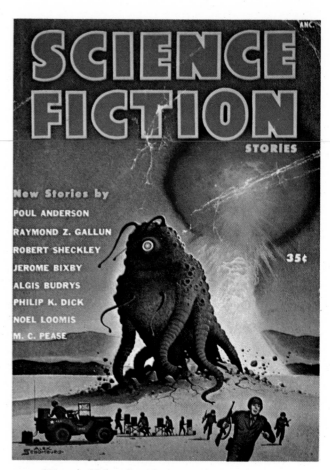

1953 (No. 1) (Schomburg)

January, 1955 (No. 3) (McCauley)

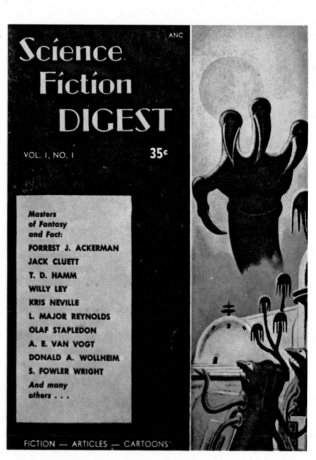

February, 1954 (Vol. 1, No. 1) (Martin)

THE FORGOTTEN ENEMY
CHECKMATE MORNING
FOR HUMANS ONLY
MISTER KOWTSHOOK
COME BLOW YOUR HORN

by Arthur C. Clarke
by John Jakes
by Alfred J. Coppel, Jr.
by John Christopher
by Milton Lesser

PLUS OTHER STORIES

AND FEATURES

ALL NEW STORIES

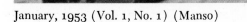

January, 1953 (Vol. 1, No. 1) (Manso)

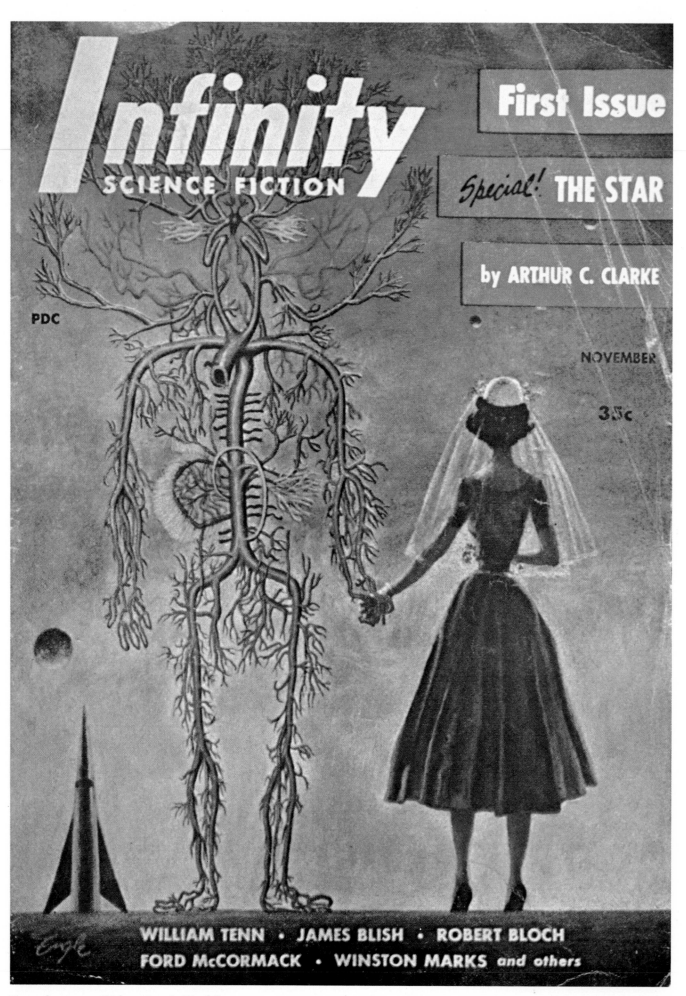

The cover shows the magazine masthead:

Infinity
SCIENCE FICTION

First Issue

Special! **THE STAR**

by **ARTHUR C. CLARKE**

PDC

NOVEMBER

35c

WILLIAM TENN • JAMES BLISH • ROBERT BLOCH
FORD McCORMACK • WINSTON MARKS and others

November, 1955 (Vol. 1, No. 1) (Engle)

October, 1956 (Vol. 1, No. 1) (Emshwiller)

December, 1956 (Vol. 1, No. 1) (Freas)

March, 1957 (Vol. 1, No. 1) (Unknown)

Spring, 1957 (Vol. 1, No. 1) (Ryan)

VANGUARD

science fiction

JUNE
35c

FIRST ISSUE: KORNBLUTH · JONES · DEL REY · DE CAMP

SOS: PLANET UNKNOWN
By A. Bertram Chandler

EDITED BY JAMES BLISH

June, 1958 (Vol. 1, No. 1) (Emshwiller)

fields as well as in science fiction; paperback books and their racks were crowding into limited space. The corner drugstore began to reduce its paperbacks to a sketchy collection, if it carried any, and the magazine and paperback-book stores were still largely in the future, at least in the greater part of this nation. The American News Company, long the principal distributor of magazines and paperback books, quit the distributing business in the fifties, and its successors were less thorough and less interested in the smaller publications from which they earned only pennies.

One editor and publisher of two second-rate science fiction magazines told me in the middle fifties that he could break even if he sold approximately 40 percent of the magazines he printed; that was true, as well, of paperback books. Because of economies in printing and increases in prices, the break-even point today may be a bit lower. The great success stories in publishing have been written by those magazines which, like *Playboy*, found a market for what it offered and sold virtually 100 percent of what it printed. For smaller publications the secret of survival was the identification of those four places out of ten where a prospective reader would see the magazine and purchase it before the retailer noticed it growing old on his stands, tore off the cover, and returned it for credit.

Publishers have used a variety of gimmicks to offset the basic inadequacies of distribution: they promote subscriptions, they date magazines later than their distribution so that they will seem current longer (have a longer shelf life), they go bimonthly to extend their newsstand sales period, they turn to paperback-book publication because paperbacks are undated and may stay on the book racks until sold or dog-eared. . . . But all ultimately fail before the indifference of the distributor, who sometimes finds it more profitable (or less expensive) to bundle an entire shipment of a science fiction magazine and send it to one outlet rather than to divide it into packages of two to twenty-five magazines according to a record of previous sales.

Edmund Cooper

Jim Harmon

Andrew J. Offut

Bob Shaw

Tom Scortia

John Brunner

Robert Silverberg

Harlan Ellison

Kate Wilhelm

Lloyd Biggle, Jr.

Dr. Jesse Bone

David R. Bunch

Keith Laumer

Joanna Russ

Tom Purdom

R. A. Lafferty

Fred Saberhagen

Terry Carr

Thomas M. Disch

Joseph Green

Piers Anthony (Jacob)

Lawrence Janifer

Alexei Panshin

Larry Niven

Greg Benford

Peter S. Beagle

Gardner Dozois

H. H. Hollis

Christopher Priest

Gene Wolfe

Dean R. Koontz

Jack Wodhams

David Gerrold

Joe Haldeman

Barry Malzburg

Jerry Pournelle

The bigger paperback houses and magazines solved the problem by creating their own distribution systems—the major paperback publishers customarily sell more than 60 percent of their printings—but the science fiction magazines have never involved a sufficient profit to justify their own distribution system or effective distribution by another system. The fact that the magazine with the largest circulation, *Analog*, is owned by Condé Nast probably is no coincidence. (John Campbell once remarked that he sometimes wondered whether Condé Nast hired him to edit *Analog* or he hired them to take care of the problems while he had the fun.) Ultimately, faced by the apparently unchangeable facts of publishing life, the magazines may disappear.

One lingering result of the sudden expansion of science fiction magazines followed by their equally sudden demise was the psychology of failure that pervaded the field. The feeling that science fiction was doomed to experience inevitable cycles of boom and bust meant that the good times that would come later would be greeted by publishers and writers alike with cautious skepticism or outright suspicion.

Aside from the brief broad availability of science fiction, the publishing boom of the early fifties had two positive aspects. The first was the attraction of a bold new clutch of science fiction writers: in 1950 came the first stories of Reginald Bretnor, Miriam Allen DeFord, Gordon Dickson, John Jakes, Richard Matheson, Ward Moore, Chad Oliver, Mack Reynolds, Frank Robinson, and Cordwainer Smith (Paul Linebarger). Some of them were new to authorship; some, like Bretnor, Miss DeFord, and Moore, were new only to science fiction. All, doubtless, found in the new spirit of the times an inspiration to produce science fiction, and in the magazines a place to have their fiction published and encouragement to produce more.

In 1951 came the first stories of John Christopher (C. S. Youd), Charles Beaumont, Harry Harrison, Zenna Henderson, J. T. McIntosh, Dean McLaughlin, Walter M. Miller, Jr., Kris Neville, Alan Nourse, Edgar Pangborn, E. C. Tubb, and F. L. Wallace. In 1952 came the flood: Jerome Bixby, A. J. Budrys, Mark Clifton, Mildred Clingerman, Ted Cogswell, Philip K. Dick, Philip José Farmer, Daniel Galouye, Randall Garrett, Ron Goulart, Frank Herbert, Arthur Porges, Robert Sheckley, Evelyn E. Smith, Jerry Sohl, Theodore Thomas, and Frederik Pohl writing under his own name. In 1953 the tide began to retreat: Brian Aldiss, Raymond Banks, Marion Zimmer Bradley, Tom Godwin, Joe Hensley, Anne McCaffrey, Winston K. Marks, Arthur Sellings, Kurt Vonnegut, Jr., James White, Robert F. Young; and Charles Eric Maine (D. McIlwaine) in England. In 1954 came Doris P. Buck, Kenneth Bulmer, Edmund Cooper, Avram Davidson, Jim Harmon, Andrew Offut, and Bob Shaw; in 1955, John Brunner, Robert Silverberg, and Henry Slesar; in 1956, Christopher Anvil, J. G. Ballard, Harlan Ellison, and Kate Wilhelm. In 1957 came Lloyd Biggle, Jr., J. F. Bone, and David R. Bunch: and a major British astronomer named Fred Hoyle published his first science fiction novel, *The Black Cloud.*

And then the tide ebbed: In 1958 there was Kit Reed; in 1959, Keith Laumer and Joanna Russ. In 1960 came Ben Bova, Tom Purdom, and R. A. Lafferty; in 1961, Michael Moorcock and Fred Saberhagen; in 1962, Terry Carr, Thomas M. Disch, Joseph Green, and Roger Zelazny; in 1963, Piers Anthony (Jacob), Lawrence Janifer, Alexei Panshin, and Norman Spinrad; in 1964, Larry Niven and Keith Roberts; in 1965, Greg Benford; in 1966, Peter Beagle, Gardner Dozois, H. H. Hollis, Christopher Priest, and Gene Wolfe; in 1967, Jack Wodhams and Dean Koontz; in 1968, James Tiptree, Jr., and Sterling Lanier; in 1969, David Gerrold, Joe Haldeman, and Barry Malzberg. The major new writers of the seventies have yet to identify themselves, although one, Jerry Pournelle, was named the first winner of the world convention's annual John W. Campbell Award for best new author, and was elected president of SFWA. Other names to watch for include, in no particular order. William E. Cochrane, Geo. Alec Effinger, George Zebrowski, Pamela Sargent, Edward Bryant, James B. Hemesath, Ken McCullough, James Sallis, Josephine Saxton, Chelsea Quinn Yarbro, Vonda N. McIntyre, and Doris Piserchia (whose first story actually appeared in 1966).

The second positive aspect of the publishing boom was the addition to science fiction of second and third voices. For a dozen years science fiction had been articulated almost entirely by John Campbell, in *Astounding* words; by 1950 science fiction had other voices, other words. The literary science fiction story had found a home in *The Magazine of Fantasy and Science Fiction,* and the sociological story and the satire in *Galaxy.* To provide a place for creative work to be published is second only to creation itself; without an opportunity to be published fiction might just as well not be written.

Through the fifties *Astounding, Galaxy,* and *The Magazine of Fantasy and Science Fiction* established three new frontiers for the limitless realms of science fiction; from those frontiers they pushed forward in diverging directions. They tripled science fiction's potential audience and tripled the number of writers attracted to it.

They would be joined in the sixties by a fourth world and a new exploring party.

CHAPTER 12
ALTERNATE WORLDS:
1949-1965

In 1949 the highway of science fiction, constructed by Hugo Gernsback in 1926 with the creation of *Amazing Stories* and resurfaced and broadened by John Campbell when he became editor of *Astounding Stories*, arrived at an intersection in time and space from which three main routes and a number of smaller byways extended into the future, through unknown countrysides and into strange lands.

To switch metaphors, Gernsback ended the forgotten diaspora of science fiction readers and writers with his creation of a new Jerusalem, and Campbell gave a Zionist movement new leadership, new vigor, and new direction. In 1949 a science fiction homeland had grown large enough, strong enough, sure enough to tolerate a variety of viewpoints, a diversity of goals.

For twenty-three years science fiction had been held together by a remarkable unity created out of a kind of fraternity of the elect among readers and writers alike, built with the cumulative effects of one concept developing out of another and forming a foundation for a third. Now, as the fifties began, as science fiction expanded, its significant characteristic became its growing variety; science fiction began to explode with new magazines, new ideas, new techniques.

Up to 1949 John Campbell and his favorite writers—Doc Smith, Williamson, Simak, De Camp, Russell, del Rey, Leinster, Hubbard, Asimov, Heinlein, Sturgeon, Van Vogt, and the Kuttners writing under their pseudonyms—had achieved, through their published stories, a kind of consensus definition of science fiction: imagination leavened with pragmatism. But *Astounding*'s dominant position did not exclude other options: *Famous Fantastic Mysteries* offered old-fashioned romantic fantasy; *Planet Stories* and *Amazing Stories* provided adventure among the stars; *Thrilling Wonder Stories* and *Startling Stories* offered fantasy *and* adventure; and an offbeat story might find a place anywhere, even in *Astounding*.

But with the publication of *The Magazine of Fantasy and Science Fiction* in 1949 and of *Galaxy Science Fiction* in 1950, significant alternatives to *Astounding*'s consensus appeared. The definition of science fiction broadened, new writers with different ideas about how to write and what to write about developed or were attracted, new readers found in the new variations and permutations of science fiction something that appealed to them. Science fiction writers, from H. G. Wells through Murray Leinster and Clifford Simak to Ward Moore and Philip K. Dick, have considered the possibility that there may exist, side by side with our Earth, separated from it by time or dimension, alternate worlds split off by moments of great (or small) historic actions or decisions, and that upon occasion, by traveling in time or chancing upon some gateway or crossroads, we can pass from one world to another. In 1949 and 1950 science fiction created two such alternate worlds.

The Magazine of Fantasy and Science Fiction, created by Anthony Boucher and J. Francis McComas with the help of publisher Lawrence Spivak, was based on the belief that science fiction could be literature and that a literary approach that included fantasy would be viable on the newsstands. In the Boucher-McComas magazine, the distinction between science fiction and fantasy was not as great as it would have been in *Astounding:* literary science fiction tends to resemble fantasy. The distinction between science fiction and fantasy is worth exploring in more detail, because it helps explain the new territory explored by *The Magazine of Fantasy and Science Fiction.*

Anthony Boucher

The wellsprings of science fiction are in the mind; of literature, in the heart. Science fiction appeals to the intellect and achieves its effects through the tensions created by treating an imaginative concept naturalistically, through the disproportion observed between man and the universe, between man's lifetime and eternity, between his accomplishments and his dreams; literature appeals to the emotions and achieves its effects through the analysis of character and the interplay of language. Science fiction and literature seem poles apart. Fantasy and literature, on the other hand, are inseparable; fantasy, which is concerned with the conflict between man and his imagination, which deals with the fanciful explanations man has created to rationalize himself, his origin, and his fate, and the mysterious forces that act upon him and his world—that is, with myth and legend—has as long a history as literature itself; they are interwoven and in some ways identical. Insofar as we dare to generalize about so diverse and so undefinable a phenomenon, we might say that science fiction is a social vision, a public vision; fantasy is always personal and private. Science fiction concerns man's dreams of reality; fantasy, the reality of man's dreams.

Fall 1949 (Vol. 1, No. 1)
(Photo: Bill Stone)

Science fiction has difficulty being literary in the traditional sense. First of all, it deals not with the known but the unknown, and the specifications of the unknown require explanation; such explanations are not narrative, but they can be and should be the stuff on which narrative is built. The best contemporary science fiction has learned how to describe its milieus economically, how to suggest more than it describes, how to imply more than it suggests. In inexperienced or careless hands, this can result in a reliance upon science fiction conventions, some of them the accretion of a century and a half of explanations of the ways in which physical processes (such as a rocket in space) or psychic powers (such as telepathy) operate; some the educational experiences (mechanization, technology, robots) of several generations; some a shorthand (space warp, time track, tractor beam, force field, blaster) of a genre which tends to baffle and repel the noninitiate. All art has similar conventions, it is true, but the best science fiction can achieve its effects without resorting to its own jargon.

Science fiction changed, nevertheless, after the creation of the science fiction magazine: authors became aware that their readers had changed. Verne and Wells wrote for a general audience for whom everything had to be explained and, in some instances, simplified. Asimov, Heinlein, Sturgeon, and Van Vogt wrote for a science fiction reader, self-selected through his purchase of a science fiction magazine; they could assume a relatively sophisticated audience—sophisticated at least in science fiction terms—and a basic understanding of the concepts with which science fiction had been dealing for a dozen years or more.

Earlier writers had focused on technology itself, upon broad social patterns, upon invention, upon adventure. In the thirties main-current science fiction writers began to narrow their aim to a single idea and the consequences of an idea carried out in its purest form to its ultimate outcome. In one sense science fiction became a Platonic fiction dealing with the ideals, even in characterization, of which the physical representations we see around us are only imperfect copies; in another sense, eschatological fiction dealing with last or final things. Virtually every story in *The Science Fiction Hall of Fame,* if dissected, will reveal at its heart a single idea.

In science fiction the idea became king; the situation, superior to the character; the character, a kind of purified vehicle for the idea. This offends literary critics and literary readers; they are accustomed to reading about complex characters in familiar surroundings and to concerning themselves with the way these characters change or are revealed during the course of the narrative. In science fiction it has not mattered (until recently) how complex or how sensitive a character was if he was wrong in the eyes of the universe, if he held views that were in conflict with the physical laws governing the world we know; and the usual science fiction story shows relatively uncomplex characters in unfamiliar surroundings, moved by familiar emotions to unusual actions. In science fiction, that is, the characters remain the same and the environment changes. As readers, we cannot have both changed environments and changing characters or we have no reference points at all; we lose not only standards for understanding the meaning of change but meaning itself. Ultimately, of course, it is environment that matters to science fiction, to us, and to the human race.

Thus science fiction tends to take man's basic emotions and impulses as constants; characters tend to take the roles of ideas; and unperceptive critics accuse them of being wooden or cardboard. Sometimes they are; usually they are more important as representatives than as individuals, and their feelings are important only insofar as they are typical and lead to actions which mean survival or death for the group. One of the frissons provided by this kind of science fiction is to see humans subordinating their small passions to the greater cause of human survival, as in Clarke's "Rescue Party" (see Chapter 13), or sacrificing themselves to that cause as in Bester's "Adam and No Eve" or Asimov's "Founding Father."

Boucher and McComas, however, believed that science fiction could be literature, in part by reducing or eliminating the inbred coventions—if you hope to appeal to a general audience, you must not rely on any specialized understanding—or using them for their myth value; in part by insisting on skillful writing and a greater concern for the complexities of character and of language; in part by associating science fiction with more literary works in the fantasy tradition within the pages of the same magazine and by reprinting stories from the experimental mainstream; in part by critical or biographical headnotes for each story; and in part by a conscious attempt to broaden the mainstream's critical vision to include *The Magazine of Fantasy and Science Fiction* and thereby science fiction itself.

McComas, who wrote a couple of early science fiction stories under the name of Webb Marlowe and five later under his own name, had as his chief credential the editing, with Raymond J. Healy, of *Adventures in Space and Time*. But the character of the magazine was established, I believe, by Anthony Boucher, an erudite, gentle, creative man, author of some thirty science fiction and fantasy stories but better-known as an author of mystery novels and short stories under the pseudonym of H. H. Holmes (his *Rocket to the Morgue* already has been described) and a reviewer, particularly of mystery stories (at one time he was reviewing as Anthony Boucher for *The New York Times* and H. H. Holmes for the New York *Herald Tribune*). The Holmes pseudonym was taken from a famous Chicago murderer. Actually Boucher itself was a pseudonym derived from a family name. His real name was William Anthony Parker White, and he took a pen name when he checked the Library of Congress catalog and found seventy-five writers named William White.

The Magazine of Fantasy and Science Fiction succeeded, not in any spectacular financial way—though it managed to survive and become one of the top three science fiction magazines in spite of a word-rate consistently a cent or more under the other two—but in attracting literary interest, literarily inclined authors, and literary (or at least more literate) stories. One of the continuing surprises in science fiction is the financial sacrifices science fiction authors will accept for an appreciative editor.

In the first issue—Fall 1949—when it was called *The Magazine of Fantasy,* publisher Lawrence E. Spivak wrote:

> . . . In this new periodical, the *Magazine of Fantasy*, I hope to satisfy every aspect of that demand for the finest available material in stories of the supernatural. I hasten to point out that by "the supernatural" I mean all of the world of fantasy, from the thrilling to the chilling, from the comic to the cosmic—whatever our senses may reject, but our imagination logically accepts. . . .

> To authors who have long wished to try their hand at this sort of thing and found the usual markets closed to such experiments, let me assure you that the latchstring is out and the welcome mat freshly dusted. . . .

And as if to clarify further what Spivak meant by "the supernatural," the sec-

Winter-Spring 1950 (Salter)

ond issue, Winter-Spring 1950, was retitled *The Magazine of Fantasy and Science Fiction.*

The magazine brought out of hiding a number of competent and sometimes exciting new writers, and obtained new kinds of stories from older writers, such as Ed Hamilton. It reprinted Defoe, Dickens, Stevenson, London, Wodehouse, Saki, J. B. Priestley, C. S. Forester, John Collier, Howard Fast, George P. Eliot, Howard Schoenfeld, and others. It introduced Kris Neville, H. Nearing, Jr., Idris Seabright (pseudonym for Margaret St. Clair), Richard Matheson, Arthur Porges, Mildred Clingerman, Reginald Bretnor, Zenna Henderson, and others; provided a temporary home for the work of Ray Bradbury; began serializing Heinlein's juvenile novels as adult science fiction; and got exciting new stories from such writers as Poul Anderson and Alfred Bester.

And then there were two alternate worlds.

Boucher, who became sole editor of the magazine in 1954, retired in 1958 and died in 1968. The magazine's tone and tradition were carried on by a succession of editors, among them, Robert Mills, who had been managing editor from the beginning and editor of *Venture;* Avram Davidson; and Ed Ferman.

The third alternate world was created in 1950 when H. (for Horace) L. Gold, with World Editions, Inc. and later with printer-publisher Robert Guinn, produced *Galaxy Science Fiction.* Gold had been a free-lance writer and editor in a variety of fields, including science fiction and fantasy, publishing stories under the name of Clyde Crane Campbell in 1934–35 and under his own name in 1938–41 and 1943, as well as later. Like John Campbell and Tony Boucher, he had clearly defined ideas about what a good science fiction story was and how it could be pushed into new shapes and create new effects.

Galaxy wanted well-written stories, but it was not willing, as perhaps *The Magazine of Fantasy and Science Fiction* sometimes was, to accept literary quality as a substitute for narrative excitement. The evolution of the science fiction hero began with Mary Shelley's tormented scientist and continued through Poe's natural aristocrat of sensibilities, Verne's middle-class engineers, Wells's common man, Burroughs' adventurers, Gernsback's inventors, Campbell's engineers and meritocrats, and Boucher's man of sensibilities. Now Gold's vision focused not on the adventurer, the inventor, the engineer, or the scientist, but on the average citizen. "The bluntest, truest statement about the human race," Gold wrote to me once, "is this: It will accept and try to adapt to anything immutable. You could say with almost total accuracy that the race's motto is that what can't be cured must be endured." Gold wanted stories about characters who accept their situations and endure, who try to adjust to them, "because the permutations are as limitless as the number and complexity of the persons living in that environment. The attempt to adjust may be doomed, just as they often are under, say, the various dictatorships we've spawned, yet the great majority will try its damnedest to get along somehow."

Opposed to this, Gold wrote, was the story of the rebel, the misfit.

Alfred Bester

Robert P. Mills

Avram Davidson

Edward L. Ferman

Horace Gold

October, 1950 (Vol. 1, No. 1) (Stone)

The exceptions, the rebels and misfits who beat their heads against walls, who fight City Hall, who want snow in the summer, who uncharacteristically subordinate their own lives to principles, philosophies, causes of all sorts—these are the ones science fiction has hitherto written about nearly exclusively. Sure, they also include the history-makers among the outcasts, but that's not the point.

There are only so many varieties of misfit, from the most passively humanitarian to the most destructively antisocial.

Work through the list, as s-f has done, and you come back to the beginning and can only go through it again—and again—and again. Somebody had to break the suicidal trunk-to-tail procession. I may have been the biggest single editorial influence in doing so. At any rate, it pleases me to believe I was, and still am, and who would I be hurting if I'm wrong?

Now don't demand that I be inflexible and apply this standard in every case, without exception. I'm not inflexible about anything except my refusal to be inflexible. The built-in conflict can be made brilliantly new by virtuoso treatment, as in GRAVY PLANET and THE DEMOLISHED MAN. Wouldn't I have been a damned fool to have insisted otherwise? But I can't build a magazine on virtuoso treatment and so, in the main, the orientation must be toward the individual treatment, the personal conflict, the interaction of character and extrapolated background. . . .

November, 1950 (Sibley)

And yet it was the virtuoso treatment, the "Gravy Planets" and the "Demolished Men," that established *Galaxy*'s dominant tone. Consciously or unconsciously, Gold encouraged a satirical approach. Inevitably, much of what *Galaxy* printed continued to be traditional for a time, but the different stories created the magazine's tone: bright, bitter, mocking, savage, satirical, dynamic. . . .

In the first issue of October 1950, Gold established *Galaxy*'s position with respect to science fiction in his editorial, which said, in part:

Science fiction, everybody agrees, or seems to, has finally come of age. Hollywood, radio, book publishers, and the slick magazines are all, with the usual degraded exceptions, buying and treating science fiction intelligently.

GALAXY *Science Fiction* proposes to carry the maturity of this type of literature into the science fiction magazine field, where it is now, unfortunately, somewhat hard to find. It establishes a compound break with both the lurid and stodgy tradition of s-f publishing. From cover design to advertising selections, GALAXY *Science Fiction* intends to be a mature magazine for mature readers . . . mature in reading; age alone is no assurance of maturity. . . .

January, 1952 (Sibley)

Galaxy provided a home for the blackest visions of the late Cyril Kornbluth, such as "The Marching Morons," and the gentle, mind-expanding concepts of Clifford Simak in the novel that opened in the first issue, *Time Quarry* (published in book form as *First He Died* and *Time and Again*), *Ring Around the Sun,* and *Here Gather the Stars* (book title: *Way Station*). But its initial success in finding its own voice came with the publication of the 1952 serial *Gravy Planet* (book title: *Space Merchants*) by Frederik Pohl and Cyril Kornbluth, a savage satire about a crowded, despoiled, overpopulated world of the future controlled by the advertising agencies. On its own (and with later books by Pohl and Kornbluth and Pohl alone) this novel created a whole new mode of science fiction by returning to the satire, the anti-utopia, but with the addition of science fiction's concern for extrapolation and scientific credibility. It also found its distinctive voice in the pyrotechnics of Alfred Bester's 1952 serial about crime and detection in a telepathic society, *The Demolished Man.*

At its worst, *Galaxy* and the new satirical mode could descend into a kind of self-parody, like the winner of a 1955 *Galaxy* novel contest, Edson McCann's *Preferred Risk,* about a world run by insurance companies (actually it was written by Pohl and Lester del Rey when Gold grew desperate because no suitable novels had been submitted). At its best it could rise to the distilled emotion and subtle social comment of Fritz Leiber's "Coming Attraction," a short story (which appeared in *Galaxy*'s second issue) about a postatomic-war America in which guilt and radiation lead to a society where sex lurks behind masks and lascivious lettering, delinquency and male-female wrestling. A visiting Englishman becomes intrigued by one masked young woman until, at the end:

I leaned forward and ripped the mask from her face.

I really don't know why I should have expected her face to be anything else. It was very pale, of course, and there weren't any cosmetics. I suppose there's no point

June, 1952 (Emshwiller)

in wearing any under a mask. The eyebrows were untidy and the lips chapped. But as for the general expression, as for the feelings crawling and wriggling across it—

Have you ever lifted a rock from damp soil? Have you ever watched the slimy white grubs?

I looked down at her, she up at me. "Yes, you're so frightened, aren't you?" I said sarcastically. "You dread this little nightly drama, don't you? You're scared to death."

And I walked right out into the purple night, still holding my hand to my bleeding cheek. No one stopped me, not even the girl wrestlers. I wished I could tear a tab from under my shirt, and test it then and there, and find I'd taken too much radiation, and so be able to ask to cross the Hudson and go down New Jersey, past the lingering radiance of the Narrows Bomb, and so on to Sandy Hook to wait for the rusty ship that would take me back over the seas to England.

Other writers brought stories to *Galaxy* that Campbell had found unsatisfactory, or concepts that *Astounding* found uncongenial. Isaac Asimov submitted such novels as *Tyrann* and *The Caves of Steel;* Heinlein, *The Puppet Masters* and several important shorter works; Ted Sturgeon, who worked as a consultant for the magazine in its early days, a series of novelettes and short novels, including *Baby Is Three*. Damon Knight had stories in *Galaxy*, as did James Blish ("Surface Tension"), Murray Leinster, Ray Bradbury ("The Fireman" which was expanded into the book *Fahrenheit 451*), William Tenn (Phil Klass), Gordon Dickson, Poul Anderson, and others, including myself.

THE WORLD OF OCTOBER 2052 By WILLY LEY

Galaxy's second anniversary cover was a tribute to the people who were making the magazine a success. Key to the Emshwiller painting:

1. Fritz Leiber
2. Evelyn Paige
3. Robert A. Heinlein
4. Katherine MacLean
5. Chesley Bonestell
6. Theodore Sturgeon
7. Damon Knight
8. H. L. Gold
9. Robert Guinn
10. Joan De Mario
11. Charles J. Robot
12. Cyril Kornbluth
13. E. A. Emshwiller
14. Willy Ley
15. F. L. Wallace
16. Isaac Asimov
17. Jerry Edelberg
18. Groff Conklin
19. John Anderson
20. Ray Bradbury
21. Bug Eye
22. W. I. Van der Pool
23. Poul Anderson

Galaxy discovered or uncovered or attracted a series of brilliant new writers, such as Robert Sheckley, whose bright, clever stories represented *Galaxy* at its brightest and cleverest; J. T. McIntosh; Alan Nourse; F. L. Wallace; A. J. Budrys, who worked for *Galaxy* as an assistant editor; Dan Galouye; Raymond Banks; John Christopher; Evelyn E. Smith; Lloyd Biggle, Jr.; and others.

Horace Gold

All significant magazines probably are directed by creative editors, though the early science fiction magazines were more important for their existence than for their editing. Hugo Gernsback's *Amazing Stories* was primarily a reprint magazine for its first year, and even when it began buying new fiction Gernsback and T. O'Conor Sloan selected what they wanted from a pile of submissions. Harry Bates, first editor of *Astounding Stories*, paid well for the times but also was satisfied to wait for submissions, and F. Orlin Tremaine sought "thought-variant" stories for *Astounding* but according to authors active at the time was not significantly involved with them in suggesting ideas or revisions for making stories better or more acceptable. John Campbell created a new pattern for science fiction editors with his voluminous interchange of ideas, Tony Boucher impressed his personality on his magazine through his selections and his correspondence, but Horace Gold may have been the most creative of all: he cudgeled and cajoled writers into creating something different. He worked closely with Alfred Bester, he told me once, in the creation of *The Demolished Man*; in *The Worlds of Science Fiction*, Bester later recorded from his notebook: "A crime story set in a future in which crime no longer exists because the police have time-scanners and can go back into the past and ferret out evidence to convict. (I remember mentioning this to Horace Gold of *Galaxy Magazine*. He said the time-scanner gimmick was pretty dull, but would like me to do a crime story in a future which made crime difficult for more original reasons. That eventually led to a novel called *The Demolished Man*.)" Gold had stories rewritten for him by the authors and by others, he rewrote portions himself, and he changed endings and titles freely—sometimes without notifying the author.

Anthony Boucher and
L. Sprague de Camp

Gold wrote to me once: ". . . a story is a fluid thing right up to the moment it hits the press." And later: "The blunt truth is that I'm putting out a better magazine than the material that's available. How do I do it? Any editor can, if he's willing to suffer the sweats and shakes that operating so deviously causes."

Creativity can be overdone—particularly when it comes to the words of others—and gradually the special brand of excitement generated by the early *Galaxy* began to fade. A confident, dynamic man in his own environment, Gold for many years was psychologically unable to leave his Stuyvesant Town apartment on Manhattan's 14th Street. He used his apartment as a gathering place for writers and as an office, and he used the telephone as an extension of his voice for long conversations—many of them long distance—about writing and stories. (My first encounter with Gold was by phone, a long-distance call from out of nowhere about the first story I had submitted to *Galaxy*, a short novel called *Breaking Point*—which eventually was published in *Space Science Fiction*, but that's another story.) He wrote long, savage rejection slips, and his acceptances sometimes were little better. As time passed, his temper seemed to grow shorter, his seclusion more complete, his notes of acceptance or rejection more waspish.

Gentle Tony Boucher would write a rejection that sounded like an acceptance. About one of my stories he wrote: "Gunn's STILLED PATTER is a very great deal of fun—& yet not quite believable, even on its own light level. I kept thinking of too many loopholes, other things that wd be bound to happen. But for its valiant onslaught on the cheerful baby books let a father of 2 offer his warmest thanks."

Horace Gold wrote an acceptance that sounded like a rejection, and his rejections seemed written with acid: it was not enough to reject, the author had to be punished so that he would never sin again. About a short novel called "Medic" which formed a central portion of my novel *The Immortals*, Gold wrote to my agent:

There's no sense going through the thing point by point. It won't convince Jimmie, after the ineffectiveness of the hours I put in corresponding with him about the footless nature of the extrapolation. Even if it could, I wouldn't know how to go about helping him make it valid and believable. Some of the scenes are very good and the blind girl was handled with restraint and considerable affection. The rest of it—well, it's a shame he had to put in so much time on something I can't use. That's from my point of view, of course. From his and yours, I feel pretty sure you'll sell it somewhere . . . but I hope neither of you consider that proof that I was wrong in objecting to the illogicality of the idea and the wildness of the development. . . .

One of the amusing anecdotes of science fiction developed around Gold's submission to Fred Pohl's first *Star Science Fiction Stories* anthology of a clever little story, "The Man with English," about a person injured in a fall whose nerve fibers are switched in an operation so that his senses are reversed—he sees light as dark, feels heat as cold, tastes sweet as salt. After a second operation he wakes up and asks, "What smells purple?" In an inspired moment, Pohl called Gold on the telephone to tell him that the story was good but needed some changes, and then went through the story word by word editing everything. Came the final stroke: Pohl told Gold he had decided to change the title to "The Man with Something on the Ball."

Even such retribution could not balance the scales, and writers, who on the whole are neurotics requiring frequent reassurance, began to refuse to submit themselves to Gold's whipping block or their stories to his surgery.

They did Gold an injustice. I thought he provided excitement and a dynamic new force in science fiction, even though he may have been tempted into dangerous practices in his drive toward perfection.

Gold left the magazine at the end of 1960, and Fred Pohl succeeded him. A basically kinder—or more realistic—editor, Pohl continued the magazine in its original tradition but with more friends, fewer enemies, and a greater tolerance for variety. But sales slowly dropped, and eight years later Robert Guinn sold the magazine and its sister publications to the Universal Publishing Company; Pohl, who had been editing the magazines from his home in Red Bank, New Jersey, resigned rather than come in to New York every day. Ejler Jakobsson, a long-time pulp editor and writer, took over with the help of Judy-Lynn Benjamin (now Mrs. Lester del Rey) as managing editor and del Rey as a part-time assistant. Mrs. del Rey is now an editor for Ballantine Books, and James Baen has replaced Jakobsson as editor of *Galaxy*.

Inevitably, the stories that were rejected by *Astounding, The Magazine of Fantasy and Science Fiction,* and *Galaxy* found their markets, if at all, in the publications that lived in the shadow of the Big Three. Two such magazines were *If*, which was sold by the Quinn Publishing Company to *Galaxy* and later, under Pohl's editorship, won several Hugo awards; and the shorter-lived *Venture Science Fiction*, a companion to *The Magazine of Fantasy and Science Fiction*. They stood out from the other magazines partly because of their editors but largely because of their willingness to pay a fraction of a cent more a word than their competitors (usually two cents a word rather than a cent or a cent and a half); and their tolerance for experimentation and more literate writing.

A fourth alternate world appeared in 1951. It seemed like a radical experiment at the time: a book composed of never-before-published stories, that contradiction in terms, an original anthology. It was a response to three facts of science fiction publishing: the success of the anthology, the increasing difficulty in finding unanthologized stories worth reprinting, and inadequate distribution of magazines. Raymond J. Healy, who had co-edited the big postwar anthology, *Adventures in Time and Space,* commissioned and solicited original fiction from a variety of science fiction writers and published them in a book entitled *New Tales of Space and Time* (see Chapter 11).

Later Twayne Publishing Company put together two or three hard-cover volumes of short novels by different authors, built around the physical facts of another world, but the idea of the original anthology was maintained in its first form when Fred Pohl began editing a series of volumes for Ballantine Books in the early fifties. *Star Science Fiction Stories,* published in 1952, was the first volume in an annual series which started by offering five cents a word or more for short stories, but gradually the rates dropped to about that of the better-paying magazines. A volume or two of *Star Short Novels* also came out,

January, 1957 (Vol. 1, No. 1) (Emshwiller)

May, 1953 (Phillips)

Philip José Farmer

beginning in 1953. The series was discontinued when Pohl became editor of the *Galaxy* magazines, succeeding Gold.

The principle had been proved sound, however: anthologies of original materials sold better than magazines, probably because they remained longer on the book racks; being undated, they weren't automatically returned when a new issue arrived.

The next major venture into the original anthology was the *Orbit* series, edited by Damon Knight for Putnam in hard covers and by Putnam's paperback firm, Berkley, in paperback. Launched in 1966 as an annual, the anthology became a semiannual publication in 1968. The *Orbit* series was the first, I think, to actively encourage new writing, even experimental writing; one year its stories received the majority of Nebula Award nominations by members of the Science Fiction Writers of America.

Orbit illustrated another aspect of book publication: it relaxed the taboos that had inhibited science fiction in strange ways almost from its magazine beginnings: the natural functions of the body had been studiously ignored, and "unnatural" emotions (except for the inexplicable lusts of bug-eyed monsters for human maidens) were seldom even the subject of veiled hints. As a consequence, this one aspect of science fiction was curiously puritanical. There were some exceptions: the brief slick experiment with *Amazing* and *Fantastic* produced some sex-oriented stories; Lester del Rey's grim, naturalistic novel, *Police Your Planet*, serialized under the pseudonym of Erik van Lhin for *Science Fiction Adventures*, a magazine Del Rey was editing at the time; some sexed-up and abortive science fiction novels in the later fifties; and stories with explicit physical or sexual content in *Venture* and perhaps one or two other magazines about the same time. Tony Boucher thought that *New Tales of Space and Time* broke some taboos—some of the few taboos, he said, that existed in science fiction. Everything else could be explored fictionally except the physical aspects of life; it was a kind of bondage in the midst of what prided itself on being the freest of genres.

Let us be fair: in most science fiction stories sex and other bodily functions have no point and thus no place—in the scientific romance, the gadget story, the space opera, most philosophical stories. The inclusion of such physical actions and reactions often are worse than pointless—they are a distraction within the main-current science fiction story. Only in certain sociological stories do they have a significant place. "It is nearly impossible to mix sex and science fiction," Groff Conklin wrote in his 1946 anthology, *The Best of Science Fiction*. But writers ultimately resent even the most padded handcuffs.

Philip José Farmer made a breakthrough in 1952 with a *Startling Stories* short novel, later expanded into a novel, entitled *The Lovers*, which described a love affair between an earthling from a puritanical culture and a beautiful female-shaped insect parasite of a species called "lalitha"; the lalitha can breed only by mating with a human male, but she then dies and the larvae feed off her flesh until mature enough to emerge. The drinking of a foul liquor exuded by a beetle prevents pregnancy, but the hero waters his mistress's beetle juice, thinking he is breaking her addiction, and she becomes pregnant and dies. A new Romeo, a newer Juliet.

Farmer has gone on to write other taboo-breaking science fiction, including, in the sixties, some that is frankly pornographic and much admired by critic Leslie Fiedler.

Norman Spinrad

Ted Sturgeon was exploring his own concern for different kinds of human, nonhuman, and interspecies relationships in a series of stories and novels involving many of the possible permutations of male-female-third party combinations such as "The Girl Had Guts," "Affair with a Green Monkey," *Venus Plus X, Some of Your Blood,* and *More than Human.* And Heinlein, ever the trailbreaker, dealt with taboo material and themes in *Glory Road, Stranger in a Strange Land,* and *I Will Fear No Evil.* My own first novel, *This Fortress World,* was in part an attempt to write a naturalistic space opera.

The rationale for the new freedom was clear: sexual relationships and bodily functions are as much a part of the natural world as electricity, nuclear reactions, and evolution; and a fiction, particularly a science fiction, that ignores them is going to be strangely unrealistic and incomplete. The problem—it was a serious artistic problem—was how to deal with these new-old matters in a way that did not overwhelm the story and the reader. Reaction is a law of human nature as well as of physics, and some reactions to the taboos of science fiction, once the walls had been breached, may have been artistically excessive. The cause of frankness in science fiction was adopted by the young Turks of what has been called the "New Wave," which has added to the controversy over whether science fiction and sexual frankness can coexist. But contemporary science fiction seems capable of handling the matter with proper perspective, even with much of the new wave involved in exploration of the physical and intimate psychological realities of the future. One such novel—in which theme and method merge—is Norman Spinrad's *Bug Jack Barron.*

The shattering of taboos reached its sixties' peak in Harlan Ellison's *Dangerous Visions* anthology of original fiction, and in his own writing, typified by his Nebula Award short novel, *A Boy and His Dog.* In announcing his anthology, Ellison urged writers to send him stories that were too bold and too frank for science fiction magazines. As he has related it, with the same vigor with which science fiction magazines told writers they couldn't write about certain subjects or use certain material, he told writers "to get it on, to really do it." The critical and popular success of the anthology not only led to two sequels, *Again, Dangerous Visions* and *Last Dangerous Visions,* but may have contributed to the lowering of barriers elsewhere. *Galaxy,* for instance, began including some hitherto taboo scenes and stories, including serialization of Heinlein's *I Will Fear No Evil;* and a few references to physical relationships have even crept into the once immaculate pages of *Analog.*

The original anthology is perpetuated by Robert Silverberg's *New Dimensions,* Harry Harrison's *Nova,* Terry Carr's *Universe,* Damon Knight's *Orbit,* and a host of one-shot specials in hard cover and paperback, many of them edited by indefatigable Roger Elwood. More such publications can be expected. New American Library has published several *Clarion* anthologies that include the student stories produced by the novel and successful Clarion Science Fiction Writers Workshop. Today the science fiction magazine is one of the few remaining markets for the short story. Its future seems uncertain: it may follow the other category magazines and general fiction publications into the rosy realm of nostalgia, although it may be too soon to say for certain that it is doomed. But it is not too soon to speculate that the future of the short story may lie in the publication which finds a place on the paperback rack rather than the magazine stand.

The fifth alternate world for science fiction in printed form has become the book. The paperback field began expanding rapidly in the midsixties, as paperback publishing itself grew more adventurous, with large advances and larger

Harlan Ellison

print orders and even advertising budgets for major books. At the same time a major new market for science fiction began to grow among the alienated and affluent young. At one time the alienated were a minority which turned to science fiction magazines in desperation: to find a world which accepted them and a world they could accept, which was more exciting and more satisfying than the reality around them. Now the alienated are a substantial minority if not yet a majority—a subculture which finds in science fiction a banner to rally under, and in science fiction a concern for life and for different life styles, a missionary spirit for justice, individual merit, and ecology, and a tradition of criticizing and satirizing what is wrong in contemporary society. The subculture is familiar with paperback books but not magazines (television is its form of cheap, serial entertainment): according to a 1972 questionnaire, a science fiction class of 150 read some 400 magazines a year but more than 2300 paperback books. The subculture had money; paperback books began to sell in substantial quantities. *Publishers Weekly* reported the publication of 170 paperback science fiction books in 1969, 188 in 1970, 223 in 1971, and a cutback to 154 in 1972. *Locus* counted 191 new titles and 280 reprints published in 1973. Of all books of fiction published in 1971, 8.9 percent were science fiction.

Rod Serling

The hard-cover publishers became involved more slowly, but today many major hard-cover publishers have science fiction lines, and publication has increased from 56 books in 1969 to 81 each in 1970 and 1971, and 90 in 1972. Locus (whose figures are larger, and perhaps more accurate) listed 155 new titles and 35 reprints for 1973. Compare that to a total of 41 hard-cover and paperback books combined in 1949, 60 in 1950, and 57 in 1951, science fiction's previous boom period. At that time four mystery novels were published for every science fiction book; today the ratio is about two to one.

One might speak of science fiction on television as another alternate world if that world were not so inadequately realized, so self-imitative. Science fiction and television have suffered through some twenty years of courtship and rejection, drawn to each other time and again for a brief, troubled season and then separating, more in despair than in anger, to find true happiness and success apart.

Richard Deacon and friend in 1964 *Twilight Zone* production, "The Brain Center at Whipples."

Television seemed created for science fiction: its flickering images were both science and fantasy, modern magic and the promise of the future, like science fiction itself. Today, with contemporary concern for the problems of accelerating change and the ways in which today's decisions will shape tomorrow's world, science fiction's place on television seems even more obvious.

But on television, as in films, dramas which can be called good science fiction are inexplicably scarce—or perhaps their scarcity can be explained as a lack of understanding about science fiction by those who adapt it for the visual media, and this in turn leads to cheapening or adulteration or reduction to the least common denominator of horror or terror or comic-strip wonder. Occasionally, to be sure, a good show or a modestly effective though uneven series has come along. Most of them have been anthology shows, or science fiction adaptations on general dramatic anthologies such as Playhouse 90 or Desilu Playhouse or General Electric Theatre, or an occasional science fiction special. Now, with the recent trend toward the made-for-television movie, many producers are turning for material to science fiction and fantasy, but with the usual high proportion of the inadequate and the utterly awful.

The fantastic element in science fiction drew television from the first—the kind of wonderful whimsies or modern fairy tales that became such perennial children's classics as *The Wizard of Oz, Alice in Wonderland,* or *Peter Pan.* Science fiction and fantasy always have been considered the special kingdom of the young, and television turned first to such juveniles as "Space Cadet" (1950) and "Captain Video" (1949 and 1950).

Children's programming always seemed to have a niche for science fantasy, and because it was broadcast at unpopular hours or simply because it was for children it has seemed relatively immune to ratings: between 1956 and 1966 have come such series as "Superman," "Voyage to the Bottom of the Sea," "Lost in Space," and "Land of the Giants," not to mention innumerable cartoon adventures.

For whatever reason, no adult science fiction series ever has been a "hit"—

Gene Roddenberry

LEFT: *Star Trek's* Starship *Enterprise*. BELOW: Mr. Spock (Leonard Nimoy) and Captain John Kirk (William Shatner) of the *Enterprise*

not, at least, in the way that detective shows have achieved popular success, western shows have reckoned their longevity not just in years but in decades, and medical shows have ranked at the top of the Nielsens. I speak from experience: I had an ABC-TV Movie of the Week adapted from one of my novels and the next year produced as a weekly, hour-long series. It was called "The Immortal," and it died in fifteen weeks.

More successful shows have run for at most two or three seasons, collected their small but loyal band of followers, and then vanished from the air: "Out There," "Tales of Tomorrow," "One Step Beyond," "Outer Limits," "Time Tunnel," "Star Trek," "The Invaders," "The Prisoner," and Rod Serling's "Twilight Zone" and "Night Gallery." I mention Rod Serling not only because his has been the only name intimately associated with a major series but because his shows have shown more understanding of science fiction and more respect for the written word than any of the others, with the possible exception of Gene Roddenberry and "Star Trek." The success of "Star Trek" in syndication, with its own fandom (sometimes called "Trekkies") and conventions with attendance in the thousands, has created a new interest in science fiction, with the same seemingly inevitable disappointments: several series pilots by Roddenberry have not been picked up, and Harlan Ellison disowned his syndicated series "The Starlost" when the concept was compromised.

These are the alternate worlds of science fiction. But what of the future? Do these worlds have a future? Does science fiction, which has made the future its special province, have a future?

CHAPTER 13
THE SHAPE OF
THINGS TO COME

ALTHOUGH science fiction writers may toy with time, putter about in the past, or transport themselves to alternate worlds, their real home is the future. Other arenas are pleasant resorts or creative playgrounds, but the missionary aspect of the science fiction writer, as contrasted with his artistic aims, his practical needs, or his sportive moments, demands an opportunity to urge salvation, a change in ethics or morals or religions, a new way of thinking or a new way of life itself. . . . Science fiction writers, as a group, have an ineradicable need to urge or to warn, and only the future can be changed. As Edmund Crispin has pointed out, "Science fiction is the last refuge of the morality tale."

In their concern about the future, science fiction writers have developed a consensus scenario. With remarkable agreement, particularly in the early years of Gernsback and then Campbell, science fiction writers evolved what Donald Wollheim calls "the full cosmogony of science-fiction future history." Story by story, through acceptance and further development by other writers (and its reverse, rejection and disuse), through accretion that future history was written.

Wollheim dates the "cosmogony" from the publication of Asimov's *Foundation* trilogy in the early forties:

Donald A. Wollheim

First we have the initial voyages to the moon and to the planets of our Solar System. In this sequence we also include stories of the contact of man with intelligent species elsewhere in this system—Martians, Jovians, Venusians, if any. Stories of the first efforts to set up terrestrial bases on such planets. Stories of the first colonies of such worlds, their problems internal and external, their conflicts with the parent world, their breakaway or interplanetary commerce, spaceship trade lanes, space pirates, asteroid mining, the weird wonders of the Outer Planets, and so forth.

Second, the first flights to the stars. The problem of whether science can ever exceed the speed of light—a very important one where the problem of colonization is concerned. Starships, ships that must travel centuries and contain generations, descended from the original crews. Other planets of other stars. Intelligences on such planets and our problems with them or against them. Human colonies on other starry systems. Contact with Mother Earth, independence or dependence. Commerce—exploitation or otherwise.

Third, the Rise of the Galactic Empire. The rise of contact and commerce between many human-colonized worlds or many worlds of alien intelligences that have come to trust and do business with one another. The problem of mutual relations and the solution, usually in the form of treaties or defensive alliances. Implacable aliens in the cosmos who must be fought. The need for defense. The rise of industrial or financial or political powers, the eventual triumph of one and the establishment of a federation, a union, an alliance, or an autocratic empire of worlds, dominated usually from Old Earth.

Fourth, the Galactic Empire in full bloom, regardless of what form it takes. Com-

merce between worlds an established fact, and adventures while dealing with worlds in and out of the Empire. The farthest planets, those of the Galactic Rim, considered as mavericks. The problems of aliens again outside the Empire, and outside our own galaxy. Politics within the government setup, intrigues, and dynasties, robotic mentalities versus human mentalities. "Terra-forming" worlds for colonization. The exploration of the rest of the galaxy by official exploration ships, or adventurers, or commercial pioneers.

Fifth, the Decline and Fall of the Galactic Empire. Intrigue and palace revolt. Breakaway planets. The alliance of worlds strained beyond its limits by rebellion, alien wars, corruption, scientific inability to keep up with internal or external problems. The rise of restless subject worlds. Decline, then loss of contact with farthest worlds, crumbling of commerce, failure of space lanes, distrust, finally worlds withdrawing into themselves as the empire/alliance/federation/union becomes an empty shell or is destroyed at its heart.

Sixth, the Interregnum. Worlds reverting to prespace-flight conditions, savagery, barbarism, primitive forms of life, superstition. Worlds taking to barbarian raids on defenseless isolated planets, hastening the downfall of knowledge. Fragments of space flight, fragments of empire, some starships, some efforts to revive. Thousands of years of loss of contact. Humanity in this period becomes indigenous to most of the habitable planets of the galaxy, forgetting origins. Evolutionary changes may take place. Alterations of form to fit differing world conditions—giant men, tiny men, water-dwelling men, flying men, mutations.

Seventh, the Rise of a Permanent Galactic Civilization. The restoration of commerce between worlds. The reexploration of lost and uncontacted worlds and the bringing them back to high-technology, democratic levels. The efforts to establish trade between human worlds that no longer seem kin. Beating down new efforts to form empires, efforts which sometimes succeed and revert to approximations of the previous period, with similar results. The exploration of other galaxies and of the entire universe.

Eighth, the Challenge to God. Galactic harmony and an undreamed-of high level of knowledge leads to experiments in creation, to harmony between galactic clusters, and possible explorations of the other dimensions of existence. The effort to match Creation and to solve the last secrets of the universe. Sometimes seeking out and confronting the Creative Force or Being or God itself, sometimes merging with that Creative First Premise. The end of the universe, the end of time, the beginning of a new universe or a new time-space continuum.

Wollheim's "cosmogony" begins with man's conquest of space, perhaps because a consensus future history of man on Earth is not nearly as easy. Once into space, man will be increasingly difficult to wipe out and among the countless stars everything that can happen will happen, but his colonization of his solar system, much less the stars, is uncertain. Before he can conquer space he must conquer war and avoid other man-made and natural catastrophes; he must cope with the Malthusian pressures of overpopulation and diminishing natural resources; he must stop polluting; he must find a way of living with his machines, of living in his cities; he must learn, that is, to understand and to control himself. (But Heinlein has expressed another view: "This world's used up. Let's go find another.") Out of these kinds of conflicts have come innumerable stories of man on Earth, man who never gets into space or whose travels in space are unimportant to the story: Man and his society, for instance, in which the situation is concerned with man's efforts to shape his society or be shaped by it, natural extensions of historical societies or current trends as well as "what if" kinds of possibilities created around entirely different interrelationships between individuals or groups. Often, however, such explorations of different social possibilities are translated, for credibility, to other planets in a populated galaxy.

Critic Darko Suvin has said that "a literary genre is a collective system of expectations in the readers' minds stemming from their past experience with a certain type of writing, so that even its violations—the innovations by which every genre evolves—can be understood only against the backdrop of such a system." but science fiction has evolved more than other genres—the western, the mystery, the gothic—perhaps because it is based not upon traditional elements but upon change ushering man into an uncertain future. The development of a consensus future history was the natural outcome of the science fiction process.

The construction—or foreseeing—of man's future history continues; fragments still are being written; stories and novels are being fitted into the framework,

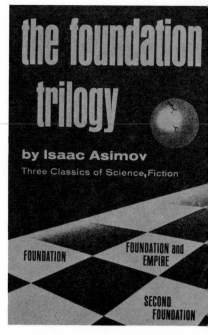

Science Fiction Book Club edition

filling it in, expanding its concepts, sometimes illuminating its assumptions or extending its conclusions. The value of such a framework for the science fiction writer is clear: just as the writer of historical fiction has all history and its varied civilizations in which to find or fit his plot and can play it against the reader's memory and his understanding of historical trends, so the science fiction writer has a future history of vast scope and unlimited possibilities in which to find or fit his story and can play it against the reader's understanding of future history or his comparisons with actual history. As Isaac Asimov has said, history may not repeat itself but "similar broad responses frequently occur under similar broad stimuli. If you stand far away from the great and variegated story of man and squint your eyes so that you drown out the details and see only the broad blocks of color, various repetitive patterns do appear."

And, accepting a future history which scarcely seems to limit his choices, the science fiction writer is not faced, each time he writes a story, with the task of creating the universe anew. Moreover, pragmatically speaking, the future history has proved its right to survive by surviving. It is superior because it is fittest; it must be considered the true book of the future because it has resisted every attempt to rewrite it.

And yet some brilliant writer may come along tomorrow and point out, beyond argument, a fallacy in the consensus future history and, on the spot, the history will be rewritten. As Wollheim has pointed out, "science fiction builds upon science fiction." Concepts grow out of other concepts, to expand them, to extend them, or to contradict them; future histories use devices and techniques pioneered by other authors, fans grow into new writers, authors stand on each other's shoulders. A consensus future history developed because it had to. And yet all of this is not to suggest that writers display a slavish subservience toward the consensus: as many authors depart from the consensus as use it and each writer who develops a consistent series of future history stories— Heinlein, Poul Anderson, Gordon Dickson, Cordwainer Smith, and many others —creates his own future historical circumstances and peoples it with his own personages and influences.

But there is, behind the basic scenario, a vision of man, a philosophy, which is at the same time arrogant and humble. It is based upon a concept of man as an animal selected by environmental pressures for intelligence, aggressiveness, possessiveness, and survival, but also an animal whose passions, aspirations, and understanding have given him a tragic nobility: he may not be divine but in his hubris and his understanding he partakes of divinity; he has eaten of the tree of life and of the tree of knowledge of good and evil; he is a creature who can dream of greatness and understand that it is only a dream.

"Man is the only animal that laughs and weeps," Hazlitt wrote; "for he is the only animal that is struck with the difference between what things are, and what they ought to be."

Viewed as an animal, man must continue to expand his domain, to extend his ecological range, to push out his territory; or he must find an innocuous ecological niche in another society, like the ant or the housefly, where he is too difficult or too expensive to eradicate; or he must ingratiate himself into a superior culture, like the dog or the cat; or he must die. Such as been the evolutionary history of Earth, of which man is a part. Both evolutionary and recorded history confirm a picture of man as a creature which must be dominant, which eliminates competing species, which has found ways of existing wherever endurance, adaptability, or intelligence can fit him to the environment or environment to him. This is science fiction's traditional vision of man as he faces the universe.

In Arthur C. Clarke's "Rescue Party," for instance, members of a race who "had been lords of the Universe since the dawn of history," to whom "had been given all knowledge—and with infinite knowledge went infinite responsibility," discover that Earth's sun is to become a nova in seven hours and that Earth has a civilization. It is one of the greatest tragedies of their history, but they can only examine each of the 8 billion solar systems in the galaxy at intervals of about a million years, and 400,000 years ago Earth had showed no signs of intelligent life. In such a short span intelligence and civilization could not be expected to develop. Their spaceship searches an abandoned Earth, which has developed a great, worldwide civilization, and finally discovers in the lonely space far beyond Pluto "thousands of tiny pencils of light." The leader of the alien survey ship comments:

"I wonder what they'll be like?" he mused. "Will they be nothing but wonderful engineers, with no art or philosophy? They're going to have such a surprise when Orostron reaches them—I expect it will be rather a blow to their pride. It's funny how all isolated races think they're the only people in the Universe. But they should be grateful to us—we're going to save them a good many hundred years of travel."

Alvaron glanced at the Milky Way, lying like a veil of silver mist across the vision screen. He waved towards it with a sweep of a tentacle that embraced the whole circle of the Galaxy, from the Central Planets to the lonely suns of the Rim.

"You know," he said to Rugon, "I feel rather afraid of these people. Suppose they don't like our little Federation?" He waved once more towards the star-clouds that lay massed across the screen, glowing with the light of their countless suns.

"Something tells me they'll be very determined people," he added. "We had better be polite to them. After all, we only outnumber them about a thousand million to one."

Rugon laughed at his captain's little joke.

Twenty years afterward, the remark didn't seem so funny.

In Heinlein's juvenile novel, *Have Spacesuit—Will Travel*, a teen-ager is faced with the terrible responsibility of convincing a Council of Three Galaxies that humanity, even though quarrelsome, combative, and probably a danger to all other intelligent creatures, should not be destroyed, that it should be allowed time to mature, to improve, to fit itself for living in an alien, civilized universe. Feeling the unfairness of a situation in which he has been chosen to represent all of mankind, to defend its right to survive, the boy finally bursts out:

"It's not a defense, you don't *want* a defense. All right, take away our star—you will if you can and I guess you can. Go ahead! We'll *make* a star! Then, someday, we'll come back and hunt you down—all of you!"

Nobody bawled me out. I suddenly felt like a kid who has made a horrible mistake at a party and doesn't know how to cover it up. But I meant it. Oh, I didn't think we could *do* it. Not yet. But we'd try. "Die trying" is the proudest human thing.

Pride has been a major philosophic aspect of science fiction, pride not so much in the qualities a creature must have to survive, though survival is basic, but pride in the qualities a creature that must survive can develop and sustain in spite of unrelenting adversity. Man, says the science fiction main current, must be tough and aggressive, but his glory is that he can temper his toughness and aggressiveness with an appreciation for beauty, with artistic creativity, with self-sacrifice, with love. And that paradox is what it means to be truly human.

Science fiction, for all its fantasy, sprang out of naturalism, which viewed man as another animal conditioned by his environment and no more responsible for his actions than any other animal, and it is through fantastic subject matter treated naturalistically that science fiction has achieved some of its finest effects. But the science fiction philosophy has moderated its naturalism, its Darwinism, with rationalism.

Leo Rosten concluded a recent book with a story about Destiny:

Destiny came down to an island, centuries ago, and summoned three of the inhabitants before him. "What would you do," asked Destiny, "if I told you that tomorrow this island will be completely inundated by an immense tidal wave?" The first man, who was a cynic, said, "Why I would eat, drink, carouse, and make love all night long!" The second man, who was a mystic, said, "I would go to the sacred groves with my loved ones and make sacrifices to the gods and pray without ceasing." And the third man, who loved reason, thought for a while, confused and troubled, and said, "Why I would assemble our wisest men and begin at once to study how to live under water."

That man, who loved reason, is the very model of a modern science fiction writer. The spirit he represents finds alien the dismal view of man displayed by the nonscience fiction writer when he ventures into the genre, like that of Aldous Huxley in *Brave New World* or Nevil Shute in *On the Beach*; it is not so much that their view of man is tragic nor even that they perceive him as an emotional rather than a rational being, but that they underestimate him. If

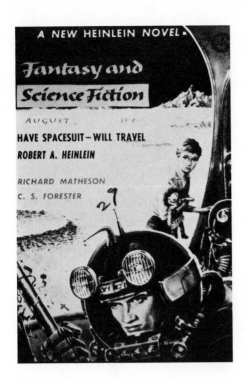

threatened by destruction, man, science fiction says, will not surrender peace-
fully; he will struggle to the end, studying how to live under water, on a
frozen or a flaming Earth, in outer space, on the most hostile worlds. And it
seems to me that this is the truer picture of man's character. It is not unique to
science fiction, of course. "I decline to accept the end of man," William Faulkner
said in his 1950 Nobel-laureate speech. "I believe that man will not merely endure: he will prevail." And Dylan Thomas wrote:

> Do not go gentle into that good night,
> Old age should burn and rave at close of day;
> Rage, rage against the dying of the light. . . .

But rationalism—the belief that the mind is the ultimate judge of reality and
can be relied upon to provide an answer to any problem—even rationalism modified by experimentalism, does not describe completely science fiction's philosophic
position. It has been tempered by a more contemporary philosophy—existentialism. Jean-Paul Sartre described existentialism in these terms:

Atheistic existentialism, of which I am a representative, declares with greater con-
sistency that if God does not exist there is at least one being whose existence comes
before its essence, a being which exists before it can be defined by any conception of it.
That being is man or, as Heidigger has it, the human reality. What do we mean by
saying that existence precedes essence? We mean that man first of all exists, encounters
himself, surges up in the world—and defines himself afterwards. . . .

Man is nothing else but that which he makes of himself. . . . If, however, it is true
that existence is prior to essence, man is responsible for what he is. Thus, the first
effect of existentialism is that it puts every man in possession of himself as he is, and
places the entire responsibility for his existence squarely upon his own shoulders.

And, when we say that man is responsible for himself, we do not mean that he is
responsible only for his own individuality, but that he is responsible for all men. . . .
When we say that man chooses himself, we do mean that every one of us must choose
himself; but by that we also mean that in choosing for himself he chooses for all
men. . . .

This is not to suggest that existentialism changed science fiction, but that
science fiction arrived at the existential position relatively independently. Man,
science fiction said before Sartre, is responsible. Even if he is a conditioned animal, by reason of his passions and his understanding he is free; he has free
will; he can choose between actions and between fates. And even in a hostile
universe deserted by God or meaning, he still must struggle to remain human,
to do the human thing. That human thing may be to keep evolving, to keep
improving, to explore the ultimate potential of the human form, the human
mind, the human spirit, or of intelligence itself. In this sense, the arrogance of

229

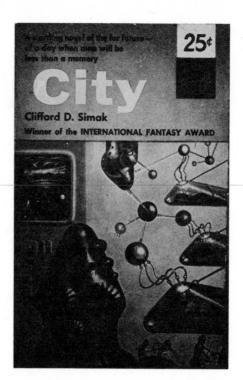

the science fiction man is a kind of humility before the blind creative processes which produced him, and a determination to prove worthy; and if some alien race or the machine itself proves to be superior, better fitted to think, to understand, to create, to survive, then man has a responsibility to step aside and, perhaps wearily, perhaps gratefully, lay down the earthling's burden.

In a story called "Resurrection" (or "The Monster"), A. E. van Vogt illustrated science fiction's pride in humanity and its still-unrealized potential: An alien spaceship descends upon an Earth where life has been unexpectedly wiped out by a cosmic storm. The aliens recreate men from fragments of bone and destroy them when they suggest danger; each resurrected man has greater powers until the fourth understands the situation at the moment of his rebirth, vanishes instantly, and revives the rest of mankind to fulfill their interrupted destiny.

Other stories demonstrate science fictional man's concern for the survival of his successor if not himself. In a lecture at the University of Kansas, Arthur Clarke pointed out that Nietzsche called man a rope stretched between the animal and the superhuman; Clarke suggested that man may be the organic phase between the inorganic. "Once you make a machine which can learn . . . there is no end to the process." The intelligent machine may be man's successor. "It's hard to see how on a lifeless planet an IBM computer could evolve without passing through the organic phase first."

In a collection of stories called *City*, Clifford Simak saw robots and dogs as man's successors. In John Campbell's "Twilight," it was too late for dogs: "as man strode toward maturity, he destroyed all forms of life that menaced him" and eventually all other forms of life. Man was dying because he had lost his curiosity; but there were still the perfectly operating machines, and the visitor to this distant future leaves that era a legacy:

> So I brought another machine to life, and set it to a task which, in time to come, it will perform.
> I ordered it to make a machine which would have what man had lost. A curious machine.

On a more immediate level, science fiction tests mankind and the future against the principles of scientific positivism, a philosophy which rejects metaphysics and believes that knowledge is based only on sense experience and scientific experiment and observation. The key to understanding the serious, main-current science fiction speculation about the future and man's role in it is pragmatism. Through the Augean stables of traditional literature, John Campbell's *Analog* diverted the Peneus and Alpheus rivers of realism: "It is not what you believe to be true that will determine your or humanity's success but what works," the magazine said. A substantial body of science fiction is dedi-

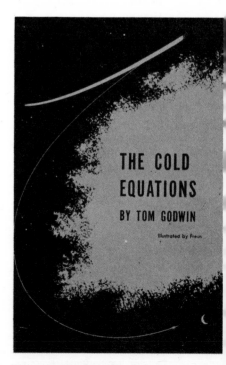

THE COLD
EQUATIONS
BY TOM GODWIN

Illustrated by Freas

cated to undermining prejudice and prior judgments, romanticism and senti-
mentality; and many writers have made livings by asking themselves what
mankind and its folk wisdom hold dear, and by demonstrating fictionally that
the opposite makes more sense.

Tom Godwin's "The Cold Equations" is the quintessential expression of this
approach: a girl, hoping to see her brother who is a member of an advance
group on a frontier planet, stows away aboard a one-man emergency delivery
ship sent out by an interstellar liner with vital serum for another group on the
planet. The amount of fuel necessary to reach the planet has been carefully cal-
culated by computer because of frontier necessity which Godwin spends much
of the story justifying. Interstellar regulations state that a stowaway must be jet-
tisoned immediately upon discovery; if not the ship will crash and instead of
one person dying eight will die. The cold equations say that the girl must leave
the ship, that she must die; and she does.

That is looking at humanity from the viewpoint of the universe: the universe
doesn't care whether individuals live or die, whether mankind itself survives;
its cosmic processes involve the titanic birth and death of suns, of galaxies, and
of a universe itself slowly running down toward the universal heat death called
entropy, and even for these things it does not care. Those who infer purpose or
concern in the universe may find comfort but they also assume risk; and what
they hazard is not merely their lives and the lives of others but the waste
of those lives, those human purposes, those human efforts, through willful
ignorance.

"The whole intricate question of method, in the craft of fiction, I take to be
governed by the question of the point of view—the question of the relation in
which the narrator stands to the story," Percy Lubbock wrote more than fifty
years ago in his classic study of *The Craft of Fiction*. The kinds of viewpoints
that science fiction adopts, however, are more than questions of narration; in a
larger sense, irrespective of the point of view from which the story is narrated,
the viewpoints of science fiction, whether implied or actual, have made science
fiction what it is—markedly different from any other kind of fiction—and more
than anything else, subject or scene, have created the effects science fiction
achieves.

The critically different viewpoints of science fiction (which some critics call
its "distancing" effect) place the reader at a position remote from the human

View of Earth from
the moon (NASA)

race: for the first time, perhaps, he is able to see man—and himself—from afar
and judge objectively his potential and his accomplishments, his history and his
prospects. The most distant, most objective view is the indifference of the universe. Another, a bit closer and a bit more subjective, is the view of man
from space. One of the reasons for getting into space is to attain this perspective, and one of the values of the space program was the photographs of Earth
from space, along with the comments of the astronauts.

Even from this group of extroverted pragmatists came such remarks as Neil
Armstrong's "I remember on the trip home on Apollo 11 it suddenly struck me
that that tiny pea, pretty and blue, was the Earth. I put up my thumb and
shut one eye, and my thumb blotted out the planet Earth. I didn't feel like a
giant. I felt very, very small." To Bill Anders the sight of Earth from space
evoked "feelings about humanity and human needs that I never had before."
Rusty Schweickart said, "I completely lost my identity as an American astronaut.
I felt a part of everyone and everything sweeping past me below." Or Tom Staf-
ford: "You don't look down at the world as an American but as a human
being." Michael Collins: "I knew I was alone in a way that no earthling had
ever been before." Or Ed Mitchell: "You develop an instant global consciousness, a people orientation, an intense dissatisfaction with the state of the world
and a compulsion to do something about it."

Where were man's monuments? Where were the signs of his civilization? "Is
there life on Earth?" I. S. Shklovskii and Carl Sagan ask in their book *Intelligent
Life in the Universe,* and go on to remark, "For all our feelings of self-impor-
tance, we are only a kind of biological rust, clinging to the surface of our
small planet, and weighing far less than the invisible air which surrounds us."
And they searched photographs taken by the Tiros and Nimbus series of satel-
lites for signs of life on Earth, including photographs of the eastern seaboard of
the United States and the southern tip of India and the island of Ceylon. "The
regions depicted in these photographs are among the most heavily populated
and densely vegetated areas of the Earth; yet even close inspection shows no
sign of life at all. New York appears deserted; India and Ceylon appear barren . . . when the resolution is no better than a few kilometers, there is no sign
of life on Earth."

Or man can look back at man from space, as I did in "The Cave of Night,"
a story about the first man to venture into space, who gets stranded up there
and cannot get back:

"An hour ago, I saw the sun rise over Russia. It looks like any other land from
here, green where it should be green, farther north a sort of mud color, and then white
where the snow is still deep.

"Up here, you wonder why we're so different when the land is the same. You think: we're all children of the same mother planet. Who says we're different? . . .

"Don't want anyone feeling sorry for me. . . . I've seen the stars, clear and undiminished. They look cold, but there's warmth to them and life. They have families of planets like our own sun, some of them. . . . They must. God wouldn't put them there for no purpose. . . . They can be homes to our future generations. Or, if they have inhabitants, we can trade with them: goods, ideas, the love of creation. . . .

"But—more than this—I have seen the Earth. I have seen it—as no man has ever seen it—turning below me like a fantastic ball, the seas like blue glass in the sun . . . or lashed into gray storm-peaks . . . and the land green with life . . . the cities of the world in the night, sparkling . . . and the people. . . ."

The farther into space one travels the less significant become the passions and agonies of man, and the only matter of importance in the long morning of man's struggle to survive is his survival so that his sons could be seeded among the stars, just as the only importance of the long, terrible efforts of gilled creatures to live upon the land was that they became the ancestors of all air breathers, including man, and the only importance to the life of a man is what he passes on to his children or the children of his race in the form of a physical, genetic, or intellectual legacy.

In 1969 Ray Bradbury said, "Space travel says you can live forever. Now we are able to transport our seed to other worlds. We can be sure that this miraculous gift of life goes on forever."

Another detached viewpoint of science fiction is the future. Much of science fiction has looked back at man from this vantage place: from this viewpoint the important function of the present is to make possible the future—or at least not to make it impossible. Ted Sturgeon made use of this viewpoint in his 1947 story "Thunder and Roses." The United States had been attacked with atomic bombs from both the East and the West; it was doomed, although there still were a few survivors, some of them searching for the secret trigger to launch the atomic weapons of the United States in a retaliation that would destroy all life on Earth. One woman, a popular singer, tries to get across the message that "we must die—without striking back."

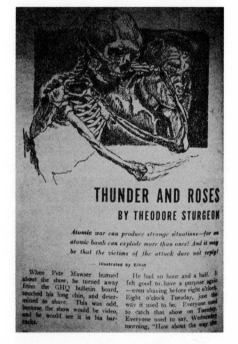

From *Astounding*, November, 1947 (Elliot)

"Let us die with the knowledge that we have done the one noble thing left to us. The spark of humanity can still live and grow on this planet. It will be blown and drenched, shaken and all but extinguished, but it will live if that song is a true one. It will live if we are human enough to discount the fact that the spark is in the custody of our temporary enemy. Some—a few—of his children will live to merge with the new humanity that will gradually emerge from the jungles and the wilderness. Perhaps there will be ten thousand years of beastliness; perhaps man will be able to rebuild while he still has his ruins. . . ."

He looked down through the darkness at his hands. No planet, no universe, is greater to a man than his own ego, his own observing self. These hands were the hands of all history, and like the hands of all men, they could by their small acts make human history or end it. Whether this power of hands was that of a billion hands, or whether it came to a focus in these two—this was suddenly unimportant to the eternities which now enfolded him. . . .

"You'll have your chance," he said into the far future. "And by Heaven, you'd better make good."

Here is science fiction pointing out the ultimate horror of holocaust—the horror is not just that so many will die so horribly and so painfully (all men are doomed to die, and few deaths are easy), but that they destroy the future of mankind—all the unachieved potential, all the untested possibilities, all the art and love and courage and glory that might be; it is not just that some idiot kind of total warfare might destroy the present—but that it might destroy eternity. From this viewpoint, from the viewpoint of our distant descendants, no matter what their alien forms, ways, beliefs, the ultimate crime is not murder but lack of foresight, which leads to an emphasis on solving contemporary situations with ultimate solutions, no matter what the risk to life or civilization—a kind of romantic idiocy. In a metaphorical sense, science fiction might be considered letters from the future, from our children, urging us to be careful of their world. By writing about a future, no matter how pessimistically or in how cautionary a vein, science fiction might be considered an optimistic fiction.

A final detached viewpoint is that of the alien—sometimes the alien to our society such as the visitor from the future, as in Fredric Brown's "Dark Interlude"; or the visitor from a distant planet as in Robert Sheckley's "Love, Inc."; or the Earth man in another society as in his "The Language of Love" or Roger Zelazny's "A Rose for Ecclesiastes"; sometimes the exterrestrial beings who visit Earth for conquest or exploration or judgment, as in Murray Leinster's "Nobody Saw the Ship" or Ross Rocklynne's "Jackdaw" or Gordon Dickson's "Dolphin's Way," or Jack Williamson's *The Trial of Terra;* or the alien conquerors of Arthur Clarke's *Childhood's End;* or the ultimate alien of Eric Frank Russell's "Hobbyist." From the alien viewpoint we can see clearly the relativity of our most cherished beliefs; the ridiculousness of our traditions, our mores, and our concerns; and the temporality of our societies. We can learn to share the broader vision that encompasses all living creatures, all thinking beings—which by extension renders trivial the minor differences between races or individuals.

These viewpoints—and there are others and many variations—help determine much of a reader's reaction to science fiction. Some readers welcome perspective on themselves or on humanity; some find it painful or silly or are unable to make the kind of imaginative leap necessary to dissociate themselves from their perennial earthbound conceptions. Edmund Crispin pointed out in his *Literary Supplement* article:

> All these things being thus, it would be surprising if science fiction were to be popular. Nobody can take altogether kindly to the thesis that neither he personally, nor anyone else whatever, runs much risk of unduly bedazzling the eye of eternity. . . . The best-seller lists are scarcely, if one comes to think of it, the place to look for fiction which instructs us, no matter how cheerfully, in how completely trivial we all are. . . . In medieval times Man was commonly visualized as being dwarfed against a backdrop of stupendous spiritual or supernatural agencies; yet not dwarfed ultimately, since the Christian religion consistently averred him to be a special creation. From the Renaissance onwards that backdrop shrank, or was more and more ignored, with a corresponding gain in stature to the actor in front of it. What science fiction has done, and what makes it egregious, is to dwarf Man all over again (this time without compensation) against a new great backdrop, that of environment. Leopold Bloom has Dublin, and Strether has Edwardian England, and Madame Bovary has provincial France; but the relative nonentities in science fiction have the entire cosmos, with everything that is, or conceivably might be, in it.

A revolution was inevitable against the cold inhumanity of a viewpoint which could equate the Vietnam War with Wat Tyler's Rebellion, discrimination with serfdom, individual tragedy with the crushing of a cockroach; which could consider mass starvation as a possible long-term good, plague as a genetic boon and humanitarianism as genetic suicide, and war as a means of redressing Malthusian imbalances. Although science fiction has been consistently egalitarian, libertarian, and fraternitarian (except in some foreign countries, notably the Soviet Union, where Marxist criteria get first consideration), its penchant for the long view ultimately created a new breed of writers who focused their concerns on the short term, on individuals and their inalienable worth, on men's passions and perplexities rather than their intellects. Beginning about the middle of the sixties, primarily in England in Michael Moorcock's state-subsidized

Michael Moorcock

J. G. Ballard

Brian Aldiss

Harlan Ellison

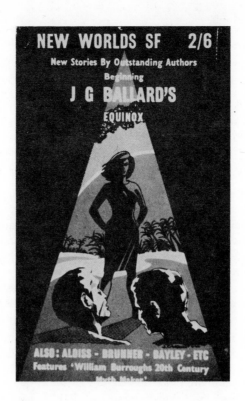

LEFT: American edition, March, 1960 (Vol. 1, No. 1) (Freas) RIGHT: British version, May-June, 1964 (Cawthorn)

New Worlds, through the writing of J. G. Ballard and Brian Aldiss, in part by John Brunner and Moorcock himself; publicized by Judith Merril in her later *Best of the Year* anthologies and her collection *England Swings SF* and named by her the "New Wave"; welcomed in this country by stylists such as Harlan Ellison, Norman Spinrad, Thomas Disch, and a host of younger writers; encouraged by the Milford Science Fiction Conferences, Clarion Science Fiction Writers Workshops and their successors, and *Orbit* and *Dangerous Visions*—the new wave broke over science fiction and left some spluttering older writers and fans in its path.

The new wave was more than a reaction to the scientific positivism that had become the main current of science fiction; it was a response of younger writers to the spirit of the times, which was rejecting intellectualism as a blind alley and which demonstrated itself in a willingness to sacrifice the universities to end the war in Vietnam, to trade the classroom and the book for the experience, to seek answers in drugs and meditation rather than in study and experiment, to put together new groupings rather than improve old ones. "I think therefore I am" became "I feel therefore I am," and this shift from rationalism to sensationalism (stressing the overriding importance of feeling: "feeling good," "feeling right," "grokking," and "vibes," good and bad) found its way into science fiction.

Tom Godwin's "Cold Equations" ends:

A cold equation had been balanced and he was alone on the ship. Something shapeless and ugly was hurrying ahead of him, going to Woden where its brother was waiting through the night, but the empty ship still lived for a little while with the presence of the girl who had not known about the forces that killed with neither hatred nor malice. It seemed, almost, that she still sat small and bewildered and frightened on the metal box beside him, her words echoing hauntingly clear in the void she had left behind her:

I didn't do anything to die for—I didn't do anything—

J. G. Ballard's "Terminal Beach" also deals with death, not directly but symbolically through the wanderings of a man named Traven among the sterile, incomprehensible structures on Eniwetok, where a hydrogen bomb was exploded in a post-war test. The story is evocative and its meaning comes, elusively, through descriptions of a psychological numbness to death and a premonition of atomic catastrophe. Traven's wife and six-year-old son were killed in an automobile accident, but this seems to Traven only part of what he calls the pre-Third—the two decades between 1945 and 1965 "suspended from the quivering volcano's lip of World War III." Traven has come to Eniwetok for a purpose he does not understand and moves aimlessly around the island. The story ends:

As the next days passed into weeks, the dignified figure of the [dead] Japanese sat in his chair fifty yards from him, guarding Traven from the blocks. Their magic still filled Traven's reveries, but he now had sufficient strength to rouse himself and forage for food. In the hot sunlight the skin of the Japanese became more and more bleached, and sometimes Traven would wake at night to find the white sepulchral figure sitting there, arms resting at its sides, in the shadows that crossed the concrete floor. At these moments he would often see his wife and son watching him from the dunes. As time passed they came closer, and he would sometimes turn to find them only a few yards behind him.

Patiently Traven waited for them to speak to him, thinking of the great blocks whose entrance was guarded by the seated figure of the dead archangel, as the waves broke on the distant shore and the burning bombers fell through his dreams.

Some readers have objected to what they considered the inconclusiveness, the willful obscurity, the pointlessness, and the aping of mainstream experimental techniques at the expense of content—all of which they consider typical of the new wave. Younger writers, I suspect, have been increasingly impatient with the bad writing that gets printed as science fiction and with the disrepute that comes along with its pulp origins; in addition to their chafing at publishing restraints, they have shared, as well, a hankering for status and critical recognition which comes more with form than substance. But I have the feeling that the deeper objections of fans and writers were stirred by the shift in viewpoint, both the shift in the viewpoint of detachment and the narrative viewpoint.

Daniel Keyes

Professor Arthur Mizener has divided contemporary fiction into four main types: realistic, romantic, subjective, and southern (the last falls outside the framework of the other three, and we will ignore it). They can be distinguished, Mizener says, by their attitude toward objective common sense: the realistic story makes us feel that objective common sense will not only be correct about how things will turn out, but right and wise in understanding that they must turn out that way; the romantic story makes us feel that objective common sense is likely to be correct about how things will turn out, but will miss the real meaning of things because it will not take into account the feelings of the central character; and the subjective story makes us feel that what men dream is so important, and therefore so real, that the objective world of common sense, however resistant to men's desires, does not finally count.

All of these traditions coexist in contemporary fiction, but science fiction, in the Campbellian tradition, is primarily realistic; science fiction in the tradition of the scientific romance of the early pulp magazines was primarily romantic. The writers of the new wave seem primarily subjectivists—a thoroughly respectable literary position but one which is foreign not only to main-current science fiction but to science itself. It is not alien, however, to fantasy, which always has been subjective. Besides insinuating a mainstream viewpoint into science fiction, the new wave also has brought in a concern for technique, for stream of consciousness and interior monologue, shifting viewpoints and symbols and metaphors, for complex characters explicating their lives on a treadmill of meaningless days, for little people or strange people caught up in the innumerable folds of an inexplicable world, for a life or a way of life that is static, trapped, or doomed. . . .

Samuel Delaney

"I Have No Mouth And I Must Scream," writes Harlan Ellison.

The objection of many older science fiction readers and newer readers who found the traditional science fiction more to their tastes was directed at the external manifestations of technique and their consequences, but I suspect that the real difference lay in the viewpoint behind the techniques: the subjective, nonscientific, feelings-are-more-important-than-thinking viewpoint. Many of the younger writers have picked up, or reinvented, Heinlein's 1947 term for science fiction, "speculative fiction," on the grounds that "science fiction" is too narrow to cover the various kinds of fiction that qualified under any reasonable definition but included no science. Their motivations probably are a bit more complex: the term "science fiction" is not broad enough to cover the kind of fiction they wished to write, and a new name suggested new possibilities and new directions—and concealed the shameful pulp origins.

By now the waves have quieted. Writers who want to do new things, experimental things, are doing them; writers who want to say new things, difficult things, outrageous things, are saying them. Many of these new voices are finding new audiences: young people, particularly, are finding the new subjective writers appealing. College book stores report that science fiction as a whole is selling remarkably well, but some speculative and introspective science fiction is selling even better; the reverse is true in the general market where the more traditional *Analog* is by far the best-selling magazine, and DAW books, published by Donald A. Wollheim, stressing traditional science fiction stories and covers, are a surprising sales phenomenon.

The net result has been, in spite of the outcries of the traditionalists, an increase in the audience for science fiction; the dividing line between the traditional and the new is blurring, and the differences may be striking to the informed, but the similarities are greater to the reader who is merely looking for something different in reading matter. Readers drawn to "speculative fiction" by *New Worlds* or *Dangerous Visions* or *Orbit*, or even *Stranger in a Strange Land*, may push on into the other terra incognita of science fiction and scarcely notice when they cross the border.

Another effect of the new wave has been an increased freedom within the field to experiment, to use unfamiliar techniques and unusual subject matter—in other words, to liberate still further what has always prided itself as being the freest medium for fiction. The final shape of science fiction—or speculative fiction—is still unclear. Isaac Asimov has speculated that we may be entering a fourth stage in science fiction's literary history: style-dominant. But I think that is an expression of alarm; even speculative fiction is concerned more than anything else with content, though the content may be unfamiliar or difficult to decipher and the style sometimes may seem to overpower it. The art of writing (science fiction writers traditionally have been more concerned with storytelling than with art) insists that style grows out of and informs subject; this may not always seem true in times of experimentation and reaction, but fundamental principles cannot long be ignored.

What we may anticipate in science fiction is a greater concern with language, character, and subjective reality on the part of many traditional science fiction writers who find their work downgraded for lack of concern for writing skill; we may also find a greater concern for content and objective reality in many writers of speculative fiction, though some will continue to push on with wilder journeys into the outer reaches of experiment. Already such trends are apparent. Greater variety will be tolerated, even encouraged, in subject, approach, and style; an increasing number of writers will be difficult or impossible to categorize. The goal will be the ideal of the mainstream: each writer with his individual vision, his individual voice.

Roger Zelazny

ABOVE: Kurt Vonnegut, Jr., who wrote science fiction (*The Sirens of Titan* and other novels) before he found a larger audience in the mainstream of modern fiction

237

But what of science fiction and the mainstream?

The mainstream seems stagnant, scarcely moving at all; or, if it is moving, it is eddying into little ponds and strange pockets without any clearly defined current. It is not going anywhere. Mainstream vigor seems to come from its contacts with popular culture: motion pictures, folk heroes, commercials, radio, television, comic strips, advertisements, modern myths, rock music and musicians, detective stories, science fiction. . . . We live in a pop culture—is there any other kind?—where soup cans are art and commercials are the most skillful art forms on television; literature is only beginning to recognize these facts. It is almost as if contemporary fiction has gone as far as it can go in the examination of character, even of abnormal character, and now its major prospect is, as Stanley Elkin has prophesied, the exploration of language itself. The alternative is to turn to the sources of energy in our culture—the myths and concerns people live by—and try to consider them, to use them as the stuff of fiction.

Increasingly mainstream writers are turning to the themes and concepts of science fiction: Barth, Borges, Boulle, Burroughs, Burgess, Golding, Hersey, Lessing, Nabokov, Percy, Pynchon, Rand, John Williams, Colin Wilson, Wouk, Vercors, Vonnegut, Voznesensky. . . . What they are finding are not only the excitement of unexplored territory (unexplored, that is, by mainstream writers), but subjects which are significant, which deal with the problems of our times and are not tracked over with literary footprints, which have the evocative power of a freshly minted metaphor. And although these writers may be dealing with science fiction themes and concepts at the level of myth rather than as serious subjects for speculation, as time passes they may be expected to become as knowledgeable about content and idea as they are about technique, if they can shed the prejudices of the literary culture.

As the drunken hero of *God Bless You, Mr. Rosewater* says to a convention of science fiction writers:

I love you sons of bitches. You're all I read any more. You're the only ones who'll talk about the *really* terrific changes going on, the only ones crazy enough to know that life is a space voyage, and not a short one, either, but one that'll last for billions of years. You're the only ones with guts to *really* care about the future, who *really* notice what machines do to us, what wars do to us, what cities do to us, what tremendous misunderstandings, mistakes, accidents and catastrophes do to us. You're the only ones zany enough to agonize over time and distances without limit, over mysteries that will never die, over the fact that we are right now determining whether the space voyage for the next billion years or so is going to Heaven or Hell.

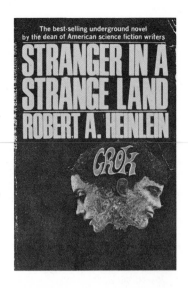

Frank Herbert

The author of those lines, Kurt Vonnegut, Jr., obtained his first recognition in science fiction magazines and paperbacks, although he later insisted that he not be labeled a science fiction writer and made his reputation in the mainstream.

Other science fiction writers are being read outside the category, and if they are not exactly welcomed into the mainstream by critics and other writers, their right to be there is not being challenged; in some ways the emergence of science fiction books into the mainstream is being recognized as a sign of vigor and strange merit in science fiction itself.

The broad appeal of Heinlein's *Stranger in a Strange Land* and Frank Herbert's *Dune*—"good examples," *Time* magazine has said, "of how public concerns and infatuations catch up with the science-fiction imagination"—already has been noted. They are not alone: Asimov's *Foundation* trilogy and Pohl and Kornbluth's *Space Merchants* have almost never been out of print since their appearance in book form in the early fifties, and Arthur Clarke's *Childhood's End* has gone through eighteen printings. "Walter M. Miller Jr.'s *A Canticle for Leibowitz*, an extraordinary novel even by literary standards," *Time* notes, "has flourished by word of mouth for a dozen years." Add to these such books as Daniel Keyes's *Flowers for Algernon*, Ursula K. Le Guin's *Left Hand of Darkness*, Robert Silverberg's *Tower of Glass*, most of the books of Ray Bradbury (who was one of the earliest admitted to be writing literature), and those of Samuel Delaney, Roger Zelazny, and Harlan Ellison, which are not far behind, along with others whose first books are yet to come.

As the science fiction writer becomes more concerned with character, with language, with technique, he will be better-accepted by nonscience fiction readers and critics. Kingsley Amis has written:

> These cardboard spacemen aren't enough,
> Nor alien monsters, sketched in rough,
> Character's the essential stuff.

But science fiction writers might be cautioned not to sell their birthright for a mess of pottage, not to sacrifice the concern for idea that made science fiction distinctive and relevant (their birthright, that is, is a pot of message), but to develop it further along the lines that Amis suggests in another poem, "Science Fiction":

Walter M. Miller, Jr.

> What makes us rove that starlit corridor
> May be the impulse to meet face to face
> Our vice and folly shaped into a thing,
> And so at last ourselves. . . .

Meanwhile, mainstream writers will continue their explorations of what previously was the exclusive preserve of the science fiction writer—the future and other lands unknown—and they will do so with increasing sophistication.

In the middle the two will meet and be virtually indistinguishable.

A genre called science fiction will continue to exist, I believe, although the magazines in which it is published may not survive. John Campbell died July 11, 1971; what will happen to *Analog* under his successor, Ben Bova? (At this writing, *Analog* circulation is rising and the magazine remains vital.) For sentimental as well as practical reasons, I hope that *Analog* and the other magazines prosper, but science fiction will survive in some form, in magazines perhaps, in paperbacks and hard-cover books almost certainly, and in other forms as yet unforeseen.

Ben Bova

The unity of science fiction, however, will begin to disintegrate without the magazines as a focus; the new wave is a portent. The consensus future and the philosophical position on which it was built will begin to fall apart as science fiction splinters into a hundred markets, into a thousand disparate, individual visions.

Beyond this the shape of things to come grows blurred, and the long journey, the odyssey of science fiction, from Homer to Hamilton, Heinlein, Herbert, and Harlan, has reached if not an end at least a pause, a place to sit for a moment and contemplate the future. Tomorrow the endless voyage begins again. . . .

APPENDIX

NEBULA AWARD WINNERS

1 9 6 5
BEST NOVEL: *Dune,* by Frank Herbert
BEST NOVELLA: "The Saliva Tree," by Brian W. Aldiss
"He Who Shapes," by Roger Zelazny (Tie)
BEST NOVELETTE: "The Doors of His Face, The Lamps of
His Mouth," by Roger Zelazny
BEST SHORT STORY: " 'Repent, Harlequin!' Said the
Ticktockman," by Harlan Ellison

1 9 6 6
BEST NOVEL: *Flowers for Algernon,* by Daniel Keyes
Babel-17, by Samuel R. Delany (Tie)
BEST NOVELLA: "The Last Castle," by Jack Vance
BEST NOVELETTE: "Call Him Lord," by Gordon R. Dickson
BEST SHORT STORY: "The Secret Place," by Richard McKenna

1 9 6 7
BEST NOVEL: *The Einstein Intersection,* by Samuel R. Delany
BEST NOVELLA: "Behold The Man," by Michael Moorcock
BEST NOVELETTE: "Gonna Roll the Bones," by Fritz Leiber
BEST SHORT STORY: "Aye, and Gomorrah," by Samuel
R. Delany

1 9 6 8
BEST NOVEL: *Rite of Passage,* by Alexei Panshin
BEST NOVELLA: "Dragonrider," by Anne McCaffrey
BEST NOVELETTE: "Mother to the World," by Richard Wilson
BEST SHORT STORY: "The Planners," by Kate Wilhelm

1 9 6 9
BEST NOVEL: *The Left Hand of Darkness,* by Ursula K.
Le Guin
BEST NOVELLA: "A Boy and His Dog," by Harlan Ellison
BEST NOVELETTE: "Time Considered as a Helix of
Semi-Precious Stones," by Samuel R. Delany
BEST SHORT STORY: "Passengers," by Robert Silverberg

1 9 7 0
BEST NOVEL: *Ringworld,* by Larry Niven
BEST NOVELLA: "Ill Met in Lankhmar," by Fritz Leiber
BEST NOVELETTE: "Slow Sculpture," Theodore Sturgeon
BEST SHORT STORY: No award

1 9 7 1
BEST NOVEL: *A Time of Changes,* by Robert Silverberg
BEST NOVELLA: "The Missing Man," by Katherine MacLean
BEST NOVELETTE: "The Queen of Air and Darkness,"
by Poul Anderson
BEST SHORT STORY: "Good News From the Vatican,"
by Robert Silverberg

1 9 7 2
BEST NOVEL: *The Gods Themselves,* by Isaac Asimov
BEST NOVELLA: "A Meeting With Medusa," by Arthur
C. Clarke
BEST NOVELETTE: "Goat Song," by Poul Anderson
BEST SHORT STORY: "When it Changed," by Joanna Russ

1 9 7 3
BEST NOVEL: *Rendezvous With Rama,* by Arthur C. Clarke
BEST NOVELLA: "The Death of Dr. Island," by Gene Wolfe
BEST NOVELETTE: "Of Mist, and Grass, and Sand,"
by Vonda N. McIntyre
BEST SHORT STORY: "Love Is the Plan, the Plan Is Death,"
by James Tiptree, Jr.
BEST DRAMATIC PRESENTATION: "Soylent Green," by Stanley
R. Greenberg from the novel *Make Rome, Make Room,*
by Harry Harrison

1 9 7 4
NOVEL: *The Dispossessed* by Ursula K. Le Guin
NOVELLA: "Born with the Dead" by Robert Silverberg
NOVELETTE: "If All the Stars Are Gods" by Gordon Eklund
and Gregory Benford
SHORT STORY: "The Day Before the Revolution"
by Ursula K. Le Guin
GRAND MASTER (for lifetime achievement, first time
awarded): Robert Heinlein
DRAMATIC PRESENTATION: *Sleeper* by Woody Allen

HUGO AWARDS

1 9 5 3: Philadelphia (Philcon II)
NO. 1 FAN PERSONALITY: Forrest J. Ackerman
INTERIOR ILLUSTRATOR: Virgil Finlay
COVER ARTIST: Ed Emshwiller and Hannes Bok (tie)
EXCELLENCE IN FACT ARTICLES: Willy Ley
NEW SCIENCE FICTION ARTIST OR AUTHOR: Philip José Farmer
PROFESSIONAL MAGAZINE: *Galaxy* and *Astounding Science-
Fiction*
NOVEL: *The Demolished Man* (Alfred Bester)

1 9 5 4: San Francisco (SFCon)
No Awards were given this year.

1 9 5 5: Cleveland (Clevention)
NOVEL: *They'd Rather Be Right* (Mark Clifton and Frank
Riley)
NOVELETTE: "The Darfsteller" (Walter M. Miller, Jr.)
SHORT STORY: "Allamagoosa" (Eric Frank Russell)
PROFESSIONAL MAGAZINE: *Astounding Science-Fiction*
ILLUSTRATOR: Frank Kelly Freas
AMATEUR PUBLICATION: *Fantasy Times* (James V. Taurasi,
ed.)

1 9 5 6: New York (NyCon II)
NOVEL: *Double Star* (Robert A. Heinlein)
NOVELETTE: "Exploration Team" (Murray Leinster)
SHORT STORY: "The Star" (Arthur C. Clarke)
FEATURE WRITER: Willy Ley
PROFESSIONAL MAGAZINE: *Astounding Science-Fiction*
ILLUSTRATOR: Frank Kelly Freas
MOST PROMISING NEW AUTHOR: Robert Silverberg
AMATEUR PUBLICATION: *Inside* and *Science Fiction
Advertiser* (Ron Smith, ed.)
CRITIC: Damon Knight

1 9 5 7: London (Loncon I)
PROFESSIONAL MAGAZINE, AMERICAN: *Astounding Science-
Fiction*
PROFESSIONAL MAGAZINE, BRITISH: *New Worlds Science
Fiction*
AMATEUR PUBLICATION: *Science Fiction Times* (James V.
Taurasi)

1 9 5 8: Los Angeles (Solacon)
NOVEL: *The Big Time* (Fritz Leiber)
SHORT STORY: "Or All the Seas With Oysters" (Avram
Davidson)
PROFESSIONAL MAGAZINE: *Magazine of Fantasy and Science
Fiction*
ILLUSTRATOR: Frank Kelly Freas
MOTION PICTURE: *The Incredible Shrinking Man*
(Richard Matheson)
MOST OUTSTANDING ACTIFAN: Walter A. Willis

1 9 5 9: Detroit (Detention)
NOVEL: *A Case of Conscience* (James Blish)
NOVELETTE: "The Big Front Yard" (Clifford D. Simak)
SHORT STORY: "The Hell-bound Train" (Robert Bloch)
ILLUSTRATOR: Frank Kelly Freas
PROFESSIONAL MAGAZINE: *Magazine of Fantasy and Science
Fiction*
AMATEUR PUBLICATION: *Fanac* (Terry Carr and Ron Ellik,
eds.)
MOST PROMISING NEW AUTHOR: Brian W. Aldiss

1 9 6 0: Pittsburgh (Pittcon)
NOVEL: *Starship Troopers* (Robert A. Heinlein)
SHORT FICTION: "Flowers for Algernon" (Daniel Keyes)
PROFESSIONAL MAGAZINE: *Magazine of Fantasy and Science
Fiction*
AMATEUR PUBLICATION: *Cry of the Nameless* (F. M. Bushby,
ed.)
ILLUSTRATOR: Ed Emshwiller
DRAMATIC PRESENTATION: *The Twilight Zone* (Rod Serling)
SPECIAL AWARD: Hugo Gernsback as "The Father of
Magazine Science Fiction"

1 9 6 1: Seattle (Seacon)
NOVEL: *A Canticle for Leibowitz* (Walter M. Miller, Jr.)
SHORT STORY: "The Longest Voyage" (Poul Anderson)
PROFESSIONAL MAGAZINE: *Analog Science Fact–Science Fiction*
AMATEUR PUBLICATION: *Who Killed Science Fiction?* (Earl Kemp, ed.)
ILLUSTRATOR: Ed Emshwiller
DRAMATIC PRESENTATION: *The Twilight Zone* (Rod Serling)

1 9 6 2: Chicago (Chicon III)
NOVEL: *Stranger in a Strange Land* (Robert A. Heinlein)
SHORT FICTION: The Hothouse Series (Brian W. Aldiss)
PROFESSIONAL MAGAZINE: *Analog Science Fact–Science Fiction*
AMATEUR MAGAZINE: *Warhoon* (Richard Bergeron, ed.)
PROFESSIONAL ARTIST: Ed Emshwiller
DRAMATIC PRESENTATION: *The Twilight Zone* (Rod Serling)

1 9 6 3: Washington D.C. (DisCon)
NOVEL: *The Man in the High Castle* (Philip K. Dick)
SHORT FICTION: "The Dragon Masters" (Jack Vance)
DRAMATIC AWARD: No award
PROFESSIONAL MAGAZINE: *Magazine of Fantasy and Science Fiction*
AMATEUR MAGAZINE: *Xero* (Dick Lupoff, ed.)
PROFESSIONAL ARTIST: Roy G. Krenkel
SPECIAL AWARDS: P. Schuyler Miller (For Best Book Reviews) Isaac Asimov (For Distinguished Contributions to the Field)

1 9 6 4: Oakland (Pacificon II)
NOVEL: *Way Station* (Clifford D. Simak)
SHORT FICTION: "No Truce With Kings" (Poul Anderson)
PROFESSIONAL MAGAZINE: *Analog Science Fact–Science Fiction*
PROFESSIONAL ARTIST: Ed Emshwiller
BOOK PUBLISHER: Ace Books
AMATEUR PUBLICATION: *Amra* (George Scithers, ed.)

1 9 6 5: London (Loncon II)
NOVEL: *The Wanderer* (Fritz Leiber)
SHORT FICTION: "Soldier, Ask Not" (Gordon R. Dickson)
PROFESSIONAL MAGAZINE: *Analog Science Fact–Science Fiction*
PROFESSIONAL ARTIST: John Schoenherr
BOOK PUBLISHER: Ballantine Books
AMATEUR PUBLICATION: *Yandro* (Robert and Juanita Coulson, eds.)
DRAMATIC PRESENTATION: *Dr. Strangelove* (Stanley Kubrick)

1 9 6 6: Cleveland (Tricon)
NOVEL: *And Call Me Conrad* (Roger Zelazny) tie
Dune (Frank Herbert) tie
SHORT FICTION: " 'Repent, Harlequin', Said the Ticktockman" (Harlan Ellison)
PROFESSIONAL MAGAZINE: *If*
PROFESSIONAL ARTIST: Frank Frazetta
AMATEUR MAGAZINE: *Erb-dom* (Camille Cazedessus, Jr., ed.)
BEST ALL-TIME SERIES: The Foundation Series (Isaac Asimov)

1 9 6 7: New York (NyCon III)
NOVEL: *The Moon Is a Harsh Mistress* (Robert A. Heinlein)
NOVELETTE: "The Last Castle" (Jack Vance)
SHORT STORY: "Neutron Star" (Larry Niven)
PROFESSIONAL MAGAZINE: *If*
PROFESSIONAL ARTIST: Jack Gaughan
DRAMATIC PRESENTATION: *The Menagerie* (Star Trek)
AMATEUR PUBLICATION: *Niekas* (Ed Meskys and Felice Rolfe, eds.)
FAN ARTIST: Jack Gaughan
FAN WRITER: Alexei Panshin

1 9 6 8: Oakland (Baycon)
NOVEL: *Lord of Light* (Roger Zelazny)
NOVELLA: "Weyr Search" (Anne McCaffrey) tie
"Riders of the Purple Wage" (Philip José Farmer) tie
NOVELETTE: "Gonna Roll the Bones" (Fritz Leiber)
SHORT STORY: "I Have No Mouth, and I Must Scream" (Harlan Ellison)
DRAMATIC PRESENTATION: *City on the Edge of Forever* (Star Trek; Harlan Ellison)
PROFESSIONAL MAGAZINE: *If*
PROFESSIONAL ARTIST: Jack Gaughan
AMATEUR PUBLICATION: *Amra* (George Scithers, ed.)
FAN ARTIST: George Barr
FAN WRITER: Ted White

1 9 6 9: St. Louis (St. Louiscon)
NOVEL: *Stand on Zanzibar* (John Brunner)
NOVELLA: "Nightwings" (Robert Silverberg)

NOVELETTE: "The Sharing of Flesh" (Poul Anderson)
SHORT STORY: "The Beast That Shouted Love at the Heart of the World" (Harlan Ellison)
DRAMA: *2001: A Space Odyssey* (Arthur C. Clarke and Stanley Kubrick)
PROFESSIONAL MAGAZINE: *Magazine of Fantasy and Science Fiction*
PROFESSIONAL ARTIST: Jack Gaughan
AMATEUR PUBLICATION: *Psychotic* (Science Fiction Review) (Dick Geis, ed.)
FAN WRITER: Harry Warner, Jr.
FAN ARTIST: Vaughn Bode
SPECIAL AWARD: Armstrong, Aldrin, Collins (For the Best Moon-landing Ever)

1 9 7 0: Heidelberg (Heicon '70 International)
NOVEL: *The Left Hand of Darkness* (Ursula K. Le Guin)
NOVELLA: "Ship of Shadows" (Fritz Leiber)
SHORT STORY: "Time Considered as a Helix of Semi-Precious Stones" (Samuel R. Delany)
DRAMATIC PRESENTATION: Television Coverage of Apollo XI Flight
PROFESSIONAL MAGAZINE: *Magazine of Fantasy and Science Fiction*
PROFESSIONAL ARTIST: Frank Kelly Freas
AMATEUR MAGAZINE: Science Fiction Review (Dick Geis, ed.)
FAN WRITER: Bob Tucker
FAN ARTIST: Tim Kirk

1 9 7 1: Boston (Noreascon)
NOVEL: *Ringworld* (Larry Niven)
NOVELLA: "Ill Met in Lankhmar" (Fritz Leiber)
SHORT STORY: "Slow Sculpture" (Theodore Sturgeon)
DRAMATIC PRESENTATION: No award
PROFESSIONAL ARTIST: Leo and Dianne Dillon
PROFESSIONAL MAGAZINE: *Magazine of Fantasy and Science Fiction*
AMATEUR MAGAZINE: *Locus* (Charles and Dena Brown, eds.)
FAN WRITER: Dick Geis
FAN ARTIST: Alicia Austin

1 9 7 2: Los Angeles (L.A.Con)
NOVEL: *To Your Scattered Bodies Go* (Philip José Farmer)
NOVELLA: "The Queen of Air and Darkness" (Poul Anderson)
SHORT STORY: "Inconstant Moon" (Larry Niven)
DRAMATIC PRESENTATION: *A Clockwork Orange* (Stanley Kubrick)
AMATEUR MAGAZINE: *Locus* (Charles and Dena Brown, eds.)
PROFESSIONAL MAGAZINE: *Magazine of Fantasy and Science Fiction*
PROFESSIONAL ARTIST: Frank Kelly Freas
FAN ARTIST: Tim Kirk
FAN WRITER: Harry Warner, Jr.

1 9 7 3: Toronto (Torcon 2)
NOVEL: *The Gods Themselves* (Isaac Asimov)
NOVELLA: "The Word for World Is Forest" (Ursula Le Guin)
NOVELETTE: "Goat Song" (Poul Anderson)
SHORT STORY: "Eurema's Dam" (R. A. Lafferty) tie
"The Meeting" (Frederik Pohl and C. M. Kornbluth) tie
DRAMATIC PRESENTATION: *Slaughterhouse-Five*
PROFESSIONAL EDITOR: Ben Bova
PROFESSIONAL ARTIST: Frank Kelly Freas
AMATEUR MAGAZINE: *Energumen* (Mike and Susan Glicksohn, eds.)
FAN WRITER: Terry Carr
FAN ARTIST: Tim Kirk
JOHN W. CAMPBELL AWARD FOR BEST NEW WRITER: Jerry Pournelle
TORCON AWARD: *L'Encyclopaedie De L'Utopie et de la Science Fiction* (Pierre Versins)

1974
NOVEL: *Rendezvous With Rama*, Arthur C. Clarke
NOVELLA: "The Girl Who Was Plugged In," James Tiptree, Jr.
NOVELETTE: "The Deathbird," Harlan Ellison
SHORT STORY: "The Ones Who Walk Away from Omelas," Ursula K. LeGuin
PROFESSIONAL EDITOR: Ben Bova
PROFESSIONAL ARTIST: Frank Kelly Freas
DRAMATIC PRESENTATION: *Sleeper*
FANZINE: *Algol* (Andrew Porter, ed.) and *The Alien Critic* (Richard E. Geis, ed.)
FAN WRITER: Susan Wood
FAN ARTIST: Tim Kirk
SPECIAL AWARD: artist Chesley Bonestell
JOHN W. CAMPBELL AWARD FOR BEST NEW WRITER: Spider Robinson and Lisa Tuttle

SCIENCE FICTION THEMES

As science fiction has developed over the past two centuries certain basic themes—
in the broadest sense, what the story is about—have evolved. Each theme incorporates
a basic aspect of change—something new has been introduced into experience
which makes things happen—because this is the nature of science fiction. Examples
offered are illustrative rather than exhaustive, and in some cases a story might fit
under several themes: the stories come first and the categories come afterwards.

THEME	EXAMPLES
1. FAR TRAVELING (changing the scene); the wonders of the world (or the universe); *voyages extraordinaire;* space travel; travel into the very large or the very small; time travel; alternate worlds or universes.	Poe, *The Narrative of Arthur Gordon Pym* Verne, *Journey to the Center of the Earth* Doyle, *The Lost World* Wells, *The Time Machine* Heinlein, "Universe" Clark and Kubrick, *2001: A Space Odyssey* Niven, *Ringworld*
2. THE WONDERS OF SCIENCE (changing the tools); wonderful inventions; gadgets; also the opposite of all this: the Mad Scientist and the terrible invention; uncontrolled technology; change gone wild.	Shelley, *Frankenstein* Verne, *From the Earth to the Moon* Wells, "The Land Ironclads" or "The New Accelerator" Wells, *The Invisible Man* Wells, *The Island of Doctor Moreau* Sherred, "E for Effort"
3. MAN AND THE MACHINE similar to THE WONDERS OF SCIENCE but in this case the emphasis is upon the relationship between man and his creation.	Forster, "The Machine Stops" Čapek, *R.U.R.* Campbell, "Twilight" Heinlein, "The Roads Must Roll" Williamson, "With Folded Hands . . ." Asimov, *I, Robot*
4. PROGRESS (change itself) and its opposite: regression or deterioration; utopias and anti-utopias; man's condition will become better if only, or man's condition will grow worse, if. . . .	Bellamy, *Looking Backward* Wells, *When the Sleeper Wakes* and *The Shape of Things to Come* Huxley, *Brave New World* Orwell, *1984* Pohl and Kornbluth, *The Space Merchants* Vonnegut, *Player Piano*
5. MAN AND HIS SOCIETY similar to PROGRESS except that the purpose (which shines through) is descriptive rather than satirical.	Verne, *The Begum's Fortune* Wells, "The Country of the Blind" Van Vogt, *The Weapon Shops* Leiber, "Coming Attraction" Bradbury, *Fahrenheit 451* Gunn, *The Joy Makers* Heinlein, *Stranger in a Strange Land*
6. MAN AND THE FUTURE similar to PROGRESS but omits any element of satire and emphasizes plausibility.	Asimov, *Foundation* Stapledon, *Last and First Men* Dickson, *Dorsai*
7. WAR (changing the weapons or the nature of war), sometimes leading to Armageddon.	Wells, *The War in the Air* Hubbard, *Final Blackout* Sturgeon, "Thunder and Roses"
8. CATACLYSM (changing physical conditions) and catastrophe.	Wells, "The Star" Balmer and Wylie, *When Worlds Collide* Stewart, *Earth Abides* Christopher, *No Blade of Grass*
9. MAN AND HIS ENVIRONMENT similar to CATACLYSM but the process is slower and less final; may concern the earth, the solar system, the universe and its natural laws, and the consequences of actions; often focuses on "the way things work."	Wells, "The Sea Raiders" Leinster, "The Mad Planet" Asimov, "Nightfall" Blish, "Surface Tension" Godwin, "The Cold Equations" Clarke, *The Sands of Mars* Herbert, *Dune*
10. SUPERPOWERS (changing abilities) such as strange talents; invisibility; immortality; mental control over people, things, events; prevision.	Wells, "The Strange Case of Davidson's Eyes" Haggard, *She* Huxley, *After Many a Summer Dies the Swan* Gunn, *The Immortals* Robinson, *The Power* Clifton and Riley, *They'd Rather Be Right*

THEME	EXAMPLES
11. SUPERMAN similar to SUPERPOWERS but the pattern of powers add up to a new genus which breeds true.	Wells, *The Food of the Gods* Stapledon, *Odd John* Van Vogt, *Slan* Sturgeon, *More Than Human* Clarke, *Childhood's End*
12. MAN AND ALIEN (changing the cast): invasion; contact; conflict; alien problems, thoughts, ways of life.	Wells, *The War of the Worlds* Leinster, "First Contact" Clement, *A Mission of Gravity* Heinlein, *The Puppet Masters* De Camp, *Rogue Queen* Dickson, "Dolphin's Way" Le Guin, *The Left Hand of Darkness*
13. MAN AND RELIGION (changing man's beliefs): beginnings (where did we come from?), meanings (why are we here?), and endings (where do we go from here?) including eschatology; beliefs and reality.	Wells, "The Lord of the Dynamos" Blish, *A Case of Conscience* Del Rey, "For I Am a Jealous People" Bester, "Adam and No Eve" Asimov, "The Last Question" Anderson, *Tau Zero*
14. MISCELLANEOUS glimpses of the future or the past; incidents; anecdotes; adventures; slices of life.	Wells, "The Grisly Folk" Heinlein, "It's Great to Be Back" Kipling, "With the Night Mail" Poe, "Melonta Tauta" Clarke, "Sunjammer"

A SHORT HISTORY OF WESTERN CIVILIZATION, SCIENCE, TECHNOLOGY, AND SCIENCE FICTION

DATE	EVENT	PERSON	WORK	AUTHOR
Prehistory	Discovery of fire, agriculture, domestication of animals, wheel, village.			
c. 4000 B.C.	Towns develop in Mesopotamia.			
2600 B.C.	Great pyramid completed by first machine: masses of people obeying one man.	Khufu or Cheops		
c. 1900–1400 B.C.	Stonehenge built on Salisbury Plain, England.			
c. 1750–1500 B.C.	Zenith of Minoan culture on Crete.			
c. 1200 B.C.	Trojan wars.		*Precursors of science fiction*	
850–600 B.C.	Homeric Greece.		*Iliad* and *Odyssey*	Homer
753 B.C.	Rome founded.	Romulus and Remus		
6th C. B.C.	Permanence is illusion; only reality is change.	Heraclitus		
5th C. B.C.	Atomic structure of matter.			
400–270 B.C.	Rome conquers Italy.			
c. 387 B.C.	Plato founds Academy.	Plato	*The Republic*	Plato
c. 300 B.C.	Geometry.	Euclid		
3rd C. B.C.	Hydrostatics.	Archimedes		
c. 230 B.C.	Earth's circumference.	Eratosthenes		
27 B.C.	Roman Empire established.	Augustus	*Aeneid*	Vergil
100–475	Goths, Vandals, and Huns raid Roman Empire.		*Metamorphoses*	Apuleius
165			*A True History*	Lucian of Samosata
306–337	First Christian emperor.	Constantine I		
c. 340	Monasticism develops.			
410	Rome sacked by Visigoths.	Alaric		
449	Angles, Saxons, Jutes begin conquest of Britain.			

DATE	EVENT	PERSON	WORK	AUTHOR
6th C.	Water wheel.			
687	Frankish kingdoms united.	Pepin of Héristal		
8th C.	Stirrup.			
700–730			*Beowulf*	
711	Moors invade Spain.			
732	Saracens stopped at Tours.	Charles Martel		
9th C.	Rudder.			
802–835	Vikings begin raids on England and Europe.			
800	Charlemagne crowned Emperor of the West.			
c. 850	Feudalism develops in Europe.			
962	Holy Roman Empire founded.			
1000	Christians expect end of world. Hindu-Arabic numerals in Europe.			
c. 1085	First university founded (Bologna).			
1066	Normans conquer England.			
1095	Crusades begin.			
11th C.	Movable type.	Pi-Sheng		
12th C.	Windmill.		*Nibelungenlied* Arthurian romances *Parzival*	Chrétien de Troyes Wolfram von Eschenbach
1273	*Summa Theologica*	Aquinas		
1295	Marco Polo returns from China.			
c. 1298	Spinning wheel.			
c. 1300	Renaissance begins.			
14th C.	Gunpowder introduced in Europe. Mariner's compass in use.			
1321	*The Divine Comedy*	Dante		
1337	Hundred Years' War begins.			
1339, 1353	*Tales, Decameron*	Boccaccio		
1347	Black Death strikes Europe.			
c. 1371	*The Voiage and Travaille of Sir John Mandeville*			
15th C.	Age of Exploration begins.			
c. 1450	Printing press.	Gutenberg		
1470			*Le Morte D'Arthur*	Mallory
1492	Europe discovers America.	Columbus		
1497	Vasco da Gama sails for India.			
1501–1502	East coast of South America explored.	Amerigo Vespucci		
1516			*Utopia*	More
1517	Protestant Reformation begins.	Luther		
1520	Rifle.	Kotter		
1532			*Orlando Furioso*	Ariosto
1543	*De Revolutionibus Orbium Coelestium*	Copernicus		
1556	*De Re Metallica*	Agricola		
1559	Scientific map-making.	Mercator		
c. 1589	Knitting machine.	Lee		
1589–1592	Laws of motion.	Galileo		
1590	Microscope.	Jansen		
1600	*De Magnete*	Gilbert		
1605			*Don Quixote*	Cervantes
1608	Telescope.	Lippershey		
1609–1619	Laws of planetary motion.	Kepler		
1614	Logarithms.	Napier		

DATE	EVENT	PERSON	WORK	AUTHOR
1619	Analytic geometry.	Descartes		
1620	*Novum Organum*	Bacon		
1623			*The City of the Sun*	Campanella
1627			*The New Atlantis*	Bacon
1628	Circulation of the blood.	Harvey		
1634			*Somnium*	Kepler
1636	Micrometer.	Gascoigne		
1638			*The Man in the Moone*	Godwin
1638, 1640			*A Discourse Concerning a New World*	Wilkins
1643	Barometer.	Torricelli		
1657			*Voyage to the Moon*	De Bergerac
1661	Reflecting telescope.	Gregory		
1662	Pressure and volume of gases.	Boyle		
c. 1670	The calculus.	Newton		
1687	*Principia Mathematica*	Newton		
1690	Wave theory of light.	Huygens		
1691			*A Voyage to the World of Cartesius*	Daniel
1703			*Iter Lunare: or, a Voyage to the Moon*	Russen
1719			*Robinson Crusoe*	Defoe
1726			*Gulliver's Travels*	Swift
1731	Sextant.	Hadley		
1732	Threshing machine.	Menjies		
1733	Weaving machine.	Kay		
1735	Law of electrical charges. *Systema Naturae:* taxonomy. Chronometer.	Du Far Linnaeus Harrison		
1740	*Pamela,* the first English novel.	Richardson		
1741			*A Journey to the World Underground*	Holberg
1745	Planetary formation by stellar collision.	Buffon		
c. 1750	Industrial Revolution begins.			
1751			*John Daniel*	Morris
1752			*Micromegas*	Voltaire
1755	Solar and planetary formation by gaseous condensation.	Kant		
1763			*Reign of King George VI: 1900–1925*	Anonymous
1764	*The Castle of Otranto,* first Gothic novel.	Walpole		
1765	Steam engine.	Watt		
1767	Spinning jenny.	Hargreaves		
1771			*Memoirs of the Year Two Thousand Five Hundred*	Mercier
c. 1775	Mesmerism (hypnotism).	Mesmer		
1776	*Wealth of Nations* Declaration of Independence	Smith Jefferson		
1777	Circular saw.	Miller		
1780	Steel pen.	Harrison		
1783	Steamboat. Balloon. Parachute.	D'Abbans Montgolfiers Lenormand		
1784	Iron plow.	Small		
1785	Power loom. *Times* of London.	Cartwright		
1789	French Revolution.			
1792	True nature of combustion. Non-Euclidean geometry.	Lavoisier Gauss		
1793	Cotton gin.	Whitney	*A Voyage to the Moon*	Aratus
1795	Modern geology.	Hutton		
c. 1796	Lithography.	Senefelder		

DATE	EVENT	PERSON	WORK	AUTHOR
1798	*An Essay on the Principle of Population*	Malthus		
	Mass production through interchangeable parts.	Whitney		
1799	Napoleon takes over France.			
1800–1825	Latin American nations gain independence.			
1800	Electric battery.	Volta		
1802	Atomic theory.	Dalton		
	Dark lines in solar spectrum.	Wollaston		
1803	Louisiana Purchase.	Jefferson		
1807	Practical steamboat.	Fulton		
1810	Breech-loading rifle.	Hall		
1812	Storage battery.	Ritter		
1813			*A Flight to the Moon*	Fowler
1815	Stratigraphic dating.	Smith		
1816	Bicycle.	Von Sauerbronn	*Science fiction*	
1817			*Frankenstein*	Shelley
1819	Stethoscope.	Laennec		
1820	Cultivator.	Burden	*Symzonia*	Seaborn
1821	*Saturday Evening Post* founded.			
1822	Electric motor.	Faraday		
	Camera.	Niepce		
1823	Calculating machine.	Babbage		
1824	Electromagnet.	Sturgeon		
	Cement.	Aspdin		
1825	Tractor.	Keeley		
1826	Reaper.	Bell	*The Last Man*	Shelley
1827	Law of electrical conduction.	Ohm	*A Voyage to the Moon*	Atterley (Tucker)
1828	Synthesis of organic compound.	Wohler		
1830			*The Moon Hoax*	Locke
1831	Electromagnetic induction.	Faraday		
	Revolver.	Colt		
1832	Electric generator.	Pixii		
1833			"Ms. Found in a Bottle"	Poe
1835	Telegraph.	Morse	"Hans Pfaall"	Poe
1836			"Three Hundred Years Hence"	Griffith
1838			*Arthur Gordon Pym*	Poe
1839	Electrotype.	Jacobi		
1840s	First law of thermodynamics.	Von Mayer, Joule, Von Helmholtz		
1842	Anesthesia (ether).	Long	"Locksley Hall"	Tennyson
			Zanoni	Bulwer-Lytton
1844			"Rappaccini's Daughter"	Hawthorne
			"The Balloon Hoax"	Poe
1845	Potato blight begins in Ireland.			
c. 1846	Nitroglycerin.	Sobrero		
1848	*Communist Manifesto*	Marx, Engels		
1849	Safety pin.	Hunt	"Melonta Tauta"	Poe
	Rifle bullet.	Minie		
1850	Second law of thermodynamics.	Clasius		
1850s	Science of spectroscopy.	Kirchhoff and Bunsen		
1852	Passenger elevator.	Otis		
	Chemical valence.	Frankland		
1854	Firearm magazine.	Smith and Wesson		
1855	Boolean algebra.	Boole	"The Bell Tower"	Melville
	Science of oceanography.	Maury		
1856	Steel-making.	Bessemer		
1858	Sleeping car.	Pullman	"The Diamond Lens"	O'Brien

DATE	EVENT	PERSON	WORK	AUTHOR
1859	*Origin of Species* Internal combustion engine.	Darwin Lenoir		
1860	Steam warship.	Ericsson		
1861	Organic chemistry.	Kekule		
1862	Dynamite. Machine gun.	Nobel Gatling		
1863	Smokeless powder.	Schultze	*Five Weeks in a Balloon*	Verne
1864	First Communist International. Typewriter. Mathematical theory of electromagnetic radiation.	Marx Mitteshofer Maxwell	*A Journey to the Center of the Earth*	Verne
1865	Laws of genetics.	Mendel	*From the Earth to the Moon*	Verne
1866	Submarine telegraph.	Field	*Alice in Wonderland*	Carroll (Dodgson)
1867	*Das Kapital*	Marx		
1868	Lawn mower. Refrigerator car.	Hills David	*The Steam Man of the Prairies*	Ellis
1869	Suez Canal completed. Periodic table of the elements.	De Lesseps Mendelejeff	*The Brick Moon*	Hale
1870	Celluloid.	Hyatt	*Twenty Thousand Leagues Under the Sea*	Verne
1870–71	Franco-Prussian War.			
1871	Paris Commune. Germany and Italy unified.		*The Coming Race* "The Battle of Dorking"	Bulwer-Lytton Chesney
1872	Motion pictures.	Muybridge and Isaacs	*Erewhon*	Butler
1874	Barbed wire.	Gidden		
1876	Telephone. Four-cycle gas engine.	Bell Otto	*Frank Reade and His Steam Man of the Prairies*	Enton
1877	Microphone. Electric welding.	Edison Thomson	*Off on a Comet*	Verne
1879	Incandescent lamp. Cash register.	Edison Relty	*Frank Reade, Jr., and His Steam Wonder*	Noname (Senarens)
1880	High-speed internal combustion engine.	Daimler		
1881	Russia's Alexander II assassinated.	"People's Will"		
1883	Rayon. *Ladies' Home Journal* founded.	Swan Curtis		
1884	Linotype. Paper from wood pulp. Steam turbine. Transfinite math. and set theory. Ionization.	Mergenthaler Dohl Parsons Cantor Arrhenius		
1885	Motorcycle. Rabies vaccine. Transformer.	Butler Pasteur Stanley	*Flatland*	Square (Abbott)
1886	Halftone engraving. Aluminum electrolyte process. *Golden Argosy* founded.	Ives Hall Munsey	*Robur the Conqueror* *She*	Verne Haggard
1887	Disc record. Propagation of radio waves.	Berliner Hertz	*A Crystal Age*	Hudson
1888	Pneumatic tire. Kodak. Fountain pen.	Dunlop Eastman and Walker Waterman	*Looking Backward* *Dr. Jekyll and Mr. Hyde*	Bellamy Stevenson
1889	*Munsey's Magazine* founded.	Munsey	*Connecticut Yankee in King Arthur's Court*	Twain
1890			*News From Nowhere*	Morris
1891	Oil-cracking process. Color photography. Oceangoing submarine. *The Strand Magazine* founded.	Dewar Eastman and Goodwin Holland and Lake Newnes		
1893	Commerical adding machine. Coke oven.	Burroughs Hoffman		
1894			"The Stolen Bacillus"	Wells

DATE	EVENT	PERSON	WORK	AUTHOR
1895	Radio telegraph. X rays Photoelectric cell.	Marconi Roentgen Elster and Geitel	*The Time Machine*	Wells
1896	·Radioactivity in uranium. *Golden Argosy* becomes *Argosy.* Discovery of electron.	Becquerel Munsey Thomson	*The Island of Dr. Moreau*	Wells
1897	Tousey dime novels discontinued.	Tousey	*The Invisible Man* *The War of the Worlds* *The Story of Ab*	Wells Wells Waterloo
1898			*Edison's Conquest of Mars*	Serviss
1899	Permanent court of arbitration established at The Hague.		*When the Sleeper Wakes*	Wells
1899–1902	Boer War.			
1900	Caterpillar tractor. Cellophane. Rigid airship. Quantum theory.	Holt Brandenberger Zeppelin Planck	*The Lost Continent*	Hyne
1901	McKinley assassinated. Mercury vapor lamp.	Hewitt	*The First Men in the Moon* *The Purple Cloud*	Wells Shiel
1902	Radio telephone.	Fessenden	*The Lake of Gold*	Griffith
1903	Airplane. Nature of radioactive disintegration.	Wrights Rutherford	*The Food of the Gods* *A Round Trip to the Year 2,000* "The Land Ironclads"	Wells Cook Wells
1904	Vacuum-tube diode. Entente Cordiale, later Triple Entente. *The Popular Magazine* founded.	Flemming France, England, Russia Street & Smith		
1905	Theory of Relativity. *All-Story Magazine* founded. *The Monthly Story Magazine* founded.	Einstein Munsey	*A Modern Utopia* *The Master of the World* *Ayesha* *Before Adam*	Wells Verne Haggard London
1906	Vacuum-tube triode. *Railroad Man's Magazine* founded. *Dreadnaught* launched. *People's Magazine* founded.	De Forest Munsey Britain Street & Smith	*In the Days of the Comet*	Wells
1907	Vacuum cleaner. Helicopter. Bakelite. *Monthly Story* becomes *Blue Book.*	Spangler Carnu Baekeland		
1908	*The Cavalier* founded.	Munsey	*The War in the Air*	Wells
1909	Robert Perry reaches North Pole.		*A Columbus of Space* "The Machine Stops"	Serviss Forster
1910	Discovery of cosmic rays.	Gockel		
1911	Amundsen reaches South Pole. Combine. Gyrocompass. Air conditioning. Cloud chamber.	Holt Sperry Carrier Wilson	*Ralph 124C 41+* *The Hampdenshire Wonder*	Gernsback Beresford
1912			*Darkness and Dawn* *Under the Moons of Mars* *Tarzan of the Apes* *The Lost World*	England Burroughs Burroughs Doyle
1913	X-ray tube (hot filament). Multirotored airplane. Planetary atom. Atomic number.	Coolidge Sikorsky Bohr Moseley		
1914	Tank.	Swinton	*At the Earth's Core*	Burroughs
1914–1918	World War I.		*The World Set Free*	Wells
1915	Radio-tube oscillator. Arc searchlight. *Detective Story Monthly* founded.	DeForest Sperry Street & Smith	*Polaris of the Snows* *The Scarlet Plague*	Stilson London
1916	Stainless steel.	Bearley		
1917	Communist revolution in Russia.		*Messiah of the Cylinder*	Rousseau
1918	Mass spectroscope. Electric toaster. Expanded galaxy.	Dempster Strite Shapley	*Palos of the Dog Star Pack* *The Moon Pool*	Giesy Merritt

DATE	EVENT	PERSON	WORK	AUTHOR
1919	*The Outline of History.* *Western Story Magazine* founded.	Wells Street & Smith	"Dagon" "The Girl in the Golden Atom" "The Runaway Skyscraper"	Lovecraft Cummings Leinster
1920	League of Nations established.		*A Voyage to Arcturus*	Lindsay
1921	*Love Story Magazine* founded.	Street & Smith	*R.U.R.* *The Blind Spot* *Back to Methuselah*	Čapek Hall and Flint Shaw
1922	Radar. USSR established.	Taylor and Young		
1923	TV iconoscope scanner. Beer-hall putsch: *Mein Kampf.* *Weird Tales* founded. "Scientific Fiction" number of *Science and Invention.*	Zworykin Hitler Gernsback	*Men Like Gods*	Wells
1924	Lenin dies; Stalin wins power struggle. Existence of other galaxies.	 Hubble	*The Land that Time Forgot* *We*	Burroughs Zamyatin
1924–1926	Wave mechanics in atomic theory.	De Broglie & Schroedinger		
1925	Quantum mechanics in atomic theory.	Heisenberg		
1926	"Conditioned Reflexes" Liquid-fueled rocket. *Amazing Stories* founded.	Pavlov Goddard Gernsback		
1928	TV image pickup tube. Differential analyzer computer. Electric shaver.	Farnsworth Bush Schick	*Skylark of Space* "Armageddon—2419" *Crashing Suns*	Smith Nowlan Hamilton
1929	Stock market crash. *Science Wonder Stories* founded. Penicillin.	 Gernsback Fleming	*The Planet of Peril*	Kline
1930	*Astounding Stories* founded. Cyclotron.	 Lawrence	*Last and First Men* *The Iron Star*	Stapledon Taine (Bell)
1931	Postulation of neutrino.	Pauli		
1932	Discovery of the neutron. Discovery of the positron.	Chadwick Anderson	*Brave New World* *When Worlds Collide* *Pirates of Venus*	Huxley Balmer and Wylie Burroughs
1933	Nazis take over Germany.	Hitler	*Lost Horizon*	Hilton
1934	Creation of transuranic elements.	Fermi	*The Shape of Things to Come* *The Legion of Space* *The Mightiest Machine,* "Twilight"	Wells Williamson Campbell
1935	Nylon. Synthetic rubber.	Carothers Carothers and Colliers	*It Can't Happen Here* *The Circus of Dr. Lao*	Lewis Finney
1937	Campbell named editor of *Astounding.*		*To Walk the Night*	Sloane
1938	Nuclear fission of uranium. Xerography.	Meitner, Hahn, and Strassman Carlson	*Out of the Silent Planet* *Galactic Patrol*	Lewis Smith
1938–1942	Boom in science fiction magazines.			
1939	FM broadcasting. Betatron. Electron microscope. First world sf convention.	Armstrong Kerst Zworykin	"Black Destroyer" *Lest Darkness Fall*	Van Vogt De Camp
1939–1945	World War II.			
1940			*Final Blackout* "The Roads Must Roll"	Hubbard Heinlein
1941			"Nightfall" "Microcosmic God"	Asimov Sturgeon
1942	Controlled fission of uranium.	Fermi and others	"Nerves" "Foundation"	Del Rey Asimov
1944	*The Pocket Book of Science Fiction*	Wollheim	"Deadline" *Rebirth*	Cartmill McClary
1945	Atom bomb.	Oppenheimer and others	"The Piper's Son"	Padgett (Kuttner)
1946			"Vintage Season" *Mr. Adam*	O'Donnell (Moore) Frank

DATE	EVENT	PERSON	WORK	AUTHOR
1947	Carbon-14 geologic dating. *The Best of Science Fiction* *Adventures in Time and Space*	Libby Conklin Healy and McComas	*1984* *What Mad Universe?*	Orwell Brown
1948	Transistor.	Bardeen, Brattain, and Shockley	*Walden Two* "That Only a Mother" "Scanners Live in Vain"	Skinner Merril Smith (Linebarger)
	Holograph.	Gabor	"Mars Is Heaven"	Bradbury
1949	Communists take over China. *Magazine of Fantasy and Science Fiction* founded.	Boucher and McComas		
1949–1953	Boom in science fiction magazines.			
1950	*Galaxy Science Fiction* founded.	Gold	"The Little Black Bag" "Born of Man and Woman" "Coming Attraction"	Kornbluth Matheson Leiber
1951	Nuclear-fission reactor. Hydrogen bomb. *New Tales of Space and Time*	Atomic Energy Commission Healy	"The Quest for Saint Aquin"	Boucher
1952			*The Space Merchants*	Pohl and Kornbluth
			The Demolished Man *Player Piano* "The Lovers"	Bester Vonnegut Farmer
1953	*Star Science Fiction* created.	Pohl	*Childhood's End*	Clarke
1954	Maser.	Townes	*Fahrenheit 451* "The Cold Equations"	Bradbury Godwin
1955	Antiproton produced.	Segre	"The Country of the Kind"	Knight
1957	Sputnik launched.	USSR	"Call Me Joe"	Anderson
1958	Explorer I launched.	USA	*A Case of Conscience*	Blish
1959	Far side of moon photographed.	USSR	*Starship Troopers*	Heinlein
1960	Laser.	Maiman	*A Canticle for Leibowitz*	Miller
1961	First man in orbit.	Gargarin	*Stranger in a Strange Land*	Heinlein
1962	" Beginnings of new wave."		*A Clockwork Orange* *The Man in the High Castle*	Burgess Dick
1963	Discovery of quasars.	Matthews and Sandage	*Way Station* "A Rose for Ecclesiastes"	Simak Zelazny
1964			"Terminal Beach" "Soldier, Ask Not"	Ballard Dickson
1965			*Dune*	Herbert
1966	*Orbit* founded.	Knight	*Flowers for Algernon*	Keyes
1967	RNA deciphered.	Harker and others	*The Einstein Intersection* *Lord of Light*	Delaney Zelazny
	Dangerous Visions Human heart transplant.	Ellison Barnard	"I Have No Mouth and I Must Scream"	Ellison
1968	RNA synthesized.	Merrifield, Herschman, and others	*Stand on Zanzibar* *Rite of Passage*	Brunner Panshin
1969	First men on the moon.	Armstrong, Aldrin, and Collins	*The Left Hand of Darkness*	Le Guin
1970			*Ringworld*	Niven
1971	Mariner 9 orbits Mars.	NASA	*A Time of Changes* *To Your Scattered Bodies Go*	Silverberg Farmer
1972			*The Gods Themselves*	Asimov
1973			*Rendezvous with Rama*	Clarke

INDEX